THE ARDEN S[...] COLLEGE

GENERAL EDITORS:
RICHARD PROUDFOOT, ANN THOMPSON
and DAVID SCOTT KASTAN

CYMBELINE

THE ARDEN SHAKESPEARE

* Second Series

THE ARDEN EDITION OF THE
WORKS OF WILLIAM SHAKESPEARE

CYMBELINE

Edited by
J. M. NOSWORTHY

The Arden website is at
http://www.ardenshakespeare.com

The general editors of the Arden Shakespeare have been
W. J. Craig and R. H. Case (first series 1899-1944)
Una Ellis-Fermor, Harold F. Brooks, Harold Jenkins and
Brian Morris (second series 1946-82)

Present general editors (third series)
Richard Proudfoot, Ann Thompson and David Scott Kastan

This edition of *Cymbeline*, by J. M. Nosworthy
first published in 1995 by Methuen & Co. Ltd
Editorial matter © 1955 Methuen & Co. Ltd

Published by The Arden Shakespeare
Reprinted 2002

Arden Shakespeare is an imprint of Thomson Learning

Thomson
High Holborn House
50-51 Bedford Row
London WC1R 4LR

Printed in Croatia

British Library Cataloguing in Publication Data
A catalogue record for this book is available from the
British Library
Library of Congress Cataloguing in Publication Data
A catalogue record has been requested

ISBN 1-903436-02-8 (pbk)
NPN 9 8 7

TO

MY WIFE

SWINDON COLLEGE REGENT CIRCUS	
Cypher	20.02.04
	£7.99

CONTENTS

PREFACE

THE present edition of *Cymbeline* aims at adhering to the 1623 Folio text as closely as modern conventions will allow. The distinctive punctuation of the original, including its picturesque and sometimes expressive use of brackets, has, in general, been retained except when such retention would be likely to mislead the present-day reader. Conjectural emendations have been admitted to the text only when Folio readings seemed hopelessly unsatisfactory, but the more credible conjectures of the commentators have been recorded in the footnotes where I have also aired a few suggestions of my own, for what they are worth.

The length of the play has inevitably imposed brevity of annotation. The following abbreviations have been used: *O.E.D.* (The Oxford English Dictionary); F (The Shakespeare Folio of 1623); Abbott (E. A. Abbott, *A Shakespearean Grammar*, 1879); Simpson (Percy Simpson, *Shakespearean Punctuation*, 1911); *E.E.* (Elizabethan English); *P.E.* (Present-day English). Reductions of Shakespearean play titles are in accordance with C. T. Onions, *A Shakespeare Glossary*.

Professor Ellis-Fermor's tactful guidance and patient wisdom have been of incalculable value to me throughout my editorial endeavours, and Dr Harold Brooks's close criticism and wealth of helpful suggestion have been quite invaluable. I am also much indebted, for help of various kinds, to Professor Kenneth Muir, Professor H. G. Wright, Dr Alice Walker, Dr W. A. Armstrong, Mr J. Earnshaw, Mr David Hoeniger, Dr G. K. Hunter, Mr J. F. Kermode, Mr J. C. Maxwell, and Dr Josef Raith. My wife has shed light on many of the play's dark places. Lastly, it is only fitting that I should record admiration and gratitude for the labours of Edward Dowden whose edition of *Cymbeline* in the original series appeared just fifty years ago.

The 1960 revision corrected a number of errors, the detection of which was almost wholly due to the vigilance of Mr J. C. Maxwell. Some notes were added, together with a brief addition to the stage history. All the reviews that I have seen have been just and helpful, and if I have here failed to utilize many excellent suggestions, it is due neither to arrogance nor to ingratitude. It seems to me that, at this stage, an editor should still abide by his original decisions, unless these are demonstrably wrong. All those decision were, at the time, endorsed by that wisest of *Cymbeline* scholars, the late Professor Una Ellis-Fermor. Our collaboration was harmonious, memorable, and, in retrospect, heart-warming. This will perhaps explain and excuse my reluctance to alter.

J. M. Nosworthy

INTRODUCTION

THE sovereign difficulty of *Cymbeline* lies in the absence of hard facts relating to the play. Its inclusion in the Folio of 1623 is a guarantee that it is mainly, if not wholly, the work of Shakespeare, and there is good reason for believing that it was written and performed before September 1611. In the face of other uncertainties, however, this knowledge cannot be said to get us very far. We still lack decisive evidence for the exact date of composition, and we cannot be entirely sure about the sources from which Shakespeare derived the main elements of his plot. Criticism, too, has sometimes had to own itself confounded when it has asked why Shakespeare fashioned the play as he did, or even why he fashioned it at all. Perhaps it is through our lack of adequate knowledge that several of the plays seem to pose this last question: *Troilus and Cressida*, for example, or *Measure for Measure*, or *Timon of Athens*, or even *Hamlet*. *Cymbeline* is a less complex document than any of these, but like them it has the appearance of being the outcome of some peculiar, and perhaps decisive, turning point in Shakespeare's private or professional life, and if it were possible, by external reference, to ascertain more about his aim and methods in this play, much that remains obscure concerning his final years as a dramatist might be clarified.

Although *Hamlet, Troilus and Cressida*, and *Measure for Measure* furnish an ample background to Shakespeare's work as a whole, and although the plays written after 1600 are more personal than those written before that date, the Jacobean Shakespeare is a more anonymous and more enigmatic person than the Elizabethan one. We know that he was writing plays down to, and perhaps beyond, 1611, and we know, with reasonable certainty, what those plays were. Their order of composition is rather less clearly defined, and, for want of an absolutely reliable chronology, we cannot always distinguish the exact relation of the plays one with another. Hence *Cymbeline* has to be studied against a not quite definite background, which allows us to take only a certain amount for granted. We have, nevertheless, the consolation of knowing that years of minute scholarly research have marshalled a body of minor evidence and hypothesis into a pattern imperfect in detail but seemingly reliable in its general outline.

I. TEXT

Cymbeline presents no major textual problems, though it leaves room for certain differences of opinion. The play was not printed in Shakespeare's lifetime, but first appeared in the Folio of 1623, this text serving as the sole authority for all subsequent editions. Act and scene divisions are carefully marked in the Folio, and the verse is correctly lined throughout. Save for isolated verbal problems, some of which are more apparent than real, the text is a pure one and must be accounted a faithful reproduction of Shakespeare's original. Sir Walter Greg holds that the Folio text was set up from a prompt-book, and thinks that the hand of the book-keeper is apparent in the stage directions which begin by being terse and end by being elaborate.[1] In the first two acts we find brief directions such as: *Enter Imogen in her Bed, and a Lady* and *Iachimo from the Trunke*, which differ markedly from such later directions as: *Enter in State, Cymbeline, Queene, Clotten, and Lords at one doore, and at another, Caius Lucius, and Attendants* or *Enter Aruiragus, with Imogen dead, bearing her in his Armes*. The last act affords two curiously elaborate directions and Greg is led to conclude that the book-keeper began by scoring out Shakespeare's directions and substituting shorter ones of his own, but abandoned this practice when he discovered that it was superfluous. Greg sums up his position thus: 'On the whole the text, which is fully divided into acts and scenes, suggests to me a prompt-book that has taken over progressively more of the author's original directions for production.'[2]

An alternative and, to my mind, more satisfactory explanation has been suggested to me privately by Dr Alice Walker, who finds certain features of the Folio text difficult to reconcile with the prompt-book theory. Dr Walker points out that, for a text based on a theatrical prompt-book, *Cymbeline* is inordinately long, and there is little else that suggests serious preparation for use in the playhouse. A book-keeper would normally have eliminated the superfluous and, apparently, discarded Dutchman and Spaniard in I. v and would have added reminders of properties, flourishes for royal entries, and the customary alarums, etc. for the battle scenes. The general tidiness of the Folio text argues against the compositor's use of foul papers or autograph fair copy, and Dr Walker's conclusion is that the actual copy was a scribe's transcript of difficult foul papers which had preceded the prompt-book. As Dr Walker points out, the choice of such a manuscript as Folio 'copy' would have been a natural one and in accordance with the proclaimed

1. W. W. Greg, *The Editorial Principle in Shakespeare* (1952), p. 150.
2. *Loc. cit.*

principles of Heminge and Condell. It is, I imagine, possible that the book-keeper made the adjustments which Greg mentions in a transcript of this kind, but if so they appear to have been casual rather than systematic.

If Dr Walker is, as I think, correct, any theory of non-Shakespearean interpolation would apparently go by the board. It is unthinkable that a professional scribe engaged on the transcription of foul papers would add a scene, a couplet or even a phrase to what stood in the manuscript before him. He would copy ill-written words wrongly and would occasionally lapse into error through relaxing his attention, but the total of error would be inconsiderable. On the whole, then, it seems probable that the Folio preserves a highly reliable copy, and that any doubts attaching to authorship must be referred to the foul papers themselves. It is possible that these were the work of Shakespeare and a co-adjutor, though I can find neither bibliographical nor stylistic evidence to support this view. Heminge and Condell seem to me to have dealt faithfully with Shakespeare and with his public, and the only way in which they exceeded their mandate was in grouping *Cymbeline* with the tragedies and giving it the head-title and running-title of *The Tragedie of Cymbeline*. It is possible that this incorrect location was the result of late receipt of the 'copy' in the printing-house.

The Folio text of *Cymbeline* was apparently set throughout by Jaggard's Compositor B. The pages reveal the neatness and symmetry that are characteristic of his work as a whole. His various habits, as defined by Dr Alice Walker—free use of parenthesis and reluctance to italicize place-names and territorial titles—are readily apparent. Dr Walker has established that his settings from Quarto copy are often perfunctory and high-handed, that he carried more in his head than he could memorize, frequently omitted lines and words, and was 'prone to memorial reconstructions and even deliberate bodging'.[1] It does not follow that Compositor B treated manuscript copy in quite the same way since, by its very nature, it compelled him to decipher word by word or even letter by letter. I suspect that a general principle is involved, and that really difficult copy imposes its own restraints. I am therefore sceptical about omissions and such like in *Cymbeline*, though, in the light of Dr Walker's findings, vigilance is clearly necessary. There are eight questionable readings, of which three certainly require emendation. All of these, if wrong, could result from misreading of manuscript copy. Literal errors total about thirty. There are

---

1. Alice Walker, *Textual Problems of the First Folio*, p. 11.

apparently about seven word omissions and about four interpolations, together with twelve alterations. This means a total of some sixty errors, yielding the comparatively satisfactory average of two per page.

2. DATE

Various dates for the composition of *Cymbeline* have been put forward. Malone, who first attempted to place the plays in chronological order, successively favoured 1604, 1605, and 1609, and this last date, which has been generally accepted, is probably not far wrong. The extreme forward limit is established by an abstract of the play preserved in a commonplace book kept by Dr Simon Forman, a schoolmaster who, in later life, turned to magic and quackery. In April 1611, or thereabouts, Forman began to jot down details of the plays that he saw performed at the Globe Theatre. On 20 April, he saw *Macbeth*, on the 30th an anonymous lost play dealing with the reign of Richard the Second, and on 15 May, *The Winter's Tale*. When and where he saw *Cymbeline* he does not specify, but it was probably in the same theatre at about the same time. It could not have been very much later, for Forman died, by accident or design, when crossing the Thames in a boat on 8 September 1611. His account of *Cymbeline*, long thought to be a forgery but now known to be genuine,[1] is interesting enough to merit quotation in full:

of Cimbalin king of England

Remember also the storri of Cymbalin king of England in Lucius time. howe Lucius Cam from Octauus Cesar for Tribut and being denied after sent Lucius w^t a greate Armi of Souldiars who landed at milford hauen, and Affter wer vanquished by Cimbalin and Lucius taken prisoner and all by means of 3 outlawes of the wch 2 of them were the sonns of Cimbalin stolen from him when they were but 2 yers old by an old man whom Cymbalin banished, and he kept them as his own sonns 20 yers w^t him in A cave. And howe on of them slewe Clotan that was the quens sonn goinge To milford hauen to sek the loue of Jnnogen the kings daughter. and howe the Jtalian that cam from her loue conveied him selfe into A Cheste, and said yt was a chest of plate sent from her loue & others to be presented to the Kinge. And in the depest of the night she being aslepe, he opened the cheste & cam forth of yt. And vewed her in her bed and the markes of her body, & toke a wai her braslet & after Accused her of adultery to her loue &c. And in thend howe he came w^t the

1. See R. W. Hunt and J. Dover Wilson, *The Review of English Studies* (1947), xxiii, pp. 193–200.

Romains into England & was taken prisoner and after Reueled
to Innogen, Who had turned her self into mans apparrell & fled
to mete her loue at milford hauen, & chanchsed to fall on the
Caue in the wods wher her 2 brothers were & howe by eating a
sleping Dram they thought she had bin deed & laid her in the
wods & the body of cloten by her in her loues apparrel that he
left behind him & howe she was found by lucius &c.[1]

The backward date is about 1606. This date receives strong, if
not conclusive, support from an interesting feature in Shakespeare's
use of Holinshed's *Chronicle*. The story in v. iii, of how

> Two boys, an old man twice a boy, a lane;
> Preserved the Britons, was the Romans' bane.

comes not, as we might expect, from Holinshed's account of early
British history, but from the section dealing with the reign of King
Kenneth in his History of Scotland. Though it would be rash to set
down any hard and fast rules about Shakespeare's reading of Holinshed, it seems reasonably safe to assume that he did not give much
detailed attention to these Scottish matters until he needed them
for stage purposes. In short, his first extensive use of the Scottish
chronicle was for *Macbeth*, and the odds are strongly in favour of the
view that the striking episode from it that appears in *Cymbeline* was
an overflow from the material so patiently gleaned for the tragedy,
which, consequently, must be reckoned the earlier of the two plays.
And the generally accepted date for *Macbeth*, though some critics
demur, is 1606.[2] The view that *King Lear*, which belongs to 1605 or
1606, also helps to establish a terminal date is less convincing. It is
possible that Shakespeare came across the *Cymbeline* material in
Holinshed when he was assembling early British history for use in
King Lear, but we should beware of assuming Shakespeare's wholesale dependence on books. The stories, to any educated Elizabethan, were old and familiar ones.

It appears, then, that *Cymbeline* belongs to a period in Shakespeare's working life for which scholarship accepts the following
approximate pattern:

Antony and Cleopatra 1606–7; *Coriolanus* 1607–8; *Timon of Athens*
1607–8; *Pericles* 1608–9; *Cymbeline* 1609–10; *The Winter's Tale*
1610–11.[3]

---

1. I have silently corrected one or two trivial errors which occur in the original
manuscript.

2. Professor J. Dover Wilson (New Shakespeare *Macbeth*) argues for *c.* 1601.
Professor Muir (Arden *Macbeth*) reverts to the traditional date.

3. See J. G. McManaway, 'Recent Studies in Shakespeare's Chronology' in
Shakespeare Survey, 3, pp. 22–33.

This chronological pattern rests on a pitifully slight body of external evidence, but it is one that can be amply supported by internal evidence. It is endorsed, for instance, by the elaborate verse tests devised and rigorously applied by nineteenth-century investigators. These are somewhat out of favour nowadays, but they cannot be wholly set aside, for, though they can obviously have little relevance to negative arguments, their positive application is probably as wide as that of any other stylistic determinant. On a more general reckoning, any objective critic would, I think, agree that *Cymbeline* has sufficient points of contact with *Antony and Cleopatra* on the one hand, and with *Pericles* and *The Winter's Tale* on the other, for it to be certain that all these plays belong to one fairly narrow area of Shakespearean chronology. The theory that Shakespeare abandoned tragedy and, turning to a more romantic kind of drama, produced *Pericles*, *Cymbeline*, *The Winter's Tale*, and *The Tempest* in unbroken succession is an inherently likely one, powerfully substantiated by indisputable similarities of style, matter, characterization, and outlook, but, like all generalizations, it must not be trusted over far. In any case, it serves only to narrow down the range of the inquiry, and does not, in itself, settle individual dating problems. *The Winter's Tale* seems (in Autolycus' threat that the Shepherd's son 'shall be flay'd alive; then 'nointed over with honey, set on the head of a wasp's nest') to be using up a scrap left over from the *Cymbeline* source material, and, partly for that reason, is usually regarded as the later of the two plays. However, we have also to admit the possibility that Shakespeare owed the name 'Belarius' to the Bellaria of Greene's *Pandosto*, which was his source for *The Winter's Tale*, so that the evidence can point either way. My own guess is that the composition of the two plays was more or less simultaneous or, at any rate, that both had been written, revised, and prepared for the stage before either was actually performed, with consequent cross-fertilization.[1] This view, which, once again, leaves the dates open, tallies with the attractive theory, put forward by Professor G. E. Bentley, that the impending acquisition of the Blackfriars private theatre led, in the spring and summer of 1608, to discussions among the King's Players as a result of which Shakespeare was henceforth to write with the Blackfriars in mind, and not the Globe, and that *Cymbeline*, *The Winter's Tale*, and *The Tempest*, in that order, were the fruits of that decision.[2]

1. I am assuming that Shakespeare, whether in London or elsewhere, was not idle during the period (summer 1608–Dec. 1609) when plague put a stop to play-acting in London.

2. G. E. Bentley, 'Shakespeare and the Blackfriars Theatre' in *Shakespeare Survey*, 1, pp. 38–50.

Bentley says nothing about their respective dates, but the application of his theory would, I think, suggest 1608 for the first play of
the series. Yet the theory itself is vulnerable. It makes no provision
for *Pericles*, and in assuming that Shakespeare suddenly and willingly deserted his old audience to cater for the more sophisticated
spectators at the Blackfriars it seems to me to run counter to what
we know, or conceive, of the man. Finally, the grounds for supposing that the plays in question were written specifically for Blackfriars—it will be recalled that it was at the Globe that Forman saw
The Winter's Tale and, presumably, *Cymbeline*—are far from conclusive. I would concede, however, that the acquisition of the Blackfriars may have induced Shakespeare to pen dual-purpose plays,
for such, most emphatically and triumphantly, the Romances are.

The remaining evidence is slight. That which *Pericles* may be
supposed to afford is neither here nor there; for that play presents
its own very vexed problems, few of which have been settled to the
general satisfaction of Shakespeareans. Professor A. H. Thorndike's
theory that *Cymbeline* was written after, and in the pattern of,
Beaumont and Fletcher's *Philaster*, another play of uncertain date,
is relevant to the present problem only if it is wrong, as I think it
is.[1] *Philaster* is accorded some complimentary verses in John
Davies's *The Scourge of Folly*, which was registered on 8 October
1610. Hence, if *Philaster* was influenced by *Cymbeline*, and not vice
versa, the latter play must have been on the boards in or before
1610.

Any attempt at close dating must necessarily be approximate
and impressionistic. The only claim that can be advanced with
real confidence is that *Cymbeline* falls within the range 1606–11.
I am inclined to accept 1608 or 1609 as the most probable date, but
the best that can be said for this conclusion, in our present state of
knowledge, is that it is the one least likely to be wrong.

3. SOURCES

The identification of the sources used by Shakespeare for
Cymbeline poses problems as baffling as those of dating. There can
be no reasonable doubt that he was indebted to Holinshed's
Chronicles, but the debt is a relatively slight one, for the historical
matter serves merely to round off a play that is mainly concerned
with specifically comic or romantic themes, namely, the wager-
story and the story of Belarius and the kidnapped princes. The

1. See A. H. Thorndike, *The Influence of Beaumont and Fletcher on Shakespeare*
(1901).

view that Shakespeare took the first of these directly from the *Decameron* is open to certain serious objections, whilst for the second nothing that can really be termed a source has, as yet, been identified.

Holinshed supplied Shakespeare with what is, at best, a confused account of a reign so uneventful that it had defeated the inventive powers of generations of quite imaginative chroniclers.[1] Cymbeline, son of Theomantius, became king in 33 B.C., and died after reigning for thirty-five years, leaving two sons, Guiderius and Arviragus. He was brought up in Rome and was absolved, by Augustus Caesar, of obligation to pay tribute. Subsequently tribute was demanded and refused, but Holinshed comments: 'I know not whether Cymbeline or some other British prince refused tribute.' Like the earlier chroniclers, he eventually makes the refusal come from Guiderius, and tells of Caesar's consequent attempts to invade Britain. Still uncertain, he relates how, according to British chroniclers, the Romans were twice defeated in pitched battles, but remarks that Latin sources claimed ultimate victory for the Romans. This generally disjunctive report bristles with glaring inconsistencies of time and circumstance which Holinshed makes no attempt to reconcile.

But Shakespeare knew something of these matters from other sources. He had browsed in other chronicles, and it is quite likely that he had read the two 'tragedies' of Guiderius printed in the additions made to the *Mirror for Magistrates*[2] by Thomas Blenerhasset and John Higgins. Higgins's contribution, printed in 1587, is based substantially on the account given by Geoffrey of Monmouth, but Blenerhasset, a young soldier stationed in Guernsey, whose additions to the *Mirror* appeared in 1578, tells us: 'I had not those Chronicles which other men had: my Memorie and Inuention were vnto me in stead of *Grafton, Polidore, Cooper*, and suche like.' But, as it turned out, his invention served him far better than his memory, and his sensational story of Guiderius' defeat of Roman armies thirty thousand strong, of his dreams of world conquest, and of his challenge to meet Claudius Caesar in single combat affords a classic instance of the uninhibited workings of the imagination of Renaissance man.[3]

If Shakespeare read all these accounts, or only a representative

1. The relevant passages are reprinted by W. G. Boswell-Stone in *Shakespeare's Holinshed* (1896).

2. See, further, Appendix A (*c*).

3. Blenerhasset was, perhaps, confused rather than inventive. Many of the feats that he attributes to Guidericus were attributed to King Arthur by Malory and the chroniclers.

selection of them, he must have been sorely puzzled. And Spenser's *Faerie Queene*, which he certainly knew, did nothing to set his mind at rest, for in the 'chronicle of Briton kings' that constitutes the tenth canto of Book II of his poem, Spenser generates further error by making Arviragus the brother to Cymbeline:

> Next him *Tenantius* raignd, then *Kimbeline*,
>   What time th' eternall Lord in fleshly slime
>   Enwombed was, from wretched *Adams* line
>   To purge away the guilt of sinfull crime:
>   O joyous memorie of happy time,
>   That heavenly grace so plenteously displayd;
>   (O too high ditty for my simple rime.)
>   Soon after this the *Romanes* him warrayed;
> For that their tribute he refused to let be payd.
>
> Good *Claudius,* that next was Emperour,
>   An army brought, and with him battell fought,
>   In which the king was by a Treachetour
>   Disguised slaine, ere any thereof thought:
>   Yet ceased not the bloudy fight for ought;
>   For *Aruirage* his brothers place supplide,
>   Both in armes, and crowne, and by that draught
>   Did drive the *Romanes* to the weaker side,
> That they to peace agreed. So all was pacifide.   (50–1)

For this part of the plot, then, Shakespeare found himself confronted with the contradictions of the chronicles, Holinshed's confessed uncertainty, Spenser's error (or omission), and, perhaps, Blenerhasset's unbounded imagination. In his wise way, he made no attempt to reconcile them. He knew, presumably, that the dramatic plot that he was presenting called for a king and two princes, and cut the knot by accepting Cymbeline as the father of Arviragus and Guiderius and by making him, and not his son, refuse the tribute. Hence, it may be said that the pseudo-history in the play has no real source, and the most that we can allege is a general dependence on Holinshed.

This use of Holinshed in the wider sense does not extend very far. It covers a substantial part of III. i, where Cymbeline, the Queen, and Cloten defy Lucius, Caesar's ambassador, and occurs also in the account of the battle in v. iii. The second of these scenes, as already noted, comes not from Holinshed's section on early Britain but from his story of how a Scottish husbandman named Hay, together with his two sons, helped to rout the Danish invader at the Battle of Luncarty in A.D. 976. The fact that an episode so widely separated in time and place from Cymbeline and his England found its way into the play at all shows just how little attention Shakespeare chose to pay to purely historical considerations. For the rest, Holinshed may have afforded him a phrase here and there, and must certainly have supplied him with the names of most of the characters. The location of these personal names in Holinshed is, however, sufficient to show that Shakespeare read round and about his chosen topic. All of them belong to the pseudo-history of early Britain, but are fairly widely distributed.[1]

The alleged sources for the wager plot range from Boccaccio's *Decameron*, which, in the view of most critics, has the strongest claim, to the homespun tale 'told by the Fishwife of Stand on the Green' in *Westward for Smelts* written by one Kind Kit of Kingston. As there is no reliable evidence to show that *Westward for Smelts* was printed before 1620, Shakespeare's supposed obligations to Kind Kit can be discounted from the start.[2] Perhaps we should absolve him from a debt to anything but his memory and his wide reading, for it seems hardly necessary to postulate an exact source for a story that had such general currency.

The wager story was not, perhaps, a tale which held children from play, but there is abundant evidence that it had enjoyed widespread popularity for at least four centuries before Shakespeare handled it. Versions of the tale are extant in practically every language known to the Elizabethans. The earliest reputable literary versions to appear were French ones, and the first quarter of the thirteenth century produced such adaptations as *Roi Flore et la belle Jeanne*, *Guillaume de Dôle*, Gerbert de Montreuil's *Roman de la Violette*, *Le Conte de Poitiers*, and a *Miracle de Notre-Dame* by Gautier de Coincy.[3] These, like most of the other versions, are hardly relevant to the present inquiry since there exists no reason for supposing that they were known to Shakespeare. If, in fact, Shakespeare borrowed from any specific literary source, his area of choice cannot have been very wide; and we may safely eliminate all possibilities save three: Boccaccio's *Decameron*, the prose tale of *Frederyke*

1. J. P. Brockbank, 'History and Histrionics in *Cymbeline*', *Shakespeare Survey*, 11, pp. 42–9, shows that Shakespeare's debt to Holinshed, especially for Brutan matter, was general and fairly extensive. He concludes that Wilson Knight is substantially correct in regarding *Cymbeline* as a historical play.

2. Both Malone and Steevens mention an edition of 1603, but modern opinion is sceptical. *Westward for Smelts* was not registered before 1620. The problem, if it exists, involves *The Merry Wives of Windsor* as well as *Cymbeline*, but the first-named, though it lacks any established source, cannot have owed anything to Kind Kit.

3. These, with many others, constitute the so-called 'Wager-cycle'. There are detailed studies by R. Ohle, Gaston Paris, Bertil Malmberg, and others. The basic story could as well cover *Measure for Measure* as *Cymbeline*.

of Jennen, and that inevitable and embarrassing shadow, a lost version in prose, verse, or play form.

Boccaccio's version is the only one which displays anything approaching the same order of genius as Shakespeare's. In the ninth novel of the second day he tells how some Italian merchants, meeting in an inn at Paris, discuss the chastity and fair dealing of their wives. When Bernabo of Genoa dares to extol his wife's virtue, he is immediately challenged by Ambrogiuolo of Piacenza and retorts by proposing a wager which is accepted. Ambrogiuolo then goes to Genoa, bribes a poor woman who has received kindnesses from Bernabo's wife, Zinevra, and is carried in a chest to Zinevra's bed-chamber. When Zinevra is asleep, he emerges from the chest, observes carefully the details of the chamber, observes further that on the lady's left breast is a mole surrounded by a few golden hairs, steals a purse, a gown, a ring, and a girdle, and returns to the chest, which is later carried away by the old woman.

So Ambrogiuolo returns to Paris, summons the merchants, and tells his deceitful tale. Bernabo dismisses his description of the bed-chamber and his tokens as insufficient proof, but accepts the mole as damning evidence. He accordingly pays the wager and sets out for Genoa to wreak his vengeance on Zinevra. But he stops some twenty miles from Genoa, and sends a trusted servant to tell of his impending return, instructing the servant, at the same time, to bring Zinevra from Genoa and to kill her as soon as they come to a suitably lonely place. The servant obeys all these instructions except the last. Zinevra pleads for her life and prevails upon the servant both to spare her and to lend her clothes. Bernabo is told that his lady has been killed and her body left for wolves to devour.

Zinevra now assumes the guise of a common sailor and, under the name of Sicurano da Finale, enters the service of a Catalonian gentleman, in whose company she sails to Alexandria where she finds favour with the Sultan. She is sent by the Sultan on a special mission to the fair at Acre; and there meets Ambrogiuolo, who is displaying the very purse and girdle that he filched from her bed-chamber. She questions him and he laughingly discloses the trick that he has played on Bernabo. Zinevra then persuades Ambrogiuolo to return with her to Alexandria, and arranges for Bernabo to be brought thither. After she has prevailed upon Ambrogiuolo to tell his tale to the Sultan, she confronts him with Bernabo, and he is forced to re-tell his story. Zinevra now reveals her true identity and consents to become reconciled with Bernabo. But Ambrogiuolo's crime is not pardoned: he is tied to a stake, his naked body smeared with honey, and is left to hang until he shall drop to

pieces. And the moral, says Boccaccio, is that in such a way the
deceiver lies at the mercy of the deceived.

This story is, *mutatis mutandis*, sufficiently close to what is, in
effect, the central plot of *Cymbeline* to warrant the assumption that
Shakespeare was acquainted with the relevant section of the
Decameron, but certain reservations have to be made. There is little
evidence to show that he read Italian and no English translation of
the *Decameron* appears to have been published before 1620. The
French versions of Laurent du Premierfaict and Antoine le Maçon
furnish a possible *tertium quid*. Maçon's translation first appeared in
1545, and the fact that it was reprinted sixteen times during the
century argues great popularity and wide currency. The possibility
that Shakespeare drew upon an English source has received slight
attention from successive editors and critics of the play, notwithstanding the fact that George Steevens drew attention to the existence of such a source nearly two hundred years ago.

The English prose tale noted by Steevens is a little pamphlet
entitled *Frederyke of Jennen* which was first printed at Antwerp in
1518 and reprinted in London in 1520 and 1560.[1] It was translated from a fairly elaborate Dutch version, which, in its turn,
derived from a Low German one. This, too, was preceded by a
version in High German, and it seems likely that this goes back to
an Italian tale, some form of which served Boccaccio's turn. There
can be little doubt that *Frederyke of Jennen* was popular in England
throughout the sixteenth century. In the famous letter written by
Master Robert Laneham to his fellow-gildsman, Master Humfrey
Martin, in 1575, we find mention of Captain Cox of Coventry who
had 'great ouersight . . . in matters of storie', and among the books
that Laneham believed him to have 'at hiz fingers endz' was
'Frederik of Gene'. *Frederyke of Jennen* is, in fact, just such a tale as
we might expect Shakespeare to have picked up in his youth.

Frederyke of Jennen is, in essence, the same as the *Decameron* story,
though it is less artistic, more prolix, and betrays signs of mistrans-
lation. Its differences lie in points of detail, and it is significant that
at several points it agrees with *Cymbeline* while differing from
Boccaccio. Whereas in the *Decameron* all the merchants are Italian,
in *Frederyke of Jennen* we find that 'foure ryche marchauntes
departed out of diuers countreis' and that they comprise a Spaniard, a Frenchman, a Florentine, and a Genoese. This will account
for what is otherwise inexplicable, the fact that the company in
Philario's house comprises Iachimo, a Frenchman, a Dutchman,

---

1. Reprinted here (see Appendix A (*b*)) from Dr Josef Raith's *Aus Schrifttum
und Sprache der Angelsachsen*, Bd. IV (Leipzig, 1936) with corrections from the
British Museum copy. 'Jennen' is Genoa.

and a Spaniard, of whom the last two are mutes. This is the most striking detail, but there are others. In *Cymbeline* and *Frederyke of Jennen*, but not in Boccaccio, the wager is first suggested by the villain, and the odds first proposed correspond: five thousand guilders against a like sum in the tale, and ten thousand ducats against 'gold to it' in the play. (Boccaccio: five thousand florins to one thousand.) The villain of *Frederyke of Jennen*, like Iachimo, declares that he has lost the wager the moment that he sets eyes on the heroine. The heroine is asked to receive the chest into safe keeping (by an old woman bribed by the villain in the prose tale) and is told, as Imogen is told, that it contains jewels and plate. In both texts, she answers that she will guard it willingly and will even keep it in her own chamber. The villain of the tale, Johan of Florence, immediately realizes that the mark on the heroine's body will be accepted as decisive evidence: 'now haue I sene a pryuy token, wherby he shall byleue me that I haue had my pleasure of his wyfe': so Iachimo:

> Here's a voucher,
> Stronger than ever law could make; this secret
> Will force him think I have pick'd the lock, and ta'en
> The treasure of her honour.

The tale states emphatically that Johan on his return called the hero, Ambrose, aside to tell him privately of his success, so that only Ambrose, Johan, and, presumably, their host, who held the stakes, knew who had won the money: so in *Cymbeline* the Frenchman, Spaniard, and Dutchman are omitted, and only Posthumus and Philario hear Iachimo's story. This seems a tenuous parallel, but is, nevertheless, significant in view of the fact that in Boccaccio Ambrogiuolo deliberately summons all the merchants to hear of his success. The device by which Pisanio sends Posthumus a 'bloody cloth' to signify that Imogen has been killed is omitted by Boccaccio but appears in *Frederyke of Jennen* where the heroine's pet lamb is killed and her clothes stained with its blood. This incident may have suggested Imogen's words to Pisanio:

> Prithee, dispatch:
> The lamb entreats the butcher. Where's thy knife?

More convincing, perhaps, than any of these is the repentance of both Ambrose and Posthumus before the innocence of their wives has been established. This is clearly stated in *Frederyke of Jennen* and equally clearly expounded in *Cymbeline*, v. i. The prose tale includes a rather intrusive battle episode which may have served to colour the battle-scenes in *Cymbeline*, though these are more probably dependent on Holinshed. At the end of the tale, when the heroine appears stripped of her masculine disguise, her patron the king recognizes, or half-recognizes, her as his former servant, Frederyke, and this affords a rough parallel to Cymbeline's half-recognition of Imogen.

There are a few minor points of contact. The wager in *Cymbeline* is in ducats as against florins in Boccaccio, and guilders in *Frederyke of Jennen*, but the last-named uses the word 'ducat' freely. The general commercial tone of the prose tale—even the jewels that Johan steals are valued in ducats!—may, in part, account for Shakespeare's frequent use of cash imagery in *Cymbeline*. Posthumus' diamond ring may have been suggested by the 'rynge with a point of diamond' which belongs to Ambrose's wife. It is just possible, though hardly probable, that the 'hauen' to which Ambrose's wife makes her way directed Shakespeare's thoughts towards Milford Haven. The use of a forged letter in *Frederyke of Jennen* certainly links up with Pisanio's 'feigned letter of my master's', and there is no parallel subterfuge in Boccaccio. Finally, *Frederyke of Jennen*, by substituting an aged king for Boccaccio's sultan, and by obscuring the oriental background—we may observe that Lord Frederyke becomes the king's 'lord protectoure and defender of all my londs'—comes nearer in tone and setting to *Cymbeline*.[1]

There are, then, substantial grounds for alleging that Shakespeare owed much to *Frederyke of Jennen*, but it is not possible to eliminate the debt to Boccaccio completely. The description of Imogen's bed-chamber, for instance, owes nothing to the English tale, but we have only to glance at the *Decameron* to discover a room in which a candle is burning, which is hung with pictures, all carefully noted by Ambrogiuolo, and to recognize at once a refinement of detail that stirred Shakespeare's imagination and set the poetry flowing from his pen. There is no need to labour the other resemblances, and no obligation to prove by detailed analysis that Shakespeare had read Boccaccio's version of the story, for it is proven by the lines from *The Winter's Tale*, already quoted, in which Autolycus' threat is palpably based on Boccaccio's account of the execution of Ambrogiuolo, to which *Frederyke of Jennen* affords no parallel. The *Decameron* and the English tale are not, therefore, rival claimants, but joint claimants, and I judge *Frederyke of Jennen* to be the more immediate of the two. My impression is that, while Shakespeare was content simply to remember the *Decameron*, he

1. Many of these similarities are discussed by W. F. Thrall, '*Cymbeline, Boccaccio, and the Wager Story in England*', *Studies in Philology*, 28 (1931), pp. 639–51.

possibly glanced once more through *Frederyke of Jennen* in order to refresh his memory. That done, he combined the two, allowing some play to memories based on oral tradition, and some to his own imagination.

It will be convenient, before considering the possibility of a lost play dealing with the wager-story, to examine that strand of *Cymbeline* which is concerned with Belarius and the princes. Several alleged sources have been identified but most of them are so preposterous that they can safely be ignored. In 1887 it was suggested by R. W. Boodle[1] that Shakespeare was indebted to *The Rare Triumphs of Love and Fortune*, a romantic drama that was, apparently, performed before Elizabeth at Windsor Castle on 30 December 1582 and was printed in 1589. At the risk of seeming dogmatic, I am content to claim that Boodle was substantially correct and that Shakespeare's obligation, such as it was, was to *Love and Fortune* and to no other literary production of which we have knowledge, with, however, the reservation that I have applied to Holinshed and the wager sources, that Shakespeare relied on memories and suggestions rather than on detailed study. Precisely what led Shakespeare to this ramshackle old play in the first place, I do not pretend to know. My guess is that the demands of a sophisticated Jacobean audience, together, no doubt, with the prospect of acquiring a private theatre, made it expedient for the King's Players to contemplate the revival of some of the romantic comedies that had been popular ten or twenty years earlier. They did, in fact, revive *Mucedorus* in 1607 and there can be little doubt that this play, spineless though it is, caught the fancy of the age and maintained its popularity over a longish period.[2] Shakespeare, moreover, did not disdain to take a few suggestions from it when he wrote *The Winter's Tale* and *The Tempest*. As a chief shareholder in the King's company, Shakespeare would have a ruling voice in the selection of plays, and if this question of reviving old plays arose, it would fall to him to read them through in the hope of finding something suitable. And I assume that *Love and Fortune* was one of the plays that he considered. The King's Players did not revive it, it seems, but that did not prevent Shakespeare from turning it to his own use.

Love and Fortune tells of the love of Princess Fidelia for the seeming orphan Hermione, who has been brought up at the Court by her father, King Phizantius. Fidelia's rash and boorish brother, Armenio, learning of their love-suit, provokes trouble and secures

1. In *Notes and Queries*, VII. iv (19 Nov. 1887), p. 405.
2. The recorded performance was a Court one, but the general popularity of the play is attested by the fact that it ran to fifteen or more editions between 1610 and 1670.

the banishment of Hermione. Hermione sends a servant to instruct Fidelia to meet him at a secret place but the plan is betrayed to Armenio who follows her. Fidelia eventually receives hospitality in the cave of Bomelio, a former courtier who was banished by the father of Phizantius because of the calumnies of a faithless friend. The plot proceeds through a series of crude and improbable episodes until the lovers are re-united and the contending parties reconciled.

The general content of *Love and Fortune*, then, is sufficiently close to those two strands of *Cymbeline*, the circumstances leading up to the banishment of Posthumus and the Belarius story, which fall outside the scope of either Holinshed or the wager sources. And the resemblance extends to points of detail. It would be unwise to attach too much weight to such parallel features as a banished lover, a banished duke, a cave, and a sleeping potion, for these are part of the stock-in-trade of every writer of romance. Yet both plays present the banished lover as a pauper brought up at Court, both include a boorish brother, and both introduce Jupiter and use him, flagrantly, as a *deus ex machina*. Just as Belarius recognizes Cloten though he has not seen him for many years, so Bomelio recognizes Armenio, and just as Imogen offers her breast for the mortal stroke, so does Fidelia. In the one play the heroine is named Fidelia; in the other she assumes the name Fidele. This might be accounted co-incidence were it not for the fact that Shakespeare borrowed the name Hermione for *The Winter's Tale*. Finally, there are a few verbal parallels which, though not exact, suggest that Shakespeare recalled occasional snatches of the dialogue of *Love and Fortune*.[1] In short, the case rests on a reputable piece of cumulative evidence. Shakespeare had read or seen or acted in *Love and Fortune*, and now, in *Cymbeline*, he fashioned past experience to present needs. It cannot be denied that some of that experience had been forgotten: otherwise he could hardly have transferred the hero's name, Hermione, to the Queen in *The Winter's Tale*.

If commentators have underestimated Shakespeare's debt to *Love and Fortune*, it is partly because they have been too ready to accept the wager-story and the pseudo-history as the central elements in *Cymbeline*. This, I think, is to misunderstand Shakespeare's intentions completely. He was no longer concerned with historical drama[2] or with comedy of intrigue but with the golden inconsequences of romance, which is a thing *per se*, existing in undefined dimensions of space and time, and is devoted, to the exclu-

1. I have cited the possible parallels in my footnotes.

2. G. Wilson Knight, *The Crown of Life* (1947), interprets *Cymbeline* as a national play. See below, pp. xliii–xlv.

sion of more mundane affairs, to the adventures of princes and princesses, to the finding of long-lost children, to wizards and witches, and hermits dwelling in desert places, to the righting of old wrongs, and to the life that is happy ever after. Of the various sources that we have considered, it is *Love and Fortune* which presents this scheme of things most fully and most consistently, and which should, in consequence, be regarded as Shakespeare's primary source or impulse. The dramatic conduct of *Cymbeline* requires that Posthumus and Imogen should be parted and re-united, that Imogen's lost brothers should be found, that the wrongs done to Belarius should be set right, and that all discordant circumstances should be resolved into a final invulnerable unity. Shakespeare introduced the wager plot and the historical matter into this pattern not because they were essential to it, but because he judged them to be tractable and concordant agents of elaboration, enabling him to motivate this, to complicate that, and finally to secure that willing suspension of disbelief which constitutes poetic, and sometimes dramatic, faith.

It has occasionally been claimed that Shakespeare did not work from multiple sources but refashioned an old play of which all record has been lost. The claim rests on reputable *prima facie* grounds, for quite a substantial body of Shakespeare's work does in fact derive in this way from earlier drama, yet it is true to say that, when applied to *Cymbeline*, it is an evasion of the source problems rather than a credible solution based on detailed evidence. Those critics who have glibly postulated a pre-Shakespearean *Cymbeline* have, in fact, failed to give any substance to their case. H. R. D. Anders urged simply that 'the crudeness of some scenes and the unequal execution of the play suggest another hand' and hinted, without a shred of supporting evidence, that Beaumont and Fletcher were responsible for the pre-*Cymbeline*.[1] J. M. Robertson, a disintegrator of erratic prejudices, supposed that Shakespeare made use of a lost play by George Peele. Other critics have taken the crudeness and inequality alleged by Anders as evidence of collaborate authorship and have applied subtle and dubious stylistic criteria in their efforts to show that Shakespeare joined forces with Massinger or some other Jacobean dramatist. But present-day criticism, which recognizes that Shakespeare sometimes wrote indifferently and is content to take the rough with the smooth, is intolerant of all theories of rehandling or collaboration which rest solely on aesthetic judgments, and if the crudeness and inequality still trouble Shakespearean purists, they are nowadays more

1. In *Shakespeare's Books* (1904).

modestly diagnosed as blemishes introduced by some rather shadowy theatre hack after the play had left Shakespeare's hands.

If the foregoing analysis of the sources for *Cymbeline* is correct, it is, in itself, sufficient to demolish the pre-*Cymbeline* theory. Since Cymbeline and his sons clearly derive from Shakespeare's reading of Holinshed, it seems unlikely that they were present in the supposed play, and it is surely uneconomical to assume the duplication of matter that already existed in *Love and Fortune*. If we eliminate these, all that remains is the wager-plot for which Boccaccio and *Frederyke of Jennen* will account quite adequately. This may have served for an earlier play, but I doubt whether it would have commended itself as a likely theme to any Elizabethan dramatist before about 1595. My impression, for what it is worth, is that the wager-story has a degree of sophistication wholly alien to the spirit of artlessness that typifies the comedies of Lyly, Greene, Peele, Porter, and Wilson.

This pre-*Cymbeline* notion, then, is one which I reject as utterly superfluous, preferring to believe that Shakespeare, influenced by earlier tradition and with some measure of direct dependence on *Love and Fortune*, shaped a straightforward romance plot and imposed upon it other plot material derived from some two or three unrelated sources. The process is a very simple one, and yet is sufficient to account for the sum total of *Cymbeline*. It accords, moreover, with the method of plot construction employed elsewhere by Shakespeare, in *King Lear* and *The Tempest* for example, and is a method which the supposed author of the supposed pre-*Cymbeline* is hardly likely to have anticipated.[1] In short, the core of *Cymbeline* is Shakespearean from first to last and not even remotely suggestive of any other dramatic discipline.

4. AUTHENTICITY

Some editors and critics smell collaboration. On this point H. H. Furness is, perhaps, the most ambitious.[2] In the brief but drastic introduction to his Variorum edition of the play, he allots to Shakespeare the Imogen love story with all that directly adheres to it and some of the Holinshed scenes. Cymbeline and Belarius are credited to the collaborator, who, it seems, was also responsible for the Vision scene, and both the Soothsayer and Cornelius sections in the

---

1. *King Lear* transmutes its plot material in much the same way as *Cymbeline*. Pseudo-history (the Lear story) and Arcadian romance (the Gloster story) are combined, but in different proportions. An earlier play, which cannot have served as an immediate source, is also involved.

2. *Cymbeline*, ed. H. H. Furness (1913), pp. v–xx.

final scene. Over and above this, there are ten or twelve odd lines or couplets which Furness believes to have been foisted in by this second author.[1]

A somewhat different policy of disintegration is followed by Harley Granville-Barker[2] who, while endorsing certain of Furness's aesthetic objections, relies on more specifically dramatic criteria. He points to the structural blemishes that can be detected in the last two-thirds of the play, and particularly to the treatment of Posthumus who, after being allowed to slip from the current of the story, is at length clumsily restored to prominence. In addition, he draws attention to banalities of stagecraft and to the seeming redundancy and flatness of most of the soliloquies, and concludes that 'a fair amount of the play—both of its design and execution— is pretty certainly not Shakespeare's.'[3] Shakespeare, he thinks, may have refashioned a play planned and, in part, written by another dramatist, giving close attention only to the first two acts and thereafter handling only those sections which aroused his interest. Granville-Barker adds the fanciful suggestion that the unknown dramatist may have restored his own ineptitudes to the play 'after Shakespeare had washed his hands of the business'.

For aught that can be proved or disproved by external reference, Furness and Granville-Barker may be right, but I do not consider that they have carried their point. Occasional speeches, though trivial and uninspired, may nevertheless be Shakespeare's, and the application of purely aesthetic canons affords no proof of the contrary. Belarius, whatever strain his moralizing may impose upon our patience, cannot be dissociated from Arviragus and Guiderius or, in fact, from the main current of the plot, and no disintegrating critic has yet had the temerity to suggest that the two Princes, as the Folio text presents them, are anything but Shakespearean. Belarius, moreover, belongs beyond reasonable doubt to the Shakespearean scheme of things. In a couple of years he will have been revivified, with a firmer hand, into the hermit magician Prospero who is, by consent, as inseparable from the revealed attitude of the mature Shakespeare as he is from the practical necessities of romance convention.[4] Even as he stands in *Cymbeline*, the

1. Furness thus adds considerably to the passages rejected by Pope and Hanmer, but is not really explicit. The lack of exact correspondence between his introduction and his critical notes on this point may result from the fact that his edition appeared after his death.

2. Harley Granville-Barker, *Prefaces to Shakespeare: Second Series* (1930).

3. *Op. cit.*, p. 243.

4. We can also refer him back to Timon, to Antonio in *Twelfth Night*, to the Duke in *As You Like It*, and, more dubiously, to Polonius. Professor Ellis-Fermor suggests to me that Simonides and Cerimon in *Pericles* are also relevant.

banished hermit is strong enough to withstand Furness's charge which rests principally on a mistaken, over-earnest interpretation of Belarius' demand that Cymbeline shall pay him for the housing of the princes. 'Once a thief always a thief. He is not for an instant to be trusted,' writes Furness with a royal disregard for what is and what is not valid literary criticism.[1]

The rhyming couplets, which offend both Furness and Granville-Barker, prove nothing, for Shakespeare uses them again and again in his plays. Sometimes they serve to end a scene, sometimes to finish off a speech on an emphatic note, sometimes, as in the last act of *Macbeth*, where they serve to isolate and clarify a number of short battle scenes, they have a clearly defined dramatic function. And very often they challenge the claim of Shakespeare's quibbles to be regarded as the fatal Cleopatra for which he lost the world and was content to lose it. Several of the couplets in *Cymbeline* appear rather aimless, but their authenticity can be defended on stylistic grounds.[2]

Granville-Barker's dramatic objections are similarly vulnerable. That *Cymbeline* exhibits a certain degree of structural ineptitude may be conceded, but this can be attributed to the experimental nature of the play. Shakespeare, who had proved himself the supreme master of both tragedy and comedy, was yet unpractised in the art of blending the two in the service of romance. He undertook now to present difficult, even intractable, narrative components in a form which was quite new to him and which would clearly test his native invention severely. The resultant play prompts the further speculation that the remarkable chain of dénouements which constitutes the final scene was the goal that he had before him at the outset, and that he was content to tolerate incidental crudities for the sake of ultimate virtuosity. Be that as it may, the fact remains that he was feeling his way in a genre hitherto attempted, with still cruder manipulation, only in *Pericles*. As a tyro in tragedy, he had been able to turn for guidance to Seneca, Kyd, and, above all, Marlowe. In the hands of his predecessors tragedy had achieved efficiency, respectability, and even greatness. Similarly the varied shapes of comedy had been given reputable expression by Greene, Lyly, and Porter, not to mention the Latin writers, Terence and Plautus, whose comedies Shakespeare had studied at school. Romance, with its dispersed action and,

---

1. *Op. cit.*, p. vii. In thus treating Belarius as a real person, Furness is very much in the A. C. Bradley tradition, though he scarcely brings Bradley's perceptiveness to bear.

2. That is unless we assume that the alleged collaborator was deliberately imitating Shakespeare's bad couplets in other plays!

dramatically, disintegrating circumstances, had defeated the earlier dramatists, so that it afforded no model comparable with *The Spanish Tragedy* or *Edward the Second* or *Campaspe* or *Friar Bacon and Friar Bungay*. A tradition that rests on things no better than *Mucedorus* or Peele's *Old Wives Tale* scarcely merits the name of tradition. The Jacobean revival of *Mucedorus* is perhaps significant. It was chosen because nothing better in the same kind could be found, and it must have become evident to Shakespeare and his fellows, in or about 1607, that there was just this lacuna in dramatic literature, that the requirements of the Jacobean theatre and its audiences could not be adequately served by existing material. Sundry dramatists, notably Shakespeare and Beaumont and Fletcher, took it upon themselves to make good the deficiency. They were not, as certain critics have implied, doing something very new. On the contrary, something very old. A comparison of *Cymbeline* or *The Tempest* with *Love and Fortune* will show quite clearly that the only distinction that can be drawn is one of quality and effect.·

It is important that we should recognize from the outset that *Pericles*, *Cymbeline*, and, to a certain but insignificant extent, *The Winter's Tale* were the pioneer colonizing efforts of a Shakespeare more completely without a reputable model than he had ever been. Once this is realized, it no longer seems surprising that *Cymbeline* reveals a dramatist 'somewhat at odds with himself', as Granville-Barker puts it. Clearly this kind of excursion into unfamiliar, crudely-charted dramatic territory raises its own set of problems and difficulties which can be overcome only by methods of trial and error. The sustaining of a satisfactory tragi-comic balance is one of the problems implicit in romance material, and the achievement of a perfectly happy ending is another. The portrayal of idealized characters in unreal situations must have represented, to the Shakespeare who for some eight or ten years had been occupied almost exlusively with individual relationships, psychological probability, and the terrible logic of human destiny, a change so fundamental as to be perplexing and, at first, detrimental. Above all, perhaps, there is the structural challenge implied in the romance's demand for alienation and subsequent reconciliation. 'Once upon a time . . .', 'Far away and long ago . . .', formulas so simple and so current in fairy-tale, impose problems of space and time which sorely tax ingenuity when they are transferred to the stage. There is nothing more obviously brilliant in the whole of Shakespeare's writings than the way in which he ultimately solved this particular problem in *The Tempest*, where the enchanted island is set, without specification, between the kingdoms of Alonso and Claribel,

> She that is queen of Tunis; she that dwells
> Ten leagues beyond man's life; she that from Naples
> Can have no note, unless the sun were post—
> The man i' the moon's too slow—till new-born chins
> Be rough and razorable.

Here Shakespeare is working in a new dimension towards which he has already advanced some distance in *The Winter's Tale*. *Cymbeline*, as we might expect, offers only a halting attempt at a solution. Temporal and spatial cohesion are not achieved, and the curious imbroglio of Augustus' Rome and Cymbeline's Britain, of the dawn of the Christian era and the Renaissance, is too much at odds with the action to be convincing. We have only to set the play beside *The Tempest* to see how clumsy and palpable it all is. It is Shakespeare's way nevertheless.

Cymbeline is far from perfect, and there are these and doubtless other reasons for its imperfections. If Posthumus is restored to the central pattern so clumsily that we can almost see the puppets dallying, the explanation is surely that Shakespeare has not yet solved a novel and complex problem. The objectionable soliloquies, too, suggest a man working, not wholly confidently, in a new medium. Granville-Barker complains of the mediocre quality of certain of these, and notes that they are sometimes allotted to the most unlikely characters. He finds them so 'frankly informative' as to be strangely artless and is therefore unable to reconcile them with Shakespeare's general tendency with the soliloquy which, 'as his art matures, is both to make it mainly a vehicle for the intimate thought and emotion of his chief characters only, and to let its plot forwarding seem quite incidental to this'.[1] This tendency, as he rightly observes, is apparent in the great tragedies, but *Cymbeline* wears its rue with a curious difference.

The truth of Granville-Barker's remarks can scarcely be denied, but the basis of comparison itself is surely an invalid one, for it overlooks the distinction that must quite emphatically be drawn between the technique of tragedy, of which Shakespeare was a consummate master, and that of romantic tragi-comedy, of which he had had, as yet, little or no experience. The difficulty of striking a balance between comedy and tragedy, of using tragic incident and motive yet turning it to a comic purpose is still a relevant consideration. *Twelfth Night* represents Shakespeare's farewell to orthodox comedy, and all the plays between it and *Pericles*, whether or not they conform to the accepted tragic pattern, were written in tragic

---

1. *Op. cit.*, p. 240.

vein.[1] At the time when he set to work on *Cymbeline*, then, tragedy was Shakespeare's current medium; comedy, however congenial it may have been to him, a somewhat rusty one. The danger of tragic thought and feeling overwhelming the comic in this untried romance form was a considerable one, especially with the wager plot thrown in.[2] The wager story, as it appears in the *Decameron* and in *Frederyke of Jennen*, is a happy enough thing; yet it could very well have proved a powerful spur to tragedy for the man who had written *Othello*, with its not dissimilar theme, and had diverted the story of Lear from its relatively happy course into the ultimate regions of spiritual anguish.[3] At times *Cymbeline* does come a little nearer to tragedy than it should, notably in its portrayal of the mental tortures of Imogen and, to a lesser extent, Posthumus and Pisanio, of Cymbeline's wrath and Iachimo's villainy. To have added soliloquies directed to the same ends as those of Hamlet, Macbeth, or Iago would have been fatal. Those in *Cymbeline* may, as Granville-Barker claims, be 'simply informative' and '*ex post facto* confidences' but they are, nevertheless, Shakespeare's insurance policies, enabling him to keep tragedy at arm's length and to indicate to his audience that this sequence of banishments, plots, murders, poisons, battles, and purposed executions is less serious than it seems. And the device, though it is that of an initiate, works. In *Cymbeline*, Shakespeare secures the tragi-comic balance, even if he uses creaking kitchen scales to do so, and the play emerges clearly as a romance. If we analyse its parts, we find that it is quite a bloodthirsty affair with a cue to tragedy more powerful than we had at first supposed: if we take a detached view of the whole, we learn that we have, after all, fallen under the spell of golden unrealities.

I am inclined, therefore, to rule out the theory of collaboration and to claim that the play is Shakespearean in conception and execution. If there is alien matter in the Folio text, it must, I think, be accounted post-Shakespearean, but I cannot conceive what purpose was served by the sporadic insertion of trivial snippets. The dialogue which accompanies Posthumus' vision in v. iv may be intrusive, and many editors, including Pope, Johnson, and

1. Those which do not conform are *Measure for Measure* and *All's Well That Ends Well*. Some critics hold that these are comedies in name only.

2. I question whether the balance is achieved in *Pericles*, a play which is exquisite in its pathos. The final impression that it gives is of wrongs endured rather than of injuries resolved.

3. It may be noted that the old play of *Leir* ends happily. So does Tate's seventeenth-century adaptation of Shakespeare's play!

Steevens, have rejected it. It is probably correct to say that the majority of present-day critics endorse their view, but the authenticity of the scene has been forcefully defended, notably by Mr E. H. W. Meyerstein and Mr G. Wilson Knight, on grounds that cannot be dismissed as wholly specious.

The Vision is written in rhyming verse which has been dismissed by hostile critics, perhaps rightly, as woefully poor stuff. That does not mean, however, that it can, with certainty, be dissociated from Shakespeare on stylistic grounds. Critics have always been far too ready to throw doubt on the mature Shakespeare's excursions into rhyme, though precisely why they should assume that he was committed solely to blank verse has never been made clear.

Meyerstein[1] claims that the Vision is fine poetry, and argues that stylistic evidence shows it to be Shakespeare's, though it deliberately affects 'the language of a more simple olden time'. He sees the Vision as an integral part of the play effecting divine preservation of the best blood of Britain. Wilson Knight's more elaborate defence insists similarly on functional and stylistic integrity.[2] He maintains that this ghostly vision is 'enclosed and clasped firmly by speeches of serene deathly meditation' which appear elsewhere in the play, and shows that it conforms closely with the main body of *Cymbeline* in the information which it supplies and in the imagery which it employs. Since the gods play a big part in *Cymbeline*, and are throughout represented as responsive to supplication, it is only natural that the play should include this chanted prayer of intercession, and the appearance of Jupiter is the logical consequence of Posthumus' prayer at v. i. 7–17. Jupiter is shown to be in keeping with the play's great wealth of classical and mythological allusion, and both the eagle and the thunderbolt figure in other parts of the play. Wilson Knight regards the theophany as central and dominating in *Cymbeline* and argues that the Vision is necessary as a striking transcendental moment. A more effective point is that theophanies are common to all the romances. Diana appears in *Pericles*, and *The Tempest* presents Juno, Iris, and Ceres. He might have added Time who appears, with a somewhat different purpose, in *The Winter's Tale*, which, in its presentation of the oracle, goes half way towards a theophany. All these are significantly linked with the appearance of Hymen in *As You Like It* and, more dubiously, with that of Hecate in *Macbeth*, and Wilson Knight's claim that all these have common stylistic features is reasonably convincing. His point that, after Jupiter has mounted to his palace

1. E. H. W. Meyerstein, 'The Vision in "Cymbeline"' in *The Times Literary Supplement*, 15 June 1922, p. 396.
2. *Op. cit.*, pp. 168–202.

crystalline, the ghosts speak Shakespearean blank verse is surely a cogent one, and so too is the parallel which he establishes between the wording of the tablet laid upon Posthumus' breast and the speech of the dying Warwick in *3 Henry VI*:

> Thus yields the *cedar* to the axe's edge,
> Whose arms gave shelter to the princely *eagle*,
> Under whose shade the ramping *lion* slept,
> Whose top-branch overpeer'd *Jove's* spreading tree
> And kept low shrubs from winter's powerful wind.
>
> (v. ii. 11–15)

Wilson Knight's final assertion, that the Vision in *Cymbeline* is 'our one precise anthropomorphic expression of that beyond-tragedy recognition felt through the miracles and resurrections of sister-plays and reaching Christian formulation in *Henry VIII*' may appear extravagant, but there is much that is convincing in the patiently assembled evidence that leads him to this conclusion. Both he and Meyerstein, as we have seen, find nothing un-Shakespearean in the style of the verse, and neither does Professor Hardin Craig, who, in a brief and illuminating study of Shakespeare's bad poetry, remarks:

> All in all, it seems possible to defend the authenticity of the masque and other stylistic abnormalities on the ground that gods and those who speak to gods, especially if they themselves are spirits, must speak differently from creatures of this world.[1]

In my view, this stylistic argument can be carried further. Meyerstein's statement that the Leonati speak 'the language of a more simple olden time' is quite correct, but the precise nature of the verse that they speak has been obscured by editorial or typographical convention. Most editions print it in short lines of four and three feet, thereby implying that it is written in a kind of jingling ballad metre, but the printing of the Folio, which is followed in the present edition, shows that this is not so. What the Folio typography implies is, in fact, this:

> No more, thou thunder-master, show thy spite on mortal flies:
> With Mars fall out, with Juno chide, that thy adulteries
>   Rates and revenges.
> Hath my poor boy done aught but well, whose face I never
>   saw?
> I died whilst in the womb he stay'd, attending Nature's law:
> Whose father then (as men report thou orphans' father art)
> Thou shouldst have been, and shielded him from this earth-
>   vexing smart.

1. Hardin Craig, 'Shakespeare's Bad Poetry' in *Shakespeare Survey*, 1, p. 55.

It is now possible to detect the nature of the antiquity, for these verses are, with a very minor modification, none other than the rhyming fourteeners so popular in the 1590s. Shakespeare, then, is reaching back to a style current during his apprenticeship and employing it for a new and specific purpose. Herein lies, perhaps, the strongest evidence for the Vision's authenticity, that it is written in a style so outmoded that lesser dramatists than Shakespeare avoided it, save for purposes of burlesque. Shakespeare's way was different, and a frequent reversion to outworn styles is one of his especial characteristics.[1] It is wholly possible that he employed fourteeners for the Vision because he associated them with classical mythology. Such an association would arise almost naturally from Chapman's choice of this particular metre for his translation of *The Iliad*. It is more likely, however, that the metre of the Vision was another overflow from *Love and Fortune*, which I have claimed as one of the sources of *Cymbeline*. That play begins with a theophany, comprising Jupiter, Mercury, Vulcan, Venus, and the other gods, and, though there is greater metrical variety than we find in the Vision, a generally analogous pattern emerges. The suppliant characters employ the fourteener, and Venus' address to Jupiter affords a suggestive parallel in thought and language as well as metre:

> O thou that gouernest euery thing that Gods and men attempt,
> And with thy fearful thunderbolte their doings doost preuent,
> What hath thy daughter so deserued? what doth she silly dame,
> Before ye thus to be abused with vndeserued blame?

Jupiter replies, as in *Cymbeline*, in rhyming pentameter:

> Content ye both I'le heare no more of this,
> And Mercury surcease, call out no more:
> I haue bethought me how to woorke their wishe,
> As you haue often proou'd it heertofore.
> Heere in this land within that Princely bower,
> There is a Prince beloued of his loue,
> On whom I meane your souerainties to proue.
> Venus, for that th(e)y loue thy sweet delight,
> Thou shalt endure[2] to encrease their ioy:
> And Fortune thou to manifest thy might,
> Their pleasures and their pastimes (thou) shalt destroye,
> Ouerthwarting them with newes of freshe anoye.

There is a difference in stanzaic pattern, but this is scarcely significant. A careful comparison between the opening of *Love and*

---

1. E.g. Brutus in the Forum speech (Euphuism); the Bleeding Sergeant in *Macbeth* (Senecanism); the Pyrrhus speeches and the inner-play in *Hamlet*.
2. 'endure' *sc*. endeavour.

Fortune and the Vision in *Cymbeline* will, I think, afford compelling evidence both of the authenticity of the latter section and of Shakespeare's acquaintance with the earlier play.

It is, perhaps, the necessity of the Vision which, when all else has been said, argues most powerfully for its authenticity. It follows upon four and a half acts of bad faith, cruelty, violence, and revenge which have brought physical, mental, and spiritual confusion upon whole armies as well as upon individuals, and is succeeded by a scene of less than five hundred lines which wins significant order out of chaos. There is no reason for supposing that this change of fortune is achieved through any human agency, and we must conclude, if the play is to have any meaning for us, that the resolution of discords is the result of supernatural intervention. This is simply logical, for the situation is so fantastically chaotic that no mere human being could be expected to control it. Such disorder can be remedied only by a god, a magician, or, as in *The Winter's Tale*, by an extraordinary series of coincidences. The Jupiter of *Cymbeline* then must be regarded as the agent of regeneration. In making him, literally, the *deus ex machina*, Shakespeare flies in the face of Aristotelian doctrine, but necessity is above precept. The Vision, with its splendour of spectacle and its attendant music, is fundamentally an artistic and noble conception, and an effective solvent.

Certain critics who object to the Vision on stylistic grounds argue that Shakespeare merely sketched it, leaving the execution to some nameless hack. But we have seen that it accords with a familiar Shakespearean habit, that it establishes a suggestive link with at least one of the play's supposed sources, that it corresponds closely with the rest of *Cymbeline* in the facts which it presents and in the language and imagery which it employs, that it is a device which, whatever its spiritual purport, is a *sine qua non* of Shakespeare's romances and has earlier precedent in his work. It seems merely perverse to question its authenticity further.

5. *CYMBELINE* AND *PHILASTER*

The originality of *Cymbeline* has been called in question, notably by Professor A. H. Thorndike whose elaborately documented theory that Shakespeare was decisively influenced by Beaumont and Fletcher's *Philaster* has obtained wide acceptance.[1] There can be no doubt that a peculiar and intimate relationship exists between *Philaster* and *Cymbeline*, but I believe Beaumont and Fletcher

1. *Op. cit.*, pp. 152–60.

to have been the debtors. For a seasoned dramatist of supreme achievement to start indulging, quite suddenly, in what is apparently slavish imitation of a pair of novices would be very odd, though not, of course, impossible. Yet there is no reason for supposing that Shakespeare saw the need or felt the inclination to do anything of the kind. *Pericles*, a play of the same genre as *Cymbeline*, certainly preceded *Philaster*, and much of *Cymbeline* is already implicit in the so-called dark comedies of 1602–4.[1] If we view the play in relation to all that preceded it, we are at once made aware that its roots are firmly planted in Shakespeare's accumulated dramatic wisdom, that it is a thing which has evolved naturally, and certainly without any external *volte face*, in the mind of the creator of *King John*, *Measure for Measure*, *King Lear*, and *Timon of Athens*. And we can only ask whether Shakespeare, with Faulconbridge, Isabella, Cordelia, and Iago behind him, had need of others' guidance in his portrayal of Cloten, Imogen, and Iachimo.

Some explanation of Shakespeare's newly-acquired romance pattern, is, it may be admitted, a desideratum, but there seems little justification for making Beaumont and Fletcher responsible for this new trend. It is altogether more probable that they, like Shakespeare, were following a rehabilitated dramatic convention which accorded, conveniently, with Jacobean taste and with the increasing amenities of the stage.[2] The impact of the *Mucedorus* revival on Shakespeare's last plays cannot be ignored. Here we can detect one external circumstance which may very well have reminded him of a yet untried way of handling dramatic material, and have led him to *Pericles* and then, via *Love and Fortune*, to *Cymbeline* without further prompting.

The actual parallels between *Philaster* and *Cymbeline*, which are fairly numerous, remain, when divorced from other considerations, ambiguous evidence. But *Philaster* is clearly a play written in the shadow of Shakespeare, and its echoes of *Troilus and Cressida*, which colours a well-defined section of the fifth act, *Hamlet*, and *King Lear* can point only one way. Two of the links with *Cymbeline* seem to me to hint, though no more than that, at Shakespeare's play having been the earlier of the two. Philaster's inquiry:

1. For wider, but still pertinent discussion, see W. W. Lawrence, *Shakespeare's Problem Comedies*, and R. W. Chambers, *Measure for Measure*, in *Man's Unconquerable Mind*. There is a masterly survey of this and other problems in F. P. Wilson, *Elizabethan and Jacobean*, pp. 126–8. I am inclined to regard the dark comedies as, primarily, dramatic romances.

2. John Daye's *Humour out of Breath*, which was licensed in April 1608 and printed in the same year, seems to me to belong to the restored convention. It may well have preceded both *Cymbeline* and *Philaster*.

> Tell me gentle boy,
> Is she not paralleless? Is not her breath
> Sweet as Arabian winds, when fruits are ripe?
> Are not her breasts two liquid Ivory balls?
> Is she not all a lasting Mine of joy?   (III. i. 198–202)

recalls Iachimo's:

> All of her that is out of door most rich!
> If she be furnish'd with a mind so rare,
> She is alone th' Arabian bird; and I
> Have lost the wager.

as well as certain details from his speech in Imogen's bed-chamber. But if we cannot be sure that Beaumont and Fletcher borrowed from *Cymbeline*, we can at least surmise that

> Is she not paralleless?

and the allusion to the East, owe something, in sound and sense, to *Antony and Cleopatra* and Shakespeare's 'lass unparallel'd'. Again, we find that Philaster embraces Bellario with the words:

> 'Tis not the wealth of *Plutus*, nor the gold
> Lockt in the heart of earth, can buy away
> This arm-full from me, this had been a ransom
> To have redeem'd the great *Augustus Caesar*,
> Had he been taken.   (IV. v. 112–16)

It may be merely fanciful to detect in this an echo of *King Lear*:

> Not all the dukes of waterish Burgundy
> Can buy this unprized precious maid of me.
>   (I. i. 261–2)

but we may reasonably ask what Augustus Caesar is doing in this context, for he has not the remotest connection with the subject matter of *Philaster*. Perhaps he is there because the dramatists recalled one of the several allusions to him in *Cymbeline*.[1]

In conclusion, it is pertinent to recall what Dryden, presumably on good authority, tells us of Beaumont and Fletcher, 'The first play that brought Fletcher and him in esteem was their *Philaster*: for before that, they had written two or three very unsuccessfully.'[2] If this is true, it presents a picture of two prentice dramatists who, in 1608 or thereabouts, were struggling to keep failure at bay and searching earnestly for some dramatic model which would ensure

1. As Professor Ellis-Fermor suggests to me, 'Augustus lives to think on't' is one of the moments that catch the imagination in drama.

2. *An Essay of Dramatick Poesie* (1668).

success.[1] Out of a somewhat restricted area of choice—restricted, that is, by personal talent and inclination, public demand, theatrical policy, and amenities—certain models would readily emerge, notably Jonsonian comedy, Shakespearean tragedy, and the seemingly popular dramatic romance recently exploited by Shakespeare in *Pericles* and *Cymbeline*, and it was in the pattern of these last-named plays that I believe *Philaster* to have been conceived and executed.

6. CRITICISM

Although critics have had much to say on the origin and purpose of Shakespeare's romances as a whole, *Cymbeline* has evoked relatively little critical comment, and no completely satisfactory account of the play's quality and significance can be said to exist. Johnson discerned few virtues in it, and was content to dismiss it in one memorable paragraph:

> This play has many just sentiments, some natural dialogues, and some pleasing scenes, but they are obtained at the expense of much incongruity. To remark the folly of the fiction, the absurdity of the conduct, the confusion of the names, and manners of different times, and the impossibility of the events in any system of life, were to waste criticism upon unresisting imbecility, upon faults too evident for detection, and too gross for aggravation.[2]

Mr Bernard Shaw has denounced *Cymbeline* in equally vehement terms, and H. H. Furness came ultimately to a reluctant admission of the justice of Johnson's strictures. On the other hand, Hazlitt praised *Cymbeline* as 'one of the most delightful of Shakespeare's historical plays', adding, however, that 'it may be considered as a dramatic romance.'[3] This significant aspect of the play is one to which Johnson, writing in the Age of Reason, was blind, as his further comment on *The Winter's Tale* ('This play, as Dr Warburton justly observes, is, with all its absurdities, very entertaining') clearly shows.[4] Hazlitt exposes another weakness of the Johnsonian standpoint:

> The business of the plot evidently thickens in the last act: the

1. In 1608, Beaumont was twenty-four, Fletcher twenty-nine. One cannot believe that they were very far advanced in their profession.

2. *General Observations on the Plays of Shakespeare* (1756).

3. *Characters from Shakespeare's Plays* (1817).

4. Johnson, who had little patience with fairies and 'the fairy way of writing', found *A Midsummer Night's Dream* 'wild and fantastical'. Hurd's great apologia, *Letters on Chivalry and Romance* (1762), ends with Spenser. One wishes that he had covered the Shakespeare romances.

story moves forward with increasing rapidity at every step; its various ramifications are drawn from the most distant points to the same centre; the principal characters are brought together and placed in very critical situations; and the fate of almost every person in the drama is made to depend on the solution of a single circumstance—the answer of Iachimo to the question of Imogen respecting the obtaining of the ring from Posthumus. Dr. Johnson is of the opinion that Shakespeare was generally inattentive to the winding up of his plots. We think the contrary is true.

Hazlitt's comments, many of which are excellent, are thus directed by recognition of the romantic nature of *Cymbeline* and of the technical brilliance of the last act, and may be said to reflect a temperate Romantic attitude just as Johnson's reflect a moribund Augustanism. They represent the best that professional criticism had to offer until Harley Granville-Barker published his preface to the play.[1] Shakespeare criticism in the nineteenth century tended to be synthetic in the bad sense, and the late romances received particularly unhappy treatment. The mood of reconciliation which they reveal was extended by such critics as Furnivall, Ten Brink, Gollancz, and Dowden into the notion that they are the personal utterances of a serenely philosophical Shakespeare living in happy retirement at Stratford, that 'at last, in his Stratford home again, peace came to him, Miranda and Perdita in their lovely freshness and charm greeted him, and he was laid by his quiet Avon side.' Dowden even went so far as to devise for Shakespeare a *curriculum vitae* which designated the period of the great tragedies 'In the Depths' and that of the Romances 'On the Heights'. Side by side with this, there existed other sentimental heresies. Shakespeare's characters were regarded as real men and women, and his heroines, especially those of the Romances, were exalted into paragons of womanly virtue. *Cymbeline* was accordingly fitted into this picture of quiet serenity, though it seemed less impressive, in this respect, than *The Tempest* in which Shakespeare, under the mask of Prospero, portrayed his aged, philosophical self— or so, following the suggestion of Thomas Campbell, it was confidently claimed. It was in connection with the nineteenth-century view of Shakespeare's heroines that *Cymbeline* loomed largest, and much of what passed for criticism was, in fact, nothing more than the perverted ritual of an Imogen cult. Swinburne's rhapsody is by no means the wildest specimen of this kind of thing:

1. *Op. cit. (Cymbeline)*, pp. 234–345.

The very crown and flower of all her father's daughters,—I do not speak here of her human father, but her divine,—woman above all Shakespeare's women is Imogen. As in Cleopatra we found the incarnate sex, the woman everlasting, so in Imogen we find half-glorified already the immortal godhead of womanhood. I would fain have some honey in my words at parting . . . and I am, therefore, something more than fain to close my book upon the name of the woman best beloved in all the world of song and all the tide of time; upon the name of Shakespeare's Imogen.[1]

The inevitable reaction against nineteenth-century attitudes was forcibly presented in 1904 in Giles Lytton Strachey's *Shakespeare's Final Period*.[2] He finds the alleged transition from the grossness of *Timon of Athens*, 'this whirlwind of furious ejaculation, this splendid storm of nastiness', to the tranquillity and joy of the last four plays too sudden to be convincing. Hence he regards the Romances as the products of a decline which was already well advanced before Shakespeare wrote *Cymbeline*, a decline perceptible in *Coriolanus* and clearly evident in *Timon of Athens*. Shakespeare's final period, then, was one of frustration and disgust, broken spasmodically by 'visions of beauty and loveliness'. *Cymbeline* and its companion plays were lucid intervals in the life of a man no longer interested in life or drama, a man 'half bored to death'.

But Strachey's premises are fallacious. The view that the tragedies reflect Shakespeare's own disgust is no more tenable than that which finds subjective tranquillity in the romances, and Strachey merely drives the Victorian heresy to an opposite extreme. It is questionable, moreover, whether the mood of *Timon of Athens* is essentially more savage and disgusting than that of *Hamlet*. Grossness is more prominent and more vocal, and the hero is less rational, but these are dramatic features, not personal disclosures. *Coriolanus* and *Timon of Athens* may represent a decline, but only a partial one. If Shakespeare was losing interest, it was in tragedy, not in drama, though I prefer to believe that the abrupt transition from tragedy to romance resulted directly from his recognition that he had said all that he could say, and all that any man could say, in tragic form. The charge that *The Winter's Tale* and *The Tempest* are the work of a man half bored to death seems to me to require only a categorical denial, and the detailed analysis of *Cymbeline* which the present edition has imposed has convinced me that it is the creation of a man perpetually fascinated by his dramatic experiment, surprised and exhilarated by the new sensations and discoveries which the elaboration of his unfamiliar material has yielded.

1. *A Study of Shakespeare* (1880).   2. In *Books and Characters* (1922), pp. 47–64.

The most valuable element in Sir Arthur Quiller-Couch's study of *Cymbeline* and its fellow Romances lies in its recognition of their experimental nature, especially in relation to the new opportunities for spectacular staging which the Jacobean theatres provided.[1] Shakespeare, in Quiller-Couch's opinion, had come to realize that forgiveness is nobler than revenge and, accordingly, sought now to reach something better than tragedy. In *Cymbeline* and *The Winter's Tale*, where mis-hits jostle with mastery, the search is not quite successful, but complete success comes at last in *The Tempest*, which he considers to be Shakespeare's supreme achievement. It is a pity that his stimulating and charming essay on *Cymbeline* makes too many concessions to bad traditions of criticism. He accepts Swinburne's and Gervinus' evaluation of Imogen, and asserts that she is 'the be-all and end-all of the play'. Hence he is led to assume that the theme of *Cymbeline* is the vindication of Imogen after wrong endured, which may, perhaps, be best described as the better half of a half-truth. Be that as it may, it involves him in the precarious argument that the play's complexity of plot diverts the mind from Imogen, and, though he pays full tribute to the magnificent craftsmanship of the last act, he fails to recognize the fact that its magnificence lies not so much in its vindication of Imogen as in its resolution of the physical and spiritual complexities as a whole.

Cymbeline studies over the past twenty-five years include the quasi-philosophical interpretations advanced by Mr F. C. Tinkler, Dr E. M. W. Tillyard, Mr G. Wilson Knight, and Father A. A. Stephenson, and the more pragmatic discussions by Dr Granville-Barker and Mr E. C. Pettet. Those which are concerned with interpretation are often original and challenging, and offer many valuable incidental comments, though it must be confessed that in all of them the elaboration of the main thesis is sometimes mystifying. Tinkler sees *Cymbeline* as a continuation of Shakespeare's achievement in tragedy, and believes that the plot was deliberately chosen for the development of material that already held essential interest for him.[2] The play presents a conflict between the tendency to escape from everyday life and the tendency to remain in it, and moves towards 'a repose achieved in spite of violence, the brutal action which constitutes the substratum of experience', ending, with a suggestion of rebirth, in a static tableau from which previous suggestions of savage farce have been carefully obliterated.

1. In *Shakespeare's Workmanship* (1918). In addition to the chapter on *Cymbeline* (pp. 259–81), that on 'Shakespeare's Later Workmanship' (pp. 221–40) contains useful material.
2. 'Cymbeline' in *Scrutiny*, VII (1938), pp. 5–20.

Tinkler distinguishes this savage farce in a good deal of the earlier action, and especially in a brutal strain discernible in the verse together with exaggeration in certain of the more important speeches.

Tillyard, too, considers *Cymbeline* to be complementary to the tragedies.[1] Tragedy, he argues, implies regeneration, and it was one of Shakespeare's main concerns in these last plays to develop the final phase of his tragic pattern towards the achievement of complete regeneration. Hence each of the final plays runs through a cycle in which the main character, who is a king, falls through his own evil or error from a state of prosperity to one of great suffering which, instead of leading to total destruction, as in the tragedies, generates a transforming element of atonement, so that in the end a new and fairer prosperity results. The idyllic element in these plays is complementary to this regenerative pattern and, far from being fortuitous or trivial, has an important metaphysical function since it fosters and maintains a sense of the complexity of existence and of the different planes on which life can be lived. The plays reveal 'a new proneness to contemplation' and a state of mind which is akin to the religious.

Cymbeline, for Tillyard, represents a halting and imperfect expression of these motives. Cymbeline's regeneration is a dead thing, and the characterization as a whole, despite some minor successes, is inconsistent, with Imogen alternating between a human being and a conventional heroine of the Griselda type. Shakespeare fails to strike a balance between the realistic presentation of character used in the tragedies and the more symbolic treatment which is called for in romance. The idyllic element too, is so loosely related to the regenerative theme that neither succeeds in reinforcing the other, so that the several planes of reality end in 'the queer phantasmagoric effect of a welter of unreality rather than in a vision of those different planes standing out in sharp and thrilling contrast'.[2]

Wilson Knight also regards the final plays as a vital extension of Shakespearean tragedy, affirming that Shakespeare abandoned the tragic method in order to develop his dramatic themes in terms of myth and miracle and to establish a pattern of immortality and conquest within apparent death and failure.[3] *Cymbeline* is, in the main, a historical play in which the dramatist blends his two primary historical interests, those of Britain and Rome. Interwoven with national issues is the conflict between Posthumus, who symbolizes what is best in British manhood, and Iachimo, the

---

1. *Shakespeare's Last Plays* (1938).   2. *Op. cit.*, p. 76.
3. *Op. cit.*, pp. 129–67, and *passim*.

representative not of Rome but of the corrupt Italy of the Renaissance. National and sexual degeneration are concurrent, but Imogen and the Princes are regenerative forces and the circumstances of the play yield a massive union. The final acceptance of Posthumus' marriage with Imogen typifies the matrimonial peace of the individual, the social integrity of the nation and the union of Britain's best manhood with the essence of royalty, while the Britain–Rome union, which Wilson Knight regards as central, transfers to Cymbeline's kingdom the virtues of Augustus' empire.

Fr Stephenson repudiates Tinkler's suggestion that *Cymbeline* presents a pattern of conflict and tension, and finds in it 'the *concentrated* tranquillity of "perfect activity"'.[1] Like Tinkler and, to some extent, Wilson Knight, he holds that the imagery is the key to the understanding of the play. He finds images of worth, value, presented in many, and frequently contrasting, forms, almost ubiquitous, and these lead him to conclude that Shakespeare was preoccupied with 'the idea of an ideal perfection, an absolute value'. Dr F. R. Leavis appends an editorial caveat in which he pronounces the interpretations of both Tinkler and Fr Stephenson unconvincing.[2] Their error lies, he thinks, in attempting to impose a profound significance upon a play whose scope does not, in fact, extend beyond that of conventional romance.

In general these interpretations seem to me to emphasize certain aspects of the play, sometimes arbitrarily selected, at the expense of others of equal or greater importance. Tillyard's cyclic pattern is more clearly discernible in *The Winter's Tale*, with its powerful formulation of crime, suffering, and reconciliation in which the audience has a full share, than in either *The Tempest*, where Prospero is more effectively the hermit magician than the wronged Duke of Milan, or *Cymbeline*. Viewed in relation to the regenerative pattern Cymbeline himself is, as Tillyard concedes, an almost meaningless cipher—at best a wholly passive participant—and we find that he is no more than that if we refer him to the Shakespearean tragic norm. Then he emerges as something less than Lear's shadow, a feeble, henpecked, credulous, boring half-reflection of heroic anger and madness, whose sanity only serves to mock his impotence. If, on the other hand, we set him against the Shakespearean comic tradition, or even against the romance pattern at large, he consorts familiarly enough with the Dukes of Venice, the Leonatos, the Alonsos, the vapid old gentlemen whose only push at chance and sufferance comes from their inability to endure the

1. 'The Significance of "Cymbeline" ' in *Scrutiny*, x (1942), pp. 329–38.
2. 'A Criticism of Shakespeare's Late Plays' in *Scrutiny*, x (1942), pp. 339–45.

toothache patiently, the rulers of state who were so infinitely less vital to Shakespeare's purposes than the Portias, Beatrices, Benedicks, Imogens—and even Clotens.

The national pattern, which Wilson Knight isolates, assumes at times a rich significance. There are those moments which catch at the imagination and remind us, as they reminded Shakespeare's first audiences, that behind both Britain and Rome there lies a traditional vision for the preservation of which men have fought and died, a thing which the Sicily, Bohemia, and Naples of the later romances fail to convey. Nevertheless, this national ethos seems to me to have no more real prominence than that of regeneration. If Shakespeare intended either theme to be central, his method of presentation, with its witch-like Queen, its poisons, its caves, flowers, and music, can only be regarded as ludicrous. If he conceived of these rambling fancies as a vital extension of his tragic experience, or envisaged Cymbeline, Imogen, and Posthumus as regenerate or regenerative successors to Lear, Othello, and Cordelia, or purposed that a rather sordid little squabble over unpaid tribute, with its stylized battle, should reinforce the moral patriotism of *Henry V* or *Julius Caesar*, he was surely guilty of something for which the Johnsonian 'unresisting imbecility' is far too mild a term.

Both Tinkler and Fr Stephenson ignore so much that has immediate relevance, even in the narrow field which they survey, that the one distributes no more than a set of half-truths, while the other moves, as it were by illumination, towards the concept of 'absolute value' which, as it happens, is nearly the whole truth. Both seem to be theorizing at some considerable distance from the play itself, and Leavis applies a useful corrective by insisting on the specifically romantic character of *Cymbeline*, though there is a sad lapse of critical perceptiveness in his repudiation of a deeper significance. The distinctive feature of *Cymbeline*, as I hope to demonstrate in the remaining parts of this introduction, is that it accommodates its comic, tragic, national, regenerative, and other patterns within the strict formula of romance, yet is able to resolve them into a unity in which their individual qualities no longer matter. Meanwhile I return to the two critics who have approached the play with a suitable degree of objectivity.

Granville-Barker's *Preface* has certain obvious defects.[1] The disintegration theories which were in the air when it was written left him perplexed and over-credulous, and his discussion of the characters of the play shows that he was still responsive to the methods of A. C. Bradley, so that his Imogen, his Posthumus, his Cloten are

---

1. *Op. cit.*, pp. 234–345.

invested with a reality that can scarcely be reconciled with Shakespeare's presumed intentions. Nevertheless, his essay is of primary importance to the student of *Cymbeline*, and valuable especially for its masterly analysis of various kinds of artifice that went to the making of the play. For him, *Cymbeline* is a romance, whose chief theme is 'chastity—and married chastity, that larger virtue', and this affords him scope for much sensible critical commentary without recourse to over-subtle interpretations of the play's meaning.

Pettet's excellent study of Shakespeare's debt to the romance tradition throws into relief much that is relevant to the better understanding of *Cymbeline*.[1] He shows that the term 'romance', as applied to Shakespeare's final plays, is not merely a vague substitute for something more specific, but is exact in the restricted and historical sense of the word. These plays belong in matter and tone to a literature of love and love-making, and are concordant with a tradition that includes *Guy of Warwick*, *Sir Bevis*, Malory's *Morte d'Arthur*, and the writings of Ariosto and Tasso; a tradition into which new vigour has been infused by Sidney in the *Arcadia* and Spenser in *The Faerie Queene*. Pettet offers a useful enumeration of the elements that go to the making of full-fledged Elizabethan romance. Love is treated as a sublime and momentous experience which imposes courtesy and leads to hazardous quests. Faithful love is subjected to abnormal strain, and situations arise which bring love into conflict with friendship. Romance makes use of complex incident which frequently arises from scheming and intrigue. Coincidence and mistaken identity are agents of both complication and simplification. Ultimately the whole contorted pattern yields to poetic justice which effects the conventional happy ending. Puppet characters, usually of royal or noble birth, actuated by motives which, whether good or bad, are wholly impossible, are made to undertake fantastic adventures, often to distant parts. Exhausting journeys through woods and wildernesses are a commonplace. Later romance has, in fact, devised a conventional Gothic landscape, and admits other accretions such as the cult of dejection and a wealth of preposterous decorative incident which includes dreams, poisons, wild animals, magic, and spells.

With this pattern before us, it would be futile to deny the claim of *Cymbeline* to be regarded as, strictly, a romance. Its use of all these conventional components is too obvious to require exemplification, and the final and abiding impression which it conveys is of romance generously presented. The final 'Exeunt' is the most

1. *Shakespeare and the Romance Tradition* (1949), pp. 174 ff.

pregnant word in the play, for Shakespeare's vision did not stop
short at the tableau which he builds up in the last scene, nor even
at the 'elaborate procession, the play dissolving into pageantry', as
Granville-Barker supposes. It went further, and envisaged a set of
characters who are to live happily ever after, retreating into the
ordered and decent background of the golden world.[1] In *Cymbeline*
we are, indeed, upon enchanted ground in a world of fine fabling,
and once this is recognized, the play, on one critical level at least,
no longer calls for any defence. 'The folly of the fiction, the absur-
dity of the conduct, the confusion of the names, and manners of
different times, and the impossibility of the events in any system
of life', which Johnson regarded as defects too palpable for serious
consideration, turn out, after all, to be among the prime virtues of
conventional romance. They crave to be accepted, not excused.

7. *CYMBELINE* AS EXPERIMENTAL ROMANCE

Cymbeline, then, is almost wholly a romance. Yet random check-
ing might suggest the contrary, and if we lighted casually on Cloten
and the two Lords, on Posthumus' tirade against women, on the
Senators and Tribunes, and on the Gaol scene, we might, in-
cautiously but not wholly unreasonably, conclude that if this is
romance it has taken some decidedly slippery turns. But the temptation to fly to extremes and label it tragedy or history, as some
critics have done, must be resisted, for the most that can be safely
inferred is that *Cymbeline* divagates in some way from the accepted
romance norm and that Shakespeare here has scored only a partial
success. This, in retrospect, proves to be the case, and the superior
merits of *The Winter's Tale* and *The Tempest* can, without much risk
of contradiction, be cited as proof, for in both the romance atmosphere is more easily secured and more powerfully sustained. But
with *Cymbeline*, still more with *Pericles*, we are back at one of the
root positions of Shakespeare's art. They represent the first fruits of
a new attempt and are, in consequence, experimental to a high
degree and prone to partial or total failure. Of all Shakespeare's
enterprises, these were doubtless the most difficult. To see them as
part of a general romance tradition which had produced abundant
masterpieces in prose and verse is one thing: to see them in relation
to a thoroughly disreputable tradition of dramatic romance, which
could boast no more than a handful of minor inanities, is quite
another. Romance conventions and stage conventions did not go

---

1. The use of the final curtain in modern productions seems to me quite alien
to Shakespeare's intentions.

hand in hand, and dramatic representation of the impossible adventures of unreal people in promiscuous surroundings was a heavy undertaking. Shakespeare, who ignored the classical unities of time and place and was prepared, in the interests of the characteristic diffuseness of romance, to let even unity of action fend for itself in *Cymbeline*, yet succeeded in the end in fitting the full romance picture into the classical frame. But the technical perfection of *The Tempest* is generally admitted to verge on the miraculous, and we must be prepared for lapses at the experimental stage. And whatever our final judgment of *Cymbeline*, we must not lose sight of the fact that it was a highly significant experiment which fully vindicated itself in its successors.

The errors which Shakespeare, in undertaking something hitherto unattempted, was almost bound to commit, are easily detected and can often be readily accounted for. He saw the need for complexity of incident and assembled an elaborate body of plot material to meet this traditional demand. On the whole he chose well. The story of Belarius and the Princes was obviously a correct choice. So, too, was the Wager, although it was the kind of tale that he would earlier have converted into comedy or tragedy of intrigue, shedding most of its romance trappings in the process. These could be held together by a royal figurehead of the conventional type, but Shakespeare erred in turning Cymbeline to that purpose. Some impalpable monarch like the King Phizantius of *Love and Fortune* would have served his purpose better. It is futile to object that the Cymbeline narrative element does not harmonize with the other plots, for romance can accommodate such anomalies.[1] Nor should the flagrant anachronisms which Cymbeline brings with him trouble us. They, too, are tolerated by the convention, and must, in any case, have been relatively unobtrusive on the Jacobean stage where Romans, Italians, and Early Britons would alike wear contemporary costume. Even the choice of a historical or pseudo-historical ruler cannot be condemned, for many romances are, in fact, impossible fictions woven around real people. Cymbeline, dull though he may have been, would have served, had it not been for what he entailed—namely a retreat to some of the least romantic pages of Holinshed and a certain temptation for Shakespeare to enlarge upon Roman military and political affairs in a manner better suited to *Julius Caesar* or *Coriolanus* than to romantic drama. Briefly, romance can carry a Cymbeline

---

1. Some of the Elizabethan history plays such as *Locrine* and *Edward the Third* admit a good deal of romantic material. Greene's *James the Fourth* is historical in name only. Its purely romantic plot derives from Cinthio.

but not a Caesar; it can encompass a half-civilized Britain but not the ordered state of Rome.

There is, then, this initial error in plot selection. Other apparent defects arise from the actual presentation of material. We have noticed that Shakespeare was now confronted with the problem of blending tragedy and comedy in the right amounts and of sustaining a balance throughout the greater part of the play, and that he took the precaution of introducing explanatory soliloquies, informative asides, and other frankly unsatisfactory artifices. From this point of view they were a wise precaution, for the tragic way of writing was not yet out of his system, and without them the play would have been hopelessly overweighted with tragic matter. The precise nature of the tragi-comic fusion requisite to romance is not easy to define or calculate, but it is reasonably safe to assert that the tragic potentialities should never be made to appear anything more than potentialities and that the formal happy ending should admit an anticipatory spirit of optimism. *Cymbeline* comes near to breaking down on both counts. Its first four acts, as we have noticed, result in such wholesale chaos that order can be restored only by a beneficent but mechanical deity. Jupiter, in other words, is a heavy weight thrown into the comic scale because chaos, comparable in dimensions, but not in intensity, with the chaos of *Othello*, *King Lear*, and *Macbeth*, has overloaded the tragic one. By far the greater part of *Cymbeline* moves towards a state of anarchy proper to tragedy but dubiously valid in tragi-comedy. Our final judgment, compelled by the transforming qualities of the concluding scene, may be that the end justifies the means, but the objection that the bulk of the play is over-tragic in tone and conception still holds. Shakespeare, we may suppose, came to realize this. He knew that some kind of cataclysm was germane to his purpose in the Romances, but saw that that which *Cymbeline* presented was excessive. It is very significant that chaos in *The Winter's Tale* does not extend beyond the third act: more significant still that, in *The Tempest*, the cataclysm is reduced to a single introductory scene.

The characters in *Cymbeline* are similarly disproportionate. In overweighting the action Shakespeare also overweights the agents and there is, at times, a destructive reality about the main personages of the play. Conventional romance makes little use of characterization. As a rule, the adventures that it relates are so utterly improbable as to eliminate all possibility of depicting consistent attitudes of mind or logical patterns of behaviour. Una, Sir Guyon, and Sir Artegall in *The Faerie Queene* personify specific virtues, and very little more. They have no reality, no character, and are pre-cisely what the convention demands. This prerequisite is a thing so obvious that Shakespeare could hardly have failed to recognize it. He must also have realized, at the very outset, that it entailed one very considerable practical difficulty, that of transferring char-acters who have no character from a literary medium to a dramatic one. This meant, of course, that the symbolic puppets of romance had to be presented not as verbal pictures but as real actors. In *Cymbeline*, artifice, music, and spectacle contribute something to-wards a solution, but stage performances sometimes reveal, as the text does not, how very imperfect the illusion is. Arviragus and Guiderius, for instance, are successful as symbols. There is no damaging reality about them, they live in romantic surroundings, they speak beautiful verse and intone exquisite lyrics. Yet, on the stage they are unconvincing, an embarrassment to actor, producer, and audience.[1]

It was not simply this transmutation from one medium to an-other that defeated Shakespeare. Whether he was still responsive to the tragic view of life can be allowed to remain a moot point, but it can scarcely be gainsaid that tragic elements obtrude upon his portrayal of character in *Cymbeline*. The convention demanded symbols, the stage demanded actors. That is a practical dilemma which can be more or less overcome by compromise. But once the compromise has been achieved, a further character problem remains. The *dramatis personae* must not be too realistically por-trayed, and should, since the outcome is to be a happy one, tend towards comedy rather than tragedy. This, too, Shakespeare realized, but familiar habits overshadowed his best intentions. The minor characters go far towards fulfilling romance demands, but the central figures have, too often, a tragic reality about them.

Cymbeline, the Queen, Belarius, Arviragus, and Guiderius are quite successful pieces of romance symbolism. Since he gives his name to the play, Cymbeline should, strictly, be regarded as a central controlling force, and that, if we accept him at his nominal value, is what he is, fulfilling as he does the function of the symbolic king of fairy tale. He is a puppet who never comes to life. When con-fronted by a real situation he is helpless:

> Now for the counsel of my son and queen,
> I am amazed with matter.

If we regard him from the realistic viewpoint, he is no more than

---

1. Perhaps I exaggerate. In the performances which I have seen the Princes have been sadly unconvincing. But see p. 212.

> this witless savage, Cymbeline,
> Whose brains were ever in his consort's head.[1]

and we then see him as a feeble monarch who invites comparison
with Lear. But the comparison is invalid, in kind as well as degree.
Lear is sufficiently a human being to arouse in us feelings of pity and
terror and to hold our sympathy: Cymbeline is so unreal that our
emotions are never stirred. The unreality is apt. As a creature of
flesh and blood he is almost meaningless: as a conventional symbol
he is, at least, adequate to the existing needs.[2]

The Queen has caused many critics to take Shakespeare to task.
She is the embodiment of malevolence in the person, not of Goneril
or Lady Macbeth, but of the fairy-tale witch and, with her flowers,
her poisons, her cats and dogs, bears little or no relation to everyday experience. Since the convention required a malign puppet,
and not a woman scheming evil, she might reasonably be reckoned
a success were it not for the access of human vigour that temporarily
shatters the illusion when Caius Lucius first comes to the British
Court.

Belarius and the Princes are generally in harmony with their
unreal surroundings. The situations in which they are involved
are, for the most part, fantastic, and Shakespeare has little difficulty in relating them to their world of enchanted unrealities.
Belarius impresses us as a piece of virtue, but not as a man of character. His morality is passive, and it can, indeed, be argued that his
deeds, such as they are, are quite immoral. There is, it seems, an art
in his portrayal. His speeches consist, almost exclusively, of abstract
moral generalizations which impress us only by their ineptitude,
and clearly serve no useful ethical purpose. They enable him, however, to remain a puppet, and to retreat, at practically every turn,
from such realities as threaten his symbolic anonymity. His first
speech will serve as illustration of this:

> A goodly day not to keep house with such
> Whose roof's as low as ours! Stoop, boys: this gate
> Instructs you how t'adore the heavens; and bows you
> To a morning's holy office. The gates of monarchs
> Are arch'd so high that giants may jet through
> And keep their impious turbans on, without
> Good morrow to the sun. Hail, thou fair heaven!

1. G. B. Shaw, *Cymbeline Refinished* (1938).

2. The symbolic force of Cymbeline must not be under-estimated. In accordance with the Shakespearean doctrine of degree, the king is obviously the most
important person in the play. Though not a vital dramatic character, he fulfils
an important dramatic function as the figure in whom all resolutions and uni-
fications are made perfect.

> We house i'th'rock, yet use thee not so hardly
> As prouder livers do.

Belarius' thoughts turn at once from the concrete reality of the low-roofed cave to moral abstraction, which is fantasticated by allusion to giants and turbans. The symbolism thus acquires a romantic colouring, and we have no difficulty in accepting him, from the start, as the conventional romance hermit. The effect at which Shakespeare is aiming can be further illustrated by comparison. Timon of Athens is compelled, like Belarius, to abjure the luxuries of the city and eke out his existence in a cave. He, too, is a victim of man's inhumanity, whose undeserved sufferings provoke moral utterance. Yet there is a fundamental difference in presentation:

> Earth, yield me roots!
> Who seeks for better of thee, sauce his palate
> With thy most operant poison! What is here?
> Gold? yellow, glittering, precious gold? No, gods,
> I am no idle votarist: roots, you clear heavens!
> Thus much of this will make black white, foul fair,
> Wrong right, base noble, old young, coward valiant.
> Ha, you gods! why this? what this, you gods? Why this
> Will lug your priests and servants from your sides,
> Pluck stout men's pillows from below their heads:
> This yellow slave
> Will knit and break religions, bless the accursed,
> Make the hoar leprosy adored, place thieves
> And give them title, knee and approbation
> With senators on the bench; this is it
> That makes the wappen'd widow wed again;
> She, whom the spital house and ulcerous sores
> Would cast the gorge at, this embalms and spices
> To the April day again. Come, damned earth,
> Thou common whore of mankind, that put'st odds
> Among the rout of nations, I will make thee
> Do thy right nature.

Here, as in Belarius' speech, the object leads to the moral and the moral is elaborated. But the whole process is unified, so that Timon's thoughts do not simply stray from the concrete to the abstract, and from the abstract to the fantastic. Instead of yielding the desired object (roots), the earth yields another object (gold), and so opens up for Timon a vision of the abstract (corruption), but that vision, we observe, is presented throughout in precise terms of concrete imagery. Timon's moralizing thus stands at the opposite extreme to that of Belarius. The one enlarges a simple object into complex reality, the other tends to escape from its object into a world of turbaned giants. Herein we comprehend the distinction drawn by Shakespeare between a tragic and a romantic character. It is possible, since *Cymbeline* must have followed close upon *Timon of Athens*, that Belarius' moralizing was suggested by the like tendency in Timon, but we must beware of drawing a false analogy. In his own mind, Shakespeare has differentiated quite clearly between the crazed pessimism of Timon and the whimsical optimism of Belarius. In the realistic character morality crystallizes, in the artificial one it evaporates.

There is evident artifice in the portrayal of Arviragus and Guiderius. From time to time they exist at the level of everyday reality. Both fight valiantly in what sounds to be a very real and bloody battle, and there is nothing idyllic about Guiderius' killing of Cloten. Yet both these incidents happen off-stage, and the battle becomes real only in Posthumus' report. The stage-directions in the last act suggest that Shakespeare was at pains to indicate that the battle, as a visible stage spectacle, must, in no circumstances, hint of reality. The exploits of the two Princes, then, must be taken in relation to the stylized fantasy which is depicted rather than to the graphic details which are related. As they appear before us on the stage, they have little damaging probability about them. For the greater part they are lyrical Arcadian figures uttering gentle unrealities. We might suppose that the killing of Cloten shatters the illusion, that Guiderius' savagery is intrusive and realistic. There is little that is idyllic about the printed page:

> This Cloten was a fool, an empty purse,
> There was no money in't: not Hercules
> Could have knock'd out his brains, for he had none:
> Yet I not doing this, the fool had borne
> My head, as I do his.

The savage tone is maintained:

> With his short sword,
> Which he did wave against my throat, I have ta'en
> His head from him: I'll throw't into the creek
> Behind our rock, and let it to the sea,
> And tell the fishes he's the queen's son, Cloten;
> That's all I reck.

And again:

> I have sent Cloten's clotpoll down the stream,
> In embassy to his mother; his body's hostage
> For his return.

But what of the stage spectacle that accompanies these words? The

idyllic prince slays a grotesque monster. There is so much convention, so much poetic justice about this that we feel no pity. The
slaying of Polonius, even of Edmund, move us more. This argues,
pretty conclusively, that the illusion which has been created
remains intact. Shakespeare, with his long experience of bloodthirsty revenge tragedies, well knew that, to be rendered less
horrible, horror must be made more horrible, and it was this knowledge that helped him here. If Guiderius had simply killed Cloten
and returned to speak the lines already quoted, he would exist on
what, for convenience, we may term the plane of tragic reality, to
which Hamlet's slaying of Polonius, in conjunction with his subsequent comments, serves as a rough analogy. The proper response
would be that of Gertrude to Hamlet's action:

O, what a rash and bloody deed is this!

But Shakespeare makes sure that we do not respond in that way
simply by augmenting the horror beyond what is reasonable. He
makes Guiderius enter bearing 'Cloten's clotpoll', so that what
would otherwise be serious is rendered ludicrous or fantastic. It is
an ugly incident, but with the conventional ugliness of romance,
where heads are severed from bodies with remorseless frequency.
The stage Guiderius is, in fact, for the time being, a variant, not of
Hamlet, but of Jack the Giant-Killer or one of King Arthur's
knights.

Guiderius, then, will pass muster as an idealized character sym-
bolizing courageous action. The integrity of Shakespeare's portrayal of Arviragus can never be called into question. As commentators have remarked, Shakespeare makes neat distinction between
him and his brother. Guiderius is active, Arviragus reflective. The
distinction, however, is not very deep-rooted. The two are shown
to be alike in lyrical utterance, and are, by implication, alike in
courage. They lack any clear-cut identifying traits, and emerge as
the conventional princes of romance.

Cloten should, perhaps, be grouped with these symbolic characters though there is an apparent generosity in his presentation
which might persuade us that he is a broad comic figure, or, in
Granville-Barker's phrase, 'a comic character drawn with a
savagely serious pen'. He must be accepted as a fool positive, for
external testimony is compelling on that point. Imogen calls him
fool and complains to her woman that she is 'sprited with a fool'.
To Guiderius he appears 'some fool', 'a fool, an empty purse'. The
Second Lord's sole function, so it seems, is to furnish a running commentary on his folly. Shakespeare carefully emphasizes this aspect

of his character. But combined with his folly, there is a proneness to vice, lechery, and violence, so that the total effect should be of a grotesque. At bottom, he represents Shakespeare's first attempt to portray a creature half-brute, half-human, and is aptly defined by Granville-Barker as 'this civilized Caliban'.[1] In action and intention, he is no more than that. In his speech, however, there is a certain sophistication. He occasionally commands the outward courtly graces, and sometimes voices thoughts that strike us as lying beyond his proper intellectual range. He had a capacity for comic utterance:

> Come, there's no more tribute to be paid: our kingdom is stronger than it was at that time: and (as I said) there is no moe such Caesars, other of them may have crook'd noses, but to owe such straight arms, none.

There is comedy in this defiance, but it is, I think, concordant with his grotesque nature. The Queen in this scene (III. i) becomes, uncharacteristically, the mouthpiece of national sentiments, but Cloten, as a spokesman for regenerated Britain, fails to impress us. There is childish mockery in his speeches, and it is a child's defiance that we hear. Cloten the patriot is still Cloten the fool, and his words must be judged in relation to the tense political issue which provokes them. Then they will be seen to be rash, obtrusive, and discourteous. Yet, if he is still the semi-monster in this diplomatic milieu, there are other occasions when the character portrayal seems inconsistent or even contradictory, and one is forced to conclude that Shakespeare shaped the actor rather at odds with the initial conception. But, as we have noted, his folly and brutality are heavily emphasized, and the Cloten that Shakespeare intended can be allowed to partner the Queen his mother as one of the human impossibilities that contribute to the comic pattern. He stands rather apart from the other characters we have so far discussed in that he is a more complex symbol, but is not presented with sufficient clarity.[2] Caliban, later, is the thing itself.

Close scrutiny will reveal that there are occasions when these symbolic characters lapse into a realism which is detrimental to the romantic tone, but these, save with Cloten, are so rare that they do nothing to impair the final impression, and it would be merely pedantic to emphasize them. All things considered, Shakespeare has achieved his object and has created characters flattened, insulated, idealized, and unreal, who belong to no normal system of

---

1. *Op. cit.*, p. 304.
2. W. M. Keck, *Shakespeare Association Bulletin*, 1935, pp. 68–72, suggests that Cloten's speeches were augmented by Robert Armin. See note to v. iv. 1.

life, but to a world of romance. Against these we have to set
Posthumus, Imogen, and Iachimo, in all of whom the execution is
more patently at variance with the conception. So much emerges
from the general impression left by most of the scenes which relate
to the wager theme, and is fully confirmed on closer examination.

Iachimo is less a symbol than a stock figure, a reduced pattern
of the Italian villain. He has been compared to Edmund and Iago,
and Wilson Knight goes so far as to claim that, as a person, he is
more rounded out and more analysable. There is little justification
for either the comparison or the claim. Iachimo is a vainglorious,
self-dramatizing rogue, but his acts of villainy do not carry real
conviction. He lacks the personality, the insistent malice, the cue
to revenge, the long-term policy of evil which the tragic villains
undoubtedly possess.

> She writes so to you? Doth she?

marks the limit of his deception, and we have only to set this
against Iago's

> She did deceive her father, marrying you:

to see the lowered vitality in presentation. He sets out for Britain
confident of winning the wager on his own supposed merits, and
there is nothing specifically evil in this. It may be argued that he
has lured Posthumus into a false position, but the wager itself, however deplorable, is fair enough, and it may be noted that our villain
accepts desperately long odds. In this, he comes near to the earlier
comic villain, Shylock, whose merry bond stands only one chance
in a million of fulfilling his hopes. Such stratagems, for drama's
sake, are granted improbable success, or seeming success. Those of
Edmund and Iago, we realize, cannot possibly fail.

In the second stage of his rake's progress, he resembles more the
tragic villain, but Imogen is not deceived. He wins his wager by
resorting to the kind of trick that Iago would contemn. As
Granville-Barker observes: 'From the first there is something fantastic about the fellow, and no tragically-potent scoundrel, we
should be sure, will ever come out of a trunk.'[1] His purpose is to
win the wager, and there is no deeper malice behind his actions, no
policy aimed at Imogen's destruction. After his defeat at the hands
of the disguised Posthumus, he reflects:

> I have belied a lady,
> The princess of this country; and the air on't
> Revengingly enfeebles me.

That, so far as he is aware, is the utmost limit of his crime.

1. *Op. cit.*, p. 305.

In the last scene of the play, when confession is extorted from him, Iachimo embroiders his tale.[1] The rambling confession is really a plea for forgiveness and secures his pardon. He is evidently not, like Cloten and the Queen, a monster who must, at all costs, be exterminated. There is a place for him in the final pattern of regeneration. His villainous integrity has been stripped off him and he has proved plain fool at last.

It is not possible to accept this self-deluding, self-excusing libertine, with his small repertoire of tricks, as the thoroughbred Machiavellian villain of tragic tradition. In conception he is the mischief-maker of comedy, conventional, artificial, and inconsistent, and stands, in relation to Shakespearean character patterns, about midway between Shylock and Autolycus. In practice, however, he goes beyond convention. He carries an air of psychological probability at times, and admits touches of individualizing detail which are at odds with type portrayal. The character who can say:

> Had I this cheek
> To bathe my lips upon: this hand, whose touch
> (Whose every touch) would force the feeler's soul
> To th'oath of loyalty: this object, which
> Takes prisoner the wild motion of mine eye,
> Firing it only here, should I (damn'd then)
> Slaver with lips as common as the stairs
> That mount the Capitol: join gripes, with hands
> Made hard with hourly falsehood (falsehood, as
> With labour): then by-peeping in an eye
> Base and illustrious as the smoky light
> That's fed with stinking tallow: it were fit
> That all the plagues of hell should at one time
> Encounter such revolt

ceases to contribute to an illusion. He imposes reality upon fantasy, tragedy upon reality.

It would be unreasonable to ask that the prime force in the wager plot should be too unreal, too much the product of artifice. No dramatic artist has ever found it either easy or rewarding to present his bad characters as puppets or bare symbols. But Iachimo might have been made to conform more closely to the general pattern. His reality and occasional tragic tone mark a lapse from the world of romance to that of tragedy. Had he been more systematically portrayed, *Cymbeline* would have gained in dramatic uniformity. But it might then have been the poorer by the absence of much fine poetry.

Posthumus Leonatus should, for the purposes of conventional

1. See note to v. v. 150–209.

romance, be a *chevalier sans peur et sans reproche*. This, in fact, is how
he is first presented to us:

> a creature such
> As, to seek through the regions of the earth
> For one his like, there would be something failing
> In him that should compare.

The emphasis that is laid on his incorruptible virtue in the opening
scene must be intentional. Since Posthumus, who is quite one of the
dullest of Shakespeare's heroes, never really comes to life,[1] it should
not be difficult for him to sustain this role of perfect knighthood,
and we should never call his honour and virtue into question. But
we do. Professor W. W. Lawrence, in his most able apology, has
shown that Posthumus' actions are in accordance with the chivalric
code,[2] but much of what we see of him is diametrically opposed
both to that code and to the common functions of romance. There
is, for instance, what Lawrence calls his 'sudden and terrible sexual
jealousy'. Jealousy is too human and too much out of character:
sexuality is too real, too much at variance with the sexless pattern
of love-making which the romances present: and the terror is too
terrible. The puppet is plastered over with the cynicism of Edmund,
the pessimism of Lear, and the violence of Timon, and rants with
the incoherence of Coriolanus.

His tirade against womankind is the signal instance of Posthumus' deviation from the romantic norm. What we were told of
him in the first act has been cancelled at the end of the second by
a clumsily executed tragic soliloquy. And this impression of a
tragically debased figure persists throughout the third and fourth
acts in which he does not appear. His return in Act v does little to
restore the original conception. His repentance and melancholy
are, perhaps, the conventional romance ones. We see him mainly
as a soldier, and only at the very end as a lover. His battle narrative
is graphic and realistic. It does not aid illusion, nor, at this point in
the play, does it shatter it. It wears a look of superfluity, as if Shakespeare felt the desperate necessity of giving his hero a fair share of
the dialogue. Perhaps the earlier soliloquy originated in the same
way.[3]

The romantic heroine should be the very perfection of beauty
and virtue, the idealized, ethereal, passive princess of fairy-tale,

1. W. H. Clemen (*The Development of Shakespeare's Imagery*, p. 210) justly points
out that the colourlessness of Posthumus' character is reflected in his language.
He is given very few striking images.

2. *Shakespeare's Problem Comedies*, pp. 174–205.

3. In the play as it was first conceived, he must have been virtually a hero
without a part. As it is, he disappears for two acts.

divorced from the trivialities of everyday life. Hermione, Perdita,
and Miranda are so conceived, so fashioned. In Imogen, the conception is impaired by excessive vitality. We are several times
reminded of her symbolical significance. She is 'alone th' Arabian
bird', 'divine Imogen', and

> undergoes
> More goddess-like than wife-like, such assaults
> As would take in some virtue.

Even Cloten's gross wits perceive that

> she hath all courtly parts more exquisite
> Than lady, ladies, woman, from every one
> The best she hath, and she of all compounded
> Outsells them all.

But it is the comic heroine who resolves to ride to Milford dressed in

> A riding-suit; no costlier than would fit
> A franklin's housewife.

and who reflects:

> Best draw my sword; and if mine enemy
> But fear the sword like me, he'll scarcely look on't.

It is the indignant woman of this world who retorts upon her
father:

> I beseech you sir,
> Harm not yourself with your vexation
> I am senseless of your wrath.

who repulses Iachimo with:

> Away, I do condemn mine ears, that have
> So long attended thee.

who rounds upon Cloten with:

> His mean'st garment,
> That ever hath but clipp'd his body, is dearer
> In my respect, than all the hairs above thee,
> Were they all made such men.

and bitterly complains:

> I am sprited with a fool,
> Frighted, and anger'd worse.

Reality usurps the symbol, and it is often a tragic reality:

> False to his bed? What is it to be false?
> To lie in watch there, and to think on him?

To weep 'twixt clock and clock? If sleep charge Nature,
To break it with a fearful dream of him,
And cry myself awake? That's false to's bed, is it?

Imogen has been called a puppet, a failure. She has been exalted to the immortal godhead of womanhood. Really she is a superb accident, a Perdita or Miranda who defeated Shakespeare's intentions by coming to life. The dramatist knew well enough how to present chastity as a symbolic figure, as the passionless splendour of Valeria, in *Coriolanus*, v. iii, shows:

The noble sister of Publicola,
The moon of Rome, chaste as the icicle
That's curdied by the frost from purest snow
And hangs on Dian's temple.

but he was not yet adept at extending such a character in relation to a broad dramatic action. He tended, therefore, to fall back upon his earlier practice, in both comedy and tragedy, so that the symbol acquired a varied reality all her own. At one moment she assumes the temper of Beatrice, at another, the resourcefulness of Rosalind. She plays Cordelia to her father, but Desdemona to her husband. She is, to adapt a phrase from Keats, continually informing and filling some other body, though her primary symbolical meaning is never really lost.[1] She is, we must cheerfully admit, a character sadly out of character in this play of *Cymbeline*, and analysis shows her to be a various and erratic tissue of inconsistencies.[2] Yet the cumulative effect is enchanting, and if, on occasion, we are content to forget the play and concentrate on its heroine, no great harm is done, provided that the disproportionate response remains a private one.

8. STYLE

In *Cymbeline* Shakespeare explored a new way of using plot material within the limits of a convention which also demanded a radically different treatment of character. We have seen something of the problems that confronted him in the organization of situations and agents, and it now remains to consider the further problem of fashioning a style in harmony with romantic action and with what set out to be symbolic characters. In the mature tragedies Shakespeare devised the most supple and moving medium of communication that drama has ever known. These plays are dramatic

1. Clemen (*op. cit.*) finds that the imagery connected with Imogen 'does not go beyond the conventionalism of the Elizabethan sonnets', but I think that a new and richer significance emerges.
2. There are moments in the play when she recalls the giggling schoolgirl!

poems in the fullest sense. Action, thought, character, poetry, and imagery are so completely interfused that it is impossible to isolate any one element. Shakespeare, unless he had lapsed into that bored indifference which Strachey postulates, would certainly not wish his Romances to stand at a lower level of creation than his tragedies. He would inevitably seek to achieve the same indivisible harmony. Such is, in fact, the achievement of *The Tempest* and *The Winter's Tale*. But romance, which imposes a new species of action and a changed process of character portrayal, would, by implication, call for new forms of expression. The scene is no longer in a world of actualities, where

> Injurious Time now with a robber's haste
> Crams his rich thievery up.

but in a fairyland of unrealities.[1] The need is now for lyrical movement and lightly freighted imagery, and for the elimination of much of the rhetoric, the complexity, the sustained concretion of images that contributed so powerfully to the unity of the tragedies.

Considered in general terms, *Cymbeline* reflects Shakespeare's later style. Blank verse is handled with the utmost freedom, and run-on lines, light, weak, and double endings are marked characteristics. Ellipsis and elision contribute greatly to stylistic economy, and short speeches in particular are sometimes so concentrated as to be perplexing, thus:

> One sand another
> Not more resembles that sweet rosy lad,
> Who died, and was Fidele.

or thus:

> Thou shouldst have made him
> As little as a crow, or less, ere left
> To after-eye him.

There is no perceptible decline in technical competence, but much of the poetry seems to lack compulsion. Exquisite things are generated from time to time, but sustained inspiration is lacking.

The truth is that the Shakespeare of *Cymbeline* was a man in search of a style. In *Othello*, *Antony and Cleopatra*, and *The Tempest*, to take three diverse examples, he was able to bring a pre-existent capacity for expression to bear upon his material, so that, 'his mind and hand went together', but *Cymbeline* is transitional and experimental in style, as in other matters, and the surmise that it reveals

1. Unrealities in which injurious time plays no controlling part. *Cymbeline* has relatively few time allusions in comparison with some of the middle-period works (*2 Henry IV*; *As You Like It*; a number of the Sonnets) which seem to reflect a personal obsession.

Shakespeare committed, for once, to slow-endeavouring art is probably not far from the truth. There is evidence of an attempt to reduce tragic expression to a lower pitch. A new kind of lyrical verse is used extensively for the first time. Occasionally the strain of the endeavour is apparently too great, and we detect a slackening of effort with a consequent descent into flabby redundancies and trite couplets.

Shakespeare's relapses into tragic action and motivation inevitably affected his style, and what may be termed retrogressive expression is seen at its fullest (and richest) in Iachimo's early verse speeches. His first meeting with Imogen brings him, as we have seen, into near conformity with the tragic pattern, and thought, language, and imagery alike add further to this effect. His tortuous excogitation and self-justification are developed, just as Iago's are, in gross or bestial images:

> apes and monkeys,
> 'Twixt two such shes, would shatter this way, and
> Contemn with mows the other.
> Sluttery, to such neat excellence oppos'd,
> Should make desire vomit emptiness,
> Not so allur'd to feed.

> The cloyed will:
> That satiate yet unsatisfied desire, that tub
> Both fill'd and running: ravening first the lamb,
> Longs after for the garbage.

It is excellent writing but unfitted to the occasion. Such incongruities occur elsewhere in the play. Thus Pisanio gives tragic shape to superfluous thoughts:

> No, 'tis slander,
> Whose edge is sharper than the sword, whose tongue
> Outvenoms all the worms of Nile, whose breath
> Rides on the posting winds, and doth belie
> All corners of the world. Kings, queens, and states,
> Maids, matrons, nay, the secrets of the grave
> This viperous slander enters.

Powerful images from *Macbeth* and *Antony and Cleopatra* have intruded here.

At times Shakespeare seems to recognize that he has allowed his characters to react excessively, and then attempts, with dubious success, to relieve the tension with stylistic variation. Posthumus' wild soliloquy is a case in point:

> Is there no way for men to be, but women
> Must be half-workers? We are all bastards,

> And that most venerable man, which I
> Did call my father, was I know not where
> When I was stamp'd.

This is pure *Timon of Athens*, and the full tragic intensity is sustained over a dozen lines:

> O, vengeance, vengeance!
> Me of my lawful pleasure she restrain'd,
> And pray'd me oft forbearance: did it with
> A pudency so rosy, the sweet view on't
> Might well have warm'd old Saturn, that I thought her
> As chaste as unsunn'd snow.

But then comes a disintegrating change:

> O, all the devils!
> This yellow Iachimo, in an hour, was't not?
> Or less, at first?—Perchance he spoke not, but
> Like a full-acorn'd boar, a German one,
> Cried 'O!' and mounted.

Tragedy has given way to the bathos of mental arithmetic and grotesque imagery clumsily contrived. Thereafter, the soliloquy degenerates into an incoherent rant, and ends with a ludicrous picture of Posthumus as a writer of satirical broadsides:

> I'll write against them,
> Detest them, curse them.

It is bad tragedy and, what is worse, bad tragi-comedy.

Imogen, even in dark situations, fares better, and many of her speeches show Shakespeare moving towards more congruent utterance. The following lines are spoken when she is temporarily a tragic figure in a temporarily tragic situation:

> Why, I must die:
> And if I do not by thy hand, thou art
> No servant of thy master's. Against self-slaughter
> There is a prohibition so divine
> That cravens my weak hand: Come, here's my heart,
> (Something's afore't,—soft, soft! we'll no defence)
> Obedient as the scabbard. What is here?
> The scriptures of the loyal Leonatus,
> All turn'd to heresy? Away, away,
> Corrupters of my faith! you shall no more
> Be stomachers to my heart: thus may poor fools
> Believe false teachers: though those that are betray'd
> Do feel the treason sharply, yet the traitor
> Stands in worse case of woe.

Here the expression, in spite of a somewhat pointless echo of *Hamlet*, modifies the tragic force. The situation is made to seem serious, but not terrible or cruel. The verse moves to a tempo brisker than that of normal tragic speech, and the imagery has been perceptibly lightened, tending to be fanciful rather than imaginative, and carrying no overtones. The argument is developed logically, almost wittily, and the concretion of images is the outcome of an intellectual rather than an overwrought emotional process, so that the whole utterance is made to lack the finality of despair in, for instance, Ophelia's

> And I, of ladies most deject and wretched,
> That suck'd the honey of his music vows,
> Now see that noble and most sovereign reason,
> Like sweet bells jangled, out of tune and harsh;
> That unmatch'd form and feature of blown youth
> Blasted with ecstasy.

It is evident that Shakespeare is moving towards a new kind of tragi-comic expression. In the last stages of *Cymbeline* the task has almost been accomplished, and it is the master craftsman who emerges in Imogen's soliloquy over the headless body of Cloten, which, in my opinion, is the finest thing in the play. The situation here is complex. For Imogen it is all in deadly earnest, and she piles one tragic error upon another. To the audience, the errors are ludicrous and the whole situation farcical. If the headless corpse imparts a touch of grimness, that is soon forgotten. It is, after all, Cloten's body and we have no tears to waste on him. Shakespeare resolves the complexities with facetious grace liberating the spirit of comedy into what is ostensibly a tragic period and allowing Imogen's half-conscious thoughts free play. We can detect many elements which contribute, sometimes inexplicably, to the resultant tragi-comic unity. A play of fancy relieves the tragic note:

> These flowers are like the pleasures of the world;
> This bloody man, the care on't.

>   Good faith,
> I tremble still with fear: but if there be
> Yet left in heaven as small a drop of pity
> As a wren's eye, fear'd gods, a part of it!

Once or twice calculated anticlimax relieves the tension.

>   Pisanio,
> All curses madded Hecuba gave the Greeks,
> And mine to boot, be darted on thee!

> O Posthumus, alas,
> Where is thy head? where's that? Ay me! where's that?
> Pisanio might have kill'd thee at the heart,
> And left this head on.

Ambiguity is a conspicuously successful device:

> A headless man? The garments of Posthumus?
> I know the shape of's leg: this is his hand:
> His foot Mercurial: his Martial thigh:
> The brawns of Hercules.
>
> Damn'd Pisanio
> Hath with his forged letters (damn'd Pisanio)
> From this most bravest vessel of the world
> Struck the main-top!

These lines which have tragic validity when applied to the supposedly dead Posthumus, are merely farcical in relation to Cloten. And throughout the soliloquy, the imagery is light and is left undeveloped. It is delicately fanciful:

> 'Twas but a bolt of nothing, shot at nothing,
> Which the brain makes of fumes.
>
> as small a drop of pity
> As a wren's eye.

and the language itself admits such prettinesses as 'Ods pittikins', and 'O gods and goddesses!'.[1]

Much of *Cymbeline*, then, is written in verse which, beginning in a tragic vein, is gradually modified into a tragi-comic utterance which Shakespeare occasionally uses with sure effect. Side by side with this goes a new kind of poetry, frankly lyrical in tone, which revives the emblematic and mythological decorations characteristic of the Elizabethan Renaissance and weaves exquisite patterns round birds, beasts, and flowers. Such poetry has, of course, no relation to Shakespeare's tragic practice, and first emerges clearly in *Pericles*:

> No, I will rob Tellus of her weed,
> To strew thy green with flowers: the yellows, blues,
> The purple violets, and marigolds,
> Shall as a carpet hang upon thy grave,
> While summer-days do last.

This verse, which may, for convenience, be termed neo-Arcadian, is obviously suited to the needs of dramatic romance, and especially

---

1. The same oath is used by Scarus in *Antony and Cleopatra*, III. x. 5, but with an instructive difference.

to its more idyllic episodes. Shakespeare uses it extensively in *Cymbeline* and the play shows an increasing tendency to fuse it with the more specifically dramatic tragi-comic norm. In *The Winter's Tale* and *The Tempest* the fusion is complete and sustained.

It has sometimes been assumed that, in adopting this kind of verse for his Welsh scenes, Shakespeare was following the example of Fletcher. The surmise is credible but wholly superfluous, for the truth is that this kind of writing was new only in relation to Shakespeare's dramatic style. Amongst the Elizabethans, it was a convention—almost the convention—and assuredly Shakespeare had no need to turn to Fletcher for what had already been quite as well done by Spenser, Sidney, Barnefield, Constable, and a host of others. Nor did he need Fletcher, with or without the moral support of Beaumont, to reveal to him that such writing could be made to serve dramatic ends, for he already knew that even the turgid *Mucedorus* is relieved by such lyrical intervals as:

> When thou art vp, the wood lanes shalbe strawed
> With violets, cowslips, and swete marigolds
> For thee to trampel and to trace vpon.

This question of Shakespeare's dependence on others could be argued at great length and much ground would be covered in the process. The most sensible and probable assumption is that he relied, as he so often did, on earlier experience, and that the new strain of verse found in the Romances represents an extension of that energy which had some years previously gone to the making of *Venus and Adonis* and many of the sonnets.

It is reasonably safe to claim that *Venus and Adonis*, 'the first heir of my invention', was very much in Shakespeare's thoughts when he was writing *Cymbeline*. Both play and poem exhibit the same Arcadian features, extensive use of the pathetic fallacy and the long episodic sentence, and both move within the same range of imagery. Classical images are, of course, very conspicuous, and Wilson Knight has drawn attention to the immense wealth of classical and mythological allusion in *Cymbeline*. The floral and faunal images so ubiquitously self-evident in the play, are commonplaces of the poem, which affords horse, deer, boar, hare, fox, lark, eagle, dive-dapper, blue-veined violets, primrose bank, lily prison'd in a gaol of snow, to take only a few random examples. The emblematic force of many of these is retained in *Cymbeline*. Imogen, for example, is 'fresh lily', 'sweetest, fairest lily', 'the bird . . . that we have made so much on': her face is like the 'pale primrose', her veins like the 'azur'd harebell'. Similarly, in Arviragus'

> We are beastly; subtle as the fox for prey,
> Like warlike as the wolf for what we eat:
> Our valour is to chase what flies: our cage
> We make a quire, as doth the prison'd bird,
> And sing our bondage freely.

emblematic elements from the poem:

> But if thou needs wilt hunt, be ruled by me;
> Uncouple at the timorous flying hare,
> Or at the fox which lives by subtlety,
> Or at the roe which no encounter dare

are extended and augmented.

Parallelism of thought and phrase occurs. Adonis'

> Mine ears, that to your wanton talk attended,
> Do burn themselves for having so offended.

may be set alongside Imogen's

> Away, I do condemn mine ears, that have
> So long attended thee.

The similarity between:

> Look when a painter would surpass the life,
> In limning out a well-proportion'd steed,
> His art with nature's workmanship at strife,
> As if the dead the living should exceed.

and Iachimo's

>   A piece of work
> So bravely done, so rich, that it did strive
> In workmanship and value, which I wonder'd
> Could be so rarely and exactly wrought,
> Since the true life on't was—

together with

>   never saw I figures
> So likely to report themselves; the cutter
> Was as another Nature, dumb; outwent her,
> Motion and breath left out.

relates to a subject that Shakespeare returned to time and again, but some significance attaches to it in view of his apparent preoccupation in these last plays with artistic perfection, a preoccupation which colours the presentations of Hermione as a living statue.[1]

---

1. The detailed commentary in *The Winter's Tale*, v. ii and v. iii, is surely significant.

The kinship extends even to trite sententiae. Thus, in *Venus and Adonis*,

> Seeds spring from seeds and beauty breedeth beauty;
> Thou wast begot; to get it is thy duty.

the rhetorical pattern seems to look forward, via the Sonnets, to Belarius'

> Cowards father cowards, and base things sire base;
> Nature hath meal, and bran; contempt, and grace.[1]

It is unnecessary to dwell at length on this assumption of an earlier style in those parts of the play which concern Belarius and the Princes, and their contact with Imogen, for it is everywhere so evident that it requires no underlining. Instead let us turn to Iachimo's speech in Imogen's bedchamber, a speech which undoubtedly belongs to Shakespeare's maturity and ranks with the loveliest poetry that he ever wrote. There we shall find his dependence on the early exercise in poetic narrative reflected at practically every turn. A retrospective classical simile:

> Our Tarquin thus
> Did softly press the rushes, ere he waken'd
> The chastity he wounded.

which reverts, of course, not to *Venus and Adonis* but to *The Rape of Lucrece*, is succeeded by a standard mythological apostrophe: 'Cytherea!' Imogen, first likened to the goddess of Love, is then translated into the emblem of chastity, 'fresh lily!' The accompanying conceit:

> And whiter than the sheets!

is a palpable echo of *Venus and Adonis*:

> Who sees his true-love in her naked bed,
> Teaching the sheets a whiter hue than white.

The lines that follow are a little obscure:

> That I might touch!
> But kiss, one kiss! Rubies unparagon'd,
> How dearly they do't:

but I think, with Capell, that Iachimo kisses Imogen, and that his 'dearly' carries something of the old Elizabethan conceit of buying and selling kisses. The Elizabethan tone of 'rubies unparagon'd' calls for no comment. With

> 'tis her breathing that
> Perfumes the chamber thus:

---

1. This is one of the disputed couplets. See note to IV. ii. 26–7.

we return to *Venus and Adonis*:

> For from the stillitory of thy face excelling
> Comes breath perfumed that breedeth love by smelling.

So too with:

> th' enclosed lights, now canopied
> Under these windows, white and azure, lac'd
> With blue of heaven's own tinct.

which is strikingly reminiscent of:

> Her two blue windows faintly she up-heaveth.

In the remainder of the speech we may note the classical allusions to the Gordian knot, the tale of Tereus and Philomel; the Elizabethan, doubtless Ovidian, images of the dragons of the night and of dawn baring the raven's eye, and, above all, that typical Elizabethan interest in the veining of flowers implicit in:

> On her left breast
> A mole cinque-spotted: like the crimson drops
> I' th' bottom of a cowslip.[1]

More significant than any verbal debts is the re-emergence of that intense sensibility towards tiny things which is apparent in Shakespeare's early work. That sympathy which, in *Venus and Adonis*, goes out to 'the timorous flying hare', 'poor birds, deceived with painted grapes' and the snail, who, his

> tender horns being hit,
> Shrinks backward in his shelly cave with pain,

is everywhere apparent in *Cymbeline*: 'you bees that make these locks of counsel', 'as small a drop of pity as a wren's eye', 'thus smiling, as some fly had tickled slumber', 'our cage we make a quire, as doth the prison'd bird'. We may observe how style spreads through feeling to colour character. This acute sensibility towards flowers and small creatures in Imogen and her brothers is contrasted with the Queen's cold-blooded experiments on 'such creatures as we count not worth the hanging'. The 'violets, cowslips, and the primroses' are, for her, no more than the ingredients for distilments which she can put to baleful uses. Without pressing the point too far, we can assume that the neo-Arcadian style

---

1. As editors have duly noted, *The Faerie Queene*, VI. xii. 7, affords a parallel, but it is not necessary to suppose that Shakespeare was directly indebted to Spenser.

brought with it certain nuances that contributed to symbolic characterization. Whether these fall under the generic term of 'pathetic fallacy' it is, perhaps, wiser not to ask.

In general, *Cymbeline* moves towards a fusion of two styles, the one virtually evolved from a current medium, the other imposed by previous practice. Complete harmony is achieved sporadically, and the play, as a whole, is more unified in conception than in execution. Once or twice purely comic scenes are introduced, and these serve as foils to the tragic excesses that we have noted, but the practice of allowing one kind to cancel the other is too violent for a play of this type which calls for uniformity of presentation above everything.

9. IMAGERY

Much that relates to the imagery of the play has already received incidental notice.[1] Natural images, covering trees, flowers, and, especially, birds are very frequent. Classical images are common, and art and architecture are freely drawn upon. These are all concordant with the play's romantic function. Gross and brutal elements of imagery occur chiefly in those sections of the play which deviate into tragedy, and may, therefore, be intrusive. Images connected with buying, selling, weight, and exchange are surprisingly frequent and pervade the whole play. Professor Spurgeon thought that this possibly related to something which was 'much in Shakespeare's mind at the time', and hinted at some business transaction. This, though possible, lacks confirming evidence, and, as Miss Spurgeon concedes, such images could have been suggested by the wager story and the Roman demand for tribute. The commercial tone of *Frederyke of Jennen* may be relevant. But I am inclined to regard them as an overflow from the tragedies since, like the gross images employed by Iachimo, they are especially conspicuous in *Timon of Athens*. Their connection with the strand of imagery relating to worth or value, which Fr Stephenson segregates, is too obvious to require comment.

The various sets of images bear a more subtle relationship one to another than appears at first sight, and their contribution to the total effect is extremely important. Shakespeare several times dwells on the internal and external nature of things:

1. The writings of Wilson Knight and, to a lesser extent, Tinkler and Fr Stephenson, are relevant. Large-scale studies of Shakespeare's imagery include Caroline Spurgeon, *Shakespeare's Imagery* (1935) and Wolfgang Clemens's *Shakespeare's Bilder* (1936), the second of which has appeared in an English translation (*The Development of Shakespeare's Imagery*, 1951). E. A. Armstrong's *Shakespeare's Imagination* (1946) draws some exciting, if occasionally dubious, conclusions.

> So fair an outward, and such stuff within . . .
>
> . . . that which makes him both without and within.
>
> All of her that is out of door most rich!
> If she be furnish'd with a mind so rare,
> She is alone th' Arabian bird . . .
>
> The fashion, less without and more within.

and the idea is extended in such lines as:

> O sleep, thou ape of death, lie dull upon her,
> And be her sense but as a monument,
> Thus in a chapel lying.

These are in part value images and also connect with the play's body of architectural images, but their distinctive feature is that they are analytic, and that the division tends to be one of body and mind. Shakespeare seems to be drawing near to those metaphysical poets, Donne, Habington, Lord Herbert, and Cleveland, with whom the theme of soul and body is a constant one, save that, unlike them, he does not suggest that mind and body are separable entities. This strand of imagery is complementary to another one which is essentially conjunctive. The picture of things being joined or compounded together is a frequent one:

> I do extend him, sir, within himself,
> Crush him together, rather than unfold
> His measure duly.

As fair, and as good—a kind of hand-in-hand comparison

>   to knit their souls
> . . . in self-figur'd knot

>   from every one
> The best she hath, and she of all compounded
> Outsells them all.

>   I yoke me
> In my good brother's fault:

>   Nobly he yokes
> A smiling with a sigh;

>   I do note
> That grief and patience rooted in them both,
> Mingle their spurs together.

O, the charity of a penny cord! it sums up thousands in a trice:

>   let his virtue join
> With my request,

For condition,
A shop of all the qualities that man
Loves woman for . . .

A more precise symbolism seems to me to attach to many of those natural images which concern birds. Posthumus is represented as an eagle. He is so termed by Imogen in I. ii, and the analogy is reinforced by such remarks as that of the Frenchman, that 'he could behold the sun' with firm eyes. The fact that the eagle has other significances within the framework of the play does not diminish the force of this particular symbol, and it can be argued that these, too, are relevant to Posthumus since the eagle imagery usually bears some relation to his presence or to his values, while Jove's eagle itself is private in the sense that it belongs only to his vision. Whether this is so or not scarcely matters. The parallel between Posthumus, the 'noble lord', and the eagle, the lord among birds, would be immediately grasped by Shakespeare's audience, however considerable the degree of obscuring detail. Imogen, as Wilson Knight notes, is conceived aerially, and, as Fidele, is 'the bird . . . that we have made so much on'. Iachimo is more precise when he terms her 'alone th' Arabian bird' and, in view of her seeming destruction and restoration, this Phoenix symbol is the appropriate one.[1] For the rest, the Princes are the 'poor unfledg'd' who make their cage 'a quire', the lack of definition corresponding with their unrevealed identity. Cloten is, fittingly enough, 'a puttock'; Belarius, who is wise, is 'like a crow'; Posthumus' supposed seductress is 'some jay of Italy'; and Iachimo is, apparently, a raven.[2] The inference, I think, is that Shakespeare tended to see his characters simultaneously as human beings and as birds, so that they are given the kind of double signification that belongs to animal fables of the Æsop kind—or rather the double signification that had recently been brilliantly exploited by Ben Jonson in *Volpone*, where Volpone is the Fox, Corbaccio the Raven, Voltore the Vulture, Corvino the Crow.[3] Possibly Shakespeare followed Jonson's lead, but in a different way and for a different purpose, and I shall attempt to relate that purpose to the play as a whole in the final section of this introduction. Meanwhile it will suffice to note that the imagery of *Cymbeline*, like so much else in the play, tends to be experimental.

1. Is she so represented at IV. ii. 371–2?

I may wander
From east to occident—

She can scarcely wander westwards from Milford Haven.

2. Furness's interpretation. See note to II. ii. 49.

3. D. A. Scheve contributes an admirable note on 'Jonson's *Volpone* and Traditional Fox Lore' to *The Review of English Studies* (1950), I, pp. 252–5.

10. THE PLAY

A different aspect of Shakespeare's experimentation may be seen in the frank sensationalism of *Cymbeline*. It is not easy to determine whether sensational effects were introduced because Shakespeare saw them as an integral part of traditional romance or because he succumbed to an impulse to exploit his own virtuosity. Probably each was, in part, responsible. We may leave the point for the moment and consider instead the probable impact of *Cymbeline* upon the Jacobean audience—that is, upon people to whom Shakespeare was a writer of comedies, histories, and tragedies.

To such an audience the new play would afford a full measure of surprise, suspense, and wonder. Iachimo emerging from a trunk, an old man and two boys living in a cave, a seemingly dead heroine coming to life again, a parade of ghosts and the descent of Jupiter: these are all surprising and thrilling circumstances.[1] The Queen creates suspense. Her nature and her practices are revealed at once, and it is clear that she is plotting—but against whom? Likewise Imogen, who sets off for Milford, apparently a comic character on a tragic mission. What will the outcome be? But suspense and amazement are not limited simply to isolated episodes. They cover the whole length and breadth of the play. In the first three acts, surprise follows upon surprise, and knot after knot is tied. Act I sees the wager plot well under way. Act II introduces the demand for tribute and brings Cloten's designs upon Imogen to the forefront. Act III begins by giving the impression that neither the wager story nor the tribute incident have much further to run. The one seems to be moving towards the death of Imogen, the other to a decisive battle. Shakespeare has handled matters very cunningly. Hitherto most of his plays had been based on familiar stories, and were notable for richness of treatment rather than novelty of incident, though there had, from time to time, been surprises. But *Cymbeline* takes what was almost certainly less accessible, less familiar narrative material and immediately sets out to complicate it in a strange way. Now the Jacobean audience would look upon Shakespeare as a dramatist who, in earlier years, had luxuriated in comedy, but thereafter had given himself over wholly to the tragic vein. And here, to be sure, is another tragedy. There have been some curious incidents, some odd soliloquies and asides, but everything is

1. It is true that they are hinted at beforehand, but the hints are very slight and could easily be missed by anyone coming to the play for the first time. We are not told that Iachimo will emerge from the trunk, or that the lost Princes are living in a cave. The Imogen incident is ambiguous, but the preliminary (false) assumption that she dies of a broken heart would be perfectly reasonable.

clearly leading up to the slaying of Imogen and, no doubt, to the slaughter of many of the others in battle.

Imogen, in III. ii, sets out on her fatal journey.

> Why, one that rode to's execution, man,
> Could never go so slow.

A palpable piece of tragic irony! The more expert members of the audience nod their heads wisely—or perhaps shake them sadly. Their surmise is proving correct. The play is like to prove another *Othello*. And then—*Enter Belarius, Guiderius, and Arviragus*. Suspense and perplexity are renewed, for here are three entirely new and un-expected characters who, in their idyllic setting, are quite out of keeping with all that has gone before. Shakespeare quite artlessly discloses their identity, and therewith their importance, but what new trend their presence implies remains obscure. If the play is to end tragically, they will but delay matters. Yet tragedy itself looks a little more remote now that these idyllic, lyrical characters of hopeful seeming have been introduced. Scene iv affords contrast and complement. It advances towards tragedy and then retreats, but may be no more than a temporary lull. At the end of Act III Imogen is safely bestowed for the time being, but Cloten is in pur-suit and the suspense continues, though it is now less acute.

If the additional complications of the third act have seemed to promise some mitigation of disastrous consequences, Act IV promptly darkens the scene once more. Cloten's evil plans mis-carry and he meets his just fate, but that is of little moment. Whether Imogen dies or only appears to die is, perhaps, a little obscure for the moment, but is soon clarified. She is revived from death, however, only to fall into the tragic error of supposing that her husband has been murdered by Cloten and Pisanio. Things are moving rapidly towards disaster once again. War has broken out. It is clear that *Cymbeline* is not, after all, to be a play of the *Othello* kind. Perhaps it will end very much as *Romeo and Juliet* ends.

The beginning of Act V shows that Posthumus, too, has fallen into the tragic error of believing that Imogen is dead, and the *Romeo and Juliet* catastrophe seems imminent now. But Posthumus decides to seek death in battle, is taken prisoner, and is condemned to death by hanging. This is perplexing. Marlowe hanged the Governor of Babylon, and Kyd hanged Pedringano.[1] Cordelia was hanged. But the idea of Posthumus being turned off does not seem to fit. There have been strangely unrealistic battles, but chaos has descended and a violent end is in sight. Then, surprisingly, comes

---

1. *Tamburlaine the Great*, V. i; *The Spanish Tragedy*, III. vi.

the apparition of Jupiter with its promise of happier things, yet this may be nothing more than

> such stuff as madmen
> Tongue, and brain not.

and such it seems when the Gaolers re-enter to take Posthumus off to execution. There comes a last-minute reprieve, and then, in the final scene, the clouds disappear with a swiftness that is almost explosive.

And so, throughout this whole play, the Jacobean audience has been 'fool'd with a most false effect', and has doubtless enjoyed the experience. Shakespeare, despite hindrances, uncertainties, and lapses, has displayed brilliant technical control of the new medium. Behind the plot complication and the dénouement lies a conscious virtuosity bred of confidence and experience. The new kind of soliloquy, the treatment of time and place, and the *deus ex machina* are, I think, more defiant and more dubiously successful exercises of technical skill. Nevertheless, the Shakespeare of *Cymbeline* is very much a dramatic conjurer and we find that he remains so. In *The Winter's Tale* he further defies convention with an impossible scheme of time and place which involves the non-existent sea-coast of Bohemia and a solemn proclamation by Father Time that sixteen years have now passed by. In *The Tempest* he defies by conforming. The classical unities are rigorously observed, but in connection with an action which really falls outside time and space. Precisely why he chose, in these last plays, to exploit his so potent magic so unconstrainedly can only be conjectured. Dramatic romance afforded him the opportunity, and probably he felt that this was the proper shape for it to take. Perhaps he felt, too, that a measure of obvious virtuosity would serve as a safeguard to his own pre-eminence in plays which were tending more and more to reflect glory upon others. For the greater part of Shakespeare's career, plays had been the concern of the dramatist. Now, with the cult of the masque, and the insistent demand for music and spectacle, they were bringing distinction to others, to composers such as Ferrabosco and Robert Johnson, and to designers such as Inigo Jones. It was necessary that the ingenuity of these people should be matched, and if possible exceeded, by that of the playwright.

II. THE SIGNIFICANCE

Cymbeline is not a play which can be covered by a single brief and coherent statement of the kind which will serve for *Richard the Second*, *The Merchant of Venice*, *Julius Caesar*, or even *Othello*. To receive it as a play concerned with regeneration, or a dramatization of the national ideal, or an experimental tragi-comedy, or a conscious essay in technical virtuosity is simply inadequate. Even the term 'Romance'—so absurdly generous that it can be made to cover almost anything and will, in fact, serve for about nine-tenths of *Cymbeline*—is ultimately insufficient because the play proceeds at last to a condition or effect which, in quality if not in kind, lies beyond the romance orbit.[1] It is not just one or the other of these things but all of them, and with something else besides. In other words the play comprises so many spare parts representing so many interests, all of which are assembled in a final unity. Johnson was aware only of the dispersal of material and interests, and the terms of his solemn denunciation show just how completely it was based on a consideration of the parts. It may cheerfully be admitted that even Johnson did not realize exactly how great a tissue of incongruities the thing is. Had he done so, he might have been provoked into a more profitable curiosity about the whole. But *Cymbeline* is not a play that will readily disclose its meaning to those who apply the Johnsonian canons, for to survey the parts is to recognize that they seldom rise above a certain modest standard. The poetry, for instance, is never quite equal to Shakespeare's best. Every outstanding line can be matched by ten or twenty better in *Othello*, *Macbeth*, *Antony and Cleopatra*, or *The Winter's Tale*, and we may look in vain for lines of the magnitude of:

> Conjures the wandering stars, and makes them stand
> Like wonder-wounded hearers.

or:

> Keep up your bright swords, for the dew will rust them.

or:

> Name not the god, thou boy of tears.

or:

> . . . and yours, and yours,
> That wear upon your virgin branches yet
> Your maidenheads growing.

Yet, as Quiller-Couch wisely reminds us, the whole is greater than the sum of the parts. He assures us that the *incongruities of fact* will be found to resolve themselves into *imaginative congruity* 'if we keep our gaze loyally on Imogen'.[2] This, I think, is to exaggerate

---

1. Just as *Petrouchka* is so much more than a mere fairy-tale. In other words, the particular has been universalized, so that what nominally happened 'once upon a time' becomes valid for all ages, and for all sorts and conditions of men.

2. *Op. cit.*

Imogen's contribution to the resolution, but the general conclusion remains valid. And once this conclusion has been reached, we are able to return to a consideration of the parts and to ask those questions which Johnson failed to ask. Why is the fiction so foolish? Why this undigested gallimaufry of English, Welsh, French, Ancient Roman, Renaissance Italian? Why this impossible conduct? And why, above all, was Shakespeare so blind to faults which Dr Johnson was able to dismiss as 'too evident for detection'? The latitude of 'Romance', the experimental nature of the play, and the fact that Shakespeare was handling unfamiliar and intractable material supply only a partial answer, so that we must consider whether, after all, the dramatist knew pretty well what he was doing.

Now it happens that one of the sister arts can furnish a useful analogy. Beethoven, in his final period, displays the same arbitrary dispersal of material as we find in *Cymbeline*. The late sonatas and quartets seem to adhere to no recognized musical form; the melodies are often so artless as to appear childish; treble twitterings are followed suddenly, and without any perceptible formula, by rumblings deep in the bass; the development sometimes appears to take the form of five-finger exercises; fugal episodes have an unaccountable habit of turning into something altogether different; archaic elements are introduced; and there are remote modulations and decidedly queer harmonies. These works appear so dispersed, so spasmodic, that Beethoven's early critics were pleased to dismiss them as 'unresisting imbecility', or, rather, raving lunacy, yet they are now admitted to be among the supreme creations of the human mind, for we have come to realize that the artlessness is deliberate, that the experience is vital, and that the end in sight is a tranquillity so complete that we can never hope to encompass it. Had Shakespeare written several plays like *Cymbeline*, it is probable that, as with Beethoven, criticism would have gone more diligently in pursuit of his intentions. Since he did not, it has been customary to regard the play as an oddly unaccountable lapse which, in view of preceding tragedy and succeeding romance, may be excused but must, at all costs, be deplored. If I demur, it is because I believe that *Cymbeline*, no less than the last works of Beethoven, is a comprehensive piece of impressionism, that it finally expresses something which Shakespeare never quite achieves elsewhere, and that, when all the still valid objections have been taken into account, it must yet be reckoned among his supreme utterances.

Shakespeare's impressionism is easily apparent in those arbitrary conglomerations of conflicting fictions and manners which Johnson trounces. It is apparent, too, in the casual, sometimes wilful, way in which so much of the play is set down, so that it reads, as one critic remarks, as if Browning had written it. But it is the characterization which, perhaps above all else, most clearly reveals the customary methods of the impressionist. The critical commonplace is that the characters in *Cymbeline* are recapitulatory. This is certainly true in the sense that they are, as it were, assembled from bits and pieces of past dramatic experience, but it cannot be allowed to stand as the conclusion to that kind of criticism which finds Cymbeline a second Lear, Posthumus another Othello, Iachimo a repetition of Iago, and so on. This method, if pressed to its logical limits, would have to admit such absurdities as the claim that Belarius is Polonius, the Queen Tamora (or Lady Macbeth), and Cloten Faulconbridge (or Aaron the Moor). In fact, no character sustains his reliance on the extended patterns of the past for very long. Cloten, for instance, is at one moment a roaring boy, at another, an irregular humourist with a hint of Laertes (or is it Doctor Caius?); now he is Timon; and now Cousin Slender; once again Laertes; now Faulconbridge; and finally Aaron. Similarly Posthumus, within the range of one soliloquy (II. iv. 153–86) is Othello, and Timon, and Edmund— and Master Ford! And to this must be added that the characters have a symbolic, if not a real, life of their own.

Cymbeline in its outlook, and it is the outlook which dictates the method, is precisely what a mature dramatist, skilled in comedy and tragedy and now attempting tragi-comedy for the first time, might be expected to produce, and it is here, however persuasive appearances may be, that the play must part company, once and for all, with the romances of Beaumont and Fletcher, which cannot have derived from any settled kind of attitude to life. *Cymbeline* is purely Shakespearean in its recognition that life itself is not a coherent pattern leading by orderly degrees to prosperity, as in comedy, or to destruction, as in tragedy, but a confused series of experiences, good and evil, grave and gay, momentous and trivial. It is purely Shakespearean in its realization that when certain values—here presented as symbols—are applied, order can be won out of seemingly hopeless disorder. There is no question of an escape into romantic unreality: on the contrary, reality is presented with new intensity within the traditional romance framework. To claim that the play is universal in the absolute sense may appear extravagant in view of 'the folly of the fiction', but the spiritual experience deriving from the fiction is, perhaps, more nearly the common property of man than that which adheres to a Lear, a Brutus, or even a Benedick.

That the astonishing final scene is decisive for the winning of order out of chaos is something that admits no question, but, throughout the play, the imagery, if not the action, anticipates and contributes immensely to the ultimate unification.[1] Behind the images of within and without lies the notion of body and mind, which are nominally distinct, being one, and the images of yoking and compounding point to a preoccupation with unity in many forms, in fact to the poet's conscious attempt to unify experience as a whole. Such imagery is in complete harmony with the play's full purpose. In *Cymbeline* what seems a hopelessly varied multiplicity moves towards a great act of union, and two further images are especially relevant. The inseparable union of husband and wife is symbolized in Posthumus'

> Hang there like fruit, my soul,
> Till the tree die.

and both national and international unity are powerfully figured in:

> The lofty cedar, royal Cymbeline,
> Personates thee: and thy lopp'd branches point
> Thy two sons forth: who, by Belarius stolen,
> For many years thought dead, are now revived
> To the majestic cedar join'd: whose issue
> Promises Britain peace and plenty.

These really amount to clear statements that certain unions have been achieved. At first there are several of them: Posthumus and Imogen; Imogen and Cymbeline; Imogen and the Princes; Cymbeline and the Princes; Cymbeline and Belarius; Britain and Rome. The fantastic promiscuity of the earlier acts has now been reduced and simplified, and that, we may suppose, is enough. But Shakespeare is not satisfied until he has subsumed all these independent unions under one union, until he has presented his most complete and triumphant *vision* of unity. The moment that the family relationship is established, the whole concept of such relationship is broken down into something more absolute. Cymbeline proclaims himself

> A mother to the birth of three.

and proceeds to question those three as if they were one:

> Where? how liv'd you?
> And when came you to serve our Roman captive?
> How parted with your brothers? how first met them?

---

1. I do not accept Clemen's view (*op. cit.*, p. 209) that the imagery of *Cymbeline* shows no development.

We may note the significance of 'your three motives to the battle' and of:

> the counterchange
> Is severally in all.

Still more significant are his words to Belarius:

> Thou art my brother; so we'll hold thee ever.

followed by Imogen, also to Belarius:

> You are my father too.

The complexity of past events is narrowed down. First:

> Pardon's the word to all.

then:

> The fingers of the powers above do tune
> The harmony of this peace.

then:

> Th' imperial Caesar, should again unite
> His favour with the radiant Cymbeline.

The bird symbolism is resolved into precisely the same visionary union, though the way in which this is done is less apparent to us than it would have been to Shakespeare's first audiences. Cymbeline, who, it may have been noticed, is excluded from the series of bird symbols, is finally represented as a cedar and is also likened to the sun. Both tree and sun are important symbols since they are closely associated with the Phoenix (Imogen) which is enthroned on a tree in Heliopolis, the city of the sun.[1] The precise nature of the Phoenix tree is obscure and not a little perplexing, but the Elizabethans, with their conception of degree running through all created things, were ready enough to enthrone the Phoenix in the king of trees, the cedar. William Smith, in one of his sonnets, makes this abundantly clear:

> The Phoenix fair which rich Arabia breeds,
> When wasting time expires her tragedy;
> No more on *Phoebus*' radiant rayes she feeds:
> But heapeth up great store of spicery;
> And on a lofty tow'ring cedar tree,
> With heavenly substance, she herself consumes.[2]

---

1. See Roger L. Green, 'The Phoenix and the Tree' in *English* (1948), VII. 37, pp. 11–15.

2. *Chloris* (1596), Sonnet xxiii. Clemen (*op. cit.*, p. 206) claims that tree imagery is prevalent in *Cymbeline*, but I do not find it an especially conspicuous element.

The Imogen–Cymbeline union, then, is also the union of the Phoenix and 'the sole Arabian tree', and further the union of the bird and the sun. The restoration of Cymbeline's lost sons, too, is in exact accord with the Phoenix myth since the tree is a dry tree which is mysteriously restored. It may be merely fanciful to suggest any association between the smoking altars of the play and the fiery sacrifice of the Arabian bird, and the parallels are sufficiently strong without this. As Sir Osbert Sitwell remarks, in his essay, *Roots of the Sole Arabian Tree*, 'there can be no doubt that, to adopt the jargon of today, Shakespeare was intensely "phoenix-conscious".'[1]

The Phoenix myth is one of vast implications and these can be transferred to *Cymbeline* more or less according to taste. The danger is that a blinding fog of mysticism may result. Shakespeare's great metaphysical epithalamium, *The Phoenix and the Turtle*, should, one feels, throw some light on the significance of the symbolism in *Cymbeline*, but that poem is open to so many interpretations that its clarifying force is dubious. Its Phoenix symbols are certainly unifying ones and, like the play, it exalts love as the force which reduces all unions to one. It has lines which are valid for Posthumus and Imogen:

> So they loved, as love in twain
> Had the essence but in one;
> Two distincts, division none:
> Number there in love was slain.

and the growing together into a single unity is expressed, albeit obscurely, in:

> Reason, in itself confounded,
> Saw division grow together,
> To themselves yet either neither,
> Simple were so well compounded.

The preoccupation, here within a narrower range, seems to be with the singleness of mind and body, the singleness of man and wife, and the oneness of the many, and so it is with *Cymbeline*. Whether the poem is concerned with the marriage or the death of the lovers is a matter of dispute.[2] In *Measure for Measure* the Duke tells Claudio that it is death which makes these odds all even. But *Cymbeline* resolves the issue, and it is Shakespeare himself who suggests that the resolution of the Many into the One can be accomplished within the pattern of life itself.

---

1. In *Sing High! Sing Low!* (1944), pp. 98–105.
2. The various interpretations are outlined in Professor Hyder E. Rollins's monumental edition of Shakespeare's *Poems*.

It is not extravagant to claim that *Cymbeline*, in its end, acquires a significance that extends beyond any last curtain or final *Exeunt*. There is, quite simply, something in this play which goes 'beyond beyond', and that which ultimately counts for more than the traffic of the stage is the Shakespearean vision—of unity certainly, perhaps of the Earthly Paradise, perhaps of the Elysian Fields, perhaps, even, the vision of the saints. But whatever else, it is assuredly a vision of perfect tranquillity, a partial comprehension of that Peace which passeth all understanding, and a contemplation of the indestructible essence in which Imogen, Iachimo, atonement, the national ideal have all ceased to have separate identity or individual meaning.

CYMBELINE

DRAMATIS PERSONÆ

CYMBELINE, *King of Britain.*
CLOTEN, *Son to the Queen by a former Husband.*
POSTHUMUS LEONATUS, *a Gentleman, Husband to Imogen.*
BELARIUS, *a banished Lord, disguised under the name of Morgan.*
GUIDERIUS, } *Sons to Cymbeline, disguised under the names of Polydore*
ARVIRAGUS, } *and Cadwal, supposed Sons to Morgan.*
PHILARIO, *Friend to Posthumus,* } *Italians.*
IACHIMO, *Friend to Philario,* } *Italians.*
CAIUS LUCIUS, *General of the Roman forces.*
PISANIO, *Servant to Posthumus.*
CORNELIUS, *a Physician.*
PHILARMONUS, *a Soothsayer.*
A Roman Captain.
Two British Captains.
A Frenchman, Friend to Philario.
Two Lords of Cymbeline's Court.
Two Gentlemen of the same.
Two Gaolers.

Queen, Wife to Cymbeline.
IMOGEN, *Daughter to Cymbeline by a former Queen.*
HELEN, *a Lady attending on Imogen.*

*Lords, Ladies, Roman Senators, Tribunes, a Dutchman, a Spaniard,
Musicians, Officers, Captains, Soldiers, Messengers and other
Attendants.*

APPARITIONS

CYMBELINE

ACT I

SCENE I.—*Britain. Cymbeline's Palace.*

Enter two Gentlemen.

First Gent. You do not meet a man but frowns: our bloods
　No more obey the heavens than our courtiers
　Still seem as does the king's.
Sec. Gent. 　　　　　　　　But what's the matter?
First Gent. His daughter, and the heir of's kingdom (whom
　He purpos'd to his wife's sole son—a widow　　　　5
　That late he married) hath referr'd herself
　Unto a poor but worthy gentleman. She's wedded,

ACT I

Scene 1

S.D. *Britain . . . Palace*] *not in* F.　　1–3.] *four lines ending* Frownes. / Heauens /
Courtiers: / Kings. F.　　2. than] Than F4; Then F.

S.D. Enter two Gentlemen] This
short opening scene is characteristically Shakespearean. It is virtually a
monologue, punctuated by the Second
Gentleman's questions. The First
Gentleman's speeches are, at times,
tantalizing elliptical, and have undergone much emendation. To emend is
to miss Shakespeare's point completely. The Second Gentleman is a
stranger to the Court: his companion
has a strange tale to tell, and tells it
breathlessly, excitedly, and, at times,
rather incoherently.

1–3. *our bloods . . . king's*] F prints
'Courtiers:' which can hardly be right.
Tyrwhitt's emendation 'king' for
'Kings' has been widely accepted,
though it does little to clarify the sense.
The First Variorum prints 'courtiers''

which may be correct. The sense of the
passage is fairly obvious: the courtiers
'wear their faces to the bent of the
king's looks' as completely as our tem-
peraments follow planetary influence.
The idea is Shakespearean: cf. *Ant.*,
I. v. 55–6: 'He was not sad, for he
would shine on those / That make
their looks by his.'

6. *referr'd*] assigned. Furness points
out that Cymbeline planned to advance Imogen, but that she has
'referr'd herself', i.e. has chosen a
lower station. 'Preferr'd' (Ingleby),
'affied' or 'assur'd' (Lettsom) are
superfluous.

7–10. *She's wedded . . . heart*] Steevens
emends to 'wed' and rearranges the
lines. 'Outward' (l. 9), external, in-
sincere. 'Touch'd' (l. 10) wounded, or

3

Her husband banish'd; she imprison'd, all
Is outward sorrow, though I think the king
Be touch'd at very heart.
Sec. Gent.   None but the king?   10
First Gent. He that hath lost her too: so is the queen,
That most desir'd the match. But not a courtier,
Although they wear their faces to the bent
Of the king's looks, hath a heart that is not
Glad at the thing they scowl at.
Sec. Gent.   And why so?   15
First Gent. He that hath miss'd the princess is a thing
Too bad for bad report: and he that hath her
(I mean, that married her, alack good man,
And therefore banish'd) is a creature such
As, to seek through the regions of the earth   20
For one his like; there would be something failing
In him that should compare. I do not think
So fair an outward, and such stuff within
Endows a man, but he.
Sec. Gent.   You speak him far.
First Gent. I do extend him, sir, within himself,   25
Crush him together, rather than unfold
His measure duly.

24. far] *Ff1–2;* fair *Ff3–4.*

possibly, angered. I have preserved the punctuation of F. Simpson suggests that the semi-colon after 'banish'd' is necessary to give the proper emphasis in a run of commas.

16. *thing*] The word has a pejorative sense, cf. 'basest thing', 'disloyal thing', 'foolish thing' in the next scene. Its force as a term of abuse is made abundantly clear in *Wint.*, II. i. 82–3: 'O thou thing! / Which I'll not call a creature of thy place.'

17–54.] Wilson Knight (*The Crown of Life*) remarks that Posthumus' merit is a major theme of the play. Shakespeare intends us to accept the First Gentleman's estimate of his virtue.

21. *one his like;*] Pope alters the semi-colon to a comma, but Simpson notes

that it serves to mark off a dependent clause. In effect it implies . . . for one his like—well, there would be something lacking, etc.

22. *him . . . compare*] him chosen for comparison with Posthumus.

25. *I . . . himself*] 'I extend him within himself; my praise however extensive is within his merit' (Johnson). Dowden thinks that two senses, 'stretch out' and 'value', may be played with here. 'Extend' in combination with 'crush' in l. 26 constitutes a typical Shakespearean oxymoron of the 'most busy least' kind (*Tp.*, III. i. 15). Tinkler detects a note of strain and violence, and may be right. The underlying imagery is obscure, but the notion of stretching and crushing suggests some instrument of torture.

Sec. Gent.   What's his name and birth?
First Gent.   I cannot delve him to the root: his father
        Was call'd Sicilius, who did join his honour
        Against the Romans with Cassibelan,   30
        But had his titles by Tenantius, whom
        He served with glory and admired success:
        So gain'd the sur-addition Leonatus:
        And had (besides this gentleman in question)
        Two other sons, who in the wars o' th' time   35
        Died with their swords in hand. For which their father,
        Then old, and fond of issue, took such sorrow
        That he quit being; and his gentle lady,
        Big of this gentleman (our theme) deceas'd
        As he was born. The king he takes the babe   40
        To his protection, calls him Posthumus Leonatus,
        Breeds him, and makes him of his bed-chamber,
        Puts to him all the learnings that his time
        Could make him the receiver of, which he took,

29. *Sicilius*] The name is taken from Holinshed, but Posthumus' father has, of course, no connection with the King Sicilius who began to reign 430 B.C.

join his honour] For 'join' Jervis conjectures 'win' or 'gain', and Dowden suggests 'joy in'. For 'honour' Steevens conjectures 'banner' and Vaughan 'colour'. F, however, seems quite satisfactory. 'Honour', as Dowden suggests, can signify personal reputation or soldierly virtue.

31. *Tenantius*] Tenantius or Theomantius, the father of Cymbeline *teste* Holinshed. According to Fabyan, he was brother to Cassibelan. Shakespeare evidently followed Fabyan as he makes Cassibelan Cymbeline's uncle at III. i. 5. The rights and wrongs of the matter need not concern us. In F 'Cassibelan' is spelt 'Cassibulan'.

33. *sur-addition Leonatus*] an additional distinctive name: here an award of merit analogous to Caius Marcius' sur-addition 'Coriolanus'. Leonatus (lion's whelp) implies that he was lion-hearted. Wilson Knight com-

pares *John*, II. i. 135–42 and v. i. 57

37. *fond of issue*] 'fond of's' (Collier MS.). Usually taken to mean doting on or desirous of offspring, but the sense is surely that Sicilius had abandoned hope of having further children. In Elizabethan English 'fond' often means 'foolish' and sometimes carries a suggestion of despair, as indeed it does in P.E. 'fond hopes'.

41. *Leonatus*] Proper names are often extra-metrical in Elizabethan drama. Cf. *Arden of Feversham* where the names left the dramatist little option. Many editors have mistakenly followed Pope in omitting 'Leonatus'.

43. *Puts . . . time*] 'Puts him to' (Reed), 'learning' (Steevens). This line has been variously interpreted. 'Puts to him' must, I think, mean sets before him, and the fact that he took what was offered emphasizes his virtue. The imagery is vague, but the spring and harvest of l. 46 suggest that the learnings are likened to manure. This accords with the plant imagery found elsewhere in the play.

As we do air, fast as 'twas minister'd,   45
And in's spring became a harvest: liv'd in court
(Which rare it is to do) most prais'd, most lov'd;
A sample to the youngest, to th' more mature
A glass that feated them, and to the graver
A child that guided dotards. To his mistress,   50
(For whom he now is banish'd) her own price
Proclaims how she esteem'd him; and his virtue
By her election may be truly read
What kind of man he is.
Sec. Gent.   I honour him,
Even out of your report. But pray you tell me,   55
Is she sole child to th' king?
First Gent.   His only child.
He had two sons (if this be worth your hearing,
Mark it) the eldest of them at three years old,
I' th' swathing-clothes the other, from their nursery
Were stol'n; and to this hour no guess in knowledge   60
Which way they went.
Sec. Gent.   How long is this ago?
First Gent. Some twenty years.
Sec. Gent. That a king's children should be so convey'd,
So slackly guarded, and the search so slow
That could not trace them!
First Gent.   Howsoe'er 'tis strange,   65

59. clothes the other, from] *Rowe;* cloathes, the other from *F.*

49. *feated*] 'featur'd' (Rowe). *O.E.D.*
conjecturally interprets 'constrained
to propriety', and this seems adequate. The more mature would be
courtiers who were desperately in-
tent upon observing the finesses of
court etiquette. Posthumus was the
reflection of what they aspired to
but could not attain. Some kind of
unconscious play on 'defeated' is
possible.

50. *To his mistress*] variously interpreted, but I take it to be a conflation
of two constructions: (i) To his mistress he was . . . , (ii) As to his mistress,
well, her own price, etc. Capell prints
a dash after 'banish'd' in l. 51, and

perhaps his neat solution is a correct
one.

51. *her own price*] her own value, i.e.
the value attaching to the heir-
apparent.

60. *guess in knowledge*] This abrupt
phrase has been variously explained.
I would interpret: In the whole field of
knowledge there is not one credible
guess. There is, I think, a concealed
image: cf. 'this great gap in his
abused nature' (*Lr.*, IV. vii. 14); 'a
breach in nature' (*Mac.*, II. iii. 119);
'a gap in nature' (*Ant.*, II. ii. 223);
'beyond the mark of thought' (*ibid.*,
III. vi. 87).

63. *convey'd*] stolen.

Or that the negligence may well be laugh'd at,
Yet is it true, sir.
Sec. Gent.   I do well believe you.
First Gent. We must forbear. Here comes the gentleman,
The queen, and princess.   [*Exeunt.*

SCENE II.—*The Same.*

Enter the QUEEN, POSTHUMUS, *and* IMOGEN.

Queen. No, be assur'd you shall not find me, daughter,
After the slander of most stepmothers,
Evil-ey'd unto you. You're my prisoner, but
Your gaoler shall deliver you the keys
That lock up your restraint. For you Posthumus,   5
So soon as I can win th' offended king,
I will be known your advocate: marry, yet
The fire of rage is in him, and 'twere good
You lean'd unto his sentence, with what patience
Your wisdom may inform you.
Post.   Please your highness,   10
I will from hence to-day.
Queen.   You know the peril.
I'll fetch a turn about the garden, pitying
The pangs of barr'd affections, though the king
Hath charg'd you should not speak together.   [*Exit.*

---

68. *forbear*] withdraw.

Scene II

S.D. Enter the Queen . . . Imogen] I
have followed F in marking a new
scene at this point. Most editors dispense with it; since there is no change
of place, and Granville-Barker attributes it to an editorial slip. There is,
however, a cleared stage together with
a momentary pause in the action, and
this justifies the division, which may
relate to some original subtlety in production that is lost beyond recovery.

Imogen] This form of the name,
used throughout F, is possibly a misprint. The form found in Holinshed is

'Innogen' and Forman refers to Shakespeare's character as 'Jnnogen' (see
Introduction, p. xiv). In the 1600 Q of
Ado. Innogen, the wife of Leonato, appears as a mute, which proves, inciden-
tally, that Shakespeare associated the
name of his heroine with that of his
hero long before he wrote *Cym.* Perhaps 'Imogen' should be emended
to 'Innogen' throughout. For typographical perpetuation of a parallel
error, cf. Mrs Gaskell's *The Doom of the
Griffiths*, where Angharad, owing to
misreading of the manuscript, is converted into 'Augharad'.

3. *Evil-ey'd*] 'Evil' is monosyllabic.
5. *your restraint*] your prison.

Imo.   O
    Dissembling courtesy! How fine this tyrant   15
    Can tickle where she wounds! My dearest husband,
    I something fear my father's wrath, but nothing
    (Always reserv'd my holy duty) what
    His rage can do on me. You must be gone,
    And I shall here abide the hourly shot   20
    Of angry eyes: not comforted to live,
    But that there is this jewel in the world
    That I may see again.
Post.   My queen, my mistress:
    O lady, weep no more, lest I give cause
    To be suspected of more tenderness   25
    Than doth become a man. I will remain
    The loyal'st husband that did e'er plight troth.
    My residence in Rome, at one Philario's,
    Who to my father was a friend, to me
    Known but by letter; thither write, my queen,   30
    And with mine eyes I'll drink the words you send,
    Though ink be made of gall.

Re-enter QUEEN.

Queen.   Be brief, I pray you:
    If the king come, I shall incur I know not
    How much of his displeasure: [*Aside*] yet I'll move him
    To walk this way: I never do him wrong   35
    But he does buy my injuries, to be friends:
    Pays dear for my offences.   [*Exit.*
Post.   Should we be taking leave

28. Philario's] *Rowe;* Filorio's *Ff1–2;* Florio's *Ff3–4.*   34. *Aside*] *Rowe.*
37. S.D.] *Rowe.*

14. *O*] Capell. At the beginning of
l. 15 in F.
  18. *Always . . . duty*] Clearly the duty
of the child to the parent as set down in
the Fifth Commandment, and not, as
some editors suppose, of the wife to the
husband.
  28. *Rome*] Keightley unnecessarily
changes to 'Rome's'.
  35–7. *I never . . . offences*] He submits

to the wrongs that I do to him in order
to retain my friendship. Or possibly
the Queen simply means: he interprets my injuries as favours. The
image, derived from commerce, is a
common one in *Cym.*
  37–45.] Posthumus' parting from
Imogen recalls that of Troilus from
Cressida. Cf. *Troil.,* IV. iv. 26–
50.

As long a term as yet we have to live,
The loathness to depart would grow. Adieu!
Imo. Nay, stay a little: 40
Were you but riding forth to air yourself,
Such parting were too petty. Look here, love;
This diamond was my mother's; take it, heart;
But keep it till you woo another wife,
When Imogen is dead.
Post.   How, how? Another?   45
You gentle gods, give me but this I have,
And sear up my embracements from a next
With bonds of death! Remain, remain thou here,
                                    [*Putting on the ring.*
While sense can keep it on: And sweetest, fairest,
As I my poor self did exchange for you   50
To your so infinite loss; so in our trifles
I still win of you. For my sake wear this,
It is a manacle of love, I'll place it
Upon this fairest prisoner.   [*Putting a bracelet on her arm.*
Imo.   O the gods!
When shall we see again?

Enter CYMBELINE *and Lords.*

Post.   Alack, the king!   55
Cym. Thou basest thing, avoid hence, from my sight!
If after this command thou fraught the court

48, 54. S.D.s] *Rowe.*

45. *How, how?*] Furness thinks that we should read 'Ho, ho' meaning 'Stop!' His note is barely intelligible. It is wholly possible that the compositor set up 'Ho' as 'How', but that does not justify alteration.

47–8. *And sear . . . death*] 'cere' (Steevens); 'seal' (Eccles); 'bands' (Grant White); 'brands' (Jervis). These changes, save for that of Steevens which is merely orthographical, are unnecessary. The imagery is complex. 'Sear' means to wrap in a cerecloth, i.e. waxed linen used for shrouds, but Shakespeare simultaneously thought of the wax

used for sealing legal bonds, possibly recalling the image that he had used in *Rom.*, v. iii. 114–15: 'seal with a righteous kiss / A dateless bargain to engrossing death.'

49. *While sense . . . it on*] Change of persons occurs elsewhere in the play, and Pope's emendation 'thee on' is not required. 'Sense' and 'senseless' occur fairly frequently, cf. I. ii. 66; I. iv. 7; II. ii. 32. Sensibility plays an important part in *Cymbeline*.

56. *avoid hence*] Many editors read 'avoid! hence'. I have retained F pointing.

57. *fraught*] burden. Possibly, as

With thy unworthiness, thou diest. Away!
Thou'rt poison to my blood.

Post.   The gods protect you,
And bless the good remainders of the court!   60
I am gone.   [*Exit.*

Imo.   There cannot be a pinch in death
More sharp than this is.

Cym.   O disloyal thing,
That shouldst repair my youth, thou heap'st
A year's age on me!

Imo.   I beseech you sir,
Harm not yourself with your vexation,   65
I am senseless of your wrath; a touch more rare
Subdues all pangs, all fears.

Cym.   Past grace? obedience?

Imo. Past hope, and in despair, that way past grace.

Cym. That mightst have had the sole son of my queen!

Imo. O blessed, that I might not! I chose an eagle,   70
And did avoid a puttock.

Eccles suggests, a subjunctive. Capell's conjecture, 'fraught'st' is ugly.

59–60. *The gods . . . court!*] Dowden detects irony in l. 60, and may be right. But the lines echo, rather remotely, Hermione's parting shot in the parallel situation in *Love and Fortune*: 'Long live my Lord, long live my Ladies grace, / God send them freends as loyall in my place' (443–4).

63. *That shouldst . . . heap'st*] an octosyllabic line, supplemented by editors in various ways. Capell's 'heap'st instead' is the best of an unconvincing bunch.

64. *A year's age*] much emended, but I think that the phrase is idiomatic, meaning, as Thiselton suggests, an age of years. Shakespeare, in *AYL*, divides human life into seven *ages*, each being about ten years. Cymbeline's meaning would then be equivalent to P.E. 'You put years on me'. For similar time idioms cf. 'a winter's week' (Kyd); 'this fortnight's day' (*Arden of Feversham*); 'one seven years' (*Cor.*).

Ll. 62–4 may be compared with *Love and Fortune*: 'And thou fond girle, whose stained blood hath wrought, / How hath mine age and honor beeh abusde?' (396–7) spoken by Phizantius to Fidelia in a parallel situation.

66. *a touch . . . rare*] This, I think, can only mean 'a deeper mental anguish', or, as Dowden puts it, 'a more exquisite pain'.

68. *that way past grace*] I am past grace in that respect. Commentators have detected here, as elsewhere in *Cym.*, an allusion to Calvin's doctrine of election. It is unlikely that these bear any relation to Shakespeare's own religious convictions.

70. *O blessed . . . not*] a quibble which follows upon 'past grace' in l. 68. Imogen has admitted that, in one way, she is damned, but in another (i.e. in having avoided Cloten) she is blessed.

71. *puttock*] kite. The kite is baser than the eagle, just as in *Mac.*, II. iv. 12–13, the mousing owl is inferior to

Cym. Thou took'st a beggar, wouldst have made my throne
    A seat for baseness.

Imo.   No, I rather added
    A lustre to it.

Cym.   O thou vile one!

Imo.   Sir,
    It is your fault that I have lov'd Posthumus: 75
    You bred him as my playfellow, and he is
    A man worth any woman: overbuys me
    Almost the sum he pays.

Cym.   What? Art thou mad?

Imo. Almost, sir: heaven restore me! Would I were
    A neat-herd's daughter, and my Leonatus   80
    Our neighbour-shepherd's son!

Cym.   Thou foolish thing!—

·   *Re-enter* QUEEN.

    They were again together: you have done
    Not after our command. Away with her,
    And pen her up.

Queen.   Beseech your patience. Peace
    Dear lady daughter, peace!—Sweet sovereign,   85
    Leave us to ourselves, and make yourself some comfort
    Out of your best advice.

Cym.   Nay, let her languish
    A drop of blood a day, and being aged
    Die of this folly.   *[Exeunt Cymbeline and Lords.*

---

74. vile] *F4*; vilde *F*.   81. *Re-enter Queen*] *Dyce*; *Enter Queene F* (*after* son).

the falcon. Such distinctions were important to Shakespeare, since in his day they were thought of as applying to all created objects. See E. M. W. Tillyard, *The Elizabethan World Picture*. Also Introduction, p. lxxiii.

75. *It is . . . Posthumus*] So Hermione in *Love and Fortune* addresses King Phizantius: 'Thy selfe the roote and cause of mine owne wrong' (427).

77–8. *overbuys me . . . he pays*] He exceeds me in worth by almost the price which he is now called upon to pay, i.e., banishment. *Love and Fortune*

affords an interesting parallel. Hermione, referring to his banishment, says: 'Which loue though I am like to buye full deere, / Yet is her loue more precious then the price' (440–1). Dowden suggests 'I am worth but a small fraction of what, in giving himself, he has given for me.'

87. *advice*] consideration, reflection.

languish] Dowden notes that the verb was sometimes causal and active (as, apparently, here), though he prefers to interpret: 'languish, at the rate of a drop of blood a day'.

Queen.   Fie! you must give way.

Enter PISANIO.

Here is your servant. How now, sir? What news?   90
Pis. My Lord your son drew on my master.
Queen.   Ha?
No harm I trust is done?
Pis.   There might have been,
But that my master rather play'd than fought,
And had no help of anger: they were parted
By gentlemen at hand.
Queen.   I am very glad on't.   95
Imo. Your son's my father's friend, he takes his part
To draw upon an exile. O brave sir!
I would they were in Afric both together,
Myself by with a needle, that I might prick
The goer-back. Why came you from your master?   100
Pis. On his command: he would not suffer me
To bring him to the haven: left these notes
Of what commands I should be subject to,
When't pleased you to employ me.
Queen.   This hath been
Your faithful servant: I dare lay mine honour   105

---

89. *Enter Pisanio.*] *Dyce; after* folly *F.*   104. pleased] *F;* please *Ff3–4.*

89. *Fie! . . . way.*] F reads: 'Fye, you must give way:' and the implication is that the words are spoken to Cymbeline, with the evil purpose of augmenting his wrath. Capell, with less psychological probability, suggests that the Queen says 'Fie!' to Cymbeline, rebuking him for his cruel but feeble curse, and addresses the rest to Imogen. A third interpretation, that of Elze, who argues that the whole is spoken to Imogen, shows little understanding of the Queen's methods.

94. *help of anger*] Sidney uses the phrase. Posthumus, although he outfenced Cloten, fought half-heartedly, presumably because he was too dejected to be really angry.

96–7. *he takes . . . exile.*] Johnson, whom many editors follow, places a full-stop and dash after 'part' and an exclamation mark after 'exile', but the change seems heavy and unnecessary. Editors who retain the F reading usually explain: in drawing upon an exile he takes my father's part. But Imogen is scornful, and I think her meaning is that Cloten plays the part that might be expected of him. The frequency with which Shakespeare uses images and figures drawn from the stage justifies such an interpretation. Cf. v. v. 228.

98. *in Afric*] i.e. in some desert place. Shakespeare has much the same idea elsewhere. Cf. *Mac.*, III. iv. 104; *Cor.*, IV. ii. 23–5; *R2*, IV. i. 74.

99. *needle*] sometimes, as here, pronounced as a monosyllable.

105. *lay*] stake.

He will remain so.
Pis.   I humbly thank your highness
Queen. Pray, walk awhile.
Imo. About some half-hour hence, pray you, speak with me;
  You shall (at least) go see my lord aboard.
  For this time leave me.   [*Exeunt.*   110

SCENE III.—*The Same.*

Enter CLOTEN *and two Lords.*

First Lord. Sir, I would advise you to shift a shirt; the
  violence of action hath made you reek as a sacrifice:
  where air comes out, air comes in: there's none
  abroad so wholesome as that you vent.
Clo. If my shirt were bloody, then to shift it. Have I hurt
  him?
Sec. Lord. [*Aside*] No, faith: not so much as his patience.
First Lord. Hurt him? his body's a passable carcass, if he
  be not hurt. It is a throughfare for steel, if it be not
  hurt.   10

108–10.] *four lines ending* hence, / me; / aboord. / me. *F.*

Scene III

7. *Aside*] *Asides to l. 14 Theobald; from l. 19 to end Pope.*   9. throughfare] *F;*
thorough-fare *F3.*

108–10.] in F printed as four lines
ending 'hence,' 'me;' 'aboord.' 'me.'.
I have followed Rowe's rearrange-
ment. Many editors follow Capell and
emend 'pray you' to 'I pray you' to the
slight advantage of the metre. Dr H. F.
Brooks cogently suggests that 'pray'
was perhaps wrongly caught by the
printer from 'Pray' in l. 107, so displacing an irrecoverable dissyllable.

Scene III

Ingleby (followed by Furness) questions the authenticity of this scene and
of the similar one at the beginning
of Act II. There seems no especial

justification for this, though we
may willingly concede that 'the allusions are obscure, and the quibbles
poor.'

1–4. *Sir . . . vent*] 'The speaker advises
Cloten to shift a shirt in order to cease
reeking; otherwise he must take air in
to supply what he loses, and the outer
air is less wholesome than that of his
own sweet body' (Dowden).

8. *passable*] There is a play on several
senses: (i) tolerable, (ii) penetrable,
(iii) penetrated by rapier passes.

9. *it*] Dr H. F. Brooks suggests that
'it' may have been caught from the
previous line, displacing 'he'.

Sec. Lord. [*Aside*] His steel was in debt, it went o' th' back-
      side the town.

Clo. The villain would not stand me.

Sec. Lord. [*Aside*] No, but he fled forward still, toward
      your face.   15

First Lord. Stand you? You have land enough of your
      own: but he added to your having, gave you some
      ground.

Sec. Lord. [*Aside*] As many inches as you have oceans.
      Puppies!   20

Clo. I would they had not come between us.

Sec. Lord. [*Aside*] So would I, till you had measur'd how
      long a fool you were upon the ground.

Clo. And that she should love this fellow, and refuse me!

Sec. Lord. [*Aside*] If it be a sin to make a true election, she   25
      is damn'd.

First Lord. Sir, as I told you always, her beauty and her
      brain go not together. She's a good sign, but I have
      seen small reflection of her wit.

Sec. Lord. [*Aside*] She shines not upon fools, lest the reflec-   30
      tion should hurt her.

Clo. Come, I'll to my chamber. Would there had been
      some hurt done!

Sec. Lord. [*Aside*] I wish not so, unless it had been the fall
      of an ass, which is no great hurt.   35

19–20. oceans. Puppies!] *Capell;* Oceans (Puppies.) *F.*   34. been] *F4;* bin *F.*

11–12. *His steel ... town.*] His sword
was like a debtor who avoids his
creditors by keeping clear of the main
streets. The 'backside the town' is a
fairly common Elizabethan phrase
and here sustains the quibble on
'throughfare'.

17–18. *gave ... ground*] 'playing on
"give ground", meaning "retire", as
in *Tp.*, II. ii. 64' (Dowden).

19. *inches*] The antithesis between
'inches' and 'oceans' suggests that
there is a play on words. Inch is used
in its everyday sense and also as signifying a small island. Saint Colme's-
inch is mentioned in *Mac.*, I. ii.

25. *election*] a pun on the theolo-

gical sense. See note to I. ii. 68.

27–8. *her beauty and her brain*] Her
beauty exceeds her intelligence (or
judgement).

28. *sign*] exterior semblance, as in
Ado, IV. i. 34. Conjectural emendations 'shine' (Warburton) and 'sun'
(Staunton) are needless. There is probably some obscure play on the word.
Steevens, detecting reference to a
tavern sign, remarks that 'anciently
almost every sign had a motto, or some
attempt at, a witticism, underneath
it.' The secondary allusion may be to
one of the signs of the Zodiac. The sign
of the Virgin would be the most
apposite for Imogen.

Clo. You'll go with us?
First Lord. I'll attend your lordship.
Clo. Nay come, let's go together
Sec. Lord. Well my lord.   [*Exeunt.*

SCENE IV.—*The Same.*

Enter IMOGEN *and* PISANIO.

Imo. I would thou grew'st unto the shores o' th' haven,
  And question'dst every sail: if he should write,
  And I not have it, 'twere a paper lost
  As offer'd mercy is. What was the last
  That he spake to thee?
Pis.   It was, his queen, his queen!   5
Imo. Then wav'd his handkerchief?
Pis.   And kiss'd it, madam.
Imo. Senseless linen, happier therein than I!
  And that was all?
Pis.   No, madam: for so long

36–9. *You'll go . . . Well my lord*]
Capell gives l. 37 to the Second Lord:
Delius conjectures that l. 39 belongs to
the First Lord. Dowden accepts F dis-
tribution: 'I think Cloten addresses
the Second Lord, who is not eager to
reply; First Lord intervenes with his
assurance of attendance; Cloten still
presses for the company of Second
Lord, who then submits with a
reluctant "Well my lord".' Granville-
Barker holds much the same view and
remarks that, at l. 36, Cloten notices
the Second Lord (who has been following some paces behind) for the first
time.

Scene IV

4. *offer'd mercy*] Warburton interprets as the 'offer'd mercy of Heaven';
Heath, as a pardon to a condemned
criminal. The sense is not quite clear,
but Staunton's conjecture 'deferr'd' is
scarcely justified. Since papers and
letters figure so conspicuously in this

play, there is, perhaps, an element of
irony in Imogen's words. The paper
found by Posthumus in v. iv is, in fact,
'offer'd mercy'.

8–22.] Steevens notes a parallel
between this scene and Ceyx's parting
from Alcyone in Ovid, *Metamorphoses*
XI. The following lines from Golding's
translation, which Shakespeare knew,
are relevant: 'She lifting up her watery
eyes beheld her husband stand / Upon
the hatches, making signs by beckon-
ing with his hand, / And she made
signs to him again; and after that the
land / Was far removed from the ship,
and that the sight began / To be unable
to discern the face of any man, / As
long as e'er she could she looked upon
the rowing keel, / And when she could
no longer time for distance ken it well,/
She looked still upon the sails that
flasked with the wind / Upon the mast;
and when she could the sails no longer
find / She gat her to her empty bed
with sad and sorry heart, / And laid

As he could make me with this eye, or ear,
Distinguish him from others, he did keep   10
The deck, with glove, or hat, or handkerchief,
Still waving, as the fits and stirs of's mind
Could best express how slow his soul sail'd on,
How swift his ship.

Imo.   Thou shouldst have made him
As little as a crow, or less, ere left   15
To after-eye him.

Pis.   Madam, so I did.

Imo. I would have broke mine eye-strings, crack'd them, but
To look upon him, till the diminution
Of space had pointed him sharp as my needle:
Nay, followed him, till he had melted from   20
The smallness of a gnat, to air: and then
Have turn'd mine eye, and wept. But, good Pisanio,
When shall we hear from him?

Pis.   Be assur'd, madam,
With his next vantage.

Imo. I did not take my leave of him, but had   25
Most pretty things to say: ere I could tell him

---

9. this] *Theobald* (*Warburton*)*; his F.*   23. him?] *Rowe;* him. *F.*

---

her down. The chamber did renew
afresh her smart, / And of her bed did
bring to mind the dear departed part.'
Cf. note to II. ii. 45. Dowden compares
Ven., 817–22.

9. *this eye, or ear*] F 'his' can hardly
be correct. Of the many emendations
proposed, that of Warburton is the
simplest and best. If the compositor of
F was speaking the line over to himself, he would tend to convert 'with
this' into 'with his'.

12. *as*] Dowden takes this to mean
'so as', not 'as if'.

14–22.] The scene described and
imagery employed obviously invite
comparison with Edgar's description
of the Dover straits in *Lr.*, IV. vi, which
affords an excellent example of 'the
diminution of space', i.e. as Johnson
correctly says, the diminution of which
space is the cause: 'The fishermen that

walk upon the beach / Appear like
mice; and yond tall anchoring bark, /
Diminisht to her cock,—her cock, a
buoy / Almost too small for sight.' In
the present play this diminution is suggested by several subtle devices. Sail
contrasts with handkerchief: eye and
ear are resolved to eye alone, and then
to eyestrings, and the eye image may
be implicit in 'needle' (l. 19): similarly
the life-size figure of Posthumus yields
to crow, crow to gnat, and gnat to thin
air.

17. *eye-strings*] The eye-strings (i.e.
muscles, nerves, or tendons of the eye)
were thought to break or crack at
death or loss of sight. So in Toplady's
great *Rock of Ages* (until gentility
effected what it took to be an improvement): 'When my eye-strings break in
death'.

24. *vantage*] opportunity.

How I would think on him at certain hours,
Such thoughts, and such: or I could make him swear
The shes of Italy should not betray
Mine interest, and his honour; or have charg'd him,　30
At the sixth hour of morn, at noon, at midnight,
T' encounter me with orisons, for then
I am in heaven for him; or ere I could
Give him that parting kiss, which I had set
Betwixt two charming words, comes in my father,　35
And like the tyrannous breathing of the north,
Shakes all our buds from growing.

Enter a lady.

Lady.　　　　　　　　　　　　The queen, madam,
Desires your highness' company.
Imo. Those things I bid you do, get them dispatch'd.—
I will attend the queen.
Pis.　　　　　　　　Madam, I shall.　　*[Exeunt.*　40

28–30. *or I . . . his honour*] Imogen lapses, rather unhappily, into the Beatrice or Portia vein. It is not a most pretty thing to say and is quite out of character.

30–3. *or have charg'd . . . for him*] The times mentioned are three of the seven canonical hours of the Divine Office. The obvious interpretation is that Imogen sees herself as a goddess whom Posthumus is to worship at certain hours, but I doubt whether it is the correct one. I take 'encounter me' to mean 'join me' (cf. *O.E.D.* encounter. vb. 6 = to go to meet) and would interpret: I would have charged him to join with me in prayer at these times because I shall then be praying for him.

35. *two charming words*] words which

have the power of protecting him from evil. The parting kiss is seen as a jewel set between two charming words and the underlying image may therefore be of a brooch shaped like a lover's knot with a precious stone set in the middle.

37. *Shakes all our buds*] Love is likened to a bud in *Rom.*, II. ii. 121. Hurd's conjecture, 'checks' for 'shakes', is ingenious but unnecessary since Sonnet xviii has: 'Rough winds do shake the darling buds of May.' Warburton's 'blowing' for 'growing' is perverse. The tyrannous breathing of the north still occasionally shakes all our buds from growing in the Avon valley, as the market-gardeners declare, though in more prosaic terms.

SCENE V.—*Rome. Philario's House.*

Enter PHILARIO, IACHIMO, *a Frenchman, a Dutchman,*
and a Spaniard.

Iach. Believe it sir, I have seen him in Britain; he was then
of a crescent note, expected to prove so worthy as
since he hath been allowed the name of. But I could
then have look'd on him without the help of admiration, though the catalogue of his endowments had   5
been tabled by his side and I to peruse him by items.
Phi. You speak of him when he was less furnish'd than
now he is with that which makes him both without
and within.

Scene v

Furness, fortified perhaps by
Ingleby's comment that 'the language
of this scene presents a notable instance
of slipshod writing', relieves Shakespeare of all responsibility for the first
fifty-six lines but offers nothing that
can really be regarded as evidence.

S.D. Rome. Philario's House]
Granville-Barker observes that the
most effective way of presenting this
scene would be with the inner stage
revealed, the Dutchman and Spaniard
remaining, throughout, seated and in
the background.

Iachimo] the same as Italian
'Giacomo'. F4 reads 'Jachimo', which
Douce favours, and this might better
accord with modern convention than
'Iachimo', but some doubt attaches to
the pronounciation used by Shakespeare. Cf. the 'yellow Iachimo' of II.
iv. 166 which may be alliterative.

a Dutchman, and a Spaniard] The
introduction of these mute *dramatis
personæ* seems to establish Shakespeare's dependence on *Frederyke of
Jennen*, where the corresponding characters are four rich merchants 'out of
diuers countreis', namely Courant of
Spain, Borcharde of France, Johan of
Florence (= Iachimo), and Ambrose
of Genoa (= Posthumus). In the

Decameron the four merchants are all
Italians. Granville-Barker suggests
that the Dutchman and Spaniard may
have worn distinctive national costume or that they may have been given
an explanatory line or two, now lost.
It is possible, however, that both characters were dispensed with when the
play was actually brought to the stage.
That they were depicted as drunk past
the power of speech is not beyond
Jacobean possibility.

2. *crescent note*] growing distinction.
F3 reads 'cressent none', and F4
'crescent, none'. These served to mislead editors until Theobald restored
the text.

4–5. *help of admiration*] The phrase
seems straightforward though it so
confused Staunton that he proposed to
emend to either 'yelp' or 'whoop'.
W. W. Lloyd's 'eyes' is less preposterous but equally superfluous. For the
idiom, cf. 'no help of anger' at I. ii. 94.
Iachimo turns the phrase into a sneer,
for he thinks all men as mean and
cynical as himself. The First Gentleman has already in I. i presented the
picture of Posthumus which Shakespeare intends us to accept, and
Iachimo's disparagement in the present scene damages only himself.
'Admiration', wonder, astonishment.

French. I have seen him in France: we had very many   10
there could behold the sun with as firm eyes as he.

Iach. This matter of marrying his king's daughter, wherein he must be weighed rather by her value than his
own, words him (I doubt not) a great deal from the
matter.   15

French. And then his banishment.

Iach. Ay, and the approbation of those that weep this
lamentable divorce under her colours are wonderfully to extend him; be it but to fortify her judgement, which else an easy battery might lay flat, for   20
taking a beggar without less quality. But how comes
it he is to sojourn with you? how creeps acquaintance?

11. *behold the sun*] Dowden's tenta-
tive suggestion that 'as he' refers to
Iachimo and that Posthumus is ironically referred to as 'the sun' seems
rather strained. Posthumus is likened
to the eagle which can gaze at the sun
without blinking, as the Elizabethan
dramatists frequently remind us. The
eagle image is a vital one in *Cymbeline*:
Imogen has already told her father
that she 'chose an eagle' (i. ii. 70). See
Introduction, p. lxxiii.

14–15. *words him . . . matter*] gives him
a reputation far greater than he merits.
'From', away from, removed from: cf.
v. v. 432. Since 'matter' is used in l. 12,
it is barely possible that the compositor
set up the wrong word in l. 15. But the
sense is adequate and there is no need
to be over-curious.

16. *banishment*] Pope, assuming that
the sentence is unfinished, reads
'banishment—'.

18. *colours*] banner. Iachimo employs military imagery: 'colours',
'fortify', 'battery'.

18–19. *are . . . extend him*] greatly add
to his reputation. Various emendations have been proposed: 'aids wonderfully' (Warburton); 'are wonderful' (Capell); 'and wonderfully do'
(Eccles); 'who wonderfully do'
(Orger). In his edition Warburton

makes 'approbation' plural and is followed by Johnson, but Steevens's view
that a plural verb results from a plural
subject (i.e. his banishment (l. 16) *and*
the approbation) is surely the correct
one. For 'wonderfully' I am tempted
to read 'wonder fully'.

21. *without less quality*] The phrase
means precisely the opposite of what
it says, or so it would seem. 'less' has
been freely emended: 'more' (Rowe);
'level' (Bailey); 'self' (Bulloch); 'best'
(Vaughan). Cartwright reads 'without
less inequality' and Dowden suggests
'with, doubtless, quality'—but there
seems no escape from F reading, which
may simply be an Elizabethan double
negative of the kind that nowadays
puzzles thought. Malone's statement
that 'whenever *less* or *more* is to be
joined with a verb denoting want, or a
preposition of a similar import, Shakespeare never fails to be entangled in a
grammatical inaccuracy, or rather, to
use words that express the very contrary of what he means' is too sweep-
ing. If we could take 'without' in its
colloquial sense of leaving out of
account, we might interpret: a beggar,
leaving out of account any lower rank.

22–3. *creeps acquaintance*] Furness
pronounces the phrase incompre-
hensible, but Herford's paraphrase—

Phi. His father and I were soldiers together, to whom I
   have been often bound for no less than my life.—   25
   Here comes the Briton. Let him be so entertained
   amongst you as suits, with gentlemen of your knowing, to a stranger of his quality.

Enter POSTHUMUS.

I beseech you all be better known to this gentleman,
   whom I commend to you as a noble friend of mine.   30
   How worthy he is I will leave to appear hereafter,
   rather than story him in his own hearing.
French. Sir, we have known together in Orleans.
Post. Since when I have been debtor to you for courtesies
   which I will be ever to pay, and yet pay still.   35
French. Sir, you o'er-rate my poor kindness: I was glad I
   did atone my countryman and you: it had been pity
   you should have been put together, with so mortal a
   purpose as then each bore, upon importance of so
   slight and trivial a nature.   40
Post. By your pardon, sir, I was then a young traveller,
   rather shunn'd to go even with what I heard than in
   my every action to be guided by others' experiences:

26. Briton] *Theobald;* Britaine *F.*   28. S.D.] *Dyce; after* life, *l. 25, F.*

How have you stolen into acquaintance?—seems adequate. There is a
palpable sneer in 'creeps'. It is possible
that the phrase is not a question but an
exclamation, and that we should read
'How creeps acquaintance!' i.e. how
acquaintance grovels (in admitting
this beggar). F is erratic in its use of
interrogation marks and notes of
admiration.

27–8. *knowing*] knowledge or experience.

32. *story*] Philario perhaps plays
ironically on Iachimo's 'words him'.

33. *have known*] have been acquainted.

37. *atone*] reconcile.

38. *put together*] set against one another. Porter uses 'set together' in
the same sense in *Two Angry Women
of Abingdon*: 'Nor that same hisse

that setteth dogges together' (3021).

39. *importance*] Malone glosses as
'importunity, instigation', and both
Steevens and Dowden concur. The
alternative explanation, 'matter', 'subject', 'import', seems preferable on
general grounds. It suffices to observe
that 'importance' and 'quarrel' (l. 45)
evidently mean much the same thing.

42. *shunn'd to go even*] refused to agree.
The sense of 'go even' is established by
Tw.N., v. i. 246: 'Were you a woman,
as the rest goes even'. Staunton's conjecture 'sinn'd' is irresponsible. The
general sense of Posthumus' speech has
been the object of much dispute but, as
Furness remarks, Capell's 'rather than
appear to be guided by others' experience I avoided giving assent to what I
heard' has scarcely been improved
upon by subsequent commentators.

but upon my mended judgement (if I offend not to
say it is mended) my quarrel was not altogether   45
slight.

French. Faith yes, to be put to the arbitrement of swords,
and by such two, that would by all likelihood have
confounded one the other, or have fallen both.

Iach. Can we with manners ask what was the difference?   50

French. Safely, I think: 'twas a contention in public,
which may (without contradiction) suffer the report.
It was much like an argument that fell out last night,
where each of us fell in praise of our country mis-
tresses; this gentleman at that time vouching (and   55
upon warrant of bloody affirmation) his to be more
fair, virtuous, wise, chaste, constant, qualified and
less attemptable than any the rarest of our ladies in
France.

Iach. That lady is not now living; or this gentleman's   60
opinion, by this, worn out.

Post. She holds her virtue still, and I my mind.

Iach. You must not so far prefer her 'fore ours of Italy.

Post. Being so far provok'd as I was in France, I would
abate her nothing, though I profess myself her   65
adorer, not her friend.

44. offend not] *Rowe;* offend *F.*   54–5. country mistresses] *Theobald; hyphened F.*
64. France, I] *Rowe;* France: I *F.*

44–5. *if I offend . . . mended*] Though
his judgement is mended, he has not
changed his opinion, and still regards
the quarrel as serious. Hence the
formally apologetic 'if I offend not'.

48. *by such two*] Capell conjectures
'by such, too' which is ingenious and,
in some ways, attractive.

52. *without contradiction*] Johnson explains as 'undoubtedly': Capell more
tortuously paraphrases 'without danger of drawing on another dispute like
that which happened before'. But
surely the Frenchman simply means
that he can report the matter so
accurately and impartially that no
one will have reason to contradict
him.

53–4. *fell out . . . fell in*] Furness notes
that this repetition is not Shakespeare
at his best. Possibly the second 'fell' is
a printer's error, though the sense is
satisfactory as it stands. It is doubtful
whether a pun is intended.

57. *constant, qualified*] Capell emends
to 'constant-qualified' which nearly all
editors have accepted, but *O.E.D.*,
with its quotations from Nashe and
Richard Bernard, vindicates F 'qualified': endowed with good qualities,
accomplished, perfect.

64–95.] Posthumus' praise of Imogen recalls Collatine's similar claims
for Lucrece: see *Lucr.*, 8–42.

65–6. *though . . . friend*] There is no
point in discussing the mass of error to

Iach. As fair, and as good—a kind of hand-in-hand com-
    parison—had been something too fair, and too good
    for any lady in Britany. If she went before others I
    have seen, as that diamond of yours outlustres many   70
    I have beheld, I could not believe she excelled many:
    but I have not seen the most precious diamond that
    is, nor you the lady.

Post. I prais'd her as I rated her: so do I my stone.

Iach. What do you esteem it at?   75

Post. More than the world enjoys.

Iach. Either your unparagon'd mistress is dead, or she's
    outpriz'd by a trifle.

Post. You are mistaken: the one may be sold or given, or
    if there were wealth enough for the purchase, or   80

67–8. good—a . . . comparison—] *Camb.;* good: a . . . comparison, *F.*   69.
Britany.] Britanie; *F.*   others I] *Pope;* others. I *F.*   80. purchase] *Rowe;*
purchases *F.*

which these lines have given rise.
Crosby has demonstrated that Shakespeare sometimes uses 'though' in the
sense 'because', 'since', 'inasmuch as',
and he may do so here, though the
more obvious meaning would suffice.
'Adorer' means lover, obviously in the
best sense. 'Friend' signifies a paramour of either sex and is used by
Shakespeare in *Meas.*, I. iv. 29: 'He
hath got his friend with child.'
Middleton in *The Witch*, 489–515, lets
Francisca discourse at length about
her 'friend' and affords a nice distinction: 'When they are once Husbands,
they'll be whipd ere they take such
paines, as a *Frend* will doe.' The Frenchman has earlier referred to Imogen as
Posthumus' mistress: Posthumus now
corrects him by professing himself her
lover, not her paramour.

67–8. *a kind . . . comparison*] a comparison which claimed for her equal-
ity, not superiority.

69. *Britany*] Britain. Dowden notes
that Bacon uses both names indiscriminately.

71. *could not*] Malone reads 'could

not but' which most editors adopt.
Other conjectures are 'could' (Warburton) and 'could but' (Heath).
Ingleby has been rebuked for his
championship of the F reading in a
speech where the compositor admittedly did his worst (with punctuation at least) but I think he comes near
to the truth. If, says Iachimo, your
lady excelled many others in beauty
(as your diamond does), I still could
not believe that she excelled many in
virtue—but I have not seen the finest
diamond: no more have you seen the
most virtuous lady. Ingleby's critics
would have done well to consider
whether the emendations which they
favour do not, in fact, attribute moral
virtue to diamonds!

76. *enjoys*] possesses.

77–8. *Either . . . trifle*] If your lady is
not dead, you evidently value your
diamond above her, for, if she lives, the
world enjoys her. Iachimo's quickness
of repartee cannot conceal his ignorance and spiritual poverty.

79–80. *or if*] either if. But 'or' may be
a printer's error. Rowe omits it.

merit for the gift. The other is not a thing for sale,
and only the gift of the gods.

Iach. Which the gods have given you?

Post. Which by their graces I will keep.

Iach. You may wear her in title yours: but you know   85
strange fowl light upon neighbouring ponds. Your
ring may be stolen too: so your brace of unprizable
estimations, the one is but frail and the other casual;
a cunning thief, or a (that way) accomplished courtier, would hazard the winning both of first and last.   90

Post. Your Italy contains none so accomplish'd a courtier
to convince the honour of my mistress, if in the hold-
ing or loss of that, you term her frail: I do nothing
doubt you have store of thieves; notwithstanding, I
fear not my ring.   95

Phi. Let us leave here, gentlemen.

Post. Sir, with all my heart. This worthy signior, I thank
him, makes no stranger of me; we are familiar at
first.

Iach. With five times so much conversation, I should get   100
ground of your fair mistress; make her go back,
even to the yielding, had I admittance, and opportunity to friend.

Post. No, no.

Iach. I dare thereupon pawn the moiety of my estate, to   105
your ring, which in my opinion o'ervalues it something: but I make my wager rather against your

93. frail: I] fraile, I *F.*   96. gentlemen.] gentlemen? *F.*

85. *in title*] Dowden notes that the
image is from the title to an estate.

86. *strange fowl . . . ponds*] Iachimo's
precise meaning is obscure but is, presumably, sexual. We may equate the
strange fowl with the 'birds of prey'
in *Meas.*, II. i. 2, and the neighbouring
ponds may be equivalent to the
'peculiar river' in the same play, I. ii.
91.

87. *so your*] 'so of your' (Theobald);
'so for your' (conj. Craig). But no
supplement is required.

88. *casual*] accidental, subject to
mischance.

92. *convince*] usually glossed as overcome, defeat, but I think that convict
may be the sense here. The word
occurs in this sense in *Arden of Feversham* (1592), I. i. 375.

98–9. *at first*] from the first; cf. II. iv.
167.

100–1. *get ground*] get an advantage.
Furness derives the simile from fen-
cing, but a secondary bad sense is also
possible.

confidence than her reputation. And to bar your
offence herein too, I durst attempt it against any
lady in the world.   110

Post. You are a great deal abus'd in too bold a persuasion, and I doubt not you sustain what you're
worthy of by your attempt.

Iach. What's that?

Post. A repulse: though your attempt (as you call it)   115
deserve more; a punishment too.

Phi. Gentlemen, enough of this, it came in too suddenly,
let it die as it was born, and I pray you be better
acquainted.

Iach. Would I had put my estate and my neighbour's on   120
th' approbation of what I have spoke!

Post. What lady would you choose to assail?

Iach. Yours, whom in constancy you think stands so safe.
I will lay you ten thousand ducats to your ring, that,
commend me to the court where your lady is, with   125
no more advantage than the opportunity of a
second conference, and I will bring from thence
that honour of hers, which you imagine so reserv'd.

Post. I will wage against your gold, gold to it: my ring I
hold dear as my finger, 'tis part of it.   130

Iach. You are a friend, and therein the wiser. If you buy

---

109. herein too] *F3;* heerein to *F.*   115. repulse: though] repulse though *F.*
120. neighbour's] *Pope;* neighbors *F.*   124. thousand] *F3;* thousands *F.*

109. *herein too*] 'herein-to' (White);
'hereunto' (conj. Anon.); 'herein, so'
(conj. Vaughan). It is not easy to see
how any of these proposed emendations elucidate the text, and the F3
correction is undoubtedly right.
Iachimo may refer, in passing, to the
offence given to Posthumus earlier in
France.
    111. *abus'd*] deceived.
    112. *you sustain*] Rowe reads 'you'd'
and is followed by many editors, but
Abbott (*Shakespeare Grammar*) treats
the verb as subjunctive, representing
P.E. future, i.e. you will sustain.
    120. *neighbour's*] Since there is no
apostrophe in F, it is equally permiss-

ible to read 'neighbours" and this,
perhaps, better expresses Iachimo's
meaning.
    121. *approbation*] proof. Cf. 'ap-
provers', II. iv. 25, and 'probable', II.
iv. 115.
    124. *ten thousand ducats*] In the *Deca-
meron* the proposed wager is one
thousand florins to five thousand: in
Frederyke of Jennen each party lays five
thousand guilders. The word 'ducats'
is used freely in the latter work.
    129. *gold to it*] I take this to mean an
equal sum in gold, as one would expect
if Shakespeare followed *Frederyke of
Jennen* at this point.
    131. *a friend*] Theobald's comment

ladies' flesh at a million a dram, you cannot preserve
it from tainting; but I see you have some religion in
you, that you fear.

Post. This is but a custom in your tongue: you bear a   135
graver purpose I hope.

Iach. I am the master of my speeches, and would undergo what's spoken, I swear.

Post. Will you? I shall but lend my diamond till your
return: let there be covenants drawn between's.   140
My mistress exceeds in goodness the hugeness of
your unworthy thinking. I dare you to this match:
here's my ring.

Phi. I will have it no lay.

Iach. By the gods, it is one. If I bring you no sufficient   145
testimony that I have enjoy'd the dearest bodily
part of your mistress, my ten thousand ducats are
yours, so is your diamond too: if I come off, and
leave her in such honour as you have trust in, she
your jewel, this your jewel, and my gold are yours: 150
provided I have your commendation for my more
free entertainment.

Post. I embrace these conditions, let us have articles betwixt us. Only, thus far you shall answer: if you

152. free] *F; not in Ff2–4.*

is: 'I correct with certainty: *afraid*',
but several able editors, Johnson,
Steevens, and Malone among them,
accept the F reading which I retain.
For the conservative interpretation,
Johnson's comment will suffice: '"You
are a friend" to the lady, "and therein
the wiser," as you will not expose her
to hazard; and that you *fear* is a proof
of your *religious* fidelity.' On the other
hand, Iachimo may mean 'you are a
friend to me', i.e. you are really of my
persuasion (see *O.E.D.* 'friend', sb. 6),
taking Posthumus' reluctance to wager
the ring as a sign of tacit admission.

133. *religion*] Possibly, in Iachimo's mouth, the word means fear or
superstition. Iachimo, here at least,
conforms to the Elizabethan notion of a Machiavellian villain who

counts religion 'but a childish toy'.
137–8. *undergo*] undertake.
143. *here's my ring*] Vaughan is
wrong in supposing that Posthumus
hands the ring to Iachimo. He may, as
Capell surmises, pass it to Philario who
is to hold the stakes.
144. *lay*] wager.
148. *yours*] Warburton substitutes
'mine' and tampers with the text, but
Johnson, reverting to F, wisely comments: 'Shakespeare intended that
Iachimo, having gained his purpose,
should designedly drop the invidious
and offensive part of a wager, and, to
flatter Posthumus, dwell long upon the
more pleasing part of the representation. One condition of the wager
implies the other, and there is no need
to mention both.'

make your voyage upon her, and give me directly   155
to understand you have prevail'd, I am no further
your enemy; she is not worth our debate. If she
remain unseduc'd, you not making it appear otherwise, for your ill opinion, and th' assault you have
made to her chastity, you shall answer me with your   160
sword.

Iach. Your hand, a covenant: we will have these things
set down by lawful counsel, and straight away for
Britain, lest the bargain should catch cold and
starve. I will fetch my gold, and have our two   165
wagers recorded.

Post. Agreed.   [*Exeunt Posthumus and Iachimo.*
French. Will this hold, think you?
Phi. Signior Iachimo will not from it. Pray let us follow
'em.   [*Exeunt.*   170

SCENE VI.—*Britain. Cymbeline's Palace.*

Enter QUEEN, *Ladies, and* CORNELIUS.

Queen. Whiles yet the dew's on ground, gather those flowers;
Make haste. Who has the note of them?
First Lady.   I, madam.
Queen. Dispatch.   [*Exeunt Ladies.*

167. S.D.] *Theobald; not in F.*   168. you?] *Rowe;* you. *F.*

2. *First Lady*] *Theobald; Lady F.*

155. *make your voyage*] The image is, perhaps, from the voyage of a merchant adventurer, as Dowden suggests, but there seems to be a secondary bad sense.

164–5. *lest . . . starve*] lest cooler judgement cause you to change your mind. The phrase was, perhaps, proverbial: cf. *Arden of Feversham,* IV. ii. 22–3: 'Na, thereby lyes a bargane, and you shall not haue it fresh and fasting'.

Scene VI

1. *Whiles yet . . . ground*] Furness notes

that the specification 'whiles the dew lasteth' occurs in Arderne's recipes for oil of roses and oil of violets. Belarius, at IV. ii. 284–5, observes that 'The herbs that have on them cold dew o' th' night / Are strewings fitt'st for graves', and there may, or may not, be a sinister significance in the Queen's present requirements. The evil uses to which she puts the flowers, when viewed in relation to the floral element in the play as a whole, are symbolic of her malignant character.

Now master doctor, have you brought those drugs?
Cor. Pleaseth your highness, ay: here they are, madam: 5
                                    [*Presenting a small box.*
But I beseech your grace, without offence,
(My conscience bids me ask) wherefore you have
Commanded of me these most poisonous compounds,
Which are the movers of a languishing death:
But though slow, deadly.
Queen.   I wonder, doctor,   10
Thou ask'st me such a question. Have I not been
Thy pupil long? Hast thou not learn'd me how
To make perfumes? Distil? Preserve? Yea so,
That our great king himself doth woo me oft
For my confections? Having thus far proceeded   15
(Unless thou think'st me devilish) is't not meet
That I did amplify my judgement in
Other conclusions? I will try the forces
Of these thy compounds on such creatures as
We count not worth the hanging (but none human)   20
To try the vigour of them, and apply
Allayments to their act, and by them gather
Their several virtues, and effects.
Cor.   Your highness
Shall from this practice but make hard your heart:
Besides, the seeing these effects will be   25
Both noisome and infectious.
Queen.   O, content thee.

Enter PISANIO.

5. S.D.] *Malone.*

7. *My conscience . . . ask*] I take this to be an aside addressed directly to the audience.

10. *I wonder*] Theobald, to meet the metrical difficulty, reads 'I do wonder'.

12. *learn'd*] taught.

15. *confections*] compounded drugs.

18. *conclusions*] experiments.

try] Vaughan conjectures 'prove' here in view of 'try' at l. 21. If any change is to be made, however, that of

Walker, who proposes altering the second 'try' to 'test', seems preferable.

22. *by them*] What does 'them' refer to? Eccles thinks 'allayments'; Dowden, 'creatures'; Craig (who would read 'Allayment to their acts'), 'acts'; Furness, 'conclusions'. As I do not feel confident about any one pronoun in ll. 21-3, I hesitate to pronounce judgement. It matters little, for the general sense is clear enough.

      [Aside] Here comes a flattering rascal, upon him
      Will I first work: he's for his master,
      And enemy to my son. How now, Pisanio?
      Doctor, your service for this time is ended,   30
      Take your own way.
Cor.   *[Aside]* I do suspect you, madam;
      But you shall do no harm.
Queen.   *[To Pisanio]* Hark thee, a word.
Cor. *[Aside]* I do not like her. She doth think she has
      Strange ling'ring poisons: I do know her spirit;
      And will not trust one of her malice with   35
      A drug of such damn'd nature. Those she has
      Will stupefy and dull the sense awhile;
      Which first (perchance) she'll prove on cats and dogs,
      Then afterward up higher: but there is
      No danger in what show of death it makes,   40
      More than the locking up the spirits a time,
      To be more fresh, reviving. She is fool'd
      With a most false effect: and I the truer,
      So to be false with her.
Queen.   No further service, doctor,
      Until I send for thee.
Cor.   I humbly take my leave. *[Exit.*   45

27, 31. *Aside] Rowe.*   32. *To Pisanio] Rowe.*   33. *Aside] Capell.*

28. *Will . . . master]* The line is metrically irregular and various adjustments have been suggested: 'Will I first let them work: he's etc.' (Capell); 'Will . . . he's for his master's sake / An enemy etc.' (Pope); 'Will . . . he's factor for his master,' (Walker); 'Will . . . he's for his master and / An enemy etc.' (Anon.). Daniel, who offers no supplement, conjectures 'he's, for his master, / An enemy'. Of these proposals that of Walker seems to me immeasurably the best, since the corruption must lie in the awkward and feeble phrase 'he's for his master' where the lacuna will almost certainly be a substantive.

33–44.] Johnson found this soliloquy 'very inartificial': 'The speaker is under no strong pressure of thought; he is neither resolving, repenting, suspecting, nor deliberating, and yet makes a long speech to tell himself what he himself knows.' Other critics have concurred but, like Johnson, overlook the fact that the audience requires this information. Shakespeare has to ensure that his tragicomedy does not grow too big with the promise of disaster. Moreover, at this stage, he still keeps his audience guessing.

40. *it makes]* Vaughan takes 'it' to refer to the act of dulling the sense, but Delius's view that it refers to 'those she has' is altogether more plausible. The construction is inexact: understandably so in view of 'strange ling'ring poisons' followed by 'a drug of such damn'd nature'.

Queen. Weeps she still, say'st thou? Dost thou think in time
        She will not quench, and let instructions enter
        Where folly now possesses? Do thou work:
        When thou shalt bring me word she loves my son,
        I'll tell thee on the instant, thou art then   50
        As great as is thy master: greater, for
        His fortunes all lie speechless, and his name
        Is at last gasp. Return he cannot, nor
        Continue where he is: to shift his being
        Is to exchange one misery with another,   55
        And every day that comes comes to decay
        A day's work in him. What shalt thou expect,
        To be depender on a thing that leans?
        Who cannot be new built, nor has no friends,
        So much as but to prop him?   [*The Queen drops the box.*
                Pisanio takes it up.] Thou tak'st up   60
        Thou know'st not what: but take it for thy labour:
        It is a thing I made, which hath the king
        Five times redeem'd from death. I do not know
        What is more cordial. Nay, I prithee take it;
        It is an earnest of a farther good   65
        That I mean to thee. Tell thy mistress how
        The case stands with her: do't, as from thyself;
        Think what a chance thou changest on; but think

60. S.D.] *Malone (subst.).*   62. made] *F;* make *F2.*

47. *quench*] O.E.D. quotes this line
and defines: 'to cool down'. For the
image in association with 'folly', cf.
Ham., IV. vii. 191–2: 'I have a speech
of fire, that fain would blaze, / But that
this folly douts it.'

54. *shift his being*] Johnson glosses 'to
change his abode' and may be right,
though Furness suspects that 'Posthumus' grief lay deeper than the care
for his lodging.'

56. *decay*] 'Decay' used as a transitive
verb is fairly common in Elizabethan
literature, but here, as Eccles suggests,
it may be a noun, thus: And every day
that comes, a day's work comes to
decay in him.

58. *leans*] 'That *inclines* towards its

fall' (Johnson). Furness suggests: 'To
be a depender on one who is himself a
depender on others', but such an interpretation is at odds with ll. 59–60.

68. *what a chance thou changest on*]
Several emendations have been proposed: 'chance thou chancest on'
(Rowe); 'change thou chancest on'
(Theobald); 'chance thou hangest on'
(Daniel); 'chase thou changest on'
(Staunton); but no alteration is
required. Heath paraphrases F:
'Think on what a chance, on how promising a prospect of advancing thy
fortunes, thou changest thy present
attachment.' I suggest, with some hesitation, that 'chance' may be used in
the sense 'risk'. If so, we might para-

Thou hast thy mistress still, to boot, my son,
Who shall take notice of thee. I'll move the king   70
To any shape of thy preferment, such
As thou'lt desire: and then myself, I chiefly,
That set thee on to this desert, am bound
To load thy merit richly. Call my women:
Think on my words.   [*Exit Pisanio.*

          A sly and constant knave.   75
Not to be shak'd: the agent for his master,
And the remembrancer of her to hold
The hand-fast to her lord. I have given him that,
Which if he take, shall quite unpeople her
Of liegers for her sweet: and which she after,   80
Except she bend her humour, shall be assur'd
To taste of too.

        Re-enter PISANIO *and Ladies.*

        So, so: well done, well done:
The violets, cowslips, and the primroses
Bear to my closet. Fare thee well, Pisanio;
Think on my words.   [*Exeunt Queen and Ladies.*
Pis.   And shall do: 85

78. hand-fast] *F;* hand fast *F2.*

phrase: Consider at what risk you would change your loyalties, but consider also that you would still have your mistress, and my son to boot. Subtle insinuation of this kind accords with the Queen's character.

think] Theobald punctuates 'think;—' which Dowden, altering slightly to 'think!—', approves.

77. *remembrancer*] a person specifically engaged for the purpose of reminding. Ingleby notes that it is a law term.

78. *hand-fast*] marriage contract. The word is used in that sense by Beaumont and Fletcher. It occurs in *Wint.* but there means custody.

80. *liegers for her sweet*] Liegers (usually spelt ledgers in P.E.) means resident ambassadors. Schmidt cites many examples of 'sweet' used substantively in the sense of lover or mistress. Hence, her husband's representative who, according to the Queen, is his sole 'remembrancer'.

85. *And shall do*] The verse is metrically defective but the various emendations proposed do little to improve matters. Dowden offers a well-reasoned explanation: 'I conjecture that the Queen's speech ended with "Think on my words, Pisanio," and that the printer, finding "Pisanio" above the speech that followed, took this for the speech-heading, which he found repeated before the word "And", whence it was omitted after "words".'

But when to my good lord I prove untrue,
I'll choke myself: there's all I'll do for you.   [*Exit.*

SCENE VII.—*The Same.*

Enter IMOGEN *alone.*

Imo. A father cruel, and a step-dame false,
A foolish suitor to a wedded lady,
That hath her husband banish'd:—O, that husband,
My supreme crown of grief! and those repeated
Vexations of it! Had I been thief-stolen,   5
As my two brothers, happy: but most miserable
Is the desire that's glorious. Bless'd be those,
How mean soe'er, that have their honest wills,
Which seasons comfort.—Who may this be? Fie!

Enter PISANIO *and* IACHIMO.

Pis. Madam, a noble gentleman of Rome,   10

Scene VII

7. desire] *F2;* desires *F.*   Bless'd] *Pope;* Blessed *F.*

86–7.] 'Did William Shakespeare write this doggerel?' asks Furness. The probable answer is 'Alas, yes!' These lines serve, at least, to emphasize Pisanio's unswerving loyalty and, as an overflow to pent-up rage, are not without dramatic force.

Scene VII

1–9.] Ingleby regards these lines as 'either rough notes for a speech, or the remains of a speech cut down for representation'. Neither supposition is tenable bibliographically. Imogen's grief renders her not quite coherent.

4. *those repeated*] recited or enumerated vexations. 'those' are father, step-dame, and suitor, as opposed to 'that husband'.

6–7. *but . . . glorious*] The safest interpretation is: most miserable is the unfulfilled longing that aspires to great

things. The phrase is perplexing, and may, since the F prints 'desires', require emendation. Both Vaughan and Craig would emend 'the' to 'she' and retain F 'desires'. This is ingenious but does not ring true. Hanmer prints 'degree' for 'desires'. Staunton conjectures that these words should follow 'comfort' in l. 9, but only Hudson has had the temerity to make the text conform with this suggestion.

9. *Which seasons comfort*] Knight's paraphrase will suffice: 'The *mean* have their *honest*, homely wills (opposed to the desire that's glorious) and that circumstance gives a relish to comfort.'

Fie] occasioned, probably, by her annoyance at being interrupted in her meditation, but her first glimpse of 'the yellow Iachimo' might well provoke the exclamation.

Comes from my lord with letters.

Iach.   Change you, madam:
The worthy Leonatus is in safety,
And greets your highness dearly.   [*Presents a letter.*

Imo.   Thanks, good sir:
You're kindly welcome.

Iach. [*Aside*] All of her that is out of door most rich!   15
If she be furnish'd with a mind so rare,
She is alone th' Arabian bird; and I
Have lost the wager. Boldness be my friend!
Arm me, Audacity, from head to foot,
Or like the Parthian I shall flying fight;   20
Rather, directly fly.

Imo. [*Reads*] He is one of the noblest note, to whose kind-
        nesses I am infinitely tied. Reflect upon him ac-
        cordingly, as you value your trust—

                        LEONATUS.   25

---

13. S.D.] *Capell.*   15. *Aside*] *Pope.*   24. trust—] *Boswell;* trust. *F.*

11. *Comes*] who comes. The comma after 'Rome' is in F and there is no reason for deleting it.

Change you, madam:] Most editors follow Rowe in printing 'madam?' but such deviation from F is quite unwarranted. When Iachimo first sees her, Imogen looks sad or angry or both. He bids her change her expression because he has good news for her.

15–18.] so Johan, in *Frederyke of Jennen*, is dismayed when he sees Ambrose's wife: 'The money is lost: I se it wel. For she semeth a worshypfull woman etc.' Boccaccio affords no such parallel. Johan abandons his original intentions on the spot: Iachimo's purpose is given a more subtle and extended treatment and Shakespeare keeps his audience in suspense for the time being.

17. *She is alone*] I have followed F. Craig proposes 'alone,' and Seymour 'alone;'. Neither change seems necessary.

th' Arabian bird] the phoenix. '. . . in Arabia / There is one tree, the phoenix' throne, one phoenix / At this hour reigning there' (*Tp.*, III. ii. 22–4). In *Ant.*, III. ii. 12, Agrippa says: 'O Antony! O thou Arabian bird.' For an interesting account of the Phoenix see Roger Lancelyn Green, *The Phoenix and the Tree* in *English*, vol. VII (1948), pp. 11–15. See also Introduction, pp. lxxi ff.

20. *Parthian*] The horse-archers of Parthia or Khorassan were proverbially famous for their fighting tactics. Their method was to discharge darts upon their enemy, then to evade close conflict by rapid flight during which they shot their arrows backwards. Iachimo means that, if boldness fails him, he will be forced to use indirect methods, or even to abandon his plans altogether ('Rather directly fly').

23. *Reflect upon him*] 'Reflect' according to Schmidt means 'look' and Dowden, who glosses it 'regard', rejects Ingleby's 'cast upon him some of the radiance of your favour'. But, in view of the sense of 'reflection' at I. iii. 30, Ingleby may well be right.

24. *trust*] It is clear from ll. 26–8 that Imogen reads only part of the letter

So far I read aloud.
But even the very middle of my heart
Is warm'd by th' rest, and takes it thankfully.
You are as welcome, worthy sir, as I
Have words to bid you, and shall find it so　　　　30
In all that I can do.
Iach.　　　　　　　　Thanks, fairest lady.—
What! are men mad? Hath nature given them eyes
To see this vaulted arch, and the rich crop
Of sea and land, which can distinguish 'twixt
The fiery orbs above, and the twinn'd stones　　　　35
Upon the number'd beach, and can we not

28. takes] *Pope;* take *F.*

aloud. It is possible that the second sentence is the final one of the letter and that F 'trust' is right. 'Trust' is usually explained: 'the charge entrusted to you', but some editors accept Hanmer's emendation 'truest'. 'Him' is, of course, Iachimo, but I am not sure that the first sentence refers to him, for there is no evidence that Posthumus is infinitely tied to his kindnesses. This sentence may, therefore, belong to the earlier part of the letter and refer to Philario. But perhaps this is to consider a little too curiously.

32–50.] Iachimo begins his accusation against Posthumus and employs what Dowden happily calls 'feigned soliloquy'. His method is one of innuendo and subtle suggestion. Once this is understood, many of the supposed cruxes disappear.

33. *crop*] much disputed, and emended to 'cope' (Warburton) and 'scope' (Crosby). For the various meanings of 'crop' the reader may be referred to *O.E.D.* I take it to mean 'harvest' in the present context and find no incongruity in sea, as well as land, having a harvest. Had Shakespeare intended 'crop' in any other known sense, I doubt whether he would have qualified it with the adjective 'rich'.

34. *distinguish*] distinguish orb from orb, and stone from stone.

35. *twinn'd stones*] that is, stones which are exactly alike. The 'fiery orbs' may be sun and moon. *Tim.,* IV. iii. 1–5, affords an instructive parallel which throws light on the imagery of the present passage and settles, once and for all, the sense and authenticity of 'twinn'd'. 'O blessed breeding sun, draw from the earth / Rotten humidity; below thy sister's orb / Infect the air! Twinn'd brothers of one womb, / Whose procreation, residence, and birth, / Scarce is dividant, touch them with several fortunes.' Since the idea of fruitless harvest lies behind these lines, they lend some support to my interpretation of 'crop'. We lesser mortals may draw some comfort from the fact that Coleridge took the 'twinn'd stones' to be cockle-shells!

36. *number'd*] Johnson glosses 'numerous'. The various emendations: 'cumber'd' (Staunton); 'umber'd' (Farmer); 'encumbered' (Vaughan); can be disregarded. Theobald, with the powerful support of *Lr.,* IV. vi. 20–1: 'the murmuring surge, / That on the unnumber'd idle pebbles chafes,' reads 'th' unnumbered beach', but I think he is wrong. In *Lr.* the pebbles are seen through the eyes of man: in the present context, though Iachimo is the speaker, the stones are viewed as it were through the eye of God.

> Partition make with spectacles so precious
> 'Twixt fair, and foul?

Imo.   What makes your admiration?

Iach. It cannot be i' th' eye: for apes and monkeys,
> 'Twixt two such shes, would chatter this way, and   40
> Contemn with mows the other. Nor i' the judgement:
> For idiots in this case of favour, would
> Be wisely definite: nor i' th' appetite.
> Sluttery, to such neat excellence oppos'd,
> Should make desire vomit emptiness,   45
> Not so allur'd to feed.

Imo. What is the matter, trow?

Iach.   The cloyed will—

---

37. spectacles] *F3;* Spectales *F.*

'There's a special providence in the fall of a sparrow', says Hamlet, echoing *Matthew*, x. 29. Is not the present line in some way dependent on St Matthew's next verse: 'But the very hairs of your head are all numbered'? The beach, then, is numbered, accountable, reasonable: and so, in *Tp.*, v. i. 81, we find 'the reasonable shore'. The same concept of divine order seems to underlie both adjectives.

37. *spectacles so precious*] This may mean 'with such precious organs of vision', as some commentators suppose, but I am not sure that 'spectacles' can bear such an interpretation and *O.E.D.* affords no support. Dowden offers, as an alternative, 'having shows (of earth and sky) which instruct the eyes in making distinctions', and notes that 'spectacles' in the sense of 'shows' is common in Shakespeare. I am inclined to paraphrase: Can we not distinguish between fair and foul when we are confronted with such precious spectacles as this Imogen?

38. *admiration*] wonder.

39–46.] In his previous speech Iachimo has spoken of 'our' failure to distinguish between fair and foul, but it is really Posthumus' failure that he seeks to imply. Here he attempts to make his accusation more particular,

though he is not yet prepared to state it categorically. It cannot be Posthumus' eye that is at fault, nor his judgement, nor his appetite, but, as ll. 47–50 imply, his lustful nature.

40. *two such shes*] one fair, like Imogen; the other foul.

this way] He points towards Imogen.

41. *mows*] grimaces.

42. *case of favour*] Dowden explains 'question respecting beauty or attractiveness' and notes that both 'case' and 'favour' are common in these senses.

43. *appetite*] Here 'appetite', like 'desire' in l. 45, is used, I think, in a good sense and implies natural physical desire.

45. *Should . . . emptiness*] The commentators have discussed this difficult line in fulsome detail. The general sense is 'should turn desire to loathing' or 'should destroy all desire'. The image of desire casting up nothing is sustained in the speech which follows where desire, though satiate, is at the same time insatiable and is therefore prevented from vomiting.

47. *The cloyed will*] With this Iachimo turns to lustful passion which, by implication, he attributes to Posthumus. This perverted desire is incapable of making any distinction between fair and foul. It feeds equally

That satiate yet unsatisfied desire, that tub
Both fill'd and running—ravening first the lamb,
Longs after for the garbage.

Imo.   What, dear sir,   50
Thus raps you? Are you well?

Iach.   Thanks madam, well:
[*To Pisanio*] Beseech you sir,
Desire my man's abode where I did leave him:
He's strange and peevish.

Pis.   I was going, sir,
To give him welcome.   [*Exit.* 55

Imo. Continues well my lord? His health, beseech you?

Iach. Well, madam.

Imo. Is he disposed to mirth? I hope he is.

Iach. Exceeding pleasant: none a stranger there,
So merry and so gamesome: he is call'd   60
The Briton reveller.

Imo.   When he was here
He did incline to sadness, and oft-times
Not knowing why.

Iach.   I never saw him sad.

61. Briton] *Steevens;* Britaine *F.*

on the lamb (the symbol of purity) and the garbage.

48–9. *that tub . . . running*] The image *may* be classical. The Danaides, as punishment for killing their husbands, were doomed to pour water into a bottomless vessel for eternity. Marston, in *The Fawn*, twice refers to this incident, and on both occasions, calls the vessel a tub. The source is Horace, *Carmina,* III. xi. 26.

51. *raps*] transports, possesses. Apparently the word was conflated with 'rape', as F 'rap's' suggests, though the two words are etymologically different. The fact that Shakespeare does not elsewhere use the word in the present tense is of little significance. It is so used by both Jonson and Fletcher.

Are you well?] Iachimo's first line of approach has failed. The tortuous mixture of defamation and ingratia-

tion which he has so far employed is interpreted by Imogen as symptomatic of illness (or madness).

53. *abode*] Request my man to await me where I left him.

54. *strange and peevish*] 'He is a foreigner and easily fretted' (Johnson). 'Peevish' had many meanings: 'mad', 'ill-tempered', 'childish', 'foolish', 'wayward'. As we see nothing of Iachimo's man, it is scarcely possible to be dogmatic. Hanmer supplies the superfluous emendation 'sheepish'.

59. *none*] Abbott quotes this line and glosses 'not at all'. Wyatt suggests 'none, a stranger there, so merry' but the construction is forced. If Abbott is right, as I think he is, l. 60 may mean 'so merry etc. that he is call'd'. With this speech Iachimo begins a new line of attack.

62. *sadness*] seriousness.

There is a Frenchman his companion, one
An eminent monsieur, that, it seems, much loves   65
A Gallian girl at home. He furnaces
The thick sighs from him; whiles the jolly Briton
(Your lord, I mean) laughs from's free lungs: cries "O,
Can my sides hold, to think that man, who knows
By history, report, or his own proof,   70
What woman is, yea what she cannot choose
But must be, will's free hours languish for
Assured bondage?"

Imo.   Will my lord say so?
Iach. Ay, madam, with his eyes in flood with laughter:
It is a recreation to be by   75
And hear him mock the Frenchman: but heavens know
Some men are much to blame.

Imo.   Not he, I hope.
Iach. Not he: but yet heaven's bounty towards him might
Be us'd more thankfully. In himself 'tis much;
In you, which I account his, beyond all talents.   80
Whilst I am bound to wonder, I am bound
To pity too.

Imo.   What do you pity, sir?

72–3. languish for / Assured] *Steevens;* languish: / For assured *F;* languish, / For assured *Ff2–4.*

67. *thick*] as often in Shakespeare an adjective of quantity.

the jolly Briton] so, in Under-downe's translation of the *Æthiopica,* Theagenes is called 'this jolly Thessalian'. The adjective in both contexts signifies licentious, lustful.

70. *proof*] experience, as at III. iii. 27.

72. *will's . . . languish*] 'languish' is used in its causal sense 'to make to languish' with 'free hours' as its object. It is so used in Florio's translation of Montaigne which Shakespeare had read. His 'free hours' means 'his bachelor freedom' as opposed to the 'assured bondage' of wedlock. 'Hours' is dissyllabic.

73. *Assured*] The word can mean either 'certain' or 'affianced' and it is possible that Iachimo plays on both

senses. Dyce cites examples of the second meaning from *John* and *Err.* 'Sure' in the sense of 'affianced' is common.

79–80. *Be . . . talents*] Heaven's bounty, in bestowing on him both his own great qualities and you, whom I regard as his, is beyond all computation. I have followed F punctuation except for the comma after 'his', which is Capell's. The precise meaning of 'talents' is disputed and must be left open. 'Gifts', 'riches', 'inclination', 'desires', have all been suggested, the last two by Craig who paraphrases: 'With respect to you, whom I account his beyond all reach of loose desires, Whilst etc.' If we take the word to mean 'riches', we may suspect that Shakespeare plays on 'talent', the coin.

Iach. Two creatures heartily.

Imo.   Am I one, sir?
You look on me: what wrack discern you in me
Deserves your pity?

Iach.   Lamentable! What   85
To hide me from the radiant sun, and solace
I' th' dungeon by a snuff?

Imo.   I pray you, sir,
Deliver with more openness your answers
To my demands. Why do you pity me?

Iach. That others do
(I was about to say) enjoy your—But   90
It is an office of the gods to venge it,
Not mine to speak on't.

Imo.   You do seem to know
Something of me, or what concerns me; pray you,
Since doubting things go ill often hurts more   95
Than to be sure they do—for certainties
Either are past remedies; or timely knowing,
The remedy then born—discover to me
What both you spur and stop.

Iach.   Had I this cheek

98. born—] borne. *F.*

83. *Two creatures*] Imogen is one, and the other, I think, Posthumus, whom Iachimo feigns to pity for his dereliction and may, with a certain irony, pity on account of the probable outcome of present mischief.

84–6.] 'Wrack', 'sun', and 'solace' is a Shakespearean collocation: cf. *Mac.*, I. ii. 25–8: 'As whence the *sun* 'gins his reflection / *Shipwracking* storms and direful thunders break, / So from that spring whence *comfort* seem'd to come / Discomfort swells.'

87. *snuff*] the burnt-out wick of a candle. Here used figuratively of a person who is on the point of extinction. The image is developed in ll. 108–10.

95. *doubting*] fearing.

96–8. *do*— . . . *born*—] I have accepted Dowden's pointing (which is,

on the whole, preferable to that of editors who begin the parenthesis with 'Since' in l. 95) and would paraphrase: ills or wrongs, which we know for certain, are either past remedy or may be rectified through being known in time. 'Timely knowing' is probably adjective plus noun, though participle qualified by adverb is also possible.

99. *What . . . stop*] usually taken as 'that which you both force upon me and withhold', but Johnson gives: 'What it is that at once incites you to speak and restrains you from it', and presumably takes 'what' as 'what things' with 'you' as the object. The image, as Steevens notes, is from horsemanship.

99–112.] This speech is less difficult than it appears and, like ll. 39–46, presents three things—lips, hands, and

To bathe my lips upon: this hand, whose touch   100
(Whose every touch) would force the feeler's soul
To th' oath of loyalty: this object, which
Takes prisoner the wild motion of mine eye,
Firing it only here; should I (damn'd then)
Slaver with lips as common as the stairs   105
That mount the Capitol: join gripes, with hands
Made hard with hourly falsehood (falsehood, as
With labour): then by-peeping in an eye
Base and illustrous as the smoky light
That's fed with stinking tallow: it were fit   110
That all the plagues of hell should at one time
Encounter such revolt.

---

108. by-peeping] *hyphened Knight.*   109. illustrous] *Tieck;* illustrious *F.*

---

sight—in a contrasted pattern. In short Iachimo says: If, having this lip, this hand, this object, I turn to those lips, etc., I deserve all the torments that Hell affords.

101. *every*] The early editors follow F3 which prints 'very', a reading which could well be right. F must be allowed full authority nevertheless.

104. *Firing*] F2 has what is, once again, a seemingly plausible variant— 'fixing'—but F is undoubtedly right. This object alone fires his eye. The 'object' may be Imogen's eye, which is contrasted with the 'eye base and illustrous' of ll. 108–9. Dowden explains 'motion' as 'passion', but 'wild motion' in that sense sounds a little strained. I am tempted to see a cosmic image behind this line. Iachimo thinks of his eye as a wandering star which only Imogen can fix and fire. The imagery in this scene is more complex and more concentrated than it is elsewhere in the play. A group of fire and light images can readily be isolated, and these lend support to 'firing' in the present line. 'Prisoner' plus 'firing' takes up the 'dungeon' and 'snuff' collocation in l. 87.

damn'd then] damned by so doing.

105–6. *Slaver . . . Capitol*] lavish slobbery kisses upon the lips of prostitutes.

The Capitol, or Temple of Jupiter, in Rome was approached by a flight of a hundred steps which, like the 'lips' in this context, were used by all comers.

107–8. *falsehood, as With labour*] with falsehood as with labour.

108. *by-peeping*] peeping sidelong, or clandestinely. Knight, to whom credit for the hyphen is due, wrongly states that it is in F. Of the proposed emendations only Johnson's 'lie peeping' has found many supporters. Iachimo contrasts sidelong glances with the fixed gaze of ll. 102–4, and Johnson's reading robs the contrast of much of its force.

109. *illustrous*] F reads 'illustrious' and there has been much controversy about Shakespeare's meaning, together with a few pointless emendations. 'Lack-lustre' seems to me to be the only meaning that can reasonably be connected with 'the smoky light / That's fed with stinking tallow' and what Furness says about the F form is surely right: '"illustrious" is Shakespeare's own word—or his compositor's, and is akin to *jealious, dexterious, prolixious, robustious, beautious,*—all to be found in the Folio and Quartos.'

112. *revolt*] revulsion of appetite (see *O.E.D.* 'revolt' sb. 2c).

Imo.   My lord, I fear,
   Has forgot Britain.
Iach.   And himself. Not I,
   Inclin'd to this intelligence, pronounce
   The beggary of his change: but 'tis your graces   115
   That from my mutest conscience to my tongue
   Charms this report out.
Imo.   Let me hear no more.
Iach. O dearest soul: your cause doth strike my heart
   With pity that doth make me sick! A lady
   So fair, and fasten'd to an empery   120
   Would make the great'st king double, to be partner'd
   With tomboys hir'd with that self exhibition
   Which your own coffers yield! with diseas'd ventures,
   That play with all infirmities for gold
   Which rottenness can lend Nature! Such boil'd stuff 125
   As well might poison poison! Be reveng'd,
   Or she that bore you was no queen, and you

113. himself.] *Pope;* himselfe, *F.*   122. hir'd with] *Rowe;* hyr'd, with *F.*

113. *And himself. Not I*] I have followed Pope in placing a stop after 'himself' but am not at all sure that F requires such correction. If we follow F, the speech might be paraphrased: And it is his own behaviour, not my inclination to tell tales, which pronounces the beggary of his change: but it is your charms (not my inclination) which actually draw this report from me. In that case, 'pronounce' must be regarded as plural by attraction, unless we assume that the compositor dropped an *s*, setting up 'pronounce' for 'pronounces' and, in l. 115, 'graces' for 'grace'. The fact that 'graces' governs a singular verb proves nothing, for this so-called Northern plural is very common. More persuasive is the fact that Iachimo uses 'grace' at l. 203, where, paradoxically enough, we might expect 'graces'.

120. *empery*] empire. Some editors follow Rowe and print 'empery,'. F means: A lady who is so fair and who

is fastened to an empire which would make the greatest king double, etc. Rowe's pointing changes the sense to: A lady so fair who, fastened to an empire, would, etc. But this seems to ignore the fact that Imogen, at this point in the play, is heir-apparent.

122. *tomboys*] harlots.
self exhibition] self-same allowance.
123–5. *ventures . . . Nature*] The general sense is clear, but certain details are ambiguous. Dyce glosses 'ventures' as 'lemans', Vaughan suggests 'gamblers', and Dowden thinks it may mean 'something risked in the way of trade', but all these seem less likely than Capell's 'traders'. Shakespeare may have coalesced 'ventures' with 'vendors' which was a neologism. 'Play' can be interpreted: 'toy', 'gamble', 'mock at', and any of these senses will fit the present passage.

125. *boil'd stuff*] persons who have undergone sweating treatment for venereal disease.

Recoil from your great stock.

Imo.   Reveng'd!
How should I be reveng'd? If this be true,
(As I have such a heart that both mine ears   130
Must not in haste abuse) if it be true,
How should I be reveng'd?

Iach.   Should he make me
Live like Diana's priest, betwixt cold sheets,
Whiles he is vaulting variable ramps,
In your despite, upon your purse— Revenge it.   135
I dedicate myself to your sweet pleasure,
More noble than that runagate to your bed,
And will continue fast to your affection,
Still close as sure.

Imo.   What ho, Pisanio!

Iach. Let me my service tender on your lips.   140

Imo. Away, I do condemn mine ears, that have
So long attended thee. If thou wert honourable,
Thou wouldst have told this tale for virtue, not
For such an end thou seek'st, as base, as strange.
Thou wrong'st a gentleman, who is as far   145
From thy report as thou from honour, and
Solicits here a lady that disdains

---

132. should] *F;* shall *F2.*   135. purse—] purse: *F.*

---

128. *Recoil . . . stock*] prove degenerate.

132–5. *Should . . . purse—*] F reads 'purse:' which many editors alter to 'purse?' but Simpson (pp. 71–4) gives numerous examples of the colon indicating interrupted speech, and this, I think, is the case here. I take 'Should he' to mean 'If he should', and F colon (my dash) to be the equivalent of 'but what need of further words?' The confusion of personal pronouns in this speech has troubled commentators, but it is deliberate, rhetorical, and dramatically effective.

133. *Live*] Walker conjectures 'Lie'.

134. *variable ramps*] 'Variable' may signify either 'fickle', or 'various', though the latter meaning may have

arisen slightly later than *Cymbeline.* 'Ramps', brazen women or girls.

135. *Revenge it.*] Furness suggests 'Revenge it?', making Iachimo echo Imogen's question at ll. 128–32. The suggestion, though not supported by F, is attractive, but see note to ll. 132–5 above.

139. *close*] secret.

142. *thee*] Imogen has hitherto treated him as an equal and used the polite form 'you', to which she reverts at l. 168 when he makes amends.

147. *Solicits*] F2 and its successors read 'Solicitst', a variant which has been universally accepted. The grammar of F, however, is unimpeachably Elizabethan and, as Furness wisely remarks, 'grammar is dearly pur-

Thee, and the devil alike. What ho, Pisanio!
The king my father shall be made acquainted
Of thy assault: if he shall think it fit　　　150
A saucy stranger in his court to mart
As in a Romish stew, and to expound
His beastly mind to us, he hath a court
He little cares for, and a daughter who
He not respects at all. What ho, Pisanio!　　　155
Iach. O happy Leonatus! I may say:
The credit that thy lady hath of thee
Deserves thy trust, and thy most perfect goodness
Her assur'd credit. Blessed live you long!
A lady to the worthiest sir that ever　　　160
Country call'd his; and you, his mistress, only
For the most worthiest fit. Give me your pardon.
I have spoke this to know if your affiance
Were deeply rooted, and shall make your lord
That which he is, new o'er: and he is one　　　165
The truest manner'd: such a holy witch
That he enchants societies into him:
Half all men's hearts are his.

---

154. who] *F;* whom *F2.*　　156. say:] say, *F.*　　168. men's] *F2;* men *F.*

chased in poetry at the price of invincible cacophony'. Cf. 'refts' at III. iii. 103.

151. *saucy*] impudent. E. A. Armstrong (*Shakespeare's Imagination*, p. 99) notes that Shakespeare tended to associate 'stew' in its culinary sense in brothels (or 'stews'), and that when the word was used for a brothel it revived culinary imagery. Hence 'saucy' in conjunction with 'Romish stew'.

152. *Romish*] This form is not found elsewhere in Shakespeare *teste* Furness. It is a common Elizabethanism, frequently used in a pejorative sense (as here), especially in connection with the Roman Catholic Church. There may be such implication here, though Anglicans could not afford to sneer since the stews adjoining the Globe Theatre were under the control of the Bishop of Winchester.

157–9. *The credit . . . credit*] The trust which your wife places in you deserves your trust, and your perfect integrity deserves her trust. Imogen's vehemence has shown that her credit of Posthumus is very much 'assur'd'.

161. *call'd his*] called its own. The possessive 'its' was not yet current. It is barely possible that 'his mistress' in this line signifies 'its mistress'. Cf. v. i. 20: 'Britain, I have kill'd thy mistress.'

165. *one*] above all.

166. *witch*] The word could apply to either sex.

167. *into*] unto.

168. *Half . . . his*] Furness defends F 'men' and paraphrases: 'half of all men who have manly hearts are his'. But 'men-heart' sounds a most unlikely compound, and Furness's interpretation is strained beyond all reason. The line means that every man has given

Imo.   You make amends.
Iach. He sits 'mongst men like a descended god;
        He hath a kind of honour sets him off,   170
        More than a mortal seeming. Be not angry,
        Most mighty princess, that I have adventur'd
        To try your taking of a false report, which hath
        Honour'd with confirmation your great judgement
        In the election of a sir so rare,   175
        Which you know cannot err. The love I bear him
        Made me to fan you thus, but the gods made you
        (Unlike all others) chaffless. Pray, your pardon.
Imo. All's well, sir: take my power i' th' court for yours.
Iach. My humble thanks. I had almost forgot   180
        T' entreat your grace, but in a small request,
        And yet of moment too, for it concerns:
        Your lord, myself, and other noble friends
        Are partners in the business.
Imo.   Pray, what is't?
Iach. Some dozen Romans of us, and your lord   185

169. descended] *F2;* defended *F.*

half his heart or affection to Pos-thumus.

169–71. *He sits . . . seeming*] Posthumus is, so to speak, the noblest Roman of them all, and, in order to emphasize his pre-eminence even in a Roman milieu, Shakespeare describes him as he several times describes the heroes of the Roman tragedies: cf. *Cæs.,* I. ii. 135–8; *Ant.,* v. ii. 82–92; *Cor.,* v. iv. 23–6. Another parallel, in *Cor.,* IV. vi. 90–3, may serve to clarify the meaning of the present passage: 'He is their god: he leads them like a thing / Made by some other deity than nature, / That shapes man better.' Capell's suggested reading: 'More than of mortal seeming' merits consideration, since 'seeming' in F is apparently a participle, whereas substantival use is rather more characteristic of Shakespeare. But the grammar is ambiguous in any case.

176. *Which*] I dissent from the customary view that 'which' refers to

'judgement' and prefer to relate it to 'sir', as yielding a better sense. Surely it is Posthumus who is immune from error: not Imogen's 'judgement' nor her 'election'. 'Which' for 'who' or 'that' is quite normal in Shakespeare. See Abbott, §265.

177. *fan*] winnow.

182. *concerns:*] All editors have followed Rowe in deleting the colon, thus making 'lord' (which they alter to 'lord;') the object. Furness, following H. Ingleby, has fully vindicated F, however. 'Concerns' means 'to be of importance' and is used intransitively by Shakespeare. Ingleby cites *Wint.,* III. ii. 87: 'Which to deny concerns more than avails', and Schmidt adds *LLL.,* IV. ii. 145–7: 'deliver this paper into the royal hand of the king: it may concern much.' There is a further example in *Gent.,* I. ii. 77: 'Madam, it will not lie where it concerns.'

185–93.] In Boccaccio and *Frederyke of Jennen,* the villain bribes an old

(The best feather of our wing) have mingled sums
To buy a present for the emperor:
Which I (the factor for the rest) have done
In France: 'tis plate of rare device, and jewels
Of rich and exquisite form, their values great,   190
And I am something curious, being strange,
To have them in safe stowage: may it please you
To take them in protection?

Imo.   Willingly:
And pawn mine honour for their safety, since
My lord hath interest in them; I will keep them   195
In my bedchamber.

Iach.   They are in a trunk
Attended by my men: I will make bold
To send them to you, only for this night:
I must abroad to-morrow.

Imo.   O, no, no.

Iach. Yes, I beseech: or I shall short my word   200
By length'ning my return. From Gallia
I cross'd the seas on purpose and on promise
To see your grace.

Imo.   I thank you for your pains:
But not away to-morrow!

---

193. protection?] *Theobald;* protection. *F.*   204. to-morrow!] *Knight;* to
morrow. *F.*

woman to convey a chest, in which he
lies concealed, into the heroine's house.
The chest subterfuge arouses no suspicion because the characters in both
tales belong to the merchant class. But
Iachimo, who belongs to the nobility,
is forced to invent some excuse for
carrying a large chest about with him
—or rather, Shakespeare is forced to
invent something to smooth over an
awkward detail. Despite the change,
Shakespeare's dependence on *Frederyke
of Jennen* is apparent. The contents of
the chest are stated to be jewels and
plate in both versions. Boccaccio fur-
nishes no such details.

186. *The best . . . wing*] For the image,
cf. *Ant.,* III. xii. 2–4: 'Caesar, 'tis his

schoolmaster: / An argument that he
is pluck'd, when hither / He sends so
poor a pinion of his wing.'
191. *curious, being strange*] anxious,
since I am a stranger.
193–6.] Again *Frederyke of Jennen*
affords a parallel which is not in
Boccaccio: 'Than said Ambroses wife:
"That wyll I do with a good will. And
I shall set it sure inough; for I will set
it in my chamber, that it may be the
surer kept."'
200. *short my word*] fall short of my
promise. I take this as a nonce-usage
formed on the analogy of 'scant one's
duty' and the like, and employed here
for the sake of antithesis ('short my
word': 'length'ning my return').

Iach.   O, I must madam.
    Therefore I shall beseech you, if you please   205
    To greet your lord with writing, do't to-night:
    I have outstood my time, which is material
    To th' tender of our present.
Imo.   I will write.
    Send your trunk to me, it shall safe be kept,
    And truly yielded you: you're very welcome.   210
                                    [*Exeunt.*

209. safe be] *F;* be safe *F3.*

ACT II

SCENE I.—*Britain. Before Cymbeline's Palace.*

Enter CLOTEN *and two Lords.*

Clo. Was there ever man had such luck? When I kissed
the jack upon an upcast, to be hit away! I had a hundred pound on't: and then a whoreson jackanapes
must take me up for swearing, as if I borrowed mine
oaths of him, and might not spend them at my   5
pleasure.

First Lord. What got he by that? You have broke his pate
with your bowl.

Sec. Lord. [*Aside*] If his wit had been like him that broke
it, it would have run all out.   10

Clo. When a gentleman is dispos'd to swear, it is not for
any standers-by to curtail his oaths. Ha?

ACT II

Scene 1

9, 13, 15. *Aside*] *Theobald.*

Furness questions Shakespeare's
authorship of this scene, the sole purpose of which, he thinks, is to inform us
that Iachimo's presence is not unknown at Court. The dialogue is undeniably poor stuff and there is little
internal evidence one way or the other.
Two of the topics—swearing and gentility—link up with the dialogue between Autolycus and the Clown in
Wint., v. ii. 138 f. and argue common
authorship. Something has to separate
ii. ii from i. viii, and this scene is
adequate. I think that it serves to
reinforce the impression of Cloten
that Shakespeare wished to convey,
but many commentators would dis-
agree.

1–2. *kissed . . . away*] The 'jack' or
'mistress' is the small ball at which the
players aim in the game of bowls, and
to kiss the jack is to lay one's bowl
alongside it. Some commentators take
'upcast' to signify a throw, but *O.E.D.*
defines as 'chance', 'accident'. If we
accept this latter interpretation, the
comma must follow 'jack' instead of
'upcast', for Cloten is not the kind of
person to deprecate his own skill. But I
do not find *O.E.D.* wholly convincing
on the point.

4. *take me up*] rebuke, scold.

10. *run all out*] i.e. if his wits had been
as watery as Cloten's. Dowden suggests a pun on 'run out' in the sense
'exhaust'.

45

Sec. Lord. No, my lord; [*Aside*] nor crop the ears of them.

Clo. Whoreson dog! I gave him satisfaction! Would he
    had been one of my rank!   15

Sec. Lord. [*Aside*] To have smelt like a fool.

Clo. I am not vex'd more at any thing in th' earth: a pox
    on't! I had rather not be so noble as I am: they dare
    not fight with me, because of the queen my mother:
    every Jack-slave hath his bellyful of fighting, and I   20
    must go up and down like a cock, that nobody can
    match.

Sec. Lord. [*Aside*] You are cock and capon too, and you
    crow, cock, with your comb on.

Clo. Sayest thou?   25

Sec. Lord. It is not fit your lordship should undertake
    every companion that you give offence to.

Clo. No, I know that: but it is fit I should commit offence
    to my inferiors.

Sec. Lord. Ay, it is fit for your lordship only.   30

Clo. Why, so I say.

First Lord. Did you hear of a stranger that's come to court
    to-night?

---

14. satisfaction!] satisfaction? *F.*   16, 46. *Aside*] *Pope.*   20. bellyful] *Capell;*
belly full *F.*   23. *Aside*] *Rowe.*   24. crow,] *Theobald;* crow *F.*   26. your]
F3; you *F.*   33. to-night] *F2;* night *F.*

13. *crop the ears*] 'Curtail' means
'crop' and is not connected etymologically with 'tail' as is clear from the
present context. For the joke, such as
it is, Shakespeare may have been indebted to *Mucedorus*, III. v. 50–1:
'*Segasto.* Why, sir, I bid you giue eare
to my wordes. / *Clown.* I tell you I will
not be made a curtall for no mans
pleasure.' Doubtless the Second Lord
refers to asses' ears.

14. *gave*] The later Ff read 'give', but
the F interrogation-mark after 'satisfaction' can (as often) stand for an
exclamation. Taken thus it yields a
somewhat better sense.

16. *smelt*] a quibble on 'rank' meaning 'pungent'. The same pun occurs in
AYL., I. ii. 113–14.

23. *capon*] idiot. There is a play on

the 'fool's cap' or 'coxcomb', which
also meant 'simpleton'.

23–4. *and you crow, cock,*] I take 'and'
to signify 'if', as often in Shakespeare.
Perhaps, in modern English, the line
should read 'and you crow "Cock"
with your comb on'. It is usual, however, to regard 'cock' as a vocative.

27. *companion*] low fellow. Johnson
gives this speech to the First Lord, but
the sting in the tail, to which Johnson
apparently was as impervious as
Cloten, is far more characteristic of
the Second.

28. *commit offence*] Cloten means
'offer battle' but Furness notes that the
term also bears a coarse meaning, adding: 'It is in reference to this meaning
that the Second Lord levels his sar-
casm in the next line.'

Clo. A stranger, and I know not on't?

Sec. Lord. [*Aside*] He's a strange fellow himself, and 35
knows it not.

First Lord. There's an Italian come, and 'tis thought one
of Leonatus' friends.

Clo. Leonatus? A banished rascal; and he's another,
whatsoever he be. Who told you of this stranger? 40

First Lord. One of your lordship's pages.

Clo. Is it fit I went to look upon him? Is there no deroga-
tion in't?

Sec. Lord. You cannot derogate, my lord.

Clo. Not easily, I think. 45

Sec. Lord. [*Aside*] You are a fool granted, therefore your
issues being foolish do not derogate.

Clo. Come, I'll go see this Italian: what I have lost to-day
at bowls I'll win to-night of him. Come: go.

Sec. Lord. I'll attend your lordship. 50

[*Exeunt Cloten and First Lord.*

That such a crafty devil as is his mother
Should yield the world this ass! a woman that
Bears all down with her brain, and this her son
Cannot take two from twenty, for his heart,
And leave eighteen. Alas poor princess, 55
Thou divine Imogen, what thou endur'st,
Betwixt a father by thy step-dame govern'd,
A mother hourly coining plots, a wooer

---

50. *Exeunt . . . Lord*] *Capell; Exit F.*

44. *derogate*] do anything derogatory
to your rank.

47. *issues*] actions, with a possible
play on 'issues' meaning offspring.

55–64. *Alas . . . land!*] F obscures
this passage by printing full stops after
'husband' (63) and 'honour' (65).
Much of the apparent difficulty disappears if it is clearly recognized that
the Second Lord first apostrophizes
Imogen, commenting on the trials
which she has to endure, and then
appeals to the heavens to give her the
strength to overcome them. Hence, it
is desirable, with Theobald, to place

the stop after 'make' (64). Dr H. F.
Brooks's plausible suggestion is that in
copying, or setting up, 'make. The'
was wrongly converted to 'make the'
(momentarily understood as 'thee'),
that a marginal correction indicating
a stop and capital T was inserted, and
that this was subsequently taken as
referring to 'husband, than' in l. 63. As
Dr Brooks cogently argues, F prints a
period and capital T where they are
not wanted, and prints neither where
they are wanted. Hence, it seems
highly probable that a single process of
corruption is involved.

More hateful than the foul expulsion is
Of thy dear husband, than that horrid act   60
Of the divorce, he'ld make. The heavens hold firm
The walls of thy dear honour, keep unshak'd
That temple, thy fair mind, that thou mayst stand,
T' enjoy thy banish'd lord and this great land!   [*Exit.*

SCENE II.—*Imogen's Bedchamber: a Trunk in one
part of it.*

Enter IMOGEN *in her bed, and a Lady.*

Imo. Who's there? my woman Helen?
Lady.   Please you, madam.
Imo. What hour is it?
Lady.   Almost midnight, madam.
Imo. I have read three hours then: mine eyes are weak,
Fold down the leaf where I have left: to bed.
Take not away the taper, leave it burning: 5
And if thou canst awake by four o' th' clock,

60. husband, than] *F4;* husband. Then *F.*   61. divorce he'ld make. The]
Theobald; divorce, heel'd make the *F.*   62. honour,] Honour. *F.*   64. *Exit*]
Capell; Exeunt F.

Scene II

1. woman Helen?] *F3;* woman: Helene? *F.*

Scene II

S.D. Imogen's Bedchamber] Evidently the inner-stage represented the
bedchamber. Several properties—bed,
trunk, book, taper—are employed but
there is no reason to assume that a
painted backcloth was used. Granville-
Barker points out that scenic impres-
sions here are retrospective and arise
not from what we see but from what
we hear in Iachimo's speeches in II. iv.
F direction 'Enter Imogen in her bed'
is the normal one used also by Marlowe and Heywood. Ingleby notes
several *Mac.* parallels. Shakespeare's
mind would naturally tend to stray
back to the earlier play with its some-

what similar presentation of trespass
upon the royal person, assault upon
sleeping innocence, and resolution
daunted (but not quenched) by fear
and a troubled conscience. For general
parallels with *Lucr.* and *Ven.* see
Introduction, pp. lxvii–lxx.

1. *Who's there?*] There is a shade
of anxiety in the question. The scene
is one of nervous tension throughout.

6. *four o' th' clock*] Imogen is no lie-
abed. Her four hours were, perhaps, in
accordance with pastoral convention.
In *Mucedorus,* v. i. 150, the hero pro-
mises Amadine a shepherd's life: 'To
bed at midnight, vp at fowre'.

I prithee call me. Sleep hath seiz'd me wholly.

[Exit Lady.

To your protection I commend me, gods,
From fairies and the tempters of the night,
Guard me, beseech ye! [*Sleeps. Iachimo comes from the trunk.*
Iach. The crickets sing, and man's o'er-labour'd sense   11
Repairs itself by rest. Our Tarquin thus
Did softly press the rushes, ere he waken'd
The chastity he wounded. Cytherea,
How bravely thou becom'st thy bed! fresh lily!   15
And whiter than the sheets! That I might touch!
But kiss, one kiss! Rubies unparagon'd,
How dearly they do't: 'tis her breathing that
Perfumes the chamber thus: the flame o' th' taper

7. S.D.] *Rowe.*   10. *Iachimo . . . trunk*] *Collier; Iachimo from the Trunke F.*

7. S.D. Exit Lady] Rowe's direction seems eminently reasonable. In Boccaccio a little girl ('una piccola fanciulla') sleeps with the heroine, and she figures in the text and accompanying woodcut of both the High German and Low German versions of the tale. But in the Dutch version and in *Frederyke of Jennen*, which derives from it, text and woodcut represent the heroine as sleeping alone.

9. *fairies*] often used of malignant fairies. Both Holinshed and Forman refer to the *Mac.* Witches as fairies. Imogen's prayer echoes the Collect for Aid against all Perils in the Order for Evening Prayer.

10. S.D. Iachimo . . . trunk] It was, of course, a necessary convention that Imogen should sleep undisturbed through all that follows, but Iachimo, doubtless, went stealthily about his work. The translator of the 1620 edition of the *Decameron* adds to his original the detail that the villain steps out of the chest 'in sockes made of cloath'. Professor H. G. Wright, to whom I am indebted for this point, plausibly suggests that the translator may have recalled a performance of *Cym.* See his *First English Translation of the 'Decameron'*, p. 20. Murray Abend

(*Notes and Queries*, 197, 17, p. 363) notes that this ruse is borrowed by Beaumont and Fletcher in *The False One*, II. iii, where Cleopatra, concealed in a trunk, secures entry to Cæsar's tent.

12. *Our Tarquin*] i.e. our Italian (or Roman) Tarquin. The allusion emphasizes Imogen's isolation and defencelessness.

13. *rushes*] Here, as in *Lucr.*, Shakespeare attributes an Elizabethan practice to the Romans. The anachronism is not significant.

14. *Cytherea*] Venus. Some commentators take this as an exclamation addressed to the goddess, but if this were so it would be more natural for the following line to read: 'How bravely she becomes her bed.' It is far more likely that Iachimo identifies Imogen with the goddess of beauty.

15. *fresh lily*] The lily is an emblem of chastity.

18. *How dearly . . . do't*] Some critics interpret 'do't' as 'give or take kisses'; others: 'do her lips kiss each other'. Capell adds the direction 'Kissing her', much to the disgust of Victorian critics.

19. *Perfumes*] a fairly common Elizabethan fancy found in *Ven.*, Marlowe's

Bows toward her, and would under-peep her lids,   20
To see th' enclosed lights, now canopied
Under these windows, white and azure lac'd
With blue of heaven's own tinct. But my design.
To note the chamber: I will write all down:
Such, and such pictures: there the window, such   25
Th' adornment of her bed; the arras, figures,
Why, such, and such; and the contents o' th' story.
Ah, but some natural notes about her body
Above ten thousand meaner moveables
Would testify, t' enrich mine inventory.   30
O sleep, thou ape of death, lie dull upon her,

20. lids,] *Rowe;* lids. *F.*   22. these] *F;* the *F2.*

Hero and Leander, and Marston's *Pyg-malion's Image.*

20. *Bows toward her*] Dowden suggests that Shakespeare is 'varying the vulgar error, discussed by Sir Thomas Browne, "that smoke doth follow the fairest".' Furness thinks that Iachimo's movements may blow the flame towards the bed. But the pathetic fallacy scarcely needs such explanations.

lids,] No editor has accepted F 'lids.' but it may be correct. If it is, 'To see th' enclosed lights' means 'Oh, that I might see th' enclosed lights.' Cf. the construction in ll. 16–17.

21–3. *To see ... tinct*] The imagery is complex and ambiguous. Editors have variously altered the punctuation, and Rowe's comma after 'azure' is widely accepted. In the face of much uncertainty, I have retained F pointing. Kathleen Tillotson's note on 'Windows in Shakespeare' (in Geoffrey Tillotson, *Essays in Criticism and Research,* pp. 204–7) removes much of the difficulty. Mrs Tillotson shows that 'windows' here, as elsewhere in Shakespeare, means eyelids, and that the image derives not from glass windows but from 'wooden windows' or shutters. The complete image is, I think, of windows with shutters closed and curtains drawn ('canopied')—not a very exact analogy for eyelid and eye, but one which effectively conveys the

deepness of Imogen's sleep. 'White and azure lac'd' suggests that Shakespeare had latticed shutters in mind. 'Lights' canopied with heaven's blue suggests a secondary strand of cosmic imagery, the lights in Imogen's eyes, though now enclosed, yet resembling the sun in the firmament. John Daye, *The Parliament of Bees* (MS.), Character VI, has the image: 'A pair of suns move in his sphere-like eyes.' Shakespeare certainly envisages lights far more brilliant than that of the taper, and the contrast which he presents links with those of I. vii. 86–7 and 102–10. For 'canopy' meaning firmament, cf. *Ham.* II. ii. 311–12.

23. *design.*] Some copies of F read 'designe.'; others 'design?'. Most editors lighten the pointing, but wrongly. Iachimo leaves meditating and turns to business with brisk, staccato phrases, pausing after each one to jot the details down in his notebook.

26. *figures*] not, as Furness points out, the arras figures but those of the chimney-piece. See II. iv. 82.

27. *story*] usually taken to mean the story represented in the arras, but the word could also mean 'room'.

30. *testify*] The 'natural notes' would testify above ten thousand moveables (i.e. pieces of furniture).

31. *O sleep ... death*] a translation of "Somnus mortis imago', a saw which

And be her sense but as a monument,
Thus in a chapel lying. Come off, come off;
                    [*Taking off her bracelet.*
As slippery as the Gordian knot was hard.
'Tis mine, and this will witness outwardly,   35
As strongly as the conscience does within,
To th' madding of her lord. On her left breast
A mole cinque-spotted: like the crimson drops
I' th' bottom of a cowslip. Here's a voucher,
Stronger than ever law could make; this secret   40
Will force him think I have pick'd the lock, and ta'en
The treasure of her honour. No more: to what end?
Why should I write this down, that's riveted,
Screw'd to my memory? She hath been reading late,
The tale of Tereus, here the leaf's turn'd down   45
Where Philomel gave up. I have enough:
To th' trunk again, and shut the spring of it.
Swift, swift, you dragons of the night, that dawning

33. S.D.] *Rowe.*

Shakespeare remembered from the *Sententiae Pueriles*, the first Latin book in Elizabethan grammar-schools. 'Ape' means mimic. There is irony in the phrase. As a result of Iachimo's action, Imogen is soon to sleep the sleep that is more nearly the ape of death.

32. *monument*] As Malone notes, Shakespeare was thinking of the recumbent effigies placed on the tombs of distinguished persons.

36. *As strongly . . . within*] as strongly as does his inner consciousness.

38–9. *A mole . . . cowslip*] Boccaccio's Zinevra has a mole on her left breast. Shakespeare wisely preferred this to the birthmark in *Frederyke of Jennen*, a black wart on the heroine's left arm. In the French versions of the wager-story the mole is likened to a rose and to a violet, but Shakespeare's flower analogy is almost certainly coincidental.

39–42. *Here's a voucher . . . honour*] In *Frederyke of Jennen*, Johan recognizes that the wart is decisive evidence: 'O

good lorde! What great fortune haue I. For now haue I sene a pryuy token, whereby he shall byleue me that I haue had my pleasure of his wyfe.' Ambrogiuolo, in the *Decameron*, says nothing at this point. But there is no need to assume that Shakespeare was indebted to any source.

45. *Tereus*] 'This is the tragic tale of Philomel, / And treats of Tereus' treason and his rape.' Shakespeare doubtless knew the versions of the tale by Chaucer, Gower, and Painter, but we may reasonably suppose that Imogen's book was Ovid's *Metamorphoses*. In *Tit.*, IV. i. 41, Titus asks: 'Lucius, what book is that she tosseth so?' And Lucius answers: 'Grandsire, 'tis Ovid's Metamorphoses; / My mother gave it me.' Imogen's reading matter sorts with the sustained bird imagery of the play. Its ironic relevance to the immediate situation is too obvious to require further comment.

46. *gave up*] yielded, succumbed.

48. *dragons . . . night*] I am inclined to agree with Anders that Shakespeare

May bare the raven's eye! I lodge in fear;
Though this a heavenly angel, hell is here.   [*Clock strikes.*
One, two, three: time, time!   51
                    [*Goes into the trunk. The scene closes.*

SCENE III.—*The Palace.*

Enter CLOTEN *and Lords.*

First Lord. Your lordship is the most patient man in loss,
    the most coldest that ever turn'd up ace.

49. bare . . . eye] *Steevens (conj. Theobald);* beare the Ravens eye *F.*   51. *Goes
. . . closes*] *Rowe (subst.); Exit F.*

Scene III

2. ever] *F; not in F2.*

borrowed the image from Marlowe's
Hero and Leander, I. 107–8: 'Nor that
night-wandring pale and watrie starre/
When yawning dragons draw her
thirling carre, etc.' It occurs also in
MND., III. ii. 379. Dyer (*Folklore of
Shakespeare,* p. 174) comments that
dragons are a mythological attribute
of night.

49. *bare . . . eye*] All the Folios read
'bear(e)', which Warburton defends,
but most editors accept 'bare'. Other
proposed emendations: 'dare' (Collier
MS.), 'clear' (Vaughan), 'bar' or
'bier' (Thiselton) scarcely merit consideration. Of the various appeals to
ornithology which this passage has
provoked, Dowden's is, perhaps, the
most useful: 'In Willoughby's *Ornithology,* 1678, p. 123, I find "Ravens . . .
roost (as they say) upon trees, with
their bills directed towards the Sun-
rising".' This vindicates 'bare' and
justifies Steevens's terse but admirable
paraphrase: 'that the light might wake
the raven'. The 'raven' has been variously identified with the night, the
trunk, and Pisanio, but these are irrelevant. On the other hand, Furness's
suggestion that Iachimo refers to himself as a raven is plausible: 'Verily, a

whole flock of ravens could not yearn
for dawning to bare their eyes more
bitterly than the stifled prisoner.' It
may be added that the raven, like
Iachimo, is a bird of prey and that
Furness's parallel falls into one of the
play's vital image groups. For the
human raven see Corbaccio in Jonson's *Volpone.* 'To pick out the Raven's
eyes' is noted as proverbial in Bacon's
Promus.

50. *Though . . . here*] Though this
Imogen is a heavenly angel, it is Hell
that surrounds me. An echo of *Mac.*
and, perhaps, *Doctor Faustus.*

51. *time, time!*] Ingleby supposes
that the clock strikes four, but Furness
argues for three. Argument can, however, have little force in a scene whose
fifty lines extend over more than three
(or is it four?) hours! One wonders
whether, in actual performance, the
clock was sounded at regular intervals
throughout the scene, as it apparently
was at the end of *Doctor Faustus.*

Scene III

S.D. The Palace] The action now
returns to the main-stage. Granville-
Barker suggests that, in the meantime,
the inner-stage is being converted

Clo. It would make any man cold to lose.

First Lord. But not every man patient after the noble tem-
    per of your lordship. You are most hot and furious   5
    when you win.

Clo. Winning will put any man into courage. If I could
    get this foolish Imogen, I should have gold enough.
    It's almost morning, is't not?

First Lord. Day, my lord.   10

Clo. I would this music would come: I am advised to give
    her music a mornings, they say it will penetrate.

Enter musicians.

Come on, tune: if you can penetrate her with your
fingering, so: we'll try with tongue too: if none will
do, let her remain: but I'll never give o'er. First, a   15
very excellent good-conceited thing; after, a wonderful sweet air, with admirable rich words to it, and
then let her consider.

SONG

Hark, hark, the lark at heaven's gate sings,
    And Phœbus gins arise,   20
His steeds to water at those springs
    On chalic'd flowers that lies;

7. *Clo.*] *F4; not in F.*   13. her] *F; here F2.*   16. good-conceited] *hyphened
Capell.*   after,] *Pope; after F.*

from Imogen's bedchamber to Philario's house.

    2. *ace*] Alas for Cloten's intentions at
II. i. 50–1, for he has been as unlucky
with the dice as he was at bowling.
The 'ace' is the one pip, the lowest
number on the dice. It is likely that a
pun is intended, since 'ace' and 'ass'
were alike in sound, as the Elizabethan
jingle (reprinted in Arber's *English
Garner*) shows: 'The Sound's as near in
Brace and Brass, / In Hose and Horse,
in Ace and Ass.' Shakespeare uses the
quibble in *MND.*, v. i. 312–17. Cloten
has doubtless been playing the popular
Elizabethan game of backgammon or
'tables'.

    12. *a mornings*] Theobald changes to

'o' mornings', but, as Furness notes,
the speaker's illiteracy vindicates F.

    14. *fingering*] There is a coarse pun.
Dowden supposes that the word may
imply that a harp was used, but it
could apply equally well to the lute or
the recorder, either of which is a far
more likely instrument in this context.

    16. *good-conceited*] full of pleasant
conceit or fancy. This would be a fan-
tasia for several instruments, probably
the customary consort of viols and
recorders.

    18. S.D. SONG] For a discussion of
the song see Appendix C.

    20. *gins*] an aphetic form of
'begins' (*O.E.D.*).

And winking Mary-buds begin to ope their golden
    eyes;
With every thing that pretty is, my lady sweet arise:
    Arise, arise!   25

Clo. So get you gone: if this penetrate, I will consider
    your music the better: if it do not, it is a vice in her
    ears, which horse-hairs, and calves'-guts, nor the
    voice of unpaved eunuch to boot, can never amend.
                                  [*Exeunt Musicians.*

Sec. Lord. Here comes the king.   30
Clo. I am glad I was up so late, for that's the reason I was
    up so early: he cannot choose but take this service I
    have done fatherly.

             Enter CYMBELINE *and* QUEEN.

Good morrow to your majesty, and to my gracious
    mother.   35
Cym. Attend you here the door of our stern daughter?
    Will she not forth?
Clo. I have assail'd her with musics, but she vouchsafes
    no notice.
Cym. The exile of her minion is too new,   40
    She hath not yet forgot him, some more time

23. eyes;] *Theobald;* eyes *F.*   26. *Clo.*] *Dyce; not in F.*   27. vice] *Rowe;* voyce *F.*
29. S.D.] *Theobald; not in F.*   33. S.D.] *Dyce, after l. 29 F.*   36. daughter?]
Rowe; daughter *F.*

23. *winking*] with closed eyes.

Mary-buds] marigolds. The botanical discussions to which the word has
given rise need not concern us. As
Furness remarks: 'I think the betossed
soul may find peace in *Calendula
officinalis.*'

24. *is*] Hanmer needlessly alters to
'bin', to rhyme with 'begin'. This
would certainly have fallen into the
oblivion which it merits had not
the various editions of Schubert's
famous setting perpetuated it. Schubert, of course, used a German
translation.

26 ff.] The F compositor seems to

have been nodding, with the result
that twenty or thirty lines were rather
carelessly set up. There are several evident misprints and the punctuation is
occasionally suspect.

26. *consider*] usually explained as
'requite', though Furness suggests
'appreciate'.

27. *vice*] I accept Rowe's emendation, not without misgiving. It is possible that a pun on 'voice' and 'vice' is
intended.

28. *horse-hairs, and calves'-guts*] bow-
strings and fiddle-strings.

31–2. *late . . . early*] so in *Tw.N.*, II.
iii. 8.

Must wear the print of his remembrance on't,
And then she's yours.
Queen.   You are most bound to th' king,
Who lets go by no vantages that may
Prefer you to his daughter: frame yourself   45
To orderly solicits, and be friended
With aptness of the season: make denials
Increase your services: so seem, as if
You were inspir'd to do those duties which
You tender to her: that you in all obey her,   50
Save when command to your dismission tends,
And therein you are senseless.
Clo.   Senseless? not so.

Enter a Messenger.

Mess. So like you, sir, ambassadors from Rome;
The one is Caius Lucius.
Cym.   A worthy fellow,
Albeit he comes on angry purpose now;   55
But that's no fault of his: we must receive him
According to the honour of his sender,
And towards himself, his goodness forespent on us,
We must extend our notice. Our dear son,
When you have given good morning to your mistress, 60
Attend the queen and us; we will have need
T' employ you towards this Roman. Come, our queen.
                    [*Exeunt all but Cloten.*
Clo. If she be up, I'll speak with her: if not,

42. on't] *F;* ou't *F2;* out *Rowe.*   46. solicits] *F2;* solicity *F.*   52. S.D.]
Rowe; not in F.

42. *on't*] Rowe's 'out', which many
editors follow, arises from the misprint
'ou't' in Ff 2 and 3.
   44–5. *vantages . . . Prefer*] opportunities that may recommend.
   46. *solicits*] F 'solicity' is a not impossible coinage, but the F2 variant
suggests that it is, in fact, a printer's
error. Noun substantives verbal in
form are quite common in Elizabethan
English.
   46–7. *be friended . . . season*] Rowe

(ed. 3) reads 'befriended', which
several editors follow, thus making the
phrase parenthetical. This, if F punctuation has any authority, it can
scarcely be, and the simple imperative
of the original is doubtless correct.
   51. *dismission*] rejection.
   52. *senseless*] unconscious, insensible.
Cloten takes the word in the wrong
(and right) sense.
   58. *his goodness . . . us*] in view of his
past goodness towards us.

Let her lie still, and dream. By your leave, ho!   [*Knocks.*
I know her women are about her: what   65
If I do line one of their hands? 'Tis gold
Which buys admittance (oft it doth) yea, and makes
Diana's rangers false themselves, yield up
Their deer to th' stand o' th' stealer: and 'tis gold
Which makes the true-man kill'd, and saves the thief: 70
Nay, sometime hangs both thief, and true-man: what
Can it not do, and undo? I will make
One of her women lawyer to me, for
I yet not understand the case myself.
By your leave.   [*Knocks.*   75

Enter a Lady.

Lady. Who's there that knocks?
Clo.   A gentleman.
Lady.   No more?
Clo. Yes, and a gentlewoman's son.

---

64. S.D.] *Theobald; not in F.*   66. hands?] *Pope;* hands, *F.*   68. rangers] *F;* rangers, *Collier (MS.).*   76. more?] *Rowe;* more. *F.*

67–74. *yea . . . myself*] Furness rejects these lines on the ground that they are out of character. But so are several of Cloten's other speeches. Against Furness's view it may be urged that Cloten's plan to bribe Imogen's women is the kind of detail that Shakespeare would naturally develop, at his own convenience, from the bribing of the old woman in *Frederyke of Jennen* and the *Decameron*. The authenticity of the present lines is fully vindicated by *Tim.*, IV. iii. 30 ff., where Timon speaks of gold: 'Why this / Will lug your priests and servants from your sides, . . . / This yellow slave / Will knit and break religions, bless the accursed, / Make the hoar leprosy adored, place thieves / And give them title, knee and approbation / With senators on the bench.' We may concede that sentiments which suit the disillusioned Timon accord less well with the half-witted Cloten.

68. *Diana's . . . themselves*] 'Diana's rangers' are her gamekeepers—hence, in this context, Imogen's women, who are chaste like their mistress. Some commentators take 'false' as an adjective, but this yields a poor sense, and it is altogether more likely that it is a verb. *O.E.D.* records no other example of its use reflexively, but such usage, doubtless by analogy with reflexive forms of 'betray', 'forswear', 'perjure', etc., is not remarkable.

69. *stand*] a standing-place, or hiding-place, from which huntsmen shot their prey. Helge Kökeritz ('Thief and Stealer' in *English and Germanic Studies*, III, p. 59) detects a pun on 'stealer–staler' (to stale: to urinate).

70. *true-man*] I have retained F hyphen here and in l. 71. Simpson (p. 86) notes that the hyphen is metrical in function and indicates the accentuation of compound words.

Lady. 　　　　　　　　　　　That's more
　　Than some whose tailors are as dear as yours
　　Can justly boast of. What's your lordship's pleasure?
Clo. Your lady's person, is she ready?
Lady. 　　　　　　　　Ay, 　　　　　　　80
　　To keep her chamber.
Clo. 　　　　　　　There is gold for you,
　　Sell me your good report.
Lady. How, my good name? or to report of you
　　What I shall think is good? The princess! 　　[*Exit Lady*.

Enter IMOGEN.

Clo. Good morrow, fairest: sister, your sweet hand. 　　85
Imo. Good morrow, sir. You lay out too much pains
　　For purchasing but trouble: the thanks I give
　　Is telling you that I am poor of thanks,
　　And scarce can spare them.
Clo. 　　　　　　　　Still I swear I love you.
Imo. If you but said so, 'twere as deep with me: 　　90
　　If you swear still, your recompense is still
　　That I regard it not.
Clo. 　　　　　　This is no answer.
Imo. But that you shall not say I yield being silent,
　　I would not speak. I pray you spare me: 'faith
　　I shall unfold equal discourtesy 　　　　　95
　　To your best kindness: one of your great knowing
　　Should learn (being taught) forbearance.

84. *Exit Lady*] *Capell; not in* F.　　　85. fairest:] *Theobald;* fairest, F.

77–9. *That's more . . . boast of.*] Delius
plausibly conjectures that these lines
are spoken aside: likewise ll. 80–1: 'Ay
. . . chamber'.

80. *ready*] dressed and ready to leave
her chamber. Imogen's lady takes the
word in another sense.

85. *fairest : sister*] Some editors follow
Capell in reading 'fairest sister,' but
the comma in F marks a break which
is, perhaps, best indicated nowadays
by Theobald's colon.

90. *deep*] Furness observes that
'deep' is one of Shakespeare's favourite

adjectives, and it is one which, as
Rolfe notes, he often associates with
the swearing of oaths.

91. *still*] constantly, eternally.

95. *equal discourtesy*] discourtesy
equal to your best kindness. Wyatt
claims that 'as much discourtesy as I
have shewn' is the more obvious meaning—but how more obvious?

96–7. *one of . . . forbearance*] 'Knowing' means 'knowledge', and is used
ironically, for Imogen is scornful.
Warburton's conjecture, ('being
tort') for 'being taught' is prepos-

Clo. To leave you in your madness, 'twere my sin,
    I will not.
Imo. Fools are not mad folks.
Clo.   Do you call me fool?   100
Imo. As I am mad I do:
    If you'll be patient, I'll no more be mad,
    That cures us both. I am much sorry, sir,
    You put me to forget a lady's manners,
    By being so verbal: and learn now, for all,   105
    That I, which know my heart, do here pronounce,
    By th' very truth of it, I care not for you,
    And am so near the lack of charity
    (To accuse myself) I hate you: which I had rather
    You felt than make't my boast.
Clo.   You sin against   110
    Obedience, which you owe your father; for
    The contract you pretend with that base wretch,
    One bred of alms, and foster'd with cold dishes,

108–9. charity / (To . . . myself) I] *Capell;* Charitie / To . . . my selfe, I *F.*   111.
father; for] *Rowe;* father, for *F.*

terous. Cloten takes 'forbearance' to mean 'withdrawal', but Imogen means 'abstinence'.

    100. *Fools . . . folks.*] Dowden explains, 'I am not mad, I am only a fool, and so you may safely leave me to my folly.' This is less abstruse than Steevens's paraphrase ('If I am mad, as you tell me, I am what you can never be'), but neither interpretation is wholly convincing. Theobald, following Warburton, reads 'cure' for 'are', and this reading, which receives strong but not compelling support from l. 103, is followed by many editors. Becket conjectures 'care', which is pointless; Daniel 'are not for', which is feeble and unmetrical, and Dowden 'spare'. If we are to assume a literal error, I would suggest 'awe' for 'are', but faulty punctuation in F seems to me an altogether more probable assumption. It is evident from Cloten's retort that he interrupts Imogen, and the present half-line,

therefore, may very well be unfinished. If Imogen had intended to observe that fools are not mad folks' fittest counsellors or something of the kind, all that Cloten allowed her to say would be: 'Fools are not mad folks'—'. F would normally print 'folks'' as 'folks', so that the only error would be substitution of the stop for a dash. Feste's distinction between 'a fool and a madman' (*Tw.N.*, i. v. 140 ff.) may, however, have some relevance to the present line.

    105. *verbal*] Johnson glosses as 'verbose', 'full of talk', which *O.E.D.* accepts. If this is so, the phrase in which it occurs must refer to Cloten. Knight, however, takes it as referring to Imogen, who 'now resolves to speak plainly,—to be *verbal*'.

    108–9.] F has no point after 'charity' and has a comma after 'myself'. Capell's emended punctuation, which I follow, makes 'To accuse myself' a parenthesis.

With scraps o' th' court, it is no contract, none;
And though it be allow'd in meaner parties   115
(Yet who than he more mean?) to knit their souls
(On whom there is no more dependency
But brats and beggary) in self-figur'd knot,
Yet you are curb'd from that enlargement, by
The consequence o' th' crown, and must not foil   120
The precious note of it; with a base slave,
A hilding for a livery, a squire's cloth,
A pantler; not so eminent.

Imo.   Profane fellow,
Wert thou the son of Jupiter, and no more
But what thou art besides, thou wert too base   125
To be his groom: thou wert dignified enough,
Even to the point of envy, if 'twere made
Comparative for your virtues to be styled
The under-hangman of his kingdom; and hated
For being preferr'd so well.

Clo.   The south-fog rot him!   130

116. mean?] *Pope;* meane *F.*   120. foil] foyle *F.*   127. envy, if] *F2;*
Envie. If *F.*

117–18. *On whom . . . beggary*] O.E.D.
defines 'dependency' as 'a body of
dependants; a household establish-
ment', while Deighton takes it to
signify the results of marriage in
'meaner parties'. The phrase is usually
taken to refer to 'meaner parties'
rather than to 'souls', but may, I think,
simply take up the thread of Cloten's
previous parenthesis ('Yet who than
he more mean?'), thus referring
directly to Posthumus.

119. *enlargement*] freedom of choice
or action.

120. *The consequence . . . foil*] Dowden
defines 'consequence' as 'all that follows from the fact that you are heir to
the crown'. Hanmer unnecessarily
emends 'foil' to 'soil', and Ingleby conjectures ''file'. O.E.D. defines 'foil' as
'To foul, defile, pollute', Porter (*Two
Angry Women of Abingdon*) has the substantive 'foyle' in the sense of defile-
ment. Vaughan takes 'foil' in the pre-

sent context as the foil or backing of a
jewel, and this, in view of 'the precious
note' in l. 121, seems possible, at least
as a secondary sense. The pun occurs
in Porter's play, *loc. cit.*: 'And it hath
set a foyle vpon thy fame, / Not as the
foile dooth grace the Diamond' (524–
5).

122. *A hilding . . . livery*] a worthless
fellow fit only to wear livery.

123. *pantler*] the menial who supplied bread and had charge of the
pantry.

128. *Comparative . . . virtues*] Many
commentators have missed the point
through failing to recognize that 'your'
is plural. If your respective virtues, or
qualities, were made the basis of comparison, Posthumus would be a king
and you, at best, his under-hangman.

130. *south-fog*] Elizabethan literature has many allusions to the con-
tagion brought by the south wind,
many of them derived, seemingly,

Imo. He never can meet more mischance than come
      To be but nam'd of thee. His mean'st garment,
      That ever hath but clipp'd his body, is dearer
      In my respect, than all the hairs above thee,
      Were they all made such men. How now, Pisanio!   135

Enter PISANIO.

Clo. 'His garment!' Now, the devil—
Imo. To Dorothy my woman hie thee presently.
Clo. 'His garment!'
Imo.   I am sprited with a fool,
      Frighted, and anger'd worse. Go bid my woman
      Search for a jewel, that too casually   140
      Hath left mine arm: it was thy master's. 'Shrew me,
      If I would lose it for a revenue
      Of any king's in Europe! I do think
      I saw't this morning: confident I am.
      Last night 'twas on mine arm; I kiss'd it: 145

135. Pisanio!] *Collier;* Pisanio? *F.*   136. garment!] Garments? *F;* Garment?
F2.   devil—] *Theobald;* divell. *F.*   143. king's] *Rowe;* Kings *F.*

from Virgil and Ovid. Cf. IV. ii. 349, 'the spongy south'.

133. *clipp'd*] embraced.

134. *In my respect*] in my regard.

135. *How now*] Hanmer gives these words to Cloten and is followed by Walker who emends, however, to 'How! How!' This change would be more acceptable if it were possible to ascertain the precise implication of what is, at best, a rather vague exclamation. It may, as Hanmer assumes, voice Cloten's indignation, but could as easily be prompted by Imogen's sudden realization that the bracelet is no longer on her arm.

137. *To Dorothy . . . presently*] There may be a minor inconsistency here. In II. ii the name of Imogen's attendant is Helen, but there would obviously be a company of waiting-women. 'Presently' has its usual Elizabethan meaning of 'instantly'.

138. *sprited*] Steevens's paraphrase:

'I am haunted by a fool, as by a *spright*', seems adequate though Furness finds it tame and suggests: 'I am tormented by a legion of sprights with this fool here', an alternative which I find quite unconvincing. His suggestion that Imogen is 'frighted' at the thought of the loss of her bracelet and 'anger'd' by both that and Cloten's behaviour is more plausible.

144. *confident I am.*] I have retained the punctuation of F which is perfectly satisfactory. Imogen is *confident* that she saw the bracelet that morning, but *certain* that it was on her arm the night before—a subtle distinction which is lost by those editors who omit the stop after 'am'.

145. *kiss'd*] Pope, against all authority, reads 'kissed' (a dissyllable) on metrical grounds. Other attempts to supplement the line may be ignored. The semi-colon after 'arm' indicates, as Furness wisely implies, a *mora vacua*

I hope it be not gone to tell my lord
That I kiss aught but he.
Pis.   'Twill not be lost.
Imo. I hope so: go and search.   [*Exit Pisanio.*
Clo.   You have abus'd me:
'His meanest garment!'
Imo.   Ay, I said so, sir:
If you will make't an action, call witness to't.   150
Clo. I will inform your father.
Imo.   Your mother too:
She's my good lady; and will conceive, I hope,
But the worst of me. So I leave you, sir,
To th' worst of discontent.   [*Exit.*
Clo.   I'll be reveng'd:
'His mean'st garment!' Well.   [*Exit.*   155

SCENE IV.—*Rome. Philario's House.*

Enter POSTHUMUS *and* PHILARIO.

Post. Fear it not, sir: I would I were so sure

147. he] *F;* him *F2.*   148. S.D.] *Capell; not in F.*   153. you, sir] *F3;* your
Sir *F.*

Scene IV

S.D. *Rome*] *Rowe.*   *Philario's House*] *Capell (subst.).*

or rhetorical pause: 'Last night 'twas
on mine arm; (I think it was. Yes, I'm
sure it was.) I kiss'd it.'

146–7. *I hope . . . but he*] The irony is
superb. The word 'hope' is used freely
to the end of the scene and throughout
the following one, but not always in
the same sense. The repetition of a
significant word is a favourite device of
Shakespeare's: cf. 'nothing' in *Lr.*,
'honest' in *Oth.*, 'boy' in *Cor.*, etc.

152. *my good lady*] my good friend.
Imogen uses the term ironically.

Scene IV

S.D. Philario's House] Granville-
Barker locates the action of this scene
on the inner-stage.

Enter Posthumus and Philario] The
Frenchman, Dutchman, and Spaniard
have disappeared, possibly because
Shakespeare had forgotten them. In
Frederyke of Jennen, however, Johan
takes Ambrose aside, saying, 'Bycause
that ye be a good frende of myne and
we haue kepte company togyder, and
that ye sholde not be a shamed, I call
you a syde for to shewe vnto you that I
haue wonne the money,' and this may
explain why Shakespeare dispenses
with the other characters, though he is
compelled, of course, to retain Philario
whom he has made the holder of the
stakes. Shakespeare is not following
the *Decameron* at this point, for Boccaccio specifically states that Ambro-

To win the king as I am bold her honour
Will remain hers.
Phi.   What means do you make to him?
Post. Not any: but abide the change of time,
    Quake in the present winter's state, and wish   5
    That warmer days would come: in these fear'd hopes,
    I barely gratify your love; they failing,
    I must die much your debtor.
Phi. Your very goodness, and your company,
    O'erpays all I can do. By this, your king   10
    Hath heard of great Augustus: Caius Lucius
    Will do's commission throughly. And I think
    He'll grant the tribute: send th' arrearages,
    Or look upon our Romans, whose remembrance
    Is yet fresh in their grief.
Post.   I do believe   15
    (Statist though I am none, nor like to be)
    That this will prove a war; and you shall hear
    The legion now in Gallia sooner landed
    In our not-fearing Britain than have tidings
    Of any penny tribute paid. Our countrymen   20
    Are men more order'd than when Julius Cæsar
    Smil'd at their lack of skill, but found their courage

---

i. fear'd hopes] *F2;* fear'd hope *F.*

guolo summoned together all the
merchants who were present when the
wager was laid.

    2. *bold*] confident.

    3. *means*] mediation, intercession.

    6. *fear'd hopes*] Ingleby: 'hopes
dashed with fear'; Furness: 'hopes so
encompassed with fears that the hopes
are almost lost'. The distinction which
Furness draws between the participial
and the substantival adjective is, perhaps, over-subtle. Tyrwhitt conjectures 'sear'd', which is considerably
more reasonable than Vaughan's 'fair'
though neither is necessary.

    7. *gratify*] requite. Cf. i. v. 35–7.

    14. *Or*] The word may carry its pre-
sent meaning or may be an obsolete
form of 'ere'. Theobald, who takes it in
the latter sense, emends unnecessarily

to 'E'er'. I take Philario to mean that
Cymbeline will either send the arrears
or find himself at war with Rome. 'And
I think / He'll grant the tribute:' is
a separate phrase, as F colon indicates.

    15. *their grief*] 'Perhaps this means
not the grief of the Britons, but the
grief or suffering caused by "our
Romans"' (Dowden).

    16. *Statist*] statesman, politician.

    18. *legion*] Theobald emends to
'legions' which is the form found elsewhere: cf. iii. viii. 4 and 12; iv. ii. 333;
iv. iii. 24.

    20. *any penny*] Dowden notes that the
phrase is found in North's *Plutarch*
(Life of Coriolanus) which Shakespeare had recently used.

    22. *lack of skill*] The phrase is from

Worthy his frowning at. Their discipline,
(Now wing-led with their courages) will make known
To their approvers they are people such   25
That mend upon the world.

Enter IACHIMO.

Phi.   See! Iachimo!
Post. The swiftest harts have posted you by land;
And winds of all the corners kiss'd your sails,
To make your vessel nimble.
Phi.   Welcome, sir.
Post. I hope the briefness of your answer made   30
The speediness of your return.
Iach.   Your lady,
Is one the fairest that I have look'd upon—
Post. And therewithal the best, or let her beauty

26. See! Iachimo!] *Capell;* See Iachimo. *F.*   32. one the] *Steevens;* one of the *F.*
upon—] *Ingleby;* upon *F.*

Holinshed: see Boswell-Stone, p. 8,
note 2.

23. *frowning*] Vaughan observes that
the frown is 'the proper condition of
brow and face with which to meet a
dangerous enemy', and compares *H5*,
III. i. 11–12. Cf. also v. iii. 28, 'But to
look back in frown'.

24. *wing-led*] This is the F reading.
F2 reads 'mingled' which many editors accept as a certain correction, but
which Furness, rightly I think, condemns as 'inert, dead, and un-
Shakespearian'. As Knight and others
have pointed out, a printer does not
normally substitute an uncommon
word for a common one. Even so,
'wing-led' is followed by a somewhat
dubious preposition. I suspect that
Shakespeare wrote 'winged', that the
printer set up 'wingled' and that, mis-
interpreting his own error, he subsequently added the hyphen. There is
precedent for this view in *R3*, II. i. 88,
'a winged Mercury', which appears in
Q1 of the play as 'a wingled Mercury'.

25. *approvers*] those who put them to
the proof.

26. *mend . . . world*] Furness asks: 'in
mending is there not implied a *steady
progress or improvement*, upon what the
world had hitherto found them?' But
Posthumus' meaning may be that the
Britons improve upon Nature, that
they now surpass all other peoples.

28. *corners*] quarters.

30. *hope*] probably used in the sense
'believe'.

32. *one the fairest*] The line as it stands
in F is metrically irregular. I have
accepted Steevens's emendation which
receives powerful support from I. vii.
165–6. Pope reads: 'Is of the fairest'.

upon—] The absence of a period
after this word in Ff 1–3 may or may
not indicate that Posthumus interrupts
Iachimo, but the dash introduced by
Ingleby is surely justified on purely
dramatic grounds. Iachimo begins one
of his leisurely and tortuous exposi-
tions: Posthumus eagerly breaks in.

33–5. *or let . . . with them*] Malone
compares *Tim.*, IV. iii. 115–16: 'those
milk-paps / That through the window-
bars bore at men's eyes'. There is
every reason for believing that *Timon*

Look through a casement to allure false hearts,
And be false with them.
Iach.   Here are letters for you.   35
Post. Their tenour good, I trust.
Iach.   'Tis very like.
Post. Was Caius Lucius in the Britain court
When you were there?
Iach.   He was expected then,
But not approach'd.
Post.   All is well yet.
Sparkles this stone as it was wont, or is't not   40
Too dull for your good wearing?
Iach.   If I have lost it,
I should have lost the worth of it in gold—
I'll make a journey twice as far, t' enjoy
A second night of such sweet shortness which
Was mine in Britain; for the ring is won.   45
Post. The stone's too hard to come by.
Iach.   Not a whit,
Your lady being so easy.
Post.   Make not, sir,

---

34. through] *Rowe;* thorough *F.*   36. tenour] *Theobald;* tenure *F.*   42.
gold—] Gold *F.*   46. stone's] *Rowe;* stones *F*   47. not] *F2;* note *F.*

or at least this particular scene, was
fresh in Shakespeare's mind when he
wrote *Cym.*

37. Post.] All editors follow Capell
in giving this speech to Philario, for the
very excellent reason that Posthumus'
attention is fully engaged. The reason
is, perhaps, too good. The question
could result from something which he
has read in one of his letters. And, in
any case, no man is likely to read
through one or more letters while a
mere twenty words are being spoken.

39. *approach'd*] Hanmer reads 'But
was not then approach'd' in order to
regularize the line, but a *mora vacua* is
more probable. There is a brief silence
while Posthumus takes a last look at
his letters.

41-2. *If I have . . . gold*—] Singer
emends 'have' in l. 41 to 'had' and has

been followed by most subsequent
editors, though Dowden concedes that
F may be right, explaining, 'if I have
now lost it, this means that I should
have lost, etc.' This interpretation I
find wholly adequate. It is significant
that Shakespeare's early editors accepted the line without question,
though Pope regularizes 'I have' to
'I've'. The objection to 'had' is that it
is altogether too definite for Iachimo,
who, at this point, is playing a cat-and-
mouse game. The abrupt change of
tense in l. 43 leads me to substitute
'gold—' for F 'gold,'. Most editors
alter the comma to a semi-colon or a
stop. No one seems to have thought of
altering 'I'll' (F Ile) in l. 43 to 'I'ld', a
reading which, though not really
necessary, is rather more justifiable
than the emendation of 'have'.

Your loss your sport: I hope you know that we
Must not continue friends.
Iach.   Good sir, we must
If you keep covenant. Had I not brought   50
The knowledge of your mistress home, I grant
We were to question farther; but I now
Profess myself the winner of her honour,
Together with your ring; and not the wronger
Of her or you, having proceeded but   55
By both your wills.
Post.   If you can make't apparent
That you have tasted her in bed, my hand
And ring is yours. If not, the foul opinion
You had of her pure honour gains, or loses,
Your sword, or mine, or masterless leave both   60
To who shall find them.
Iach.   Sir, my circumstances,
Being so near the truth, as I will make them,
Must first induce you to believe; whose strength
I will confirm with oath, which I doubt not
You'll give me leave to spare, when you shall find 65
You need it not.
Post.   Proceed.
Iach.   First, her bedchamber,
(Where I confess I slept not, but profess
Had that was well worth watching) it was hang'd
With tapestry of silk and silver, the story
Proud Cleopatra, when she met her Roman,   70

---

51. *knowledge*] carnal knowledge.

60. *leave*] Rowe reads 'leaves' which has been generally accepted. Furness accepts F 'leave' as a plural by proximity, but it is surely simpler to regard it as an optative: the foul opinion gains your sword or mine or else let it leave both masterless, etc.

61. *circumstances*] evidence, particulars.

68. *well worth watching*] well worth lying awake for. The more normal construction would be 'well worth the watching' and Furness suggests that

the *th* of 'worth' absorbs *the*. It seems clear, however, that Shakespeare intended the simple participle.

68–9. *it was hang'd . . . silver*] Professor H. G. Wright informs me that these 'beautifull hangings', which are not mentioned by Boccaccio, are nevertheless introduced into the English *Decameron* of 1620. It seems clear that the translator, whom Wright believes to have been Florio, added a detail derived from *Cym.*, cf. note to II. ii. 10.

70–2. *Proud . . . pride*] Iachimo's brief

And Cydnus swell'd above the banks, or for
The press of boats, or pride. A piece of work
So bravely done, so rich, that it did strive
In workmanship and value; which I wonder'd
Could be so rarely and exactly wrought,   75
Since the true life on't was—
Post.   This is true:
And this you might have heard of here, by me,
Or by some other.
Iach.   More particulars
Must justify my knowledge.
Post.   So they must,
Or do your honour injury.
Iach.   The chimney   80
Is south the chamber, and the chimney-piece,
Chaste Dian, bathing: never saw I figures
So likely to report themselves; the cutter
Was as another Nature, dumb; outwent her,
Motion and breath left out.

84. Nature, dumb; outwent] *Warburton;* Nature dumbe, out-went *F*.

description glances at Enobarbus'
account of the scene in *Ant.*, II. ii. 195–
223, and makes similar use of the
pathetic fallacy.

70. *her Roman*] In delivery a slight
emphasis on 'her' is required. Just as
Antony was Cleopatra's Roman, so
Iachimo hints that he was Imogen's.

73–4. *strive . . . value*] 'it was doubtful
which of the two, workmanship or
value, was greater' (Schmidt).

76. *was—*] Since F, for once, takes
the trouble to print an interruption as
an interruption, the proposed emendations seem more than usually gratu-
itous. Hanmer's 'was.' is the only one
that need be recorded here.

77. *might have heard*] could easily have
heard. See l. 87.

81. *chimney-piece*] here a carving or
piece of sculpture placed as an orna-
ment over the fireplace or 'chimney'.

82. *Chaste Dian*] again words to
which the actor can add a touch of
irony. Iachimo's implied contrast is

between the chaste Diana and the
adulterous Imogen.

83. *So likely . . . themselves*] They were
speaking likenesses. Hanmer's 'So
lively' is wholly unwarranted.

cutter] carver, sculptor.

84. *Nature, dumb*] Editors have ad-
justed the punctuation in various
ways. I have followed Warburton
whose reading represents the sense of
F and eliminates ambiguity. The idea
is a common Elizabethan one and is
found, for instance, in Ben Jonson's
lines on Shakespeare's portrait in F
itself. For an illuminating discussion of
the topic see Hardin Craig, *The Enchanted Glass*, pp. 216 ff. Shakespeare's
own preoccupation with art is most
evident in his very early and his very
late work. In the late plays he is, in
fact, at pains to expound aesthetic
judgements in an extra-dramatic way,
cf. the detailed comments on the
reputed statue of Hermione in *Wint.*,
v. ii. 102–13 and v. iii. 14–98, and the

Post.   This is a thing   85
Which you might from relation likewise reap,
Being, as it is, much spoke of.
Iach.   The roof o' th' chamber
With golden cherubins is fretted. Her andirons
(I had forgot them) were two winking Cupids
Of silver, each on one foot standing, nicely   90
Depending on their brands.
Post.   This is her honour!
Let it be granted you have seen all this (and praise
Be given to your remembrance) the description
Of what is in her chamber nothing saves
The wager you have laid.
Iach.   Then, if you can   95
                                    [*Showing the bracelet.*
Be pale, I beg but leave to air this jewel: see!

91. honour!] *Steevens;* honor: *F.*   95. S.D.] *Camb.; not in F.*

dialogue between the Poet and the
Painter in *Tim.*, I. i. 20–37. *Timon (loc.
cit.)* affords an exact parallel: 'I will
say of it, / It tutors nature: artificial
strife / Lives in these touches, livelier
than life.' J. M. Manly detects 'the
attitude of one who knew the feeling of
the brush in his hand' in the Siege of
Troy description in *Lucr.* The present
scene, together with the analogues
cited, suggests that, *mutatis mutandis,*
Manly's speculation is not altogether
idle.

88. *andirons*] fire-dogs. From Old
French 'andier', the English form
being due to folk-etymology.

89. *winking Cupids*] Cupids with
closed eyes, i.e. blind Cupids. Again
we have a classical allusion, however
commonplace, which carries a faint
note of irony. The Cupids were blind
to the alleged deeds in the bed-
chamber. 'Winking' may be ambiguous.

90–1. *nicely . . . brands*] It is generally
agreed that the 'brands' are not brand-
irons but the hymeneal torches associated with Cupid. The image is not
very clear, but it seems that the Cupids

were leaning on the torches. Furness
comments: 'The little Cupids stood on
one foot because the legs were crossed;
and . . . crossed legs represented sleep,
which was also indicated, by the winking eyes. The Cupids were diminutive
and the hymeneal torches were tall, so
that the figures could very properly
lean or "depend on" them.'

91. *This . . . honour!*] Several unnecessary emendations have been proposed. The phrase is ironical. For F
'honor:' Johnson and Capell read
'honour?' which may be right.

95–6. *Then, if . . . pale*] Capell's
reading, 'Then, if you can, Be pale, I
beg etc.', which some editors follow,
seems obviously correct, yet examination shows it to be curiously unconvincing. Why should Iachimo question
Posthumus' capacity for turning pale?
Moreover, 'be pale' seems an in-
credibly feeble substitute for 'become
pale' or 'grow pale'. Johnson glosses
'pale': 'forbear to flush your cheek
with rage' which suits either punctuation. I would suggest, however, that
Shakespeare uses the word here in the
sense of indifferent, unmoved, in-

And now 'tis up again: it must be married
To that your diamond, I'll keep them.
Post.   Jove!—
Once more let me behold it: is it that
Which I left with her?
Iach.   Sir (I thank her) that!   100
She stripp'd it from her arm: I see her yet:
Her pretty action did outsell her gift,
And yet enrich'd it too: she gave it me,
And said she priz'd it once.
Post.   May be she pluck'd it off
To send it me.
Iach.   She writes so to you? Doth she?   105
Post. O, no, no, no, 'tis true. Here, take this too;
                                    [*Gives the ring.*
It is a basilisk unto mine eye,
Kills me to look on't. Let there be no honour
Where there is beauty: truth, where semblance: love,
Where there's another man. The vows of women   110
Of no more bondage be to where they are made
Than they are to their virtues, which is nothing.
O, above measure false!
Phi.   Have patience, sir,

100. that!] that *F.*   102. action did] *Rowe;* action, did *F.*   106. S.D.]
Johnson.

active, and would paraphrase: Then,
if you can remain unmoved by what
I have told you, give me but leave
to air this jewel. It is possible that
'pale' carries this meaning in *Mac.*,
III. ii. 50: 'Cancel and tear to pieces
that great bond / Which keeps me
pale!'

100. *that!*] F 'that' clearly requires
some punctuation mark, and I have
preferred my own to Rowe's colon or
Johnson's stop. Iachimo is emphatic
and triumphant.

105. *She writes . . . she?*] Furness
detects deep cunning behind the question, which is designed, he thinks, to
ascertain whether Imogen's letter has
made any mention of Iachimo's repre-
hensible conduct in I. vii. This attrac-

tive suggestion receives some support
from F punctuation which hints at a
certain uneasiness behind the questions.

107. *basilisk*] a fabulous reptile
otherwise termed 'cockatrice', and a
stock-in-trade of Lyly and all Euphu-
ists. Furness notes that it was the sight
from the basilisk which was reputed
fatal, but Shakespeare's error was a
pretty common one.

110–12. *The vows . . . nothing*] Let the
vows of women be no more binding to
the recipients of them than women are
bound to their own virtues—which is
not at all. Thus (substantially)
Vaughan, who correctly treats as a
prayer or imprecation what Johnson
takes to be an aphorism.

And take your ring again, 'tis not yet won:
It may be probable she lost it: or   115
Who knows if one of her women, being corrupted,
Hath stol'n it from her?
Post.   Very true,
And so, I hope, he came by't. Back my ring,
Render me some corporal sign about her
More evident than this: for this was stol'n.   120
Iach. By Jupiter, I had it from her arm.
Post. Hark you, he swears: by Jupiter he swears.
'Tis true, nay, keep the ring, 'tis true: I am sure
She would not lose it: her attendants are
All sworn, and honourable:—they induc'd to steal it?
And by a stranger? No, he hath enjoy'd her: 126
The cognizance of her incontinency
Is this: she hath bought the name of whore, thus dearly.
There, take thy hire, and all the fiends of hell
Divide themselves between you!
Phi.   Sir, be patient: 130
This is not strong enough to be believed
Of one persuaded well of.
Post.   Never talk on't:
She hath been colted by him.
Iach.   If you seek

116. one of her] *F2;* one her *F.*

115. *probable*] susceptible of proof.

116. *one of her women*] F reads 'one her women', which Staunton, not quite convincingly, changes to 'one, her women being corrupted, Hath.' Since 'one' is sometimes printed for 'on' in F (cf. v. iv. 186 and v. v. 134), and since l. 117 is unmetrical as it stands, the following suggests itself: 'Who knows if, on her women being corrupted, / He hath stol'n it from her?' In both the *Decameron* and *Frederyke of Jennen* the villain bribes a woman in order to gain access to the heroine's bedchamber, but conducts his own theft.

120. *evident*] conclusive.

121. *by Jupiter*] The oath is a profound and solemn one, since Jupiter, within the compass of this play, is the chief of the gods. Shakespeare is usually punctilious about such details in plays which have a pre-Christian setting.

125. *sworn*] Servants in noble households formerly took an oath of fidelity when they entered upon their duties.

127. *cognizance*] O.E.D. defines as 'a device or emblem borne for distinction by all the retainers of a noble house'. The image grows out of the 'attendants' of l. 124 and is carried on to 'take thy hire' in l. 129.

132. *persuaded well of.*] 'That is, of one whom we are persuaded to think well of' (Ingleby). Many editors print 'of—' on the assumption that Posthumus interrupts Philario.

For further satisfying, under her breast
(Worthy her pressing) lies a mole, right proud   135
Of that most delicate lodging. By my life,
I kiss'd it, and it gave me present hunger
To feed again, though full. You do remember
This stain upon her?
Post.   Ay, and it doth confirm
Another stain, as big as hell can hold,   140
Were there no more but it.
Iach.   Will you hear more?
Post. Spare your arithmetic, never count the turns:
Once, and a million!
Iach.   I'll be sworn—
Post.   No swearing:
If you will swear you have not done't you lie,
And I will kill thee if thou dost deny   145
Thou'st made me cuckold.
Iach.   I'll deny nothing.
Post. O, that I had her here, to tear her limb-meal!
I will go there and do't, i' th' court, before
Her father. I'll do something—   [*Exit.*
Phi.   Quite besides
The government of patience! You have won: 150
Let's follow him, and pervert the present wrath

---

143. sworn—] *Rowe;* sworne. *F.*   148. do't, i'] doo't, i' *F;* do't; i' *Capell.*
149. something—] *Rowe;* something. *F.*

134. *under her breast*] Professor H. G.
Wright reminds me that this is at variance with II. ii. 37–8: 'On her left
breast / A mole' and remarks that both
Boccaccio ('sotto la sinistra poppa')
and his French translator, le Maçon,
say that the birthmark was *under* the
heroine's left breast. The English
Decameron of 1620 has 'a small wart
upon her left pappe' which suggests
that its author followed *Cym.,* II. ii.

135. *Worthy her pressing*] Rowe
emends to 'Worthy the pressing' which
has been widely accepted. But 'her',
I think, refers to the breast, which
is here personified, as is the mole
which is 'right proud'. In other
words, this proud mole is worthy

of the pressure of Imogen's breast.

145–6. *And I . . . cuckold*] The threat
must surely be addressed to Iachimo,
who replies 'I'll deny nothing'. Nevertheless it is odd that Posthumus, who
has hitherto addressed Iachimo as
'you', should change to 'thou'. This
may indicate an access of hatred or
contempt. Less plausibly the threat
may be taken as applying to Imogen.

147. *limb-meal*] limb from limb.

149. *I'll do something*—] So Lear, in
impotent rage, exclaims: 'I will have
such revenges on you both, / That all
the world shall—I will do such
things— / What they are, yet I know
not' (II. iv. 282–4).

151. *pervert*] divert. The proposed

  He hath against himself.

Iach.   With all my heart. [*Exeunt.*

     Re-enter POSTHUMUS.

Post. Is there no way for men to be, but women
  Must be half-workers? We are all bastards,
  And that most venerable man, which I   155
  Did call my father, was I know not where

emendations 'divert' (Jervis), 'prevent' (Heath) are superfluous.

 151–2. the present . . . himself] Thiselton remarks that 'Posthumus's wrath is not "against himself" in the ordinary sense, but against Imogen.' This may be so, but man and wife are one flesh, so that a man at odds with his wife is also at odds with himself, and, for Shakespeare, any conflict in the microcosm or little state of man was an extremely serious one. Posthumus is overwrought, is not himself, and is, therefore, liable to commit violence on his own person. Hence Philario's anxiety. Posthumus' 'present wrath' can scarcely expend itself on Imogen, who is a thousand miles away, nor is there any good reason for supposing that Posthumus' friend would wish to pervert his wrath against a wife whose guilt has been established—as Imogen's apparently has.

 152. S.D. Re-enter Posthumus] It is customary to mark Posthumus' soliloquy as a new scene, though it is not so marked in F. The question, however, is whether or not it constituted an independent scene under Shakespearean stage conditions, and I am inclined to think that it did not. If, as Granville-Barker surmises, the action of II. iv takes place on the inner-stage, Posthumus' exit at l. 149 may simply indicate that he proceeds from thence to the front of the main-stage, the place from which soliloquies were usually delivered. Hence the stage would not be cleared.

 153–4. Is there . . . half-workers?] a

question fairly often asked in medieval literature, and raised later by Sir Thomas Browne in *Religio Medici* and by Milton in *Paradise Lost*. Professor Kenneth Muir suggests to me that Shakespeare may have had Rodomont's tirade against women in Harington's translation of Ariosto's *Orlando Furioso* (XXVII. 97) in mind: 'Why did not nature rather so prouide, / Without your help, that man of man might come / And one be grafted on another's side.' I find equally possible sources in Lodge's *Rosalynde*: 'The reason was (quoth Ganimede) that they were womens sonnes, and tooke that fault of their mother, for if man had growne from man, as Adam did from the earth, men had never been troubled with inconstancie', and in Marston's *Fawne* (IV ed. Harvey Wood, p. 201): 'O heaven! that God made for a man no other meanes of procreation and maintaining the world, peopled but by weomen, etc.' The idea seems implicit in Coriolanus' 'As if a man were author of himself / And knew no other kin' (v. iii. 36–7).

 154. We . . . bastards] Attempts have been made to mend the metre: 'We are bastards all' (Pope); 'We are all bastards, all' (Capell); 'Now we are all bastards' (Vaughan). But the apparently ragged metre of F allows for pregnant pauses and emphatic delivery of the significant words 'all' and 'bastards'. Cf. Edmund on bastardy in *Lr.*, I. ii. 1–22, where similar emphasis is required.

When I was stamp'd. Some coiner with his tools
Made me a counterfeit: yet my mother seem'd
The Dian of that time: so doth my wife
The nonpareil of this. O vengeance, vengeance!   160
Me of my lawful pleasure she restrain'd,
And pray'd me oft forbearance: did it with
A pudency so rosy, the sweet view on't
Might well have warm'd old Saturn; that I thought her
As chaste as unsunn'd snow. O, all the devils!   165
This yellow Iachimo, in an hour, was't not?
Or less; at first? Perchance he spoke not, but
Like a full-acorn'd boar, a German one,
Cried "O!" and mounted; found no opposition
But what he look'd for should oppose and she   170
Should from encounter guard. Could I find out
The woman's part in me—for there's no motion

168. a German one] *Rowe;* a Iarmen on *F.*   170. for should] *Pope;* for, should *F.*
172. me—] *Pope;* me, *F.*

163-4. *the sweet . . . Saturn*] Vaughan
suggests that these words are parenthetical and that 'so rosy' runs on
directly to 'that I thought her etc.'
Alternatively we may assume the
omission of 'that' before 'the sweet
view' and of 'so' before 'that I
thought'. This, perhaps accords better
with F pointing.

168. *a German one*] Rowe's adjust-
ment of F 'a Iarman on'. 'On' for 'one'
(and *vice versa*) occurs several times in
F *Cym*. 'Iarmen' for 'German' is common in E.E. Topsell (*History of Four-
footed Beasts*) describes the swine of
nether Germany as 'fierce, strong and
very fat', which suits 'full-acorn'd
boar' but is, presumably, at variance
with the appearance and methods of
Iachimo. Dowden suggests that 'Iarman' may stand for 'german', 'germane', and would interpret as 'genuine', 'thorough', but Dr H. F. Brooks
points out (privately) that the pun
on 'boar' and 'boor', i.e. a German
or Dutch (Low German) peasant
(*O.E.D.*, sense 2), vindicates Rowe's
interpretation. Thiselton's proposal

'alarum'd on' is ingenious but unnecessary. Several other emendations,
all preposterous, have been put forward. There is a relevant parallel in
Ado, iv. i. 57–62, where Claudio says:
'Out on thee! Seeming! I will write
against it: / You seem to me, as Dian in
her orb, / As chaste as is the bud ere it
be blown; / But you are more intem-
perate in your blood / Than Venus, or
those pamper'd animals / That rage in
savage sensuality.' Here, as in *Cym.*, an
angry man is fulminating against
alleged unchastity: both men allude
to Diana: both propose to write
against something. The 'chaste bud'
and 'pudency so rosy' probably derive
from the same image, and Claudio's
'pamper'd animals' are very probably
swine.

172. *me*—] Johnson reads 'me!', but
Pope's instinct was surer. Posthumus
is far too angry to be coherent. What he
doubtless intends to say, as Schmidt
points out, is: If I could find the
woman's part in me, I would tear it
out.

motion] impulse.

That tends to vice in man, but I affirm
It is the woman's part: be it lying, note it,
The woman's: flattering, hers; deceiving, hers: 175
Lust, and rank thoughts, hers, hers: revenges, hers:
Ambitions, covetings, change of prides, disdain,
Nice longing, slanders, mutability;
All faults that name, nay, that hell knows, why, hers
In part, or all: but rather all. For even to vice   180
They are not constant, but are changing still;
One vice, but of a minute old, for one
Not half so old as that. I'll write against them,
Detest them, curse them: yet 'tis greater skill
In a true hate, to pray they have their will: 185
The very devils cannot plague them better.   [*Exit.*

179–80.] *two lines, ending* knowes, / vice F.

177. *change of prides*] Schmidt glosses: 'one excess changed for another'. Dowden hints that 'prides' may mean 'proud attire' and cites *H8*, I. i. 25, but the phrase may well refer to the varying forms which the sin of pride can assume. Cf. the 'changes' of Pride in Marlowe's *Doctor Faustus* (B text, ed. Greg, ll. 683–6): 'Sometimes, like a Perriwig, I sit vpon her Brow: next, like a Neckelace I hang about her Necke: Then like a Fan of Feathers, I kisse her; And then turning my selfe to a wrought Smocke do what I list.'

178. *Nice longing*] I agree with Furness that 'nice' here signifies 'wanton', 'lascivious'. F prints 'Nice-longing' and the hyphen should, perhaps, be retained.

179. *All faults that name*] The state of F, which ends l. 179 at 'knows' and l. 180 at 'vice' suggests that something is amiss here. The majority of editors emend l. 179 and print 'for even to vice' as a separate half-line, quite justifiably since F prints 'For'. Emendations include: 'have a name' (Dyce); 'man can name' (Walker); 'man, nay, that etc.' (Daniel), but these are not better than the reading of F2: 'that may be named', which may rest on good authority. In the final analysis, F

can be defended on the grounds that Posthumus is too angry to be coherent, so that grammatical precision is the last thing which could be expected. It is, perhaps, remotely possible that F 'name' is a noun and refers back to 'mutability' which, to the Elizabethans, was a much more comprehensive thing than the other vices cited by Posthumus, hence: All faults that mutability, nay, that Hell knows.

183. *I'll write . . . them*] E. M. W. Tillyard, *Shakespeare's Last Plays*, p. 28, suggests that Shakespeare is here satirizing the satirists of his own day. That there is a touch of the satirical poet in Posthumus is evident from his impromptu verses in v. iii. 55 ff. But see the parallel in *Ado* cited in note to l. 168.

186. *The very . . . better*] Daniel regards this line as 'the cynical note of some reader of the MS.' foisted into the text, and Furness agrees. Daniel's point that 'the speech should surely end with the rhyming couplet' would be a strong one if only it were possible to conceive of such a speech ending in a dying fall. Taken as it stands, as a final, hysterical, half-strangled outburst, the line is effective enough.

ACT III

SCENE I.—*Britain. Cymbeline's Palace.*

Enter in state, CYMBELINE, QUEEN, CLOTEN, *and Lords at one door, and at another,* CAIUS LUCIUS *and Attendants.*

Cym. Now say, what would Augustus Cæsar with us?
Luc. When Julius Cæsar, (whose remembrance yet
    Lives in men's eyes, and will to ears and tongues
    Be theme and hearing ever) was in this Britain
    And conquer'd it, Cassibelan, thine uncle,   5
    (Famous in Cæsar's praises, no whit less
    Than in his feats deserving it) for him,
    And his succession, granted Rome a tribute,
    Yearly three thousand pounds; which (by thee) lately
    Is left untender'd.
Queen.   And, to kill the marvel,   10
    Shall be so ever.

ACT III

Scene I

S.D. *Britain . . . Palace*] Malone.

Furness rather half-heartedly questions the authenticity of the whole of this scene, but it is not easy to detect the basis for his doubts. Internal evidence in favour of authenticity is strong, especially in the Queen's speech, ll. 15–34.

S.D. Enter . . . Attendants] The use of the two doors indicates that the action takes place on the main-stage.

2 ff.] For this scene and its related incidents Shakespeare uses Holinshed, but treats his sources so freely that there is little to be gained by close comparison. For the general scope of Shakespeare's debts see Introduction, pp. xvii–xix.

5. *Cassibelan, thine uncle*] Holinshed makes Cassibelan Cymbeline's great uncle, though he notes Fabyan's conjecture which Shakespeare apparently followed. See Boswell-Stone, p. 7.

6. *less*] 'Cassibelan was not only deserving of praise but also received praise equal to his merits' (Dowden). But, as Dowden observes, Shakespeare may have written 'less' in error for 'more' (see note to I. v. 21).

9. *three thousand pounds*] i.e. pounds weight of gold or silver.

10. *to kill . . . marvel*] to end the astonishment which the non-payment has caused.

74

Clo. There be many Cæsars ere such another Julius:
Britain's a world by itself, and we will nothing pay
for wearing our own noses.
Queen. That opportunity,   15
Which then they had to take from's, to resume
We have again. Remember, sir, my liege,
The kings your ancestors, together with
The natural bravery of your isle, which stands
As Neptune's park, ribb'd and pal'd in   20
With rocks unscaleable and roaring waters,
With sands that will not bear your enemies' boats,
But suck them up to th' topmast. A kind of conquest

12–14.] *four verse lines ending* Cæsars, / world / pay / Noses. F.   16. take] *F;*
take't *W. J. Craig conj.*   21. rocks] *Hanmer (conj. Theobald)*; Oakes *F.*

12–14. *There be . . . noses*] F prints as
four lines of verse. Most editors allow
Pope's arrangement which is (substantially): 'There be many Caesars /
Ere such another Julius: Britain is /
A world by itself, and we will nothing
pay / For wearing our own noses.'
Even so the verse limps, and 'Britain
is' is a barely warrantable alteration
of 'Britain's'. Since Cloten speaks in
prose throughout this scene, it seems
unlikely that Shakespeare intended
this speech as verse. The idea of
Britain being 'a world by itself' was a
popular one in Shakespeare's day and
appears in the historical plays, notably
in *R2*, II. i. 45 f. Wilson Knight (*Crown
of Life*, p. 135) likens Cloten's wit to
that displayed, under similar circumstances, by Faulconbridge, Falstaff,
and Enobarbus.
    19–23. *The natural . . . topmast*] Com-
pare Gaunt's famous lines in *R2*, II. i.
M. Paul Reyher (*Essai sur les Idées dans
l'Œuvre de Shakespeare*) quotes an
interesting parallel from Ronsard: 'le
beau pays Anglois, / Fils de Neptune,
tout environné d'onde, / Et séparé des
malices du monde.'
    19. *bravery*] defiant attitude.
    20. *As . . . pal'd in*] As it stands in F
the line is unmetrical and most editors
alter to 'ribbed and paled in'. I suggest
the reading: 'As (*sc.* as if) Neptune's

park were ribb'd and palèd in', which
makes Neptune's park the sea, not the
isle. This reading receives tolerable
support from Holinshed, who remarks
that Caesar called Britain another
world and wrote that 'he had found an
other world, supposing it to be so big,
that it was not compassed with the sea,
but that rather by resemblance the
great Ocean was compassed with
it.'
    21. *rocks*] Theobald's conjecture
(long attributed, wrongly, to Seward)
restores the sense and accords with the
alliterative pattern of ll. 20–1. Porter
and Clarke defend 'oaks' and explain:
'The sea is made by the figure of speech
here a *Parke*, and the rocks are made
the fence of oaks that pale it in.' Dowden hints that 'oaks' may be used meta-
phorically for ships of war but it is
doubtful whether E.E. admitted this
usage. I find in Tourneur's *Transformed Metamorphosis*, 81–2: 'Let
Dodon's groue be lauish in expence; /
And scaffoldize her oakes for my
defence', but this is suggestive rather
than conclusive. On the whole, it is
best to accept Theobald's reading and
assume that F 'Oakes' was an error or
invention of the printer's arising from
the earlier 'Parke'. The collocation of
rocks and 'roaring waters' is repeated
in ll. 28–30.

Cæsar made here, but made not here his brag
Of 'Came, and saw, and overcame:' with shame   25
(The first that ever touch'd him) he was carried
From off our coast, twice beaten: and his shipping
(Poor ignorant baubles!) on our terrible seas,
Like egg-shells mov'd upon their surges, crack'd
As easily 'gainst our rocks. For joy whereof   30
The fam'd Cassibelan, who was once at point
(O giglot fortune!) to master Cæsar's sword,
Made Lud's town with rejoicing-fires bright,
And Britons strut with courage.

Clo. Come, there's no more tribute to be paid: our king-   35
dom is stronger than it was at that time: and (as I
said) there is no moe such Cæsars, other of them may
have crook'd noses, but to owe such straight arms,
none.

Cym. Son, let your mother end.   40

Clo. We have yet many among us can gripe as hard as
Cassibelan: I do not say I am one: but I have a hand.
Why tribute? Why should we pay tribute? If Cæsar
can hide the sun from us with a blanket, or put the
moon in his pocket, we will pay him tribute for light: 45
else, sir, no more tribute, pray you now.

Cym. You must know,
Till the injurious Romans did extort

---

28. *ignorant*] Johnson glosses: 'un-acquainted with the nature of our boisterous seas'. Examples of the pathetic fallacy in which 'poor' is followed by another adjective are fairly common in Shakespeare.

31. *Cassibelan*] Shakespeare trans-fers to Cassibelan a feat which Holin-shed and his authorities ascribe to Nennius, Cassibelan's brother.

32. *giglot fortune*] Fortune is a 'strumpet' in *Ham.*, II. ii. 240 and II. ii. 515, and 'a rebel's whore' in *Mac.*, I. ii. 15.

33. *Lud's town*] London. According to the chroniclers, the British capital, Troynovant, was so extensively im-proved by Cymbeline's grandfather,

King Lud, that it was renamed Caer-lud or Lud's town, which latter form they alleged (quite erroneously) be-came corrupted to London.

rejoicing-fires] hyphened in F.

38. *owe*] own.

straight arms] straight and therewith strong. Dowden thinks that the idea of 'stretched' underlies the image. I take the phrase to link with 'gripe' in l. 41.

43 ff.] Cloten's verbal iteration ('Why tribute? Why should we pay tribute? etc.') is petty and malicious. Cf. Edmund in *Lr.*, I. ii. 6–10, and Macbeth in *Mac.*, III. i. 64–70.

46. *sir*] Cloten turns and addresses Cymbeline.

48. *injurious*] insulting, offensive.

This tribute from us, we were free. Cæsar's ambition,
Which swell'd so much that it did almost stretch   50
The sides o' th' world, against all colour here
Did put the yoke upon's; which to shake off
Becomes a warlike people, whom we reckon
Ourselves to be.
Clo. and Lords.   We do.
Cym.   Say then to Cæsar,
Our ancestor was that Mulmutius which   55
Ordain'd our laws, whose use the sword of Cæsar
Hath too much mangled; whose repair, and franchise,
Shall (by the power we hold) be our good deed,
Though Rome be therefore angry. Mulmutius made
            our laws,
Who was the first of Britain which did put   60
His brows within a golden crown, and call'd
Himself a king.
Luc.   I am sorry, Cymbeline,
That I am to pronounce Augustus Cæsar
(Cæsar, that hath moe kings his servants than
Thyself domestic officers) thine enemy: 65

54. be . . . Cæsar] *Globe ed.;* be, we do. Say then to Cæsar *F.*   64. moe] *F;*
more *Ff2–4.*

49–51. *Cæsar's . . . world*] The primary image is, presumably, that of
'the bubble reputation'. The idea of
fame or worth stretching beyond the
confines of the world is used elsewhere
by Shakespeare in a Roman context:
cf. *Ant.*, v. ii. 82 ff., and *Cor.*, v. vi. 126–7.

51. *against all colour*] 'Without any
pretence of right' (Johnson). There is
a pun on 'colour–collar' linking with
'yoke' in l. 52.

54. *be . . . Cæsar*] Various emendations have been proposed, of which the
one accepted here is, on the whole, the
most satisfactory. Dyce gives the words
'We do' to Cloten alone. Malone allots
the whole speech to Cymbeline and
reads 'be. We do say, then, to Cæsar
etc', which is simple but strangely unconvincing. It is, however, possible to
torture a meaning out of F if we inter-

pret: 'which, since to shake it off becomes a warlike people . . . we do
shake off'.

55. *Mulmutius*] Holinshed records of
Mulmucius Dunwallon that 'he was
the first that bare a crowne heere in
Britaine.' His laws were said to have
been translated into Latin by Gildas
Priscus and later into English by
Alfred the Great. His father, Cloton,
King of Cornwall, supplies the name
for Shakespeare's foolish prince.

57. *franchise*] free exercise.

59. *Mulmutius . . . laws*] Pope omits
'made our laws' and reads 'That Mulmutius, Who was the first etc.'.
Steevens, who makes the same cut,
reads: 'Mulmutius, Who etc.'. The
proposed changes are undeniably
reasonable since F is redundant and
unmetrical.

Receive it from me, then. War and confusion
In Cæsar's name pronounce I 'gainst thee: look
For fury, not to be resisted. Thus defied,
I thank thee for myself.

Cym.   Thou art welcome, Caius.
Thy Cæsar knighted me; my youth I spent   70
Much under him; of him I gather'd honour,
Which he to seek of me again, perforce,
Behoves me keep at utterance. I am perfect
That the Pannonians and Dalmatians for
Their liberties are now in arms: a precedent   75
Which not to read would show the Britons cold:
So Cæsar shall not find them.

Luc.   Let proof speak.

Clo. His majesty bids you welcome. Make pastime with
us a day or two, or longer: if you seek us afterwards
in other terms, you shall find us in our salt-water   80
girdle: if you beat us out of it, it is yours: if you fall in
the adventure, our crows shall fare the better for you:
and there's an end.

Luc. So, sir.

Cym. I know your master's pleasure, and he mine: 85
All the remain is 'Welcome'.   [*Exeunt.*

SCENE II.—*The Same.*

Enter PISANIO, *with a letter.*

Pis. How? of adultery? Wherefore write you not
What monster's her accuser? Leonatus!

Scene II

2. monster's her accuser] *Capell;* Monsters her accuse *F.*

66. *confusion*] destruction.

72. *he to seek*] his seeking.

73. *keep at utterance*] defend to the last ditch.

74. *Pannonians and Dalmatians*] The Pannonians inhabited Hungary. The revolt referred to appears to have taken place during the reign of Cymbeline's father, Tenantius, but it would be both idle and pedantic to probe too deeply among Holinshed's dates.

86. *All the remain*] All that remains.

Scene II

2. *Leonatus*] It is possible that Pisanio reads the name from the letter which, of course, he consults several times during the speech. It is rather unlikely

O master, what a strange infection
Is fall'n into thy ear! What false Italian
(As poisonous tongu'd as handed) hath prevail'd   5
On thy too ready hearing? Disloyal? No.
She's punish'd for her truth; and undergoes,
More goddess-like than wife-like, such assaults
As would take in some virtue. O my master,
Thy mind to her is now as low as were   10
Thy fortunes. How? that I should murder her,
Upon the love and truth and vows which I
Have made to thy command? I, her? Her blood?
If it be so to do good service, never
Let me be counted serviceable. How look I,   15
That I should seem to lack humanity
So much as this fact comes to? [*Reading*]
                    Do't: the letter
That I have sent her by her own command
Shall give thee opportunity. O damn'd paper!
Black as the ink that's on thee! Senseless bauble, 20
Art thou a feodary for this act, and look'st
So virgin-like without? Lo, here she comes.
I am ignorant in what I am commanded.

Enter IMOGEN.

17. *Reading*] *Rowe.*   23. S.D.] *Singer; after l. 22 F.*

that he would himself use this more
familiar name for his master.

7. *undergoes*] bears without flinching.

9. *take in*] conquer. See note to v. v.
401.

10. *to her*] compared to her. Not, as
Hanmer (who reads 'hers') and
Malone suppose, compared to her
mind.

17. *fact*] crime, murder.

Reading] Rowe's direction has
won general acceptance, but F does
not entirely justify it. Malone notes
that these words do not appear in the
letter as given in III. iv and it is eminently possible that Pisanio is here
giving his own paraphrase of part of
the contents.

21. *feodary*] F 'Feodarie'. The word
appears as 'fedarie' in *Measure for
Measure* and 'federarie' in *Wint.* It
means 'a feudal tenant', but Shakespeare, by false association with Latin
foedus, uses it in the sense of 'accom-
plice'.

23. *I . . . commanded*] I must pretend
I know nothing of these instructions.
Steevens's 'I am unpractised in the
arts of murder' has little to commend
it. The line could only bear that meaning if Pisanio *intended* to obey Posthumus' instructions.

S.D. Enter Imogen] 'The whole of
this scene, after the entrance of Imogen,
is a prolonged example of tragic irony'
(Wyatt).

Imo. How now, Pisanio?

Pis. Madam, here is a letter from my lord.   25

Imo. Who? thy lord? that is my lord Leonatus!
    O, learn'd indeed were that astronomer
    That knew the stars as I his characters;
    He'd lay the future open. You good gods,
    Let what is here contain'd relish of love,   30
    Of my lord's health, of his content: yet not
    That we two are asunder; let that grieve him;
    Some griefs are med'cinable, that is one of them,
    For it doth physic love: of his content,
    All but in that! Good wax, thy leave: blest be   35
    You bees that make these locks of counsel! Lovers
    And men in dangerous bonds pray not alike:
    Though forfeiters you cast in prison, yet
    You clasp young Cupid's tables. Good news, gods!

    [*Reads*] Justice, and your father's wrath (should he   40
    take me in his dominion) could not be so cruel to
    me, as you (O the dearest of creatures) would even
    renew me with your eyes. Take notice that I am in

---

34. love: of] love, of *F.*   40. *Reads*] *Capell.*   42. as you] as you: *F.*

---

26. *Who . . . Leonatus*] Dowden suggests: 'I think that "thy" and "my" are to be pronounced with emphasis— as if Imogen felt wronged by Posthumus being claimed as Pisanio's lord.' But this emphasis need not carry any suggestion of indignation.

27. *astronomer*] astrologer.

28. *characters*] handwriting, possibly with secondary allusion to astrological characters.

31. *yet not*] Tyrwhitt proposes: 'yet no; That we two are asunder, let that grieve him.' This is ingenious but unnecessary.

33. *med'cinable*] curative. The imagery of these lines, revolving round 'relish', 'health', 'physic', is characteristically Shakespearean and is used with potent effect in *Mac.*

36. *locks of counsel*] seals on secret documents, used, as Imogen at once makes clear, both for love-

letters and for legal documents.

37. *men . . . bonds*] men in danger of forfeiting bonds, whose validity depended on the waxen seal.

39. *tables*] tablets for writing.

40–3. *Justice . . . eyes*] F colon after 'as you' is evidently an error but its omission does little to help the sense. Pope reads 'but you' and Knight 'an you', a simple and credible emendation. Capell reads 'would not' for 'would'. On the whole, I think F may be allowed to stand, save for the omission of the colon. 'As' implies an antithesis. On the one hand we have Cymbeline's wrath which would destroy Posthumus: on the other, the sight of Imogen which would renew him. Hence: your father's power of destroying me is not as great as your power of restoring me. The paraphrase is admittedly loose but is, I think, implicit in Posthumus' windy verbiage.

Cambria at Milford-Haven: what your own love
will out of this advise you, follow. So he wishes you   45
all happiness, that remains loyal to his vow, and
your increasing in love.

LEONATUS POSTHUMUS.

O, for a horse with wings! Hear'st thou, Pisanio?
He is at Milford-Haven: read, and tell me   50
How far 'tis thither. If one of mean affairs
May plod it in a week, why may not I
Glide thither in a day? Then, true Pisanio,
Who long'st, like me, to see thy lord; who long'st
(O let me bate) but not like me: yet long'st   55
But in a fainter kind. O, not like me:
For mine's beyond beyond: say, and speak thick,
(Love's counsellor should fill the bores of hearing,
To th' smothering of the sense) how far it is
To this same blessed Milford. And by th' way   60
Tell me how Wales was made so happy as
T' inherit such a haven. But, first of all,
How we may steal from hence: and for the gap
That we shall make in time, from our hence-going
And our return, to excuse: but first, how get hence.   65

57. beyond beyond:] *Ritson;* beyond, beyond: *F.*

47. *your . . . love*] Thiselton's suggestion that this is a second object to
'wishes' seems to me to be correct.
Alternatively, it may be governed by
'to' (as Thiselton also suggests) or may
simply be the formal ending to the
letter.

49. *horse with wings*] E. A. Armstrong
(*Shakespeare's Imagination,* p. 38) detects
an association with the story of Icarus
suggested by the wax of ll. 35–9, thus:
wax—the winged man whose wings
were attached with wax—the winged
horse. Since Icarus fell into the sea,
the allusion to Milford-Haven would
serve to reinforce the association. See
also note to ll. 57–9 below.

51. *mean affairs*] everyday business.
55. *bate*] modify.
57. *beyond beyond*] To interpret F

comma in 'beyond, beyond' in accordance with the modern convention of
punctuation, is to prefer feeble rhetoric
to great imagery.

57–9. *speak thick . . . sense*] The wax
image, used in ll. 35–9, seems to underlie these lines. 'Love's counsellor' links
with the 'counsel' which has wax
'locks' (l. 36), and wax would suggest
not only beeswax, but also that which
fills 'the bores of hearing', i.e. ear-wax.
Cotgrave has '*Bretonner.* To speake
thicke and short; or, as we say, nine
words at once'.

64–5. *from . . . excuse*] For 'And our',
Pope substitutes 'Till our' and Capell
'To our'. Malone, who follows F, interprets 'from our' in l. 64 as 'in consequence of our'. Other interpretations
are possible. 'And our return' may be

Why should excuse be born or ere begot?
We'll talk of that hereafter. Prithee speak,
How many score of miles may we well rid
'Twixt hour, and hour?

Pis.   One score 'twixt sun and sun,
Madam's enough for you: and too much too.   70

Imo. Why, one that rode to's execution, man,
Could never go so slow: I have heard of riding wagers,
Where horses have been nimbler than the sands
That run i' th' clock's behalf. But this is foolery:
Go, bid my woman feign a sickness, say   75
She'll home to her father; and provide me presently
A riding-suit; no costlier than would fit
A franklin's housewife.

Pis.   Madam, you're best consider.

Imo. I see before me, man: nor here, nor here,

---

68. score] *misprinted* store F.   74. clock's] *Pope;* Clocks F.   79. nor . . . nor]
F2; nor . . . not F.

---

a parenthetical afterthought. Dowden
is doubtless correct in saying that 'to
excuse' is governed by 'Tell me how' in
l. 61, but Shakespeare probably paid
little heed to syntax. Imogen is excited,
and excited people are not always
strictly grammatical. The reader will
do well to accept the sweet disorder of
the whole speech without any irritable
reaching after grammatical precision.

68. *score*] F 'store' is probably due to
the compositor having taken a minu-
scule *c* for a *t*. Pisanio's reply shows
that it can scarcely be the correct
reading.

rid] F2 reads 'ride' which all editors
have accepted, but Craig's view, that
F 'rid' means dispose of, clear, is fully
vindicated by *O.E.D.* which gives 'to
rid ground', i.e. to cover ground, move
ahead, make progress, also 'to rid
space', 'to rid way'.

69. *'Twixt hour, and hour*] not, as
Hudson supposes, between the same
hours of morning and evening, but
between one hour and the next.

70. *and . . . too*] because she is riding
to her destruction. Pisanio's meaning
is caught up in the irony of 'execution'
in l. 71.

72. *riding wagers*] Furness (*Variorum*,
pp. 191–2) offers a learned note for
those who really wish to know whether
Imogen refers to horse-racing or to
matches between unmounted horses.

74. *i' th' clock's behalf*] the sands of the
hour-glass, which serves as substitute
for the clock.

78. *A franklin's housewife*] A franklin
was a freeholder who ranked below
the gentry. Furness cites Sir Thomas
Overbury's character of a *Franklin*
(*q.v.*).

79–81. *I see . . . through*] The confused
discussion to which these lines have
given rise can be ignored. F is mani-
festly corrupt, and the F2 correction is
simple and obvious. Mason offers the
lucid paraphrase: 'I see clearly the
way before me, but that to the right,
that to the left, and that behind me, are
all covered with a fog that I cannot
penetrate. There is no more, therefore,

Nor what ensues, but have a fog in thcm,   80
That I cannot look through. Away, I prithee,
Do as I bid thee: there's no more to say:
Accessible is none but Milford way.   [*Exeunt.*

SCENE III.—*Wales: before the Cave of Belarius.*

Enter BELARIUS, GUIDERIUS, *and* ARVIRAGUS.

Bel. A goodly day not to keep house with such
Whose roof's as low as ours! Stoop, boys: this gate
Instructs you how t' adore the heavens; and bows you
To a morning's holy office. The gates of monarchs
Are arch'd so high that giants may jet through   5
And keep their impious turbans on, without
Good morrow to the sun. Hail, thou fair heaven!

Scene III

2. Stoop] *Hanmer;* Sleepe *F.*

to be said, since there is no way accessible but that to Milford.' Imogen, of
course, accompanies 'nor here, nor
here' with the appropriate gestures.

Scene III

S.D. Wales . . . Belarius] This scene
would take place on the inner-stage,
with a conventional property representing the cave. Several such properties are listed in Henslowe's papers
as belonging to the Earl of Notting-
ham's players in 1598 and some of
these were evidently quite elaborate.
Forman's account (see Introduction,
p. xiv) suggests that trees were used
in the Globe performances. Belarius'
cave is traditionally that at Hoyle's
Mouth near Tenby.

Belarius] The name Bellario ap-
pears in *Philaster*, but there is no reason
to suppose that Belarius was derived
from it, especially since Greene's
Pandosto, the source of *Wint.*, affords
the name Bellaria.

2. *Stoop*] Hanmer's correction of F
'Sleepe' is generally accepted. Malone

conjectures 'Sweet' and Vaughan
'Slope' (*sc.* bow, vb). 'Creep' might be
regarded as a further possibility on
bibliographical grounds. Thiselton,
however, shows that Belarius' whole
speech owes something to Henry
Smith's sermon, *A Disswasion from
Pride*, and there we find that God
would not have Pride's favourites
come to court 'unless they hold downe
their Mace, stoope when they enter'.
Likewise, 'As the way to heaven is
narrow . . . so the gate is low, and he
had need to stoope which entreth in at
it.' Hanmer's emendation, then,
seems fully justified.

5. *jet*] strut. Cf. Smith's Sermon:
'then the rich Glutton jetted in purple
every day, but now the poor unthrift
jettes as brave as the Glutton.' Thiselton notes that Smith has several
allusions to Giants.

6. *turbans*] 'The idea of a giant was,
among the readers of romances, who
were almost all the readers of those
times, always confounded with that of
a Saracen' (Johnson).

We house i' th' rock, yet use thee not so hardly
As prouder livers do.
Gui.   Hail, heaven!
Arv.   Hail, heaven!
Bel. Now for our mountain sport, up to yond hill!   10
Your legs are young: I'll tread these flats. Consider,
When you above perceive me like a crow,
That it is place which lessens and sets off,
And you may then revolve what tales I have told you
Of courts, of princes; of the tricks in war.   15
This service is not service, so being done,
But being so allow'd. To apprehend thus,
Draws us a profit from all things we see:
And often, to our comfort, shall we find
The sharded beetle in a safer hold   20
Than is the full-wing'd eagle. O, this life
Is nobler than attending for a check:
Richer than doing nothing for a robe,

23. robe] *Bulloch conj.; Babe F.*

10–21.] The crow of l.12 is followed
by the beetle in l. 20. E. A. Armstrong
(*Shakespeare's Imagination,* p. 22) shows
that this association of bird and beetle
is a common one with Shakespeare and
notes that, as in I. iv. 15, the crow is
used to emphasize distance.

13. *That it . . . sets off*] that it is place
which both diminishes and displays to
advantage. At the back of Belarius'
sentiments lies the Shakespearean concept of degree or order which receives
its clearest absolute statement in *Troil.,*
I. iii. 83–137.

17. *allow'd*] approved, acknow-
ledged.

To apprehend thus] to view things
in this way. And it may be observed
that Shakespeare himself viewed
things in this way. Belarius expresses a
view of life which Shakespeare gives to
other characters. Cf. Gaunt in *R2,* I.
iii. 275–8: 'All places that the eye of
heaven visits / Are to a wise man ports
and happy havens. / Teach thy necessity to reason thus; / There is no virtue
like necessity.'

20. *sharded*] having shards or ely-
tra.

22. *attending for a check*] attending at
court only to receive a rebuke—or
perhaps, as Knight suggests, a reduc-
tion in rank. This has, in fact, been
Belarius' own experience.

23. *robe*] F reads 'Babe' which
Malone unconvincingly explains as a
puppet or toy. Hanmer offers 'bribe'
which many editors accept, taking the
line to mean: richer than receiving
bribes from suitors and doing nothing
in return. Other conjectures include
'bauble' (Rowe), 'brabe' *sc.* a badge
of honour (Johnson), and 'brave'
(Singer). Bulloch offers two readings,
'badge' and 'robe', and the second of
these seems to me unquestionably correct. It accords with the alliterative
pattern and makes good sense (viz.
richer than hanging about the court
just for the sake of acquiring a robe of
office) which is concordant with the
meaning of ll. 24–6. F 'Babe' could
easily arise from carelessly formed *R* in
'Robe', or, more probably, through

Prouder than rustling in unpaid-for silk:
Such gain the cap of him that makes him fine,   25
Yet keeps his book uncross'd: no life to ours.
Gui. Out of your proof you speak: we poor unfledg'd,
Have never wing'd from view o' th' nest; nor know not
What air's from home. Haply this life is best
(If quiet life be best) sweeter to you   30
That have a sharper known, well corresponding
With your stiff age; but unto us it is
A cell of ignorance, travelling a-bed,
A prison, or a debtor that not dares
To stride a limit.
Arv.   What should we speak of   35
When we are old as you? When we shall hear
The rain and wind beat dark December? How
In this our pinching cave shall we discourse
The freezing hours away? We have seen nothing:
We are beastly: subtle as the fox for prey,   40
Like warlike as the wolf for what we eat:
Our valour is to chase what flies: our cage

28. know] *F2*; knowes *F*.

misreading of *Ro* in 'Roabe' (a common spelling).

25. *Such gain the cap*] usually taken to mean: such persons have the salute of their tailors. This virtually entails the acceptance of Capell's 'makes 'em fine' (F 'makes him fine') in the same line. But is it not possible that 'gain the cap' means 'win the approval'? If so, ll. 25–6 can be paraphrased, without recourse to emendation: such activities win the approval of him that makes himself fine yet does not strike out the debts in his book of debts.

27. *proof*] experience.

33. *travelling a-bed*] probably the imaginary travel of those who have 'never wing'd from view o' th' nest'.

34. *prison, or*] Pope reads 'prison for' and Vaughan conjectures 'prison of', but I think that F is correct. The construction of the whole speech is loose, but it is 'this life' which is 'a cell of ignorance, etc.,' or rather a debtor,

since it owes them something: and yet a debtor who dare not stride beyond prescribed limits. Prisoners for debt were required to keep within fixed bounds.

37. *December?*] Some editors delete the F interrogation mark.

38. *pinching*] Armstrong (*op. cit.*, p. 42) links this adjective with the 'sharded beetle' of l. 20, and shows that the two were part of a Shakespearean associative process. He draws other examples from *2H4*, I. ii. 255–60, and *Tp.*, I. ii. 328–30.

40. *beastly*] beast-like, or, perhaps, cowardly. The latter sense is possible in Elizabethan English, and a double meaning is likely in the present context. The fox and wolf reinforce the sense of 'beast-like', while the cowardice is evident in 'Like warlike as', i.e. no more warlike than, and in the concealed oxymoron of 'cowardly valour' in 'Our valour is to chase what flies.'

We make a quire, as doth the prison'd bird,
And sing our bondage freely.
Bel.   How you speak!
Did you but know the city's usuries,   45
And felt them knowingly: the art o' th' court,
As hard to leave as keep: whose top to climb
Is certain falling: or so slipp'ry that
The fear's as bad as falling: the toil o' th' war,
A pain that only seems to seek out danger   50
I' th' name of fame and honour, which dies i' th' search,
And hath as oft a sland'rous epitaph
As record of fair act. Nay, many times,
Doth ill deserve by doing well: what's worse,
Must court'sy at the censure. O boys, this story   55
The world may read in me: my body's mark'd
With Roman swords; and my report was once
First, with the best of note. Cymbeline lov'd me,
And when a soldier was the theme, my name
Was not far off: then was I as a tree   60
Whose boughs did bend with fruit. But in one night,
A storm, or robbery (call it what you will)
Shook down my mellow hangings, nay, my leaves,
And left me bare to weather.
Gui.   Uncertain favour!
Bel. My fault being nothing (as I have told you oft)   65
But that two villains, whose false oaths prevail'd
Before my perfect honour, swore to Cymbeline
I was confederate with the Romans: so
Follow'd my banishment, and this twenty years

45. city's] *F3* (citie's); citties *F*.

50. *pain*] labour.
51. *which dies*] The antecedent is not
clear. Dowden notes that some editors
take it to be 'fame and honour', but
argues for 'pain'—'the labour perishes
without attaining fame and honour,
and its epitaph is often slander-
ous.' Ingleby unconvincingly takes
'name' as the antecedent. It may be
simply 'honour' which dies in the
search. No definite conclusion can be
drawn.

54. *deserve*] i.e., as Ingleby notes,
earn (not merit).
60–4.] Cf. *Tim.*, IV. iii. 259 ff.: 'But
myself, / Who had the world as my
confectionary, / The mouths, the
tongues, the eyes and hearts of men /
At duty, more than I could frame
employment, / That numberless upon
me stuck as leaves / Do on the oak,
have with one winter's brush / Fell
from their boughs and left me open,
bare / For every storm that blows.'

This rock, and these demesnes, have been my world,   70
Where I have liv'd at honest freedom, paid
More pious debts to heaven than in all
The fore-end of my time. But up to th' mountains!
This is not hunter's language; he that strikes
The venison first shall be the lord o' th' feast,   75
To him the other two shall minister,
And we will fear no poison, which attends
In place of greater state. I'll meet you in the valleys.
                    [*Exeunt Guiderius and Arviragus.*
How hard it is to hide the sparks of Nature!
These boys know little they are sons to th' king,   80
Nor Cymbeline dreams that they are alive.
They think they are mine, and though train'd up thus
    meanly,
I' th' cave wherein they bow, their thoughts do hit
The roofs of palaces, and Nature prompts them

74. hunters'] *Theobald;* Hunters *F;* Hunter's *F3*.   83. I' . . . bow] *Warburton;*
I' th' Cave, whereon the Bowe *F*.

71. *at honest freedom*] 'at' as in 'to live
at peace'. Belarius' way of life ('at
honest freedom') is that coveted by
Imogen in I. vii. 7–9, which she is so
soon to share.

73. *the fore-end . . . time*] my early
years.

75. *lord o' th' feast*] presumably in
accordance with pastoral convention.
At the sheep-shearing in *Wint.*
Perdita is made 'mistress o' the feast'.

77–8. *which attends . . . state*] 'attends',
is present. 'Poison' seems the obvious
antecedent, but Furness argues for
'fear', i.e. the fear of poison. I do not
see how a verb can be used in this way,
nor can I follow the glosses of 'attends'
put forward by Schmidt ('is present to
do service') and Vaughan ('attendant
who poisons'). Belarius' words are
grimly true of Cymbeline's court
where the Queen brews her 'strange
ling'ring poisons'. Dr G. K. Hunter
draws my attention to the debt to
Seneca's *Thyestes*, 391 ff. Belarius,
throughout the scene, owes much to
this source.

83. *wherein they bow*] Warburton's
emendation of F 'whereon the Bowe' is
supported by the very persuasive paraphrase: 'Yet in this very cave, which is
so low that they must bow or bend on
entering it, yet are their thoughts so
exalted, etc.' Other emendations
include: 'there, on the brow' (Theobald); 'here on this brow' (Hanmer);
'where on the bow' (Capell). Capell's
reading, which is a correction rather
than an emendation, may well be the
correct one, and may be thus explained: Their thoughts are arrows
which hit the roofs of palaces. They
are, nevertheless, arrows which remain on the bow, i.e. in the cave. The
idea is thus roughly equivalent to that
of 'travelling a-bed' in l. 33. But the
syntax remains obscure unless we
interpret 'and though' in l. 82 as 'even
though'.

84. *and Nature*] It may be relevant to
observe that emendation here would
go a long way towards resolving the
preceding crux. If we could, with confidence, replace 'and' by some such

In simple and low things to prince it, much   85
Beyond the trick of others. This Polydore,
The heir of Cymbeline and Britain, who
The king his father call'd Guiderius,—Jove!
When on my three-foot stool I sit, and tell
The warlike feats I have done, his spirits fly out   90
Into my story: say 'Thus mine enemy fell,
And thus I set my foot on's neck,' even then
The princely blood flows in his cheek, he sweats,
Strains his young nerves, and puts himself in posture
That acts my words. The younger brother, Cadwal,   95
Once Arviragus, in as like a figure
Strikes life into my speech, and shows much more
His own conceiving. Hark, the game is rous'd!
O Cymbeline, heaven and my conscience knows
Thou didst unjustly banish me: whereon,   100
At three and two years old, I stole these babes,
Thinking to bar thee of succession as
Thou refts me of my lands. Euriphile,
Thou wast their nurse, they took thee for their mother,
And every day do honour to her grave: 105
Myself, Belarius, that am Morgan call'd,
They take for natural father. The game is up.   [*Exit.*

86. Polydore] *Paladour F.*   87. who] *F; whom F2.*

adjective as 'kind', the sense would run on clearly from l. 82.

94. *nerves*] sinews.

96. *figure*] Dowden interprets as 'part enacted' and refers to *O.E.D. figure,* sb. 11.

97–8. *shows . . . conceiving*] This, according to Dowden, means that he 'exhibits his own conception of things much more than merely gives life to what I say'. I would paraphrase: shows his own conception of what is related to be greater than it really is—

which perhaps comes to the same thing.

99–107.] Ingram takes these lines to be a non-Shakespearean interpolation. Furness (p. 210) concurs, but since he has already rejected the whole scene, his opinion can only be regarded as something that 'distinction should be rich in'.

105. *her grave*] Hanmer emends to 'thy grave', but such changes of personal pronouns occur elsewhere in the play.

SCENE IV.—*Country near Milford-Haven.*

Enter PISANIO *and* IMOGEN.

Imo. Thou told'st me when we came from horse, the place
　　Was near at hand: ne'er long'd my mother so
　　To see me first, as I have now—Pisanio! man!
　　Where is Posthumus? What is in thy mind
　　That makes thee stare thus? Wherefore breaks that sigh
　　From th' inward of thee? One but painted thus　　　6
　　Would be interpreted a thing perplex'd
　　Beyond self-explication. Put thyself
　　Into a haviour of less fear, ere wildness
　　Vanquish my staider senses. What's the matter?　　10
　　Why tender'st thou that paper to me, with
　　A look untender? If't be summer news,
　　Smile to't before: if winterly, thou need'st
　　But keep that count'nance still. My husband's hand?
　　That drug-damn'd Italy hath out-craftied him,　　15
　　And he's at some hard point. Speak, man, thy tongue
　　May take off some extremity, which to read
　　Would be even mortal to me.
Pis.　　　　　　　　　　　　Please you read;
　　And you shall find me (wretched man) a thing
　　The most disdain'd of fortune.　　　　　　　　20
Imo. [*Reads*] Thy mistress, Pisanio, hath played the
　　strumpet in my bed: the testimonies whereof lie

Scene IV

3. now—] *Rowe;* now: *F.*　　22. lie] *Rowe;* lyes *F.*

The action takes place on the main stage. Granville-Barker plausibly suggests that the inner-stage with its cave would be allowed to remain in view in order to localize the scene.

　1. *came from horse*] dismounted.

　3. *now*—] Rowe's reading correctly interprets the force of F 'now:' for it is quite evident that Imogen breaks off the sentence. Further emendation is quite superfluous.

　8–9. *Put . . . wildness*] assume a less terrifying look, ere madness, etc.

　10. *my*] Pope emends to 'thy', but Imogen points the contrast between Pisanio's senses and her own.

　11. *tender'st*] Pope reads 'offer'st' in order to eliminate the 'tender'st–untender' pun. The alteration is, of course, indefensible. The grim quibble at a grim moment is entirely characteristic of Shakespeare.

　16. *at some hard point*] in a tight corner.

　17. *take . . . extremity*] lessen the shock, i.e. break the news gently.

  bleeding in me. I speak not out of weak surmises,
  but from proof as strong as my grief, and as certain
  as I expect my revenge. That part thou, Pisanio, 25
  must act for me, if thy faith be not tainted with the
  breach of hers; let thine own hands take away
  her life: I shall give thee opportunity at Milford-
  Haven: she hath my letter for the purpose: where,
  if thou fear to strike, and to make me certain it is 30
  done, thou art the pandar to her dishonour, and
  equally to me disloyal.
Pis. What shall I need to draw my sword? the paper
  Hath cut her throat already. No, 'tis slander,
  Whose edge is sharper than the sword, whose tongue 35
  Outvenoms all the worms of Nile, whose breath
  Rides on the posting winds, and doth belie
  All corners of the world. Kings, queens, and states,
  Maids, matrons, nay, the secrets of the grave
  This viperous slander enters. What cheer, madam? 40
Imo. False to his bed? What is it to be false?
  To lie in watch there, and to think on him?
  To weep 'twixt clock and clock? If sleep charge
   Nature,
  To break it with a fearful dream of him,

34–5. *slander . . . sword*] In *Wint.*, II.
iii. 85–6, the idea is presented as:
'slander / Whose *sting* is sharper than
the sword's'. Behind this lies the association of sword and serpent which we
find in the *Cym.* context. The association is, perhaps, more precisely that
between the sharpness of a sword and
the sharpness of a serpent's tooth; cf.
Lr., I. iv. 310–11: 'How sharper than a
serpent's tooth it is / To have a thank-
less child.'

 36. *worms of Nile*] The Egyptian asp
or serpent is one of the dominant
images in *Ant.*, which affords the
phrase 'the pretty worm of Nilus'.

 37–8. *belie . . . world.*] Vaughan re-
points: 'belie,—All corners of the
world,—kings, etc', thus making 'all
corners of the world' a parenthesis
meaning 'everywhere' and 'kings,

etc.' the direct object of 'belie' (telling
lies about). This seems to me un-
Shakespearean. *O.E.D.* suggests that
'belie' in this context means 'fill with
lies'. But 'belie' can also mean encompass, surround, and may surely do so
here. We have to remember that the
serpent image is still in Shakespeare's
mind. Is it not possible, then, that the
image is that of slander, like a snake,
coiled and lurking at the corners of the
world?—It may be observed that the
image is still present in 'This viperous
slander enters' in l. 39, but now in the
form of a *crawling* serpent.

 38. *states*] 'That is, persons of highest
rank' (Johnson).

 39. *secrets of the grave*] analogous to
the 'sland'rous epitaph' of III. iii. 52.

 42. *in watch*] awake.

 44. *fearful dream of him*] 'That is,

And cry myself awake? That's false to's bed, is it?   45
Pis. Alas, good lady!
Imo. I false? Thy conscience witness: Iachimo,
Thou didst accuse him of incontinency;
Thou then look'dst like a villain: now, methinks,
Thy favour's good enough. Some jay of Italy   50
(Whose mother was her painting) hath betray'd him:
Poor I am stale, a garment out of fashion,
And, for I am richer than to hang by th' walls,
I must be ripp'd:—to pieces with me!—O,
Men's vows are women's traitors! All good seeming,   55
By thy revolt, O husband, shall be thought

50. favour's] *Rowe;* fauours *F.*

fearful for him, for his safety' (Furness).

47. *Thy conscience*] addressed, I think, to Posthumus, not Pisanio. At several points in this scene Imogen addresses her absent husband, see ll. 56, 62, and 89.

50. *favour's*] countenance, appearance.

Some jay of Italy] The jay here signifies a loose woman, and, as Capell pointed out long ago, the Italian word *puta* means both jay and wanton—as Shakespeare and most of his contemporaries were doubtless well aware. Armstrong (*op. cit.*, pp. 66–71) has an extraordinarily interesting chapter on 'The Painted Jay'. He observes that Shakespeare tended to associate the bird with clothing, with serpents, with drunkenness, and with deception. In the present scene we find the serpent (ll. 34–9) and the garment (ll. 50 f.). Armstrong concludes that such image clusters are 'the unwitting self-revelation of a man who had found a painted and extravagantly dressed woman "a snake in the grass"'.

51. *Whose . . . painting*] The numerous conjectural emendations are as distressing as they are superfluous, and there is not the slightest reason for questioning the F reading, though opinions may differ as to interpretation. The jay is a 'painted bird' (and is so termed by Spenser, Chapman, and others) and the harlot's cheek (*teste* Hamlet) is 'beautied with plastering art', while 'paint' in the sense of deceive is common in Elizabethan English. With these data, it is surely not difficult to extract sense from the passage. The harlot's mother may be 'her painting' in the sense that she is her exact likeness, i.e. they are both wantons. But let Johnsonian commonsense prevail: 'The present reading, I think, may stand: "some jay of Italy" made by art the creature, not of nature, but of painting. In this sense "painting" may be not improperly termed her "mother".' Armstrong (*loc. cit.*) comments on Shakespeare's hatred of make-up, giving instances from several plays. For the association 'mother-painting', cf. ll. 2–6 of this scene.

53. *hang by th' walls*] Malone curiously accepts the theory of one Roberts that Imogen here alludes to the hangings on walls, i.e. tapestries. But the characteristic Shakespearean image is of discarded clothing or armour, cf. *Troil.*, III. iii. 151–3: 'to have done is to hang / Quite out of fashion, like a rusty mail / In monumental mockery.' Steevens cites *Meas.*, I. ii. 171: 'Which have like unscour'd armour, hung by the wall'.

Put on for villainy; not born where't grows,
But worn a bait for ladies.

Pis.   Good madam, hear me.

Imo. True honest men, being heard like false Æneas,
Were in his time thought false: and Sinon's weeping   60
Did scandal many a holy tear, took pity
From most true wretchedness: so thou, Posthumus
Wilt lay the leaven on all proper men;
Goodly and gallant shall be false and perjur'd
From thy great fail. Come fellow, be thou honest   65
Do thou thy master's bidding. When thou see'st him,
A little witness my obedience. Look,
I draw the sword myself, take it, and hit
The innocent mansion of my love, my heart:
Fear not, 'tis empty of all things, but grief: 70
Thy master is not there, who was indeed
The riches of it. Do his bidding, strike.
Thou mayst be valiant in a better cause;
But now thou seem'st a coward.

Pis.   Hence, vile instrument!
Thou shalt not damn my hand.

Imo.   Why, I must die: 75
And if I do not by thy hand, thou art
No servant of thy master's. Against self-slaughter

59. men, being heard like] *Vaughan;* men being heard, like *F.*   63. leaven on]
F; leven to *F2.*

57. *not . . . grows*] not natural but
assumed.

59. *True . . . Æneas*] F has the
comma after 'heard' and not after
'men'. I have accepted Vaughan's
punctuation, but question his paraphrase: 'Honest men when they spoke
like ("being heard like") Æneas were
in the time of Æneas thought false.'
The Sinon parallel which follows
seems to indicate the sense required:
honest men were thought false in
Æneas' day because their true words
were (wrongly) interpreted in the light
of his false ones.

60. *Sinon*] Sinon betrayed Troy into
the hands of the Greeks. Æneas'
treachery occurred later in his deal-

ings with Dido, Queen of Carthage.

63. *lay . . . men*] The image is of corruption caused by sour dough, which
Shakespeare uses elsewhere. 'Proper'
here means honest, honourable.

65. *fail*] failure. Upton's conjecture
'fall' may be disregarded.

be thou honest] equivalent, perhaps,
to: 'you, at least, be honest even
though your master is not.'

67. *A little witness*] testify somewhat
to.

77–9. *Against . . . hand*] reminiscent
of Hamlet's 'Or that the Everlasting
had not fix'd / His canon 'gainst self-
slaughter'. The prohibition is not Biblical, but the early Church laid down a
number of canons which are both

There is a prohibition so divine
That cravens my weak hand. Come, here's my heart,
(Something's afore't,—soft, soft! we'll no defence)   80
Obedient as the scabbard. What is here?
The scriptures of the loyal Leonatus,
All turn'd to heresy? Away, away,
Corrupters of my faith! you shall no more
Be stomachers to my heart: thus may poor fools   85
Believe false teachers: though those that are betray'd
Do feel the treason sharply, yet the traitor
Stands in worse case of woe.
And thou, Posthumus, thou that didst set up
My disobedience 'gainst the king my father,   90
And make me put into contempt the suits
Of princely fellows, shalt hereafter find

80. afore't] *Rowe;* a-foot *F.*   88–91.] *so Capell; three lines ending Posthumus, /
King / suites F.*   89. thou that] *Capell;* That *F.*   91. make] *Malone;*
makes *F.*

rigid and specific. Father Clifford's
note on these is given by Furness
(p. 227).

80. *Something's . . . defence*] The
parenthesis, proposed by Vaughan,
makes 'heart', and not Imogen herself,
'obedient as the scabbard'. This I take
to be the correct interpretation,
though Furness demurs. The 'defence'
is Posthumus' letter which Imogen
rather fancifully likens to protective
armour.

82. *scriptures*] That is, the letter or
writing, with a pun on holy scriptures.
Here begins a run of theological
imagery stimulated, perhaps, by the
divine prohibition of l. 78. For a
parallel association of 'heart–text–
heresy' cf. *Tw.N.*, I. v. 230–53. The
whole of this scene in *Tw.N.* abounds
in quibbles on religious terms.

85. *stomachers*] A stomacher was
worn over the breast.

86. *teachers*] The 'false teachers' are
doubtless teachers of heresy. I do not
question the accuracy of the F reading,
but the emendation 'treachers' is not
impossible in view of the lines which
follow.

88–91.] F prints as three lines ending
'*Posthumus*', 'King', 'suites'. Editorial
re-arrangements are too numerous to
specify, and I have accepted Capell's
division as being the most satisfactory
correction of what is almost certainly
corrupt in F. This involves the acceptance of Capell's 'And thou, Posthumus, thou that did'st' for F 'And thou
Posthumus, That didd'st', but his
supplement seems to me judicious.
Without it the line lacks force.

91. *make*] All editors have emended
F 'makes' in some way or other, but the
original reading may yet be the correct one. The act of disobedience is a
past action: that of contemning
'princely fellows' is one continued over
a long period, and one which is still
operative if we accept Cloten as a
'princely fellow' (which, in one sense,
he is).

92. *princely fellows*] that is, Imogen's
equal in rank. Posthumus was 'a
beggar'.

92–4. *shalt hereafter . . . rareness*] My
disobedience and contempt were the
outcome of rare qualities, and not
common acts, as you, who have taken

It is no act of common passage, but
A strain of rareness: and I grieve myself
To think, when thou shalt be disedg'd by her   95
That now thou tirest on, how thy memory
Will then be pang'd by me. Prithee, dispatch:
The lamb entreats the butcher. Where's thy knife?
Thou art too slow to do thy master's bidding
When I desire it too.

Pis.   O gracious lady: 100
Since I received command to do this business
I have not slept one wink.

Imo.   Do't, and to bed then.

Pis. I'll wake mine eye-balls out first.

Imo.   Wherefore then
Didst undertake it? Why hast thou abus'd
So many miles, with a pretence? This place?   105
Mine action, and thine own? Our horses' labour?
The time inviting thee? The perturb'd court
For my being absent? whereunto I never
Purpose return. Why hast thou gone so far,
To be unbent when thou hast ta'en thy stand,   110
Th' elected deer before thee?

Pis.   But to win time

---

103. out first] *Ingleby (conj. Johnson)*; first *F.*

---

them too much for granted, shall some day learn.

96. *tirest*] O.E.D. quotes this line and offers the definition 'to exercise oneself upon'. 'Tire' originally meant rend, tear, and was a specific term used in falconry. I think, *pace O.E.D.*, that the word retains much of its original meaning here. Posthumus is symbolized as an eagle throughout the play.

97. *pang'd*] tortured, tormented.

98. *The lamb ... butcher*] The image, though a commonplace one, may have been suggested by the stratagem employed in *Frederyke of Jennen*: 'I haue a lambe here: we shall kyll it and take his tongue; and I wyll cut a locke of my here and with the bloud anoynt my clothes; and

bere these tokens to your maister.'

103. *I'll wake ... first*] Johnson conjectures that 'out' or 'blind' (which is Hanmer's reading) should follow 'eye-balls'. The supplement is quite necessary on metrical grounds, and parallel passages strongly support 'out' which Ingleby adopts. Emendations of 'wake', of which there are several, are now rendered superfluous by O.E.D. quotations in which 'wake' is used specifically of the eyes or brain. The idea, as Furness remarks, is of a *watch* —and a torturing watch. Pisanio means: I'll rather remain awake until my eyes drop out—or, in Elizabethan terms, until my eye-strings crack.

110. *To be unbent*] 'To have thy bow unbent, alluding to an hunter' (Johnson).

To lose so bad employment, in the which
I have consider'd of a course: good lady,
Hear me with patience.

Imo.   Talk thy tongue weary, speak:
I have heard I am a strumpet, and mine ear,   115
Therein false struck, can take no greater wound,
Nor tent, to bottom that. But speak.

Pis.   Then, madam,
I thought you would not back again.

Imo.   Most like,
Bringing me here to kill me.

Pis.   Not so, neither:
But if I were as wise as honest, then   120
My purpose would prove well: it cannot be
But that my master is abus'd: some villain,
Ay, and singular in his art, hath done you both
This cursed injury.

Imo. Some Roman courtezan?

Pis.   No, on my life: 125
I'll give but notice you are dead, and send him
Some bloody sign of it. For 'tis commanded
I should do so: you shall be miss'd at court,
And that will well confirm it.

Imo.   Why, good fellow,
What shall I do the while? Where bide? How live?   130
Or in my life what comfort, when I am
Dead to my husband?

Pis.   If you'll back to th' court—

Imo. No court, no father, nor no more ado

132. court—] *Pope;* Court. *F.*

117. *tent*] a probe, or wound. Used as a verb in *Ham.*, II. ii. 626.

123. *singular*] unmatched, pre-eminent.

125. *courtezan?*] F reads 'Curtezan?' but most editors substitute a dash or a point for the interrogation mark. Such a change may find support in ll. 15–16 and 50–1, but a question which receives no answer seems more dramatically effective here. Imogen would still be reluctant to believe that Pos-

thumus had been false to her, even though she had already admitted the suspicion.

127. *Some bloody sign*] possibly suggested by the device in *Frederyke of Jennen* already cited in note to l. 98. The 'sign' used in *Cym.* is a 'bloody cloth' (see v. i. 1). Posthumus' letter (ll. 21–31) contains no specific command that a token shall be sent, but something of the kind is implied by 'and to make me certain it is done'.

With that harsh, noble, simple nothing,
That Cloten, whose love-suit hath been to me   135
As fearful as a siege.
Pis.   If not at court,
Then not in Britain must you bide.
Imo.   Where then?
Hath Britain all the sun that shines? Day? Night?
Are they not but in Britain? I' th' world's volume

134. nothing,] *Rowe;* nothing: *F.*

134. *With . . . nothing*] This line is
metrically defective and, unless it employs an oxymoron of impenetrable
subtlety, quite nonsensical. The later
Folios print 'nothing?' which adds to
the confusion. Malone's comment is:
'Some epithet of two syllables has here
been omitted by the compositor; for
which, having but one copy, it is now
vain to seek.' Various emendations,
however, testify to the subsequent
thoroughness of the search. These
include: 'harsh, nothing noble, simple
nothing' (Dowden; Ingleby); 'harsh
noble, noble simply in nothing'
(Vaughan); 'harsh—no, no noble—
simple nothing' (Perring). White,
Singer, and Furness, among others,
claim that F is perfectly satisfactory as
it stands but I cannot agree. Malone is
right about the futility of seeking, but
his 'epithet of two syllables' may be a
red herring. I suspect deeper corruption. Imogen renounces the court, the
King, and Cloten. Why, we may ask, is
the Queen omitted? She, after all, is
even more distasteful than Cloten, and
I find it incredible that she should be
left out of account. It may be observed,
without prejudice, that either 'With
that harsh Queen; that noble, simple
nothing', or 'With that harsh noble
Queen; that simple nothing', the
second half of the line referring, of
course, to 'That Cloten', might fulfil
the present needs.

137. *Where then?*] Some editors
detect contradiction between this and
the questions which follow it. Capell
emends, rather pointlessly, to 'What

then?' Hanmer gives the phrase to
Pisanio, making Imogen's speech
begin at 'Hath Britain etc.' Vaughan,
Elze, and Furness independently conjecture that ll. 138–42 ('Hath Britain
. . . out of Britain') should be given to
Pisanio, that Imogen should answer 'I
am most glad You think of other
place', and that Pisanio should resume
at 'Th' ambassador'. Such a redistri-
bution would be more convincing if it
could be shown to be bibliographically
probable. F, in my opinion, can very
well stand on its own feet. The first
question, unlike those which follow,
is not necessarily rhetorical. What
Pisanio has, in effect, said is 'You must
go abroad'. Imogen, a helpless woman
in a desperate situation, naturally asks,
'Where shall I go?' 'Where then' is
simply a request for information: then,
after a pause, she proceeds to make a
virtue of necessity.

138–42. *Day? . . . Britain*] Furness
rejects these lines as non-Shakespearean, mainly because he considers the
'swan's nest' image a degrading one.
To him it signifies 'a nest of sticks'. I
cannot help thinking that Shakespeare
was more concerned with the swans
than with the sticks. Wilson Knight
(*The Crown of Life*, p. 149) remarks that
'pool' in Shakespeare carries under-
tones suggestive of impurity and supplies several examples in addition to
the present passage. This argues for authenticity, though, perhaps, not strongly. Is it not possible that 'swan's nest' in-
corporates Shakespeare's vision of Britain as a nest of singing birds, or poets?

Our Britain seems as of it, but not in't: 140
In a great pool, a swan's nest: prithee think
There's livers out of Britain.
Pis.   I am most glad
You think of other place: th' ambassador,
Lucius the Roman, comes to Milford-Haven
To-morrow. Now, if you could wear a mind   145
Dark, as your fortune is, and but disguise
That which, t' appear itself, must not yet be
But by self-danger, you should tread a course
Pretty, and full of view; yea, haply, near
The residence of Posthumus; so nigh (at least)   150
That though his actions were not visible, yet
Report should render him hourly to your ear
As truly as he moves.
Imo.   O, for such means,

140. *of it, but not in't*] Unnecessary
emendations have been proposed.
This conception of Britain is implicit in
Holinshed: 'it is not certeine vnto
which portion of the earth our Ilands
. . . should be ascribed, bicause they
(i.e. certain authors) excluded them
. . . from the rest of the whole earth'
(Boswell-Stone, p. 10).

145. *mind*] emended to 'mien'
(Warburton); 'mine' (Theobald:
later withdrawn); 'mask' (Kinnear);
'blind' (Vaughan). F is unobjection-
able, however. 'Mind', as in such
phrases as 'to have a mind to', can
indicate inclination or purpose. 'Wear
a mind' is equivalent to 'play a part',
and the verb accords with the 'disguise' image.

147. *t' appear itself*] Abbott treats
this as reflexive.

149. *Pretty . . . view*] a notable crux.
The suggested emendations: 'privy'
(Collier); 'happy' (Cartwright);
'ready' (Bulloch); 'pertly' (Cunningham), in no way affect the fact that it is
just as possible to tread a pretty course,
a becoming course—especially for
Imogen. Dowden's suggestion that
'pretty and' is a qualifying phrase (cf.
P.E. 'lovely and' in 'lovely and warm'

etc.) may be right. Thiselton, alone
among commentators, recognizes that
much depends on our interpretation of
'tread a course'. To him the phrase
suggests an equestrian allusion, and he
thinks that the passage turns meta-
phorically on 'the tournament, in
which the combatants wore armour
which so far disguised them that they
could be recognized only by the
devices they bore, and which was to
protect that which could not be un-
covered without "selfe-danger", while
they performed the "courses" in full
view of the spectators.' To me 'tread a
course' sounds like a term connected
with hunting or some other such
sport, but I can find no evidence save
for 'course' in bear-baiting which
signifies the attack of the dogs. If
any such meaning can attach to the
phrase, 'full of view' *might*, with a
possible view to emendation, be set
alongside 'full of vent' (usually explained as a hunting term meaning
spirited, eager for pursuit) in *Cor.*,
IV. v. 238.

haply] so Pope for F 'happily'. The
change is so often necessary that it is,
ipso facto, justifiable here—but it may,
for once, be wrong.

Though peril to my modesty, not death on't,
I would adventure!
Pis.   Well then, here's the point: 155
You must forget to be a woman: change
Command into obedience: fear, and niceness
(The handmaids of all women, or, more truly,
Woman it pretty self) into a waggish courage,
Ready in gibes, quick-answer'd, saucy, and   160
As quarrelous as the weasel: nay, you must
Forget that rarest treasure of your cheek,
Exposing it (but, O, the harder heart!
Alack, no remedy) to the greedy touch
Of common-kissing Titan: and forget   165
Your laboursome and dainty trims, wherein
You made great Juno angry.
Imo.   Nay, be brief:
I see into thy end, and am almost
A man already.
Pis.   First, make yourself but like one.
Fore-thinking this, I have already fit   170

169–70.] *so Rowe;* one, / Fore-thinking this *F*.

157. *niceness*] coyness, fastidiousness, daintiness.

159. *it*] The transitional form of the neuter genitive current in Shakespeare's day: see *O.E.D.* 'Its'.

waggish] The word usually means prankish, playfully mischievous, but here, I think, it is formed directly from 'wag' in its former sense of youth, young man. Imogen is told that she must convert feminine niceness into masculine courage.

161. *quarrelous*] quarrelsome. Actually weasels are not especially quarrelsome, and, as Armstrong (*op. cit.*, p. 30) notes: 'Shakespeare's weasel belongs to folk-lore rather than to natural history.' Armstrong has a valuable chapter on 'eagle–weasel–drone' associations (pp. 25 ff.) though these have little relevance to the present passage.

163. *exposing it*] In Shakespeare's

day gentlewomen wore masks in order to preserve the complexion.

harder heart] Most early commentators agree that this refers to Posthumus. Ingleby thinks that it refers to Pisanio himself. Furness asserts that no explanation yet given seems altogether satisfactory. I consider the difficulty to be imaginary and agree with Hudson that the phrase applies to Imogen. She must expose her cheek to the sun: she must also, as implied by ll. 159–61, harden her heart, and for this there is, alas, no remedy.

165. *common-kissing Titan*] Sidney refers to the sun as 'greedy *Phoebus*'. The association with greed is implicit in *1H4*, II. iv. 133: 'Didst thou never see Titan kiss a dish of butter?' and, perhaps, in the present passage.

169–70. *one . . . this*] Rowe's punctuation. F has 'one . . . this', which Thiselton defends, taking 'Fore-think-

('Tis in my cloak-bag) doublet, hat, hose, all
That answer to them: would you, in their serving
(And with what imitation you can borrow
From youth of such a season) 'fore noble Lucius
Present yourself, desire his service: tell him   175
Wherein you're happy; which will make him know,
If that his head have ear in music, doubtless
With joy he will embrace you: for he's honourable,
And, doubling that, most holy. Your means abroad:
You have me, rich, and I will never fail   180
Beginning, nor supplyment.
Imo.   Thou art all the comfort
The gods will diet me with. Prithee away,
There's more to be consider'd: but we'll even
All that good time will give us. This attempt
I am soldier to, and will abide it with   185
A prince's courage. Away, I prithee.

180. me,] *Capell;* me *F.*

ing' to mean renouncing, forsaking.
The word *may* be used in this sense in
The Faerie Queene, IV. xii. 14: 'But
soone he gan such folly to forthinke
againe.' Thiselton's suggestion is ingenious and may very well be right,
but Rowe's alteration better fits the
immediate situation.

170. *fit*] ready, prepared.

172. *in their serving*] with their aid.

174. *such a season*] such an age.

176. *happy*] accomplished, talent-
ed.

176–7. *which will make . . . music*] The
obscurity of these lines has resulted in
such emendations as 'will make him
so' (Pope); 'well make him know'
(Vaughan); 'you'll make him know'
(Hanmer). Dowden omits F comma
after 'know' and accepts Ingleby's
paraphrase: which will make him
know whether he has an ear for music.
Deighton's 'Which he will quickly discover if he has the smallest ear for
music' seems to me far preferable, but
I would gloss 'make him know' as con-

vince him, satisfy him. Theobald's
notion, that Imogen offers her services
to Lucius as a singing-boy, is unwarranted, unless there has been revision of the text. No songs are given to
Imogen in F though we later hear how
'angel-like' she sings. In the present
passage it is presumably the musical
quality of her speaking voice that is
meant.

179. *Your means abroad*] as for your
means abroad. Staunton unconvincingly glosses 'abroad' disbursed, ex-
pended.

183. *even*] *O.E.D.* explains as act up
to, keep pace with, but Furness prefers
to take it in its primary sense, to level,
render plain, render smooth. Not all
critics accept it as a verb. Of conjectural emendations 'do even' (Eccles)
and 'even do' (Keightley) may be
noted. I am inclined to interpret the
phrase as they do, but to assume
omission of the verb.

185. *soldier to*] courageously prepared for (with 'a prince's courage').

Pis. Well, madam, we must take a short farewell,
         Lest being miss'd, I be suspected of
         Your carriage from the court. My noble mistress,
         Here is a box, I had it from the queen,   190
         What's in't is precious: if you are sick at sea,
         Or stomach-qualm'd at land, a dram of this
         Will drive away distemper. To some shade,
         And fit you to your manhood: may the gods
         Direct you to the best!
Imo.   Amen: I thank thee.   195
                                        [*Exeunt severally.*

SCENE V.—*Cymbeline's Palace.*

Enter CYMBELINE, QUEEN, CLOTEN, LUCIUS, *and Lords.*

Cym. Thus far, and so farewell.
Luc.   Thanks, royal sir:
         My emperor hath wrote, I must from hence,
         And am right sorry that I must report ye
         My master's enemy.
Cym.   Our subjects, sir,
         Will not endure his yoke; and for ourself   5
         To show less sovereignty than they, must needs
         Appear unkinglike.
Luc.   So, sir: I desire of you
         A conduct over land, to Milford-Haven.

187. *short farewell*] Dowden suggests that this means a hasty farewell, not a farewell for a short time.

190. *I . . . queen*] Craig conjectures that this is an aside, and Dowden adds that, if spoken directly, it would excite Imogen's distrust. But does Imogen know of her step-mother's dealings with poison? Surely, despite her distrust of the Queen, she believes her compounds to be cordial. Hence Pisanio's remark may, in fact, be a powerful recommendation.

Scene v
S.D. Cymbeline's Palace] The

action returns to the main-stage.

2. *wrote*] Pope alters the comma to a semi-colon. This makes the first clause an absolute one, but so much could well be implied by F pointing. The semi-colon inserted by Capell after 'hence' is scarcely warranted by either Elizabethan or modern convention.

7. *So sir:*] F punctuation shows that the phrase here means 'Very well, sir.'

8. *A conduct over land*] Conduct means escort, guard. Dyce, in his first edition, reads 'over-land', and 'overland' in subsequent editions, thus making it an adjective.

  Madam, all joy befal your grace, and you!
Cym. My lords, you are appointed for that office: 10
  The due of honour in no point omit.
  So farewell, noble Lucius.
Luc.   Your hand, my lord.
Clo. Receive it friendly: but from this time forth
  I wear it as your enemy.
Luc.   Sir, the event
  Is yet to name the winner. Fare you well.   15
Cym. Leave not the worthy Lucius, good my lords,
  Till he have cross'd the Severn. Happiness!
         [Exeunt Lucius and Lords.
Queen. He goes hence frowning: but it honours us
  That we have given him cause.
Clo.   'Tis all the better,
  Your valiant Britons have their wishes in it.   20
Cym. Lucius hath wrote already to the emperor
  How it goes here. It fits us therefore ripely
  Our chariots and our horsemen be in readiness:
  The powers that he already hath in Gallia
  Will soon be drawn to head, from whence he moves 25
  His war for Britain.
Queen.   'Tis not sleepy business,
  But must be look'd to speedily, and strongly.
Cym. Our expectation that it would be thus
  Hath made us forward. But, my gentle queen,
  Where is our daughter? She hath not appear'd   30
  Before the Roman, nor to us hath tender'd
  The duty of the day. She looks us like
  A thing more made of malice than of duty,
  We have noted it. Call her before us, for

---

17. the] *F; not in Ff2–4.* 28. would] *F; should Ff2–4.* 32. looks us] *Johnson;*
looke us *F;* lookes as *F2.*

9. *and you*] Whether this is spoken to
Cymbeline, the Queen, Cloten, or the
assembled company has been long
disputed, and long is like to be. There
seems little point in pursuing the
matter through all the emendations
which have been invoked.
 14. *event*] issue, outcome.

22–3. *It fits . . . horsemen be*] either a
subjunctive with 'that' omitted or,
less probably, an infinitive with 'to'
omitted.
 32. *She looks us like*] Some critics
interpret as 'she eyes us': others, more
plausibly, I think, explain as 'she
seems to us'.

We have been too slight in sufferance. [*Exit an Attendant.*
Queen.   Royal sir,   35
Since the exile of Posthumus, most retir'd
Hath her life been: the cure whereof, my lord,
'Tis time must do. Beseech your majesty,
Forbear sharp speeches to her. She's a lady
So tender of rebukes that words are strokes,   40
And strokes death to her.

Re-enter Attendant.

Cym.   Where is she, sir? How
Can her contempt be answer'd?
Atten.   Please you, sir,
Her chambers are all lock'd, and there's no answer
That will be given to th' loud of noise we make.
Queen. My lord, when last I went to visit her,   45
She pray'd me to excuse her keeping close,
Whereto constrain'd by her infirmity,
She should that duty leave unpaid to you
Which daily she was bound to proffer: this

---

35. slight] *F;* light *Ff2–4.*   S.D.] *Capell.*   40. strokes,] *F2;* stroke; *F.*
41. *Re-enter Attendant*] *Capell; Enter a Messenger F.*

---

35. *too slight in sufferance*] too tolerant, and too mild in our tolerance.

37–8. *the cure . . . do*] from the *Sententiae Pueriles*: 'Doloris medicus Tempus'.

41. *How*] So F, but perhaps we should interpret as an irritable exclamation and read 'How?'

44. *loud of noise*] F 'lowd of noise'. Capell's 'loudst of noise' is widely accepted, though Rowe's 'loudest noise' is bibliographically more tenable. The common Elizabethan habit of using an adjective for an abstract noun seems to me to rule out the need for emendation. The following passages from Lodge illustrate the liberties that were taken: 'Tut, Sylla's sparkling eyes should dim with clear / The burning brands of their consuming light' (*The Wounds of Civil War*). 'Blush, day's eternal lamp, to see thy

lot / Since that thy clear with cloudy darks is scar'd' (*The Discontented Satyr*). 'Some, well I wot, and of that sum full many, / Wish'd or my fair or their desire were less' (*Scilla's Metamorphosis*). For Shakespearean examples see Abbott, par. 5. It seems possible that the crucial 'All cruels else subscribe' in *Lr.*, III. vii, may be an extreme instance. Vaughan defends F on the ground that 'loud' is used substantivally in Holland's *Plinie*, x. 29: 'For at one time you shall heare her voice ful of loud, another time as low'. Furness suggests that 'ful of loud' here may be a misprint for 'full oft loud'.

49. *bound*] Dowden asks: 'Does this mean bound in duty? or is the sense "ready", "willing", as often?' I imagine that this particular duty was one of the restrictions imposed on

She wish'd me to make known: but our great court   50
Made me to blame in memory.
Cym.   Her doors lock'd?
Not seen of late? Grant heavens, that which I fear
Prove false!   [*Exit.*
Queen. Son, I say, follow the king.
Clo. That man of hers, Pisanio, her old servant,   55
I have not seen these two days.
Queen.   Go, look after:
                                        [*Exit Cloten.*
Pisanio, thou that stand'st so for Posthumus—
He hath a drug of mine: I pray his absence
Proceed by swallowing that. For he believes
It is a thing most precious. But for her,   60
Where is she gone? Haply, despair hath seiz'd her:
Or, wing'd with fervour of her love, she's flown
To her desir'd Posthumus: gone she is,
To death, or to dishonour, and my end
Can make good use of either. She being down,   65
I have the placing of the British crown.

Re-enter CLOTEN.

How now, my son?
Clo.   'Tis certain she is fled:

51. to blame] *F4;* too blame *F.*   56. *Exit Cloten*] *Capell; Exit after* days *F.*
57. Posthumus—] Posthumus, *F.*

Imogen following her dereliction.
    51. *to blame*] F prints 'too blame', a common error resulting from the fact that 'to' and 'too' were confused, so that 'blame' was taken as an adjective.
    56. *Go, look after:*] Vaughan argues that Cloten's exit is (as F indicates) after 'days' and that the Queen then turns to an Attendant with: 'Go, look after / Pisanio, thou, that stands so for Posthumus etc.' This is ingenious but tampers somewhat with the text. The exits marked in F are not always strictly timed and are obviously unreliable in such examples as the present one. The Queen tells Cloten to follow the King: instead he remains to

discuss a matter of secondary importance: the Queen impatiently dismisses him a second time. This seems the more essentially dramatic interpretation and one which is, in some measure, supported by ll. 67-9.
    57. *stand'st so*] so steadfastly supportest.
    Posthumus—] I have substituted a dash for F comma. The Queen, I think, begins an imprecation or threat against Pisanio, then suddenly recalls the probable effect of the drug which she has given him. If this interpretation is accepted, the change of personal pronoun no longer presents any difficulty.

Go in and cheer the king, he rages, none
Dare come about him.
Queen.   [*Aside*] All the better: may
  This night forestall him of the coming day!   [*Exit.*   70
Clo. I love, and hate her: for she's fair and royal,
  And that she hath all courtly parts more exquisite
  Than lady, ladies, woman, from every one
  The best she hath, and she of all compounded
  Outsells them all. I love her therefore, but   75
  Disdaining me, and throwing favours on
  The low Posthumus, slanders so her judgement
  That what's else rare is chok'd: and in that point
  I will conclude to hate her, nay indeed,
  To be reveng'd upon her. For, when fools   80
  Shall—

Enter PISANIO.

Who is here? What, are you packing, sirrah?
Come hither: ah, you precious pandar! Villain,

69. *Aside*] *Globe ed. (conj. S. Walker).*   82. pandar!] *Capell;* Pandar, *F.*

70. *This night forestall*] The Queen
hopes that the violence of Cymbeline's
wrath will prove fatal to him. Wyatt,
seeking a strained figurative meaning,
interprets 'the coming day' as Imogen's succession to the throne. The
Queen's lines are doubtless an aside, as
Walker conjectures, but are not so
marked in F.

71–5. *I love ... Outsells them all*] Mary
Johnston (*Times Literary Supplement*,
22 Jan. 1938, p. 60), writing in support
of Cunningham (see note following)
demonstrates Shakespeare's debt to
Catullus, *Carmina* 85 and 86. No. 85
runs: 'Odi et amo: quare id faciam,
fortasse requiris. / Nescio, sed fieri
sentio et excrucior', and the relevant
lines from No. 86 are: 'Lesbia formosa
est, quae cum pulcherrima tota est, /
Tum omnibus una omnes surripuit
Veneres.' This second passage is also
recalled in *Tp.*, III. i. 46–8: 'but you,
O you, / So perfect and so peerless, are
created / Of every creature's best.' Cf.
also Sidney, *Arcadia* (1598), I. i. 75:

'She is her selfe of best things the collection.'

73. *Than lady, ladies, woman*] Johnson
glosses 'than any lady, than all ladies,
than all womankind', and is vindicated by the parallel in *All's W.*, II. iii.
201–2 (noted by Tollet): '*Lafeu.* Are
you companion to the Count Rou-
sillon? / *Parolles.* To any count, to all
counts, to what is man.' Several emendations have been proposed, of which
the least absurd are 'Than any lady,
winning' (Hanmer); 'Than lady (vb)
Ladies; winning' (Warburton). Henry
Cuningham (*Times Literary Supplement*, 13 Nov. 1937, p. 871) extravagantly conjectures: 'Than all the
ladies; and won from every woman /
The best she hath.' The conjectures of
Elze—'Than lady, lassie, woman'—
and Sprenger—'Than, birlady, any
woman'—are worth recording as cau-
tionary examples.

81. *packing*] scheming, deceiving:
cf. 'this packing evil' in *Edward III*,
II. ii. 7. Dowden notes that the word

Where is thy lady? In a word, or else
Thou art straightway with the fiends.
Pis.   O, good my lord!
Clo. Where is thy lady? or, by Jupiter—   85
I will not ask again. Close villain,
I'll have this secret from thy heart, or rip
Thy heart to find it. Is she with Posthumus?
From whose so many weights of baseness cannot
A dram of worth be drawn.
Pis.   Alas, my lord,   90
How can she be with him? When was she miss'd?
He is in Rome.
Clo.   Where is she, sir? Come nearer:
No farther halting: satisfy me home,
What is become of her?
Pis. O, my all-worthy lord!
Clo.   ⸰   All-worthy villain!   95
Discover where thy mistress is, at once,
At the next word: no more of 'worthy lord!'
Speak, or thy silence on the instant is
Thy condemnation and thy death.
Pis.   Then, sir:
This paper is the history of my knowledge   100
Touching her flight.   [*Presenting a letter*

---

85. Jupiter—] *Boswell;* Iupiter, *F.*   101. S.D.] *Malone; not in F.*

could also signify 'running away'.

85. *or, by Jupiter*—] so Boswell and most subsequent editors, but would not 'or—by Jupiter etc.' be a somewhat more effective reading?

86. *villain*] Walker proposes 'villanie' and other proposals have been made on metrical grounds, but 'villain' as a trisyllable was not uncommon in Shakespeare's day.

87. *heart*] The accuracy of F has never been questioned, but its reading seems a little dubious in view of 'heart' in l. 88, which may have caught the compositor's eye. It is conceivable that the original read 'mouth' or 'lips', though deliberate iteration is equally possible.

92. *Come nearer*] come to the point.

93. *home*] thoroughly.

100. *This paper*] This is evidently the 'feigned letter' of v. v. 279, but whether 'feigned' there signifies forged or dissembling is not clear. The letter which Pisanio now hands to Cloten may be forged, though Cloten claims to recognize Posthumus' handwriting. The information which it contains is evidently the same as that in the letter to Imogen at III. ii. 40–8, and it is possibly that very letter. Imogen discards it at III. iv. 83, and we may reasonably assume that the cautious Pisanio would not leave such an incriminating document lying about for anyone to find.

Clo.   Let's see't: I will pursue her
    Even to Augustus' throne.
Pis.   [*Aside*] Or this, or perish.
    She's far enough, and what he learns by this
    May prove his travel, not her danger.
Clo.   Hum!
Pis. [*Aside*] I'll write to my lord she's dead: O Imogen,   105
    Safe mayst thou wander, safe return again!
Clo. Sirrah, is this letter true?
Pis. Sir, as I think.
Clo. It is Posthumus' hand, I know't. Sirrah, if thou
    wouldst not be a villain, but do me true service,   110
    undergo those employments wherein I should have
    cause to use thee with a serious industry, that is,
    what villainy soe'er I bid thee do, to perform it,
    directly and truly, I would think thee an honest
    man: thou shouldst neither want my means for thy   115
    relief, nor my voice for thy preferment.
Pis. Well, my good lord.
Clo. Wilt thou serve me? For since patiently and con-
    stantly thou hast stuck to the bare fortune of that
    beggar Posthumus, thou canst not in the course of   120
    gratitude but be a diligent follower of mine. Wilt
    thou serve me?
Pis. Sir, I will.
Clo. Give me thy hand, here's my purse. Hast any of thy
    late master's garments in thy possession?   125

102. *Aside*] *Rowe.*   105. *Aside*] *Theobald.*   113. do, . . . it] *Theobald;* do . . .
it, *F.*

102. *Or this, or perish*] Johnson thinks
that these words should be assigned to
Cloten, but they are at least equally
appropriate to Pisanio. Whether
Rowe is right in treating them as an
aside remains a moot point, since some
force attaches to Dowden's suggestion
that they 'are meant to deceive Cloten
by apparent reluctance in showing a
letter which Pisanio believes can really
do no harm to Imogen'.

104–5. *Hum! . . . dead*] Armstrong
(*op. cit.*, p. 44) notes that 'hum', a
neutral word, 'became attached to the

Death category of images through
adventitious associations'. He shows
that in twelve of the twenty contexts in
which Shakespeare uses this word
death or sleep imagery is present.

109 ff.] The change from verse to
prose at this point is cited by Fleay in
support of his contention that *Cymbeline* was written at different times,
the prose part being the later. Fleay's
methods are, however, so subjective
and variable that little reliance can be
placed on them.

111. *undergo*] undertake.

Pis. I have my lord, at my lodging the same suit he wore
   when he took leave of my lady and mistress.
Clo. The first service thou dost me, fetch that suit
   hither, let it be thy first service, go.
Pis. I shall, my lord.   [*Exit.*   130
Clo. Meet thee at Milford-Haven! (I forgot to ask him
   one thing, I'll remember't anon) even there, thou
   villain Posthumus, will I kill thee. I would these
   garments were come. She said upon a time (the bit-
   terness of it I now belch from my heart) that she   135
   held the very garment of Posthumus in more respect
   than my noble and natural person; together with
   the adornment of my qualities. With that suit upon
   my back, will I ravish her: first kill him, and in her
   eyes; there shall she see my valour, which will then   140
   be a torment to her contempt. He on the ground,
   my speech of insultment ended on his dead body,
   and when my lust hath dined (which, as I say, to
   vex her I will execute in the clothes that she so
   prais'd) to the court I'll knock her back, foot her   145
   home again. She hath despis'd me rejoicingly, and
   I'll be merry in my revenge.

Re-enter PISANIO, *with the clothes.*

   Be those the garments?
Pis. Ay, my noble lord.
Clo. How long is't since she went to Milford-Haven?   150
Pis. She can scarce be there yet.
Clo. Bring this apparel to my chamber, that is the second
   thing that I have commanded thee. The third is,
   that thou wilt be a voluntary mute to my design.

147. *Re-enter* . . .] *Capell; Enter Pisanio. F.*

131. *I forgot to ask*] The one thing
which Cloten forgot to ask is probably,
as Eccles suggests, 'How long is't since
she went to Milford-Haven?' Thiselton remarks: 'As to the rest of this
speech, Pisanio evidently overhears
Cloten.' Some such assumption is
necessary to account for Pisanio's
knowledge of Cloten's 'unchaste purpose' at v. v. 282–5, but we cannot, in
the nature of things, suppose that Pisanio hears the whole speech, and it is
sufficient to assume that he returns at
about l. 142. In the last act he says nothing of Cloten's plan to murder Posthumus. The brutality of this speech recalls the revolting treatment of Lavinia
by the sons of Tamora in *Tit.*, II. iii.

Be but duteous, and true preferment shall tender   155
itself to thee. My revenge is now at Milford: would
I had wings to follow it! Come, and be true.   [*Exit.*
Pis. Thou bid'st me to my loss: for true to thee
Were to prove false, which I will never be,
To him that is most true. To Milford go,   160
And find not her whom thou pursuest. Flow, flow,
You heavenly blessings, on her! This fool's speed
Be cross'd with slowness; labour be his meed!   [*Exit.*

SCENE VI.—*Wales: before the Cave of Belarius.*

Enter IMOGEN, *in boy's clothes.*

Imo. I see a man's life is a tedious one,
I have tir'd myself: and for two nights together
Have made the ground my bed. I should be sick,
But that my resolution helps me: Milford,
When from the mountain-top Pisanio show'd thee,   5
Thou was within a ken. O Jove! I think
Foundations fly the wretched: such, I mean,

Scene VI

S.D. *before . . . Belarius*] Capell.   *Enter . . . clothes*] Rowe; Enter Imogen alone. F.

155. *duteous, and true preferment*] The punctuation proposed by Walker (duteous and true, preferment) misses the point. Cloten opposes the preferment which he can bestow to that which Posthumus can only promise without hope of fulfilment.

160. *To him*] Variously identified with God, with Jove, and with Posthumus. Thiselton observes that Pisanio could not apply the epithet 'most true' to Posthumus, nor could he say that he would never be false since he has already disobeyed his master's instructions. This is most true, but it concerns the letter rather than the spirit. In the broad sense, Pisanio's loyalty to Posthumus is unimpeachable. As Malone remarks: 'Pisanio notwithstanding his master's letter, commanding the murder of Imogen,

considers him as *true*, supposing, as he has already said to her, that Posthumus was abused by some villain, equally an enemy to both.'

Scene VI

2. *tir'd*] F 'tyr'd'. Most editors interpret as 'wearied' but Collier and Singer treat the word as an abbreviation of 'attired'. I accept both interpretations. Surely this is one of Shakespeare's more preposterous puns. Imogen is not without her moments of broad humour.

4. *helps*] cures.

6. *within a ken*] within view.

7. *Foundations*] a quibble on two meanings: (i) security, (ii) an institution such as a hospital. The latter sense is reinforced by allusion to sickness and beggars.

Where they should be reliev'd. Two beggars told me
I could not miss my way. Will poor folks lie,
That have afflictions on them, knowing 'tis   10
A punishment, or trial? Yes; no wonder,
When rich ones scarce tell true. To lapse in fulness
Is sorer than to lie for need: and falsehood
Is worse in kings than beggars. My dear lord,
Thou art one o' th' false ones! Now I think on thee,   15
My hunger's gone; but even before, I was
At point to sink, for food.—But what is this?
Here is a path to 't: 'tis some savage hold:
I were best not call; I dare not call: yet famine,
Ere clean it o'erthrow Nature, makes it valiant.   20
Plenty and peace breeds cowards: hardness ever
Of hardiness is mother. Ho! who's here?
If any thing that's civil, speak: if savage,
Take, or lend. Ho! No answer? Then I'll enter.
Best draw my sword; and if mine enemy   25
But fear the sword like me, he'll scarcely look on't.
Such a foe, good heavens!   [*Exit, to the cave.*

---

11. *trial*] test of faith or virtue.

Yes; no] F semi-colon disposes of Hanmer's 'yet no', which is otherwise convincing.

12. *To lapse in fulness*] to lie when prosperous.

13. *Is sorer*] 'Is a *greater* or *heavier* crime' (Johnson).

16. *even before*] only a moment ago.

17. *for food*] for lack of food. Cf. *AYL.*, II. vii. 104.

23–4. *If . . . lend*] Several emendations have been proposed but none is required. Dowden's suggestion that 'or' means 'ere', of which it was a

variant form, entails what is practically a grammatical impossibility. Imogen anticipates speech from civil (i.e. civilized) people; action from savage. If savage, she asks them either to take her life (or her purse) or to give her food (or possibly aid). 'Lend', in Shakespeare and elsewhere, often means simply 'give', and if we take it as applying to assistance in general rather than to food in particular, we may note that 'to lend aid' is still a rather more common idiom than 'to give aid'.

SCENE VII.—*The same.*

Enter BELARIUS, GUIDERIUS, *and* ARVIRAGUS.

Bel. You, Polydore, have prov'd best woodman, and
Are master of the feast: Cadwal and I
Will play the cook and servant, 'tis our match:
The sweat and industry would dry and die,
But for the end it works to. Come, our stomachs   5
Will make what's homely savoury: weariness
Can snore upon the flint, when resty sloth
Finds the down-pillow hard. Now peace be here,
Poor house, that keep'st thyself!
Gui.   I am throughly weary.
Arv. I am weak with toil, yet strong in appetite.   10
Gui. There is cold meat i' th' cave, we'll browse on that,
Whilst what we have kill'd be cook'd.
Bel.   [*Looking into the cave*] Stay, come not in:

Scene VII

12. S.D.] *Dyce.*

All editors except Capell disregard
the scene division marked in the
Folios, but the indication of a fresh
scene at this point seems to me to have
a certain subtlety which is worth pre-
serving, even if it is not logically
defensible. When Imogen enters the
cave, the stage is left clear, and this is,
perhaps, sufficient justification for the
marking of a new scene. In any case,
the break directs our attention back
from the inner-stage and cave to the
main-stage where the action of what F
terms 'Scena Septima' clearly takes
place.

   1. *woodman*] hunter.

   3. *match*] agreement.

   7. *resty*] *O.E.D.* defines as 'Disin-
clined for action or exertion; sluggish;
indolent, lazy'.

   9. *that keep'st thyself*] Belarius obviously means that the cave is unoccu-
pied at the moment—though in fact is
is not. For the idiom, cf. *AYL.*, IV. iii.
82–3: 'But at this hour the house doth
keep itself; / There's none within.'

   I am throughly weary] There is a
parallel between the tiredness of the
Princes and Imogen's lassitude, and
this is apparently deliberate. Weariness tends to heighten dramatic and
poetic effect, and to enhance the unreal, idyllic atmosphere of the scene.
This kind of effect, though it is more
easily felt than explained, is one which
Shakespeare controls with palpable
success. The weariness of Macbeth,
Cleopatra, Coriolanus, with the
heightened tension which is thereby
produced, sticks in the memory.

   11. *browse*] *O.E.D.* comments that
the word properly signifies the crop-
ping of scanty vegetation, and is
used of goats, deer, and cattle. Furness remarks that, if used figuratively, the effect in Shakespeare's day
must have seemed ludicrous. But the
animal associations may well be
foremost in Guiderius' mind. The
Princes tend to think of themselves
as little better than beasts. Cf. III. iii.
39–44.

But that it eats our victuals, I should think
Here were a fairy.
Gui.   What's the matter, sir?
Bel. By Jupiter, an angel! or, if not,   15
An earthly paragon! Behold divineness
No elder than a boy!

Enter IMOGEN.

Imo. Good masters, harm me not:
Before I enter'd here, I call'd, and thought   19
To have begg'd or bought what I have took: good troth,
I have stol'n nought, nor would not, though I had found
Gold strew'd i' th' floor. Here's money for my meat,
I would have left it on the board, so soon
As I had made my meal; and parted
With pray'rs for the provider.
Gui.   Money, youth?   25
Arv. All gold and silver rather turn to dirt,
As 'tis no better reckon'd, but of those
Who worship dirty gods.
Imo.   I see you're angry:
Know, if you kill me for my fault, I should
Have died had I not made it.
Bel.   Whither bound?   30
Imo. To Milford-Haven.

18. masters] *F; master F2.*   30. Whither] *F4; Whether F.*

14. *fairy*] F 'Faiery'. I am inclined to
interpret as an abstract noun signifying enchantment, illusion. To liken
Imogen to one of the little folk in one
breath and to an angel in the next
seems odd, though the one term may
correct the other. Moreover, fairies did
eat victuals and the putting out of food
for them occurs in many bodies of
fairy lore. Hence, if the noun is here a
common one, Belarius runs counter to
popular belief.

22. *i'*] 'in' for 'on'. Boswell compares
'Thy Will be done in earth.' The
implied image may, however, be of
gold strewed *in the rushes* on the
floor.

24. *parted*] To eke out the metre
Pope reads 'parted thence' and Capell
'parted so'. Granville-Barker's suggestion that the line has 'an apologetic
hiatus' is altogether more acceptable.

25–8. *Money . . . gods*] The Princes'
attitude to money merits comparison
with that of Cloten at II. iii. 66 ff. as
pointing the contrast between virtuous
and graceless man. Arviragus' views
are literally Utopian, for More writes
of the inhabitants of his ideal common-
wealth: 'In the meane time golde and
sylver, whereof money is made, they
do so use, as none of them doeth more
esteme it, then the very nature of the
thing deserveth.'

Bel. What's your name?

Imo. Fidele, sir: I have a kinsman who
   Is bound for Italy; he embark'd at Milford;
   To whom being going, almost spent with hunger, 35
   I am fall'n in this offence.

Bel.   Prithee, fair youth,
   Think us no churls: nor measure our good minds
   By this rude place we live in. Well encounter'd!
   'Tis almost night, you shall have better cheer
   Ere you depart; and thanks to stay and eat it: 40
   Boys, bid him welcome.

Gui.   Were you a woman, youth,
   I should woo hard, but be your groom in honesty:
   I bid for you as I do buy.

Arv.   I'll make't my comfort

---

42. groom in honesty:] *F;* groom. In honesty, *Camb.;* groom.—In honesty
Tyrwhitt conj.

33. *Fidele*] Since Johnson trounces 'the confusion of the names, and manners of different times' in *Cym.*, it is worthy of note that Imogen here chooses a French name, and that she later makes similar choice (Richard du Champ) for her supposed dead master.

34. *he embark'd*] Hanmer emends to 'he embarques' and Vaughan proposes 'here embark'd'. Thiselton interprets F as 'he was to embark'. It is, however, questionable whether we have any right to expect a clear statement from Imogen at this point. She is distressed, afraid, and, as the broken sentences show, utterly weary. Moreover she would not be likely to disclose the whereabouts of Posthumus to a group of cave-dwellers of whose intentions she is not yet sure.

36. *in*] into.

41–3. *Were you . . . buy*] These difficult lines have been variously emended and interpreted. Abbott detects confusion of two constructions in 'I should woo hard, but be etc.': (i) if I could not be your groom otherwise; (ii) but in any case I would be your groom. Furness offers the attractive suggestion

that *to* is absorbed in the final *t* of 'but' and paraphrases: 'I should woo hard but to be your groom in all honesty.' 'In honesty' may mean 'in honourable wedlock' or simply 'in truth', 'indeed', but I am inclined to think that 'your groom in honesty' means your bridegroom and also your *match* or *fellow* in honesty. The phrase as it stands is too vague to admit close definition. Some editors follow Tyrwhitt in placing a full-stop after 'groom', thus connecting 'in honesty' with l. 43. Tyrwhitt also changes F 'I do buy' to 'I'd buy'. Other readings are: 'I would buy' (Hanmer); 'I'd bid . . . I'd buy' (Johnson). Dowden suggests that the first 'I' of l. 43 is perhaps an error caught from the preceding line, and proposes 'Bid for you as I'd buy', the force of 'I should' running on to the word 'Bid'. This diagnosis of error may well be correct, but does not justify any departure from F 'I do'. It does, however, suggest that the preceding 'I' may have supplanted another word— namely 'And'. l. 43 seems to me to mean that Guiderius would bid for Imogen on equal, honest terms.

43–6. *I'll make 't . . . yours*] Nicholson

He is a man, I'll love him as my brother:
And such a welcome as I'ld give to him   45
(After long absence) such is yours. Most welcome!
Be sprightly, for you fall 'mongst friends.
Imo.   'Mongst friends?
If brothers: [*Aside*] would it had been so, that they
Had been my father's sons, then had my prize
Been less, and so more equal ballasting   50
To thee, Posthumus.
Bel.   He wrings at some distress.
Gui. Would I could free't!
Arv.   Or I, whate'er it be,
What pain it cost, what danger! Gods!
Bel.   Hark, boys.
                                          [*Whispering.*

Imo. Great men,
    That had a court no bigger than this cave,   55

48. *Aside*] *Theobald.*   53. *Whispering*] *Rowe.*

supposes that these lines are spoken
partly as soliloquy, partly generally,
and finally are addressed directly to
Imogen. Vaughan proposes to read
'I love' for 'I'll love' and takes it that
ll. 44–6, following an aside, are
addressed to Imogen, so that 'I love
him' means 'I love Guiderius'. This is
strained. I cannot guess at Shakespeare's intentions, but the most effective way of presenting this speech to
my mind is for Arviragus to address
himself first to Belarius and to turn to
Imogen at l. 45 or 46.

47–8. *'Mongst friends? If brothers*] All
editors have dispensed with F's interrogation mark, but Furness offers
cogent defence: 'Is it not conceivable
that Imogen, still doubting, repeats
Arviragus' last words questioningly?'
A less bewildered person than Imogen
would naturally express at least mild
surprise on learning that mere cave-
dwellers, however much their looks
might belie their station, have friendly
intentions. It is probable that 'If
brothers' is the beginning of an un-
completed sentence. It does not seem

to have any connection with ''Mongst
friends?' unless Imogen means to
imply, with a whimsical quibble that
is not uncharacteristic, that they are
friends so long as they regard her as a
brother, but would become enemies if
they knew that she was a woman.

49. *prize*] Hanmer reads 'price'
(Theobald's conjecture) and emends
'ballasting' to 'balancing'. Theobald
conjectures 'poize' and Vaughan
'peize'. No change seems called for.
F 'prize' puns on two meanings:
(i) value, worth; (ii) the capture of a
ship (hence 'ballasting' in l. 50).

51. *wrings*] *O.E.D.* 'wring' vb 19b.
'to twist, turn, or struggle in pain or
anguish: to writhe'.

54–9. *Great men . . . twain*] The
general sense is that the greatest and
noblest of men, if transferred to an
environment as restricted as this,
would prove to be no nobler than
these two. I would paraphrase 'laying
by / That nothing-gift of differing
multitudes': renouncing the worthless
plaudits of the fickle multitude (which
exaggerate the true extent of their

That did attend themselves, and had the virtue
Which their own conscience seal'd them, laying by
That nothing-gift of differing multitudes,
Could not out-peer these twain. Pardon me, gods!
I'ld change my sex to be companion with them,   60
Since Leonatus false.

Bel.   It shall be so:
Boys, we'll go dress our hunt. Fair youth, come in;
Discourse is heavy, fasting: when we have supp'd
We'll mannerly demand thee of thy story,
So far as thou wilt speak it.

Gui.   Pray, draw near.   65
Arv. The night to th' owl and morn to th' lark less welcome.
Imo. Thanks, sir.
Arv. I pray, draw near.   [*Exeunt.*

SCENE VIII.—*Rome. A Public Place.*

Enter two Senators and Tribunes.

First Sen. This is the tenour of the emperor's writ;
    That since the common men are now in action

57. them, laying] *Hanmer;* them: laying *F.*   59. out-peer] *F;* out-peece *F2.*
62. Fair youth] *F;* Faire you *F2.*

S.D. *Rome*] *Rowe.*   *A Public Place*] *Dyce.*

virtue, which only their consciences can establish). The phrase admits other interpretations, and perhaps Dr Harold Brooks is right in suggesting that 'differing multitudes' may simply refer to the difference in the numbers of attendants.

59. *out-peer*] surpass.

61. *Leonatus false*] Malone explains as equivalent to 'Leonatus is false', which Rowe reads. Other proposals are: 'Leonatus's false' (Rowe ed. 1); 'Leonatus' false' (Walker); 'Leonate is' (Capell). The Variorum editors print 'Leonatus false—' but this has an embarrassing touch of the King

Cambyses vein. If the line is interrupted as they suppose, the requisite reading is 'Leonatus, false—'.

62. *hunt*] game, quarry.

Scene VIII

Pope and Hanmer dispense with this scene. Eccles transfers it to follow II. iv, in order to make it conform with the time sequence and order of events. Daniel, too thinks that it should belong to the earlier part of the play. There is some force in this, though *Cym.* is not a play which lends itself kindly to time-analysis. In its present setting the scene is, as Granville-Barker points

'Gainst the Pannonians and Dalmatians,
And that the legions now in Gallia are
Full weak to undertake our wars against　　　　5
The fall'n-off Britons, that we do incite
The gentry to this business. He creates
Lucius proconsul: and to you the tribunes,
For this immediate levy, he commands
His absolute commission. Long live Cæsar!　　　　10
First Tri.　Is Lucius general of the forces?
Sec. Sen.　　　　　　　　　　　　Ay.
First Tri.　Remaining now in Gallia?
First Sen.　　　　　　　　　　With those legions
Which I have spoke of, whereunto your levy
Must be supplyant: the words of your commission
Will tie you to the numbers and the time　　　　15
Of their despatch.
First Tri.　　　　　We will discharge our duty.　[*Exeunt.*

11, 12, 16. *First Tri.*] *Dyce; Tri. F.*　　14. supplyant] *Capell;* suppliant *F.*

---

out, an anti-climax. It can be argued that it has a twofold dramatic function in that it prevents the Roman invasion from lapsing for too long a period and also conveys the passing of time between Imogen's arrival at the cave and the subsequent action in IV. ii, but it is questionable whether this can override the foregoing objections. It is conceivable that this scene was an inconsequential after-thought dictated by stage requirements, that it was supplied in the form of a foul paper and inserted, rightly or wrongly, at this point. If so, it may be the work of someone other than Shakespeare. Its quality is certainly not such as to place it wholly above suspicion.

6. *fall'n-off*] revolted.

9. *commands*] Most editors read 'commends', which is, of course, the meaning, but the orthography of F can justifiably be retained. The primary sense of Latin 'mandare' is 'to give into a person's hands' and this meaning survived throughout the M.E. period. The examples of 'command' meaning 'commend' given in *O.E.D.* date from 1340 to 1500, but the spelling evidently survived longer than that. In *Ralph Roister-Doister*, printed *c.* 1567, I find: 'She dothe very well, sir, and commaunde me to you' (I. iii. 126–9). J. C. Maxwell cites an example from Middleton's *Your Fine Gallants*, I. ii. 15.

14. *supplyant*] F 'suppliant'. Capell's alteration clarifies the meaning.

ACT IV

SCENE I.—*Wales.*

Enter CLOTEN *alone.*

Clo. I am near to th' place where they should meet, if
Pisanio have mapp'd it truly. How fit his garments
serve me! Why should his mistress who was made by
him that made the tailor, not be fit too? The rather
(saving reverence of the word) for 'tis said a woman's 5
fitness comes by fits. Therein I must play the work-
man, I dare speak it to myself, for it is not vain-glory
for a man and his glass to confer in his own chamber;
I mean, the lines of my body are as well drawn as his;
no less young, more strong, not beneath him in for- 10
tunes, beyond him in the advantage of the time,
above him in birth, alike conversant in general services, and more remarkable in single oppositions;

ACT IV

Scene 1

S.D. *Wales*] *Camb.*   3. me!] *Rowe;* me? *F.*

5. *saving reverence*] Cloten apologizes
for the indecency of his puns.

6. *fitness*] sexual inclination.

9. *I mean*] Johnson and Capell make
this the end of a parenthesis which
begins at 'for it is'. I take it to be a vul-
garism equivalent to 'what I mean to
say is etc.' The punctuation of this
speech has been so variously handled
by editors that even Furness is unable
to present a full collation. Departure
from F is not really necessary. Cloten
is so much a fool positive that what he
does mean need really have very little
meaning.

10–11. *fortunes*] Furness thinks that
the plural form hints at 'opportunities
or chances of future good luck'.

11. *advantage of the time*] usually
explained as social opportunities, but
if Furness's interpretation of 'fortunes'
is correct, this phrase could well signify
present status as compared with
future opportunities.

12–13. *general services*] Eccles takes
these to be services performed on the
battlefield.

13. *single oppositions*] single combats,
duels. Capell compares *1H4*, I. iii.
99.

116

yet this imperseverant thing loves him in my despite.
What mortality is! Posthumus, thy head (which now   15
is growing upon thy shoulders) shall within this hour
be off, thy mistress enforced, thy garments cut to
pieces before thy face: and all this done, spurn
her home to her father, who may (haply) be a little
angry for my so rough usage: but my mother, having   20
power of his testiness, shall turn all into my com-
mendations. My horse is tied up safe, out, sword, and
to a sore purpose! Fortune, put them into my hand!
This is the very description of their meeting-place,
and the fellow dares not deceive me.   [*Exit.*   25

SCENE II.—*Before the Cave of Belarius.*

Enter BELARIUS, GUIDERIUS, ARVIRAGUS, *and* IMOGEN
from the cave.

Bel. [*To Imogen*] You are not well: remain here in the cave,
    We'll come to you after hunting.
Arv.   [*To Imogen*] Brother, stay here:
    Are we not brothers?
Imo.   So man and man should be;

15. is!] *Rowe;* is? *F.*   23. Fortune, put ... hand!] *Hanmer;* Fortune put ...
hand: *F.*

14. *imperseverant*] This word has
given rise to much discussion which
was silenced for a time by Dyce's
emendation 'imperceiverant'. Dyce
takes the word to mean lacking in
power to perceive, hence undiscern-
ing, undiscriminating. Both form and
meaning are, however, suspect. The
only other recorded instance of
'imperseverant' is in one of Lancelot
Andrewes's sermons, but there it
means unenduring, which can scarcely
be its meaning in *Cym.* Furness, following Steevens, claims that the prefix is
intensive, not negative, and quotes a
formidable list of *im-* and *em-* prefixes
used by Shakespeare in this way.
Imperseverant would thus mean ex-

ceedingly perseverant, i.e. stubborn,
obstinate. It is yet possible that Dyce's
interpretation is the right one, but
Furness's demonstration fully justifies
the retention of the F reading—
at least in the present state of knowledge.

18. *thy face*] Several editors accept
Warburton's emendation 'her face',
but Malone relates the F reading to
Cloten's imbecility and justly observes that 'Shakespeare, who in *The
Winter's Tale*, makes a Clown say, "If
thou'lt see a thing to talk on after thou
art dead", would not scruple to give
the expression in the text to so fantastic a character as Cloten.'

21. *power of*] control over.

But clay and clay differs in dignity,
Whose dust is both alike. I am very sick.   5
Gui. Go you to hunting, I'll abide with him.
Imo. So sick I am not, yet I am not well:
But not so citizen a wanton as
To seem to die ere sick: so please you, leave me,
Stick to your journal course: the breach of custom   10
Is breach of all. I am ill, but your being by me
Cannot amend me. Society is no comfort
To one not sociable: I am not very sick,
Since I can reason of it: pray you, trust me here,
I'll rob none but myself, and let me die,   15
Stealing so poorly.
Gui.   I love thee: I have spoke it,
How much the quantity, the weight as much,
As I do love my father.
Bel.   What? How? How?
Arv. If it be sin to say so, sir, I yoke me
In my good brother's fault: I know not why   20
I love this youth, and I have heard you say,
Love's reason's without reason. The bier at door,
And a demand who is't shall die, I'ld say
'My father, not this youth.'
Bel.   [*Aside*] O noble strain!

24. *Aside*] *Capell.*

4–5. *But clay . . . alike*] 'But' here
may have the force of 'unless', though
such an interpretation is rather at odds
with Shakespeare's notion of degree.
Deighton takes 'dust' to signify the
ashes of death, but Furness suggests
that the word is used in its Biblical
sense ('dust thou art and unto dust
shall thou return'). Cf., however, IV.
ii. 246–9.

8. *So citizen a wanton*] such a namby-
pamby. 'Wanton' meant, among
other things, a spoilt child. 'Citizen', which *O.E.D.* glosses 'Citizen-
ish, city-bred', was strongly pejorative—more so than P.E. 'bourgeois'.
Shakespeare, like most of his fellow-
dramatists, contemned the citizen
class which was affected, puritan-

ical, and hostile to the theatres.

10. *journal*] daily.

10–11. *the breach . . . all*] an aspect of
Shakespeare's view of life concordant
with his doctrine of degree.

16–18. *I love . . . father*] 'As I read
this, the sentence runs: "I love thee (I
have spoke it) as I do love my
father." Line 17 I regard as paren-
thetic' (Dowden). This is a neat solution of an awkward problem, but it is
also possible that two constructions
have been confused: (i) I love thee and
I have said how much I do so; (ii) I
love thee with as great a quantity of
love as that with which I love my
father.

24. *noble strain*] 'Strain' here signifies inherited character, and not

O worthiness of nature! breed of greatness!   25
Cowards father cowards, and base things sire base;
Nature hath meal, and bran; contempt, and grace.
I'm not their father, yet who this should be,
Doth miracle itself, lov'd before me.—
'Tis the ninth hour o' th' morn.
Arv.   Brother, farewell.   30
Imo. I wish ye sport.
Arv.   You health.—So please you, sir.
Imo. [*Aside*] These are kind creatures. Gods, what lies
    I have heard!
Our courtiers say all's savage but at court;
Experience, O, thou disprov'st report!
Th' emperious seas breed monsters; for the dish   35
Poor tributary rivers as sweet fish:
I am sick still, heart-sick; Pisanio,
I'll now taste of thy drug.
Gui.   I could not stir him:
He said he was gentle, but unfortunate;
Dishonestly afflicted, but yet honest.   40
Arv. Thus did he answer me: yet said, hereafter
    I might know more.

32. *Aside*] *Johnson.*   35. breed] breeds *F.*

impulse or feeling, as Schmidt supposes. Cf. *Lr.*, v. iii. 40: 'Sir, you have
shown today your noble strain.'

26–7. *Cowards . . . grace*] F prints
these lines with quotation-marks to
indicate that they are sententiae or
common saws. Walker traces them to
Horace, IV, Ode iv. 29: 'Fortes
creantur fortibus et bonis. / Est in
juvencis, est in equis patrum Virtus.'
Pope and Hanmer apparently, and
Furness emphatically, deny them to
Shakespeare, but they cannot be
lightly rejected since they follow a
pattern which Shakespeare employs
in *Ven.*, 167–8: 'Seeds spring from
seeds and beauty breedeth beauty; /
Thou wast begot; to get it is thy
duty.'

29. *miracle*] Since the word is not

capitalized in F it is probably a verb
meaning shows itself miraculous.

34–6. *Experience . . . fish*] Pope and
Hanmer relegate to the margin and
Furness rejects. It is hard to believe
that Shakespeare penned the ill phrase
'for the dish', but the sea-monster
image is characteristically his, as
memorable passages in the great
tragedies, especially *Lr.*, show. 'Emperious' means imperial and is in contrast to 'tributary'. I take ll. 35–6 to
mean: poor tributary rivers breed fish
as sweet as those in the emperious seas,
and have the additional virtue of not
breeding monsters.

38. *I'll now . . . drug*] Imogen
swallows the drug at this point.
    stir him] move him to tell his story.
39. *gentle*] well-born, noble.

Bel.   To th' field, to th' field!
We'll leave you for this time, go in, and rest.
Arv. We'll not be long away.
Bel.   Pray be not sick,
For you must be our housewife.
Imo.   Well, or ill,   45
I am bound to you.
Bel.   And shalt be ever.
                    [*Exit Imogen, to the cave.*
This youth, howe'er distress'd, appears he hath had
Good ancestors.
Arv.   How angel-like he sings!
Gui. But his neat cookery! he cut our roots in characters,
And sauced our broths, as Juno had been sick,   50
And he her dieter.
Arv.   Nobly he yokes
A smiling with a sigh; as if the sigh
Was that it was, for not being such a smile;
The smile mocking the sigh, that it would fly
From so divine a temple, to commix   55
With winds that sailors rail at.
Gui.   I do note

46. S.D.] *Capell; after* you *F.*   49.] *two lines ending* Cookerie? / Characters
F.   49–51. he cut . . . dieter] *given to Arviragus in F.*   50. sauced] sawc'st *F;*
sawc't *F2.*

46. *bound*] Imogen means indebted. Belarius puns on the word, giving it the meaning linked, bound in affection.

47. *appears*] Knight reads 'he appears' and Craig proposes ''t appears'. Abbott thinks that the phrase may confuse two constructions: (i) he hath had, (it) appears, good ancestors; (ii) he appears to have had. His alternative suggestion, that 'appear' may sometimes have been used as an active verb, receives no support from *O.E.D.* but is not impossible. What the sense requires is a verb signifying reveals, makes apparent, and I would tentatively suggest the reading 'approves'. Cf. iv. ii. 380 and v. v. 245.

49–51. *But . . . dieter*] Capell makes a certain correction in giving the whole of this speech to Guiderius. Characters are letters or emblems (cf. iii. ii. 28); and dieter signifies the regulator of her diet. W. H. Clemen (*op. cit.*) notes the implied contrast between Arviragus, who thinks of Imogen's singing, and Guiderius who, more practically, thinks of her cookery.

52–6. *as if . . . rail at*] printed marginally by Pope and Hanmer and rejected by Furness. There is a pretty play of imagery here which is quite in harmony with Arviragus' character, and I see no reason for doubting the authenticity of these lines. The temple image is current in *Cym.* and the storm image is characteristic of Shakespeare's final period as a whole.

That grief and patience, rooted in them both,
Mingle their spurs together.
Arv.   Grow, patience!
And let the stinking-elder, grief, untwine
His perishing root, with the increasing vine!   60
Bel. It is great morning. Come, away!—who's there?

Enter CLOTEN.

Clo. I cannot find those runagates, that villain
Hath mock'd me. I am faint.
Bel.   'Those runagates!'
Means he not us? I partly know him, 'tis
Cloten, the son o' th' queen. I fear some ambush: 65
I saw him not these many years, and yet
I know 'tis he: we are held as outlaws: hence!
Gui. He is but one: you, and my brother search
What companies are near: pray you, away,
Let me alone with him.   [*Exeunt Belarius and Arviragus.*
Clo.   Soft, what are you   70
That fly me thus? Some villain mountaineers?
I have heard of such. What slave art thou?
Gui.   A thing
More slavish did I ne'er than answering
A slave without a knock.

58. Grow, patience!] *Theobald;* Grow patient, *F.*   61. Come, away!—]
Camb.; Come away: *F.*   70. S.D.] *Rowe.*

57. *them*] i.e., as Hunter explains, the smile and the sigh, in both of which grief and patience are rooted. Pope emends to 'him' which many editors uncritically accept.

58. *spurs*] principal roots. Cf. *Tp.*, v. i. 47–8: 'and by the spurs pluck'd up / The pine and cedar'.

58–60. *Grow . . . vine*] gibbeted by Pope and Hanmer and rejected by Furness.

59. *stinking-elder*] I have retained F hyphen. *O.E.D.* gives no instance of 'stinking-elder' but quotes numerous examples of similar botanical collocations, several of which appear in Gerard's *Herbal,* 1597.

59–60. *untwine . . . vine*] 'The meaning is With the increase of the vine, or as the vine increases, let the elder untwist his perishing root. The word "with" is not to be connected with "untwine"' (Dowden). Emendation is unnecessary. 'Perishing' means destructive.

61. *great morning*] broad daylight.

69. *companies*] Walker conjectures 'company is' but the plural form is not exceptional. The word signifies followers, retainers. The Elizabethans do not always distinguish clearly between 'company' and 'companion'.

74. *A slave*] This word, like 'churl' and 'peasant', was a common term of

Clo.   Thou art a robber,
   A law-breaker, a villain: yield thee, thief.   75
Gui. To who? to thee? What art thou? Have not I
   An arm as big as thine? a heart as big?
   Thy words I grant are bigger: for I wear not
   My dagger in my mouth. Say what thou art:
   Why I should yield to thee.
Clo.   Thou villain base,   80
   Know'st me not by my clothes?
Gui.   No, nor thy tailor, rascal,
   Who is thy grandfather: he made those clothes,
   Which (as it seems) make thee.
Clo.   Thou precious varlet,
   My tailor made them not.
Gui.   Hence then, and thank
   The man that gave them thee. Thou art some fool,   85
   I am loath to beat thee.
Clo.   Thou injurious thief,
   Hear but my name, and tremble.
Gui.   What's thy name?
Clo. Cloten, thou villain.
Gui. Cloten, thou double villain, be thy name,
   I cannot tremble at it, were it Toad, or Adder, Spider,
   'Twould move me sooner.

80. thee.] thee? *F*.   82. grandfather:] *F2;* Grandfather? *F*.

abuse. Mason's suggestion that the
two words should be italicized, as
being a mere repetition of Cloten's
'slave' in l. 72, is wholly fanciful.

76–9. *Have not . . . mouth*] Cloten is
challenged in terms similar to those in
which he himself challenged Rome at
III. i. 35–47.

81. *clothes*] Cloten is so foolish that
he has doubtless forgotten that they
are not his clothes but Posthumus'.
Some commentators think that Shakespeare was guilty of an oversight, but
the point is an academic one. Cloten
may, after all, simply mean: do not
my clothes tell you that I am from the
Court? There is no reason for supposing that he is clad in Posthumus'
'meanest garment'.

84. *My tailor*] 'My' is emphatic.

89. *Cloten . . . villain*] 'Does Guiderius
jestingly take "Cloten, thou villain" as
the name, and improve on it by his
"Cloten, thou double villain?" Or is
"thou double villain" only a retort for
"thou villain"?' (Dowden).

90. *Toad . . . Spider*] This dubious
line has been variously emended:
'toad, adder, spider' (Pope); 'Toad,
Adder or spider it would' (Hanmer).
Capell omits 'or Adder, Spider' altogether. Dowden ingeniously but unconvincingly suggests, 'Toad, or atter-
spider'. It might be argued that the
compositor's eye caught the *ad* of
'Toad', that he then set up 'Adder' in
mistake for 'Spider', and finally
covered his tracks by tacking 'Spider'

Clo.   To thy further fear,   91
  Nay, to thy mere confusion, thou shalt know
  I am son to th' queen.
Gui.   I am sorry for't: not seeming
  So worthy as thy birth.
Clo.   Art not afeard?
Gui. Those that I reverence, those I fear: the wise: 95
  At fools I laugh: not fear them.
Clo.   Die the death:
  When I have slain thee with my proper hand,
  I'll follow those that even now fled hence:
  And on the gates of Lud's town set your heads:
  Yield, rustic mountaineer.   [*Exeunt, fighting.*   100

Re-enter BELARIUS *and* ARVIRAGUS.

Bel. No company's abroad?
Arv. None in the world: you did mistake him sure.
Bel. I cannot tell: long is it since I saw him,
  But time hath nothing blurr'd those lines of favour
  Which then he wore: the snatches in his voice,   105
  And burst of speaking were as his: I am absolute

100. *Re-enter*] Capell; *Enter F.*

on to the end of the line, but the 'toad–
adder–spider' triplet is found elsewhere in Shakespeare, and is presumably correct in *Cym.* The possibility that 'Spider' is a direct term of
abuse (were it Toad, or Adder, thou
mere Spider) may be noted. Similar
terms of abuse are common in Jonson's *Volpone* which was a recent play.
The simplest and most satisfactory
explanation, however, is that Guiderius means: Were your name Toad,
or Adder, or even Spider (i.e. the
smallest and meanest of poisonous
creatures).

92. *mere*] absolute, complete.
97. *proper*] own.
99. *And . . . heads*] The heads of
traitors were impaled and exhibited on
London Bridge in Shakespeare's day.
100. S.D. Re-enter . . . Arviragus]
Pope begins a new scene here and is

followed by Warburton, Hanmer, and
Johnson. The probability is, however,
that Belarius and Arviragus entered at
one door as Guiderius and Cloten
went out through the other, so that the
alleged 'cleared stage' was more
apparent than real.
103. *I cannot tell*] Vaughan objects
that this contradicts what follows and
emends the punctuation. But the contradiction is a very natural and human
one. ('I wonder whether I am right.
Yes, I am sure I am.')
104. *lines of favour*] lineaments of his
countenance. *O.E.D.* cites a Stafford-
shire use of 'favour' in the sense of
family likeness, which might suit the
present context.
105. *snatches*] *O.E.D.* glosses 'A
catch, check, or hesitancy' and quotes
this line.
106. *absolute*] certain.

'Twas very Cloten.

Arv.   In this place we left them;
I wish my brother make good time with him,
You say he is so fell.

Bel.   Being scarce made up,
I mean, to man, he had not apprehension   110
Of roaring terrors: for defect of judgement
Is oft the cause of fear. But see, thy brother.

Re-enter GUIDERIUS *with Cloten's head.*

Gui. This Cloten was a fool, an empty purse,
There was no money in't: not Hercules
Could have knock'd out his brains, for he had none: 115
Yet I not doing this, the fool had borne
My head, as I do his.

Bel.   What hast thou done?

Gui. I am perfect what: cut off one Cloten's head,
Son to the queen (after his own report),
Who call'd me traitor, mountaineer, and swore,   120

112. see, thy] *Theobald;* see thy *F.*   *Re-enter . . . head*] *Capell; Enter Guiderius*
(*after* fear) *F.*

109–10. *Being . . . man*] Several commentators explain as 'being little more
than an idiot' but this would necessi-
tate 'has', and not 'had' in l. 110.
Belarius' qualifying phrase, 'I mean,
to man,' must surely establish the
meaning as 'being yet a boy, or youth'.
'Man' here I take to be manhood, cf.
v. iv. 52: 'When once he was mature
for man'.

111–12. *for defect . . . fear*] There are
numerous emendations of these difficult lines. Theobald's change of
'defect' to 'th' effect' has won fairly
wide acceptance and is superior to
'act of' (Crosby) and 'reflex of'
(Bulloch). Other proposals involve the
alteration of 'cause': 'cure' (Hanmer);
'cease' (Herr); 'salve' (Cartwright);
'loss' (Nicholson). Knight quotes with
approval the reading 'As oft' (for 'Is
oft'), explaining: on account of defect
of judgement, which defect is often the
cause of fear. Thiselton's paraphrase is

neat but strained: 'You may expect
him to be "fell", for at an age when
lack of judgement, springing from in-
experience, usually gives rise, in the
presence of "roaring terrors", to fear
which further experience shows to be
unjustified, he was absolutely un-
affected by them.' It is quite possible
that we should read 'fear—' on the
assumption that the rather sensational
entry of Guiderius puts a sudden end
to one of Belarius' customary moral
discourses.

114. *not Hercules*] Guiderius refers
not to the strength of Hercules but to
the seemingly impossible tasks which
were imposed upon him.

120. *traitor, mountaineer*] Staunton
proposes 'traitor-mountaineer', but
the term actually used by Cloten was
'villaine mountaineers' (F 'villaine-
Mountainers'). 'Mountaineer' was
evidently intended as a term of abuse
and so received. Probably it was equi-

With his own single hand he'ld take us in,
Displace our heads where (thank the gods!) they grow,
And set them on Lud's town.
Bel.   We are all undone.
Gui. Why, worthy father, what have we to lose,
But that he swore to take, our lives? The law   125
Protects not us, then why should we be tender,
To let an arrogant piece of flesh threat us,
Play judge, and executioner, all himself,
For we do fear the law? What company
Discover you abroad?
Bel.   No single soul   130
Can we set eye on; but in all safe reason
He must have some attendants. Though his honour
Was nothing but mutation, ay, and that
From one bad thing to worse, not frenzy, not
Absolute madness could so far have rav'd,   135
To bring him here alone: although perhaps
It may be heard at court that such as we
Cave here, hunt here, are outlaws, and in time
May make some stronger head, the which he hearing
(As it is like him) might break out, and swear   140
He'ld fetch us in, yet is't not probable

122. thank] *Steevens;* thanks *F;* thanks to *F3.*   127. us,] vs? *F.*   128–9. himself, . . . the law?] *Johnson;* himselfe? . . . the Law. *F;* himselfe? . . . no Law. *F2.*

valent to bandit. Cf. 'mountain-foreigner' (*Wiv.*, I. i. 164) and 'mountain-squire' (*H5*, v. i. 37).

129. *For . . . law*] The law does not protect us: then why should we be tender . . . simply because we fear the law? F2 emends 'the law' to 'no law', a change which, though superficially convincing, detracts from the effectiveness of Guiderius' argument.

132. *honour*] F 'Honor'. Theobald reads 'humour', which many editors accept, but humour, in the Jacobean (i.e. Jonsonian) sense, usually implies a fixed habit or ruling peculiarity, whereas Cloten is inconstant even in mutation. 'Honour' is not entirely

satisfactory, but I hesitate to change it since I find that in Chettle's *Hoffman*, 278–9, 'a witlesse foole', who like Cloten is a prince, is addressed as: 'thou vnshapen honor, my states shame, / My ages corsiue, and my blacke sinnes curse.' Ackermann proposes 'horror' in the Chettle passage, but 'honor', in contrast to 'shame', is clearly correct, though I do not understand its exact meaning. Thiselton explains 'his honour' as the title of a nobleman. I think that Belarius may mean Cloten's code or conception of honour—which is somewhat Falstaffian.

137. *It may be heard*] It may have been heard.

To come alone, either he so undertaking,
Or they so suffering: then on good ground we fear,
If we do fear this body hath a tail
More perilous than the head.

Arv.   Let ordinance   145
Come as the gods foresay it: howsoe'er,
My brother hath done well.

Bel.   I had no mind
To hunt this day: the boy Fidele's sickness
Did make my way long forth.

Gui.   With his own sword,
Which he did wave against my throat, I have ta'en   150
His head from him: I'll throw't into the creek
Behind our rock, and let it to the sea,
And tell the fishes he's the queen's son, Cloten,
That's all I reck.   [*Exit.*

Bel.   I fear 'twill be reveng'd:
Would, Polydore, thou hadst not done't: though valour
Becomes thee well enough.

Arv.   Would I had done't: 156
So the revenge alone pursued me! Polydore,
I love thee brotherly, but envy much
Thou hast robb'd me of this deed: I would revenges,
That possible strength might meet, would seek us
    through   160
And put us to our answer.

Bel.   Well, 'tis done:
We'll hunt no more to-day, nor seek for danger
Where there's no profit. I prithee, to our rock,
You and Fidele play the cooks: I'll stay
Till hasty Polydore return, and bring him   165
To dinner presently.

Arv.   Poor sick Fidele!

154. reck] *Pope;* reake *F.*

145. *ordinance*] that which is or-
dained by Fate.
146. *foresay*] *O.E.D.* gives 'to say
beforehand, foretell, predict', but
'determine' or 'will', as suggested by
Dowden, seems preferable here.

149. *Did . . . forth*] 'made my walk
forth from the cave tedious' (Johnson).
160. *possible strength*] the strength or
resources available to us.
seek us through] Vaughan proposes
'seek us three'.

I'll willingly to him; to gain his colour
I'ld let a parish of such Clotens blood,
And praise myself for charity.   [*Exit.*
Bel.   O thou goddess,
Thou divine Nature; thou thyself thou blazon'st   170
In these two princely boys: they are as gentle
As zephyrs blowing below the violet,
Not wagging his sweet head; and yet, as rough,
(Their royal blood enchaf'd) as the rud'st wind
That by the top doth take the mountain pine   175
And make him stoop to th' vale. 'Tis wonder
That an invisible instinct should frame them
To royalty unlearn'd, honour untaught,
Civility not seen from other, valour
That wildly grows in them, but yields a crop   180
As if it had been sow'd. Yet still it's strange
What Cloten's being here to us portends,
Or what his death will bring us.

Re-enter GUIDERIUS.

Gui.   Where's my brother?

167. *to gain his colour*] to restore the colour to his cheeks.

168. *I'ld . . . blood*] so F, but 'Cloten's' or 'Clotens'' are both possible readings. To let blood is a surgical term, here used figuratively in the sense 'slaughter'. To save Fidele, Arviragus would gladly slaughter a whole parish of Clotens. For similar use of the collective noun cf. v. v. 304 and Shylock's 'wilderness of monkeys.' (*Mer.V.*, III. i. 127–8).

169–83.] Idyllic poetry such as this abounds in the Romances. Some critics detect the dramatist's submission to the influence of Fletcher. Yet, paradoxically enough, Shakespeare, being least himself, is most himself. It is a far cry from this speech to Enobarbus' opulent description of Cleopatra in *Ant.*, II. ii, yet analysis of the two discloses common use of words and images. I note: (i) Nature; (ii)

gentle / delicate; (iii) violet / flower-soft; (iv) wind; (v) stoop / bend; (vi) wonder, strange / strange; (vii) invisible; (viii) frame.

170. *Thou . . . thou*] Pope alters 'thou thyself' to 'how thyself' and most editors follow his lead. F2: 'Nature; thy self' has won few supporters. Vaughan follows F but would punctuate, 'Thou, divine Nature thou, thyself thou blazon'st'. I have retained F unchanged. Editors have been unnecessarily suspicious. The line seems awkward, but if it read 'I myself I blazon' or 'he himself he blazons' it would present no difficulty. It is 'thou' which nowadays confounds us.

174. *enchaf'd*] heated, aroused, angry. Cf. *Troil.*, Prol. 2: 'The princes orgulous, their high blood chafed'.

177. *instinct*] accented on the second syllable.

I have sent Cloten's clotpoll down the stream,
In embassy to his mother; his body's hostage   185
For his return.   [*Solemn music.*
Bel.   My ingenious instrument
(Hark, Polydore) it sounds: but what occasion
Hath Cadwal now to give it motion? Hark!
Gui. Is he at home?
Bel.   He went hence even now.
Gui. What does he mean? Since death of my dear'st mother
It did not speak before. All solemn things   191
Should answer solemn accidents. The matter?
Triumphs for nothing, and lamenting toys,
Is jollity for apes, and grief for boys.
Is Cadwal mad?

Re-enter ARVIRAGUS *with* IMOGEN, *dead, bearing her
in his arms.*

Bel.   Look, here he comes,   195
And brings the dire occasion in his arms
Of what we blame him for!
Arv.   The bird is dead
That we have made so much on. I had rather

---

184. *clotpoll*] thick, wooden head.
Cf. *Troil.*, II. i. 128.

186. *My ingenious instrument*] 'ingenious' is Rowe's correction of F 'ingenu-
ous'. The two words were often confused. The adjective seems to imply
that the instrument was a mechanical
one. Such things existed in and before
Shakespeare's day. Henry VIII pos-
sessed 'a virginall that goethe with a
whele without playing vpon'. Whether
Shakespeare had in mind some such
instrument or, as Hunter claims, an
Æolian harp, need not concern us.
The significant point is that the device
allows him to employ a consort of
viols in a scene set in a remote part of
Wales. Truly an ingenious instrument!

193–5. *Triumphs . . . mad*] marginal

in Pope and Hanmer and rejected by
Furness.

193. *lamenting toys*] Dowden glosses
'lamentation for trifles'. 'Toys' may,
however, be used in its musical sense,
i.e. light compositions.

194. *apes*] *O.E.D.* defines as 'fools',
citing this passage. It may, however,
mean children—or even apes!

195. *Is Cadwal mad?*] The implication of ll. 190–2 is that the ingenious
instrument plays only elegiac music.
Guiderius evidently thinks that Arviragus has set it going because Cloten is
dead.

S.D. with Imogen, dead] so F. Capell
changes to 'as dead'. Since every
body, including the audience, should
believe that she *is* dead at this point,
F may be allowed to stand.

Have skipp'd from sixteen years of age to sixty:
To have turn'd my leaping time into a crutch,　　200
Than have seen this.

Gui.　　　　　　　O sweetest, fairest lily:
My brother wears thee not the one half so well
As when thou grew'st thyself.

Bel.　　　　　　　　　O melancholy,
Who ever yet could sound thy bottom, find
The ooze, to show what coast thy sluggish care　　205
Might'st easil'est harbour in? Thou blessed thing,
Jove knows what man thou mightst have made: but I,
Thou diedst a most rare boy, of melancholy.
How found you him?

Arv.　　　　　　　　Stark, as you see:
Thus smiling, as some fly had tickled slumber,　　210
Not as death's dart, being laugh'd at: his right cheek
Reposing on a cushion.

---

205. what] *F;* that *F2.*　　206. Might'st easil'est] *Capell;* Might'st easilest *F;*
Might easil'st *F2.*

199. *sixteen years*] Arviragus should
be twenty-two, *teste* I. i. 62 and III. iii.
69 and 101. The discrepancy should
not be taken too seriously. 'Sixteen'
and 'sixty' may be a quasi-proverbial
collocation.

200. *leaping time*] the symbol of sixteen, as the crutch is of sixty.

202. *the one half*] Rowe (ed. 3) reads
'one half'.

203–6. *O . . . harbour in*] 'Belarius'
thought is, how powerless the most
friendly well-wisher is to put one who
is suffering from Melancholy in the
way of getting rid of the clogging load
of care' (Thiselton). This seems to me
a judicious interpretation which avoids
any substantial alteration of F text.

204. *sound . . . find*] For 'thy' Eccles
proposes 'the'. Vaughan suggests
'round thy bottom find'. Staunton
would substitute 'fine' for 'find'.

205. *The ooze, to show*] 'Thy ooze'
(Hudson); 'The ooze? or show'
(Capell).

coast] 'shore' (Vaughan). An indefensible change.

care] 'carrack' (Theobald); 'crare'
(Sympson). Sympson's 'crare', i.e. a
small trading vessel, has been generally accepted and has the merit of
being an intelligible and pleasing
image.

206. *Might'st easil'est*] Many editors
substantially follow F2, but I take
'thou' understood (i.e. Melancholy)
to be the subject, in accordance with
Thiselton's interpretation. S. A. Tan-
nenbaum (*Shaksperian Scraps*, 1933,
p. 110) suggests that F 'easilest' is a
misreading of 'easieest', but the resultant 'Might'st easieest' is cacophonous.

207. *I*] I know. 'ah' (Rowe, ed. 3);
'aye' (Nicholson); 'ay' (Ingleby).

211. *Not as . . . laugh'd at*] Capell
perplexingly explains 'being laugh'd
at' as 'for I saw it laugh'd at'. Eccles
proposes 'been laugh'd at' and paraphrases: 'As if some fly had only
tickled slumber, not as if death's dart

Gui.   Where?
Arv.   O' th' floor;
His arms thus leagu'd, I thought he slept, and put
My clouted brogues from off my feet, whose rudeness
Answer'd my steps too loud.
Gui.   Why, he but sleeps: 215
If he be gone, he'll make his grave a bed:
With female fairies will his tomb be haunted,
And worms will not come to thee.
Arv.   With fairest flowers
Whilst summer lasts, and I live here, Fidele,
I'll sweeten thy sad grave: thou shalt not lack   220
The flower that's like thy face, pale primrose, nor
The azur'd harebell, like thy veins: no, nor
The leaf of eglantine, whom not to slander,
Out-sweet'ned not thy breath: the ruddock would
With charitable bill (O bill, sore shaming   225

had been laugh'd at.' Two alternative
explanations are possible: (i) as if it
were not death's dart (at which he had
laughed) which tickled slumber, but
some fly; (ii) as if some fly, being
laughed at, had tickled slumber in a
manner unlike that of death's dart.

214. *clouted brogues*] rough, heavy
shoes, studded with nails. 'Clouted'
also means 'patched'.

218. *to thee*] Guiderius, of course,
turns to address the dead Fidele. The
emendations: 'near him' (Hanmer),
'to him' (Rann), etc. are superfluous.

218–29.] Compare with the equally
beautiful lines spoken by Marina over
the grave of Thaisa in *Per.*, IV. i. 14–21.
For discussion of the imagery of both
passages see Armstrong, *op. cit.*, pp.
79 ff.

221. *pale primrose*] Armstrong (p. 80)
notes that 'by reason of its paleness the
primrose is a death-flower and therefore is incorporated in image clusters
in which death is a motif.' Cf. I. vi. 83,
where flowers are more balefully
associated with death.

222. *harebell*] not the harebell, but
the bluebell or wild hyacinth accord-

ing to Ellacombe (*Plant-lore in Shakespeare*).

223. *eglantine*] sweet briar.

whom] Pope reads 'which' and
Eccles conjectures 'who'. Abbott's
explanation, that the relative is
attracted to a subsequent implied
object, is adequate.

224. *ruddock*] F 'Raddocke': the
robin redbreast. Allusions to the
robin's office of covering the dead are
to be found in Drayton and Webster,
as well as in the tale of the 'Babes in the
Wood' which serves substantially as
one of the plot elements in Yarington's
Two Lamentable Tragedies (1601).

225–7. *O bill . . . monument*] Furness
rejects these lines on the grounds that
they are utterly irrelevant. This is no
argument. They embody one of
Shakespeare's audible grumbles which
finds expression in *Ado*, v. ii. 79–82:
'If a man do not erect in this age his
own tomb ere he dies, he shall live no
longer in monument than the bell
rings and the widow weeps', and in
Ham., III. ii. 138–43: 'O heavens! die
two months ago, and not forgotten
yet? Then there's hope a great man's

Those rich-left heirs, that let their fathers lie
Without a monument!) bring thee all this;
Yea, and furr'd moss besides. When flowers are none,
To winter-ground thy corse—
Gui.   Prithee, have done,
And do not play in wench-like words with that   230
Which is so serious. Let us bury him,
And not protract with admiration what
Is now due debt. To th' grave!
Arv.   Say, where shall's lay him?
Gui. By good Euriphile, our mother.
Arv.   Be't so:
And let us, Polydore, though now our voices   235
Have got the mannish crack, sing him to th' ground,
As once to our mother: use like note and words,
Save that Euriphile must be Fidele.

memory may outlive his life half a
year: but by'r lady, he must build
churches, then, or else shall he not
suffer thinking on.'

228. *besides. When*] Theobald's
emended punctuation, 'besides, when'
has proved as insidious as it is nonsensical. The ruddock could hardly
bring moss *in addition* to flowers when
there are no flowers!

229. *To winter-ground thy corse*—]
Guiderius' terse 'Prithee, have done'
shows that Arviragus' speech is interrupted. So does the long dash which F
prints after 'Coarse'. With this double
proof before us, we must rest content
with half-knowledge or resort to guess-
work. All the proposed emendations
may therefore be dismissed as conjectures, and sadly uninspired ones.
Steevens states that 'to "winter-
ground" a plant is to protect it from
the inclemency of the winter season by
straw, etc., laid over it.' This is harmless but lacks lexical authority. My
guess, for what little it is worth, is that
Arviragus was about to say: When
flowers are none, To winter-ground
thy corse shall be itself a flower—or
something of the kind. Cf. *Ham.*, v. i.

261–3: 'Lay her i' the earth: / And
from her fair and unpolluted flesh /
May violets spring.' The hyphen in
'winter-ground' may be an error due
to the frequency of hyphens throughout the speech.

230. *wench-like words*] Shakespeare
usually allots these floral passages to
women. Gertrude, Desdemona, Cordelia, Marina, and Perdita spring to
mind.

232. *admiration*] O.E.D. sb. 2
'wonder mingled with reverence,
esteem, approbation'.

236. *Have got . . . crack*] meaning, I
think, that their voices have broken,
not that they are breaking. Hence, no
proof that the 'sixteen' of l. 199 is to be
taken literally.

237. *As once to our mother*] Pope and
most subsequent editors omit 'to', but
F yields perfect sense—as once we sang
to our mother. See Appendix C,
p. 215.

238. *Save . . . Fidele*] usually taken to
mean: Save that we must substitute
the name 'Fidele' for 'Euriphile',
though neither name occurs in the
dirge. I suggest that 'use like note and
words' is virtually a parenthesis, and

Gui. Cadwal,
    I cannot sing: I'll weep, and word it with thee;   240
    For notes of sorrow out of tune are worse
    Than priests and fanes that lie.
Arv.   We'll speak it then.
Bel. Great griefs, I see, med'cine the less; for Cloten
    Is quite forgot. He was a queen's son, boys,
    And though he came our enemy, remember,   245
    He was paid for that: though mean and mighty, rotting
    Together, have one dust, yet reverence
    (That angel of the world) doth make distinction
    Of place 'tween high, and low. Our foe was princely,
    And though you took his life, as being our foe,   250
    Yet bury him, as a prince.
Gui.   Pray you, fetch him hither,
    Thersites' body is as good as Ajax',
    When neither are alive.
Arv.   If you'll go fetch him,
    We'll say our song the whilst.—Brother, begin.
                         [Exit Belarius.
Gui. Nay, Cadwal, we must lay his head to the east,   255
    My father hath a reason for't.
Arv.   'Tis true.

---

249. 'tween] *F;* twixt *F2.*   251. you] *F;* thee *F2.*   254. S.D.] *Capell.*

that the present line means: Save that
it must be Fidele, not Euriphile, to
whom we sing. The possibility that
'Fear no more the heat o' th' sun' replaced an earlier song which contained the name 'Fidele' cannot be
ignored though it lacks proof. The
substitution of 'Fidele' for 'Euriphile'
would doubtless involve difficulties,
both metrical and musical.

241–2. *For notes . . . lie*] Furness
regards as spurious.

248. *That angel . . . world*] ' "Reverence", or due regard to subordination,
is the power that keeps peace and
order in the world' (Johnson). It is
'that angel of the world' in the sense
that it directs man towards imitation
of the divine or heavenly pattern. Cf.
Troil., I. iii. 82–136.

251. *as a prince*] not 'as befits a
prince' but 'as being a prince'. Bishop
Wordsworth compares 2 *Kings* ix. 34:
'Go see now this cursed woman,
and bury her: for she is a king's
daughter.'

252. *Thersites' . . . Ajax*] The mean
and the mighty, though Shakespeare's
portrayal of Ajax in *Troilus and
Cressida* may suggest otherwise.

255. *east*] Imogen is buried according to classical or early Celtic practice,
which was the opposite of Christian
burial. Wyatt's suggestion that Shakespeare was suiting 'the pre-Christian
period of his play' is possibly correct.
Otherwise Belarius' 'reason' defeats
conjecture, unless there is some obscure link with the Phoenix symbolism
(see Introduction, pp. lxxxi–lxxxii).

Gui. Come on then, and remove him.
Arv.   So,—Begin.

SONG

Gui.   Fear no more the heat o' th' sun,
                Nor the furious winter's rages,
            Thou thy worldly task has done,   260
                Home art gone and ta'en thy wages.
            Golden lads and girls all must,
            As chimney-sweepers, come to dust.

Arv.   Fear no more the frown o' th' great,
                Thou art past the tyrant's stroke,   265
            Care no more to clothe and eat,
                To thee the reed is as the oak:
            The sceptre, learning, physic, must
            All follow this and come to dust.

Gui.   Fear no more the lightning-flash.   270
Arv.   Nor th' all-dreaded thunder-stone.
Gui.   Fear not slander, censure rash.
Arv.   Thou hast finish'd joy and moan.
Both.   All lovers young, all lovers must
            Consign to thee and come to dust.   275

Gui.   No exorciser harm thee!
Arv.   Nor no witchcraft charm thee!
Gui.   Ghost unlaid forbear thee!
Arv.   Nothing ill come near thee!
Both.   Quiet consummation have,   280
            And renowned be thy grave!

---

257. So,—] *Capell;* So, *F.*   272. not] *F;* no *F2.*

257. S.D. Song] For discussion see Appendix C.

262. *Golden . . . girls*] 'They are in perfect health, the elements being in them, as in gold, compounded in perfect proportion' (E. M. W. Tillyard, *The Elizabethan World Picture*, p. 60).

269. *this*] 'thee' (Hanmer).

271. *thunder-stone*] thunder-bolt. Considered to be a stone and often associated with Jupiter whose im-portance in *Cym.* is now emergent.

275. *Consign*] *O.E.D.* quotes as Johnson's the definition: 'submit to the same terms with another'. In his *Dictionary*, however, Johnson cites the present line in support of 'to yield; to submit; to resign'. Further, he conjectures 'this' for 'thee'. Steevens's 'seal the same contract with thee' seems perfectly adequate.

276. *exorciser*] one who raises spirits.

Re-enter BELARIUS *with the body of Cloten.*

Gui. We have done our obsequies: come, lay him down.
Bel. Here's a few flowers, but 'bout midnight more:
The herbs that have on them cold dew o' th' night
Are strewings fitt'st for graves: upon their faces.   285
You were as flowers, now wither'd: even so
These herblets shall, which we upon you strew.
Come on, away, apart upon our knees:
The ground that gave them first has them again:
Their pleasures here are past, so is their pain.   290
          [*Exeunt Belarius, Guiderius, and Arviragus.*
Imo. [*Awakes*] Yes sir, to Milford-Haven, which is the way?
I thank you: by yond bush? pray, how far thither?
'Ods pittikins: can it be six mile yet?
I have gone all night: faith, I'll lie down and sleep.
But, soft! no bedfellow! O gods and goddesses!   295
          [*Seeing the body of Cloten.*
These flowers are like the pleasures of the world;
This bloody man, the care on't. I hope I dream:
For so I thought I was a cave-keeper,
And cook to honest creatures. But 'tis not so:
'Twas but a bolt of nothing, shot at nothing,   300
Which the brain makes of fumes. Our very eyes
Are sometimes like our judgements, blind. Good faith,
I tremble still with fear: but if there be

283. 'bout] *F*; about *F2*.   290. is] *Pope*; are *F*.   295. bedfellow!] *Rowe*; bedfellow? *F*.   S.D.] *Rowe*.

285. *upon their faces*] This phrase has provoked much discussion, mainly because Cloten is headless, therefore faceless. Some critics rather oddly take the faces to be those of the herbs. Deighton justly points out that 'upon their faces' need mean no more than 'on the front of their bodies' and that the phrase is a direction as to the strewing of the flowers. Could not the phrase mean: Lay them face downwards? An unusual position, but possibly Belarius 'hath a reason for't'. This might add point to Imogen's curious identification in ll. 308–12. Whatever the sense,

criticism has been too literal, for the headless corpse is a narrative convention only, not a stage reality.

287. *strew*] Pope reads 'strow' which rhymes with 'so' in l. 286. Shakespeare probably intended the rhyme. These lines, like 289–90, have a formal valedictory tone.

291–332.] For analysis of this speech see Introduction, pp. lxv–lxvi.

291–3. *Yes sir . . . yet?*] as spoken to one of the beggars, cf. III. vi. 8–9.

293. *'Ods pittikins*] a diminutive form of 'God's pity'.

294. *gone*] walked.

Yet left in heaven as small a drop of pity
As a wren's eye, fear'd gods, a part of it!   305
The dream's here still: even when I wake it is
Without me, as within me: not imagin'd, felt.
A headless man? The garments of Posthumus?
I know the shape of's leg: this is his hand:
His foot Mercurial: his Martial thigh: 310
The brawns of Hercules: but his Jovial face—
Murder in heaven! How—?'Tis gone. Pisanio,
All curses madded Hecuba gave the Greeks,
And mine to boot, be darted on thee! Thou,
Conspir'd with that irregulous devil, Cloten,   315
Hast here cut off my lord. To write, and read
Be henceforth treacherous! Damn'd Pisanio
Hath with his forged letters (damn'd Pisanio)
From this most bravest vessel of the world
Struck the main-top! O Posthumus, alas,   320
Where is thy head? where's that? Ay me! where's
    that?

316. Hast] *Pope;* Hath F.

304–5. *as small . . . eye*] 'It is "sacred
pity" that "engenders" drops in eyes
(*AYL.*, II. vii. 123) and Imogen pleads
but for a drop in the smallest of eyes'
(Furness).

308–32. In romance mistaken identity is sometimes carried to incredible
lengths, as here. Mr David Hoeniger
suggests that there is a parallel in the
Clitophon and Leucippe of Achilles
Tatius (Book v), where Clitophon
buries a beheaded harlot under the
impression that she is Leucippe.

310–11. *His foot . . . face—*] Hartley
Coleridge compares Hamlet's description of his father (*Ham.*, III. iv. 55–9).

311. *brawns*] *O.E.D.* defines 'Fleshy
parts, muscle: especially the rounded
muscle of the arm or leg'. Both the
thigh and the brawns would be more
in evidence if the body had been laid
face downwards (see note to l. 285).

Jovial] like that of Jove, hence
regal, god-like, with an eye to
'threaten and command'.

315. *irregulous*] coined by Shakespeare from Latin *regula* = rule and
used only here. *O.E.D.* glosses: 'Char-
acterized by absence or disregard of
rule; unruly, disorderly, lawless'.
Johnson proposes 'th' irreligious'.

316. *Hast*] F 'Hath', which Furness
defends as a singular by attraction. But
the antecedent 'thou' makes this impossible. F, I think, can be defended
only on the assumption that ll. 313–15
are parenthetical and that 'hath' is
governed by 'Pisanio' in l. 312, but
this is tortuous.

317–20. *Damn'd . . . main-top*] Madness or frenzy in Elizabethan drama
often takes the form of disconnected
echoes of earlier speeches or incidents.
Lady Macbeth in the sleep-walking
scene affords an excellent example.
Here Imogen recalls that the letters
'would be even mortal to me', that 'the
paper Hath cut her throat already',
and lets these recollections colour present reality (or seeming reality).

Pisanio might have kill'd thee at the heart,
And left this head on. How should this be, Pisanio?
'Tis he, and Cloten: malice and lucre in them
Have laid this woe here. O, 'tis pregnant, pregnant! 325
The drug he gave me, which he said was precious
And cordial to me, have I not found it
Murd'rous to th' senses? That confirms it home:
This is Pisanio's deed, and Cloten—O!
Give colour to my pale cheek with thy blood,   330
That we the horrider may seem to those
Which chance to find us. O, my lord! my lord!
[Falls on the body.

Enter LUCIUS, *Captains, and a Soothsayer.*

Cap. To them, the legions garrison'd in Gallia
After your will have cross'd the sea, attending
You here at Milford-Haven, with your ships: 335
They are in readiness.
Luc.   But what from Rome?
Cap. The senate hath stirr'd up the confiners

329. Cloten—] Cloten: F.   332. *Falls . . . body*] Globe ed.   336. are in] *F2;*
are heere in *F.*

322. *Pisanio . . . heart*] usually taken
to mean that Pisanio might have
stabbed Posthumus through the heart,
but Imogen may mean that he could
have caused Posthumus to die of a
broken heart by revealing the falsity
of Iachimo's accusation.

323. *this head*] F3 reads 'his head'.
Other proposals are 'thy head' (Hanmer); 'the head' (Knight); 'this' with
omission of 'head' (Vaughan). F may
mean 'this head of which I am speaking' or, with emphasis on 'this', 'this
head above all others' (i.e. the best of
all heads).

325. *pregnant*] usually glossed as
evident, palpable, but Furness has an
important note: 'Imogen's exclamation . . . indicates, I think, that light is
just dawning on her. The mere mention of Pisanio and Cloten . . . gives the
clue, and she suddenly realises that
these two names enfold the whole

mystery,—that they are big with the
plot against her life.'

329. *Cloten—*] I treat the sentence as
a broken one. Vaughan adheres to F
which he explains as a Shakespearean
double genitive. Pope reads 'Cloten's'
which most editors adopt.

330–2. *Give . . . find us*] There seems
no escape from the gruesome conclusion that she smears her face with
his blood, or is about to do so.

333. *To them*] Dowden explains as
'in addition to them' but it is not easy
to distinguish between the several
bodies of troops. The suggestion that
these words are misplaced from the
S.D., which would then read: *Enter
Lucius, Captains, and a Soothsayer to them,*
is tempting.

336. *are in*] The 'heere' of F is evidently an error caught from 'heere' in
the preceding line.

337. *confiners*] inhabitants.

And gentlemen of Italy, most willing spirits,
That promise noble service: and they come
Under the conduct of bold Iachimo,   340
Siena's brother.
Luc.   When expect you them?
Cap. With the next benefit o' th' wind.
Luc.   This forwardness
Makes our hopes fair. Command our present numbers
Be muster'd; bid the captains look to 't. Now sir,   344
What have you dream'd of late of this war's purpose?
Sooth. Last night the very gods show'd me a vision
(I fast, and pray'd for their intelligence) thus:
I saw Jove's bird, the Roman eagle, wing'd
From the spongy south to this part of the west,
There vanish'd in the sunbeams, which portends   350
(Unless my sins abuse my divination)
Success to th' Roman host.
Luc.   Dream often so,
And never false. Soft ho, what trunk is here?
Without his top? The ruin speaks that sometime
It was a worthy building. How? a page?   355
Or dead, or sleeping on him? But dead rather:
For nature doth abhor to make his bed
With the defunct, or sleep upon the dead.
Let's see the boy's face.
Cap.   He's alive, my lord.
Luc. He'll then instruct us of this body. Young one, 360

360. this] *F*; his *F2*.

341. *Siena's brother*] Siena was, in fact, a republic, but not for dramatic purposes. Its duke appears in Beaumont and Fletcher's *Women Pleased*.

347. *fast*] fasted.

347–8. *thus . . . Roman*] Vaughan proposes: 'thus I saw: Jove's bird the Roman'. Craig suggests: 'thus I saw Jove's bird. The Roman'. Neither change is really justified.

349. *spongy*] Wilson Knight (*The Crown of Life*, p. 165) notes that Shakespeare's use of 'sponge' and 'spongy' elsewhere is derogatory.

351. *Unless . . . divination*] For 'sins' Gould proposes 'signs'. The Soothsayer's divination is abused, for the vision portends scant success to the Roman host. He amends his interpretation at v. v. 471–7. The vision is equivocal. The flight of Jove's eagle can portend the actual descent of Jupiter upon his eagle in v. iv, where Jupiter has come to Britain to resolve conflicting issues. It also symbolizes the return and rehabilitation of Posthumus, who is elsewhere likened to an eagle.

Inform us of thy fortunes, for it seems
They crave to be demanded. Who is this
Thou mak'st thy bloody pillow? Or who was he
That (otherwise than noble Nature did)
Hath alter'd that good picture? What's thy interest   365
In this sad wreck? How came't? Who is't?
What art thou?

Imo.   I am nothing; or if not,
Nothing to be were better. This was my master,
A very valiant Briton, and a good,
That here by mountaineers lies slain. Alas!   370
There is no more such masters: I may wander
From east to occident, cry out for service,
Try many, all good: serve truly: never
Find such another master.

Luc.   'Lack, good youth!
Thou mov'st no less with thy complaining than   375
Thy master in bleeding: say his name, good friend.

Imo. Richard du Champ: [*Aside*] if I do lie, and do
No harm by it, though the gods hear, I hope
They'll pardon it. Say you, sir?

371. There is] *F;* There are *F2.*   377. *Aside*] *Rowe.*

364. *otherwise . . . did*] For 'did'
Theobald conjectures 'bid' and Hanmer reads 'did it'. An anonymous
critic proposes 'limn'd'. Dowden interprets: 'Noble Nature only took away
the life—Who mutilated the body?' Is
it not possible that the allusion is to
Imogen? Cloten's body is a 'ruin', a
'building', a 'wreck', terms which sort
ill with 'good picture'. If Imogen has
smeared her face with blood (cf. ll.
330–2), that 'good picture' may be
said to be dyed or coloured deeper
than Nature coloured it. I would suggest 'dy'd' (for 'did') as a remotely
possible emendation.

373–4. *Try . . . master*] Supplemen-
tation is unnecessary. 'The commas
punctuate Imogen's sobs' (Wyatt). I
have retained F colons, but accept
Wyatt's main contention.

377. *Richard du Champ*] See note to
III. vii. 33. Richard du Champ, i.e.

Richard Field, is an interesting choice
of name. Richard Field of Stratford-
upon-Avon was a well-known printer
in London and flourished from 1579
to 1624. He printed *Ven.* in 1593 and
Lucr. in 1594, and it is highly probable
that he and Shakespeare were friends.
It seems that Shakespeare here makes a
complimentary allusion to the printer
of the two poems which strongly influenced the style of *Cym.* The French
form may be due to the fact that
Field's wife was French or it may be
a form that he himself sometimes
affected. He certainly called himself
'Ricardo del Campo' in his Spanish
publications. No significance need
attach to the fact that 'fielde', a variant
spelling, is an anagram of 'Fidele'.
The same conclusion has been reached
independently by Robert J. Kane
in *Shakespeare Quarterly*, IV (1953), p.
206.

Luc.   Thy name?

Imo.   Fidele, sir.

Luc. Thou dost approve thyself the very same: 380
Thy name well fits thy faith; thy faith thy name:
Wilt take thy chance with me? I will not say
Thou shalt be so well master'd, but be sure
No less belov'd. The Roman emperor's letters
Sent by a consul to me should not sooner   385
Than thine own worth prefer thee: go with me.

Imo. I'll follow, sir. But first, an't please the gods,
I'll hide my master from the flies, as deep
As these poor pickaxes can dig: and when
With wild wood-leaves and weeds I ha' strew'd his grave
And on it said a century of prayers   391
(Such as I can) twice o'er, I'll weep and sigh,
And leaving so his service, follow you,
So please you entertain me.

Luc.   Ay, good youth;
And rather father thee than master thee.   395
My friends,
The boy hath taught us manly duties: let us
Find out the prettiest daisied plot we can,
And make him with our pikes and partisans
A grave: come, arm him. Boy, he is preferr'd   400
By thee to us, and he shall be interr'd
As soldiers can. Be cheerful, wipe thine eyes:
Some falls are means the happier to arise.   [*Exeunt.*

385. not] *F;* no *F2.*   387. an't] *F2;* and't *F.*   400. he is] *F2;* hee's *F.*

389. *pickaxes*] 'Meaning her fingers' (Johnson).
390. *wild wood-leaves*] The Cambridge editors favour 'wild-wood leaves', but I think F means wild
wood-leaves *and* wood-weeds.
394. *entertain*] hire, employ.
399. *partisans*] halberds.
400. *arm him*] bear him in your arms.

SCENE III.—*A Room in Cymbeline's Palace.*

Enter CYMBELINE, *Lords,* PISANIO, *and Attendants.*

Cym. Again: and bring me word how 'tis with her.
                                        [*Exit an Attendant.*
A fever with the absence of her son;
A madness, of which her life's in danger: heavens,
How deeply you at once do touch me! Imogen,
The great part of my comfort gone: my queen   5
Upon a desperate bed, and in a time
When fearful wars point at me: her son gone,
So needful for this present. It strikes me, past
The hope of comfort. But for thee, fellow,
Who needs must know of her departure, and   10
Dost seem so ignorant, we'll enforce it from thee
By a sharp torture.
Pis.   Sir, my life is yours,
I humbly set it at your will: but, for my mistress,
I nothing know where she remains: why gone,
Nor when she purposes return. Beseech your highness,
Hold me your loyal servant.   16
First Lord.   Good my liege,
The day that she was missing, he was here:
I dare be bound he's true, and shall perform
All parts of his subjection loyally. For Cloten,
There wants no diligence in seeking him,   20
And will no doubt be found.
Cym.   The time is troublesome:
[*To Pisanio*] We'll slip you for a season, but our jealousy
Does yet depend.

Scene III

S.D. *A Room*] Capell   *Enter Cymbeline* . . .] *Enter Cymbeline, Lords, and Pisanio*
F.   1. S.D.] *Dyce.*   16. *First Lord*] *Capell; Lord* F.   22. *To Pisanio*]
Johnson.

4. *touch*] wound, afflict.

19. *subjection*] obedience, duty as a
subject.

20. *wants*] "'Wants' is probably
here not impersonal, but intransitive
—'is wanting'" (Abbott).

21. *And will*] proposed emendations

are: 'He will' (Hanmer); 'And he'll'
(Capell); 'And he will' (Keightley);
"A will' (anon.), but it is probable
that the nominative is simply omitted.
Abbott gives parallel examples.

22–3. *jealousy . . . depend*] my suspicion still remains in the balance.

First Lord.   So please your majesty,
The Roman legions, all from Gallia drawn,
Are landed on your coast, with a supply   25
Of Roman gentlemen, by the Senate sent.
Cym. Now for the counsel of my son and queen,
I am amaz'd with matter.
First Lord.   Good my liege,
Your preparation can affront no less
Than what you hear of. Come more, for more you're
        ready: 30
The want is but to put those powers in motion
That long to move.
Cym.   I thank you: let's withdraw
And meet the time, as it seeks us. We fear not
What can from Italy annoy us, but
We grieve at chances here. Away!   35
        [*Exeunt Cymbeline, Lords and Attendants.*
Pis. I heard no letter from my master since
I wrote him Imogen was slain. 'Tis strange:
Nor hear I from my mistress, who did promise
To yield me often tidings. Neither know I
What is betid to Cloten, but remain   40
Perplex'd in all. The heavens still must work.
Wherein I am false, I am honest; not true, to be true.
These present wars shall find I love my country,
Even to the note o' th' king, or I'll fall in them:

---

28. *First Lord*] Malone; *Lord F.*   31. those] *F;* these *F2.*   35. *Exeunt . . .*]
Capel; *Exeunt. F.*   40. betid] *Hammer;* betide *F.*

27–8. *Now . . . matter*] F3 prints a
full-stop after 'Queen' and Pope reads
'queen:' but most editors accept
Theobald's 'queen!' All these readings mean: Would that I now had the
counsel etc. If we follow F, which is not
demonstrably wrong, it is possible that
'for the counsel' means 'for lack of the
counsel', cf. III. vi. 17 and *H5*, I. ii. 114:
'All out of work and cold for action.'
This seems to me to yield a more
vigorous continuity. 'Amaz'd with
matter' means confused with press of
business.

29. *preparation*] forces under arms.
affront] confront.
34. *annoy*] molest.
36. *I heard . . . letter*] 'Perhaps "letter" here means, not an epistle, but the
elemental part of a syllable' (Malone).
For 'I heard', Hanmer reads 'I've had'
and Mason proposes 'I had'. Mus-
grave suggests 'later' for 'letter'.
39. *often*] sometimes an adjective
and possibly so here.
44. *Even . . . king*] 'I will so distinguish myself the king shall remark my
valour' (Johnson).

All other doubts, by time let them be clear'd,   45
Fortune brings in some boats that are not steer'd. [*Exit.*

SCENE IV.—*Wales. Before the Cave of Belarius.*

Enter BELARIUS, GUIDERIUS, *and* ARVIRAGUS.

Gui. The noise is round about us.
Bel.   Let us from it.
Arv. What pleasure, sir, we find in life, to lock it
From action and adventure.
Gui.   Nay, what hope
Have we in hiding us? This way, the Romans
Must or for Britons slay us or receive us   5
For barbarous and unnatural revolts
During their use, and slay us after.
Bel.   Sons,
We'll higher to the mountains, there secure us.
To the king's party there's no going: newness
Of Cloten's death (we being not known, not muster'd
Among the bands) may drive us to a render   11
Where we have liv'd, and so extort from's that
Which we have done, whose answer would be death
Drawn on with torture.
Gui.   This is, sir, a doubt
In such a time nothing becoming you,   15
Nor satisfying us.
Arv.   It is not likely

Scene IV

S.D. *Wales ... Belarius*] Dyce.

Scene IV

2. *we find*] F2 prints 'find we' and has
a question-mark after 'adventure', a
plausible, but not inevitable, change.
The F reading implies nobly indignant
remonstration: F2 merely presents the
kind of question that has already been
sufficiently exploited in III. iii.

4. *This way*] If we do so.

6. *revolts*] rebels.

7. *During their use*] usually explained: So long as they make use of
us, but Hudson offers the acceptable
alternative: during their present
armed occupancy.

11. *render*] 'An account of our place
of abode. This dialogue is a just representation of the superfluous caution of
an old man' (Johnson).

13. *answer*] requital.

That when they hear their Roman horses neigh,
Behold their quarter'd fires; have both their eyes
And ears so cloy'd importantly as now,
That they will waste their time upon our note,   20
To know from whence we are.

Bel.   O, I am known
Of many in the army: many years
(Though Cloten then but young) you see, not wore him
From my remembrance. And besides, the king
Hath not deserv'd my service nor your loves,   25
Who find in my exile the want of breeding,
The certainty of this hard life, aye hopeless
To have the courtesy your cradle promis'd,
But to be still hot Summer's tanlings, and
The shrinking slaves of Winter.

Gui.   Than be so,   30
Better to cease to be. Pray, sir, to th' army:
I and my brother are not known; yourself
So out of thought, and thereto so o'ergrown,
Cannot be question'd.

Arv.   By this sun that shines
I'll thither: what thing is't that I never   35
Did see man die, scarce ever look'd on blood,
But that of coward hares, hot goats, and venison!

36–7. die . . . venison!] *Dyce;* dye . . . venison? *F.*

17. *their*] Rowe emends to 'the'. Furness points out that 'their' bears the same reference as in 'their quarter'd fires'.

18. *quarter'd fires*] the watch-fires in their quarters, but Rann reads 'quarter'd files', i.e. their well-disposed lines, which may be correct.

19. *so cloy'd importantly*] O.E.D. defines 'cloy'd': clogged, cumbered, burdened. 'Importantly' may mean either 'momentously' or 'urgently'. The general sense is 'so fully occupied'.

27. *certainty*] Malone interprets as consequence, result (i.e. the want of breeding which is the result of this hard life), but Vaughan's 'certain continuance' seems preferable. Vaughan

treats 'aye . . . promis'd' as a parenthesis and glosses 'But to be still' as 'to be ever only'.

29. *tanlings*] infants tanned by the sun. Winter and summer are, as Dowden notes, personified.

33. *o'ergrown*] variously interpreted as 'bearded', 'grown old', 'grown out of memory'. I incline to the last, since 'thereto' seems to link the word with 'thought'. Because of the present hurly-burly, Belarius is quite out of their thoughts: he has *also* grown out of their thoughts through his long absence.

35. *what thing is't*] probably meaning: what a disgraceful thing it is.

37. *hot*] lecherous. The goat is a symbol of lechery in *Othello.*

Never bestrid a horse, save one that had
A rider like myself, who ne'er wore rowel,
Nor iron on his heel! I am ashamed   40
To look upon the holy sun, to have
The benefit of his blest beams, remaining
So long a poor unknown.
Gui.   By heavens, I'll go,
If you will bless me, sir, and give me leave,
I'll take the better care: but if you will not,   45
The hazard therefore due fall on me by
The hands of Romans!
Arv.   So say I, amen.
Bel. No reason I (since of your lives you set
So slight a valuation) should reserve
My crack'd one to more care. Have with you, boys!   50
If in your country wars you chance to die,
That is my bed too, lads, and there I'll lie.
Lead, lead. The time seems long, their blood thinks
     scorn
Till it fly out and show them princes born.   [*Exeunt.*

---

39. *rowel*] spur.

46. *hazard therefore due*] the risk to which my disobedience exposes me.

53-4. *The time . . . born*] Hanmer prints as an aside, but the heroic tone of the couplet indicates, *me judice*, that

it was positively boomed at the audience. Its authenticity is supported by *Mac.*, v. vii. 12–13: 'But swords I smile at, weapons laugh to scorn, / Brandish'd by man that's of a woman born.'

ACT V

SCENE I.—*Britain. The Roman Camp.*

Enter POSTHUMUS *alone.*

Post. Yea, bloody cloth, I'll keep thee: for I wish'd
Thou shouldst be colour'd thus. You married ones,
If each of you should take this course, how many
Must murder wives much better than themselves
For wrying but a little? O Pisanio,   5
Every good servant does not all commands:
No bond, but to do just ones. Gods, if you

ACT V

Scene I

S.D. *Britain* . . .] *Dyce.*   1. I wish'd] *Pope;* I am wisht *F.*   3. should] *F;*
would *F3.*

Posthumus' repentance may owe
something to *Frederyke of Jennen*: 'And
whan Ambrose sawe theim [i.e. the
bloody tokens], than was he more
sorier than he was before, because that
he spake not with her before that he
caused her to be put to death, to
examyne her, wherfore John of
Florence had the Jewels.' In the
Decameron there is no repentance prior
to the reconciliation. The problem of
restoring Posthumus to the main current of the play after an absence of two
acts is a difficult one, and Shakespeare
is not wholly successful. The hero's
remorse of conscience is unconvincing.
Since he still believes in Imogen's
guilt, his attitude towards her should
remain unchanged, however much he
may repent of the supposed murder.
To term her alleged offence 'wrying
but a little' seems contrary to the moral

code of the play, though, as Professor
Ellis-Fermor points out, it is not necessarily inconsistent with the feelings of a
human being illuminated by grief and
seeing with new eyes. Certainly the
picture of a man utterly disgusted with
himself and his surroundings is admirably presented.

 1. *bloody cloth*] the 'bloody sign' of
III. iv. 127.

 I wish'd] F 'I am wisht', which
Abbott explains as equivalent to 'I
have had many a wish'. Thiselton
quotes a passage from Dekker in which
'were wisht' clearly means 'were pos-
sessed with the desire'. But even so,
'I am wisht' would surely imply 'I
have had and still have many a wish'.
Singer emends to 'I e'en wish'd' which
is credible, but I have followed Pope.

 5. *wrying*] deviating from the path
of virtue.

145

Should have ta'en vengeance on my faults, I never
Had liv'd to put on this: so had you saved
The noble Imogen, to repent, and struck   10
Me, wretch, more worth your vengeance. But alack,
You snatch some hence for little faults; that's love,
To have them fall no more: you some permit
To second ills with ills, each elder worse,
And make them dread it, to the doers' thrift.   15
But Imogen is your own, do your best wills,
And make me blest to obey. I am brought hither
Among th' Italian gentry, and to fight
Against my lady's kingdom: 'tis enough
That, Britain, I have kill'd thy mistress: peace,   20
I'll give no wound to thee: therefore, good heavens,
Hear patiently my purpose. I'll disrobe me
Of these Italian weeds, and suit myself
As does a Briton peasant: so I'll fight
Against the part I come with: so I'll die   25
For thee, O Imogen, even for whom my life

11. Me, wretch,] Me (wretch) *F.*   15. doers'] *Theobald;* dooers *F.*   19.
lady's] *Rowe;* ladies *F.*

9. *put on*] usually explained as to instigate, incite (this crime), but assume, take on myself seems equally possible.

13–15. *you some . . . thrift*] a very difficult passage. Of the mass of emendations, only Theobald's 'dreaded' for F 'dread it' merits notice. Interpretations vary, but the general trend is to interpret 'elder' (paradoxically) as 'later' and 'thrift' as 'profit, gain'. Posthumus thus says that, unlike Imogen who has been snatched hence for a little fault, he has been allowed to proceed from great to greater evil, until overtaken by a dread of sin which is beneficial. Thiselton takes 'worse' in 'each elder worse' as a verb. The phrase may be an unusual ellipsis: each worse than the elder (i.e. than the preceding one), cf. II. iv. 182–3: 'One vice, but of a minute old, for one / Not half so old as that.' If taken literally, the lines must mean that each of the

ills, or sins, is less, not greater, than its predecessor: in other words, the gods permit some persons to continue sinning in diminishing degree, so that they come, with profit, to dread sin. This, if we take it as applying not to Posthumus himself but to divine mercy in general, might be the meaning, but the interpretation is terribly strained. See note to v. v. 216.

16. *your best wills*] Johnson's conjecture 'bless'd' may well be as correct as it is inspired.

20. *mistress: peace*] Staunton conjectures 'mistress-piece' and notes that Lord Herbert refers to Elizabeth Blunt as 'the beauty and Mistress-piece of her time'. *O.E.D.* gives a similar instance from Fuller. Since the conjecture is warrantable and has been approved by sound critics, I can do no more than record my dislike.

25. *part*] side, party.

Is, every breath, a death: and thus, unknown,
Pitied, nor hated, to the face of peril
Myself I'll dedicate. Let me make men know
More valour in me than my habits show.   30
Gods, put the strength o' th' Leonati in me!
To shame the guise o' th' world, I will begin,
The fashion less without, and more within.   [*Exit.*

SCENE II.—*Field between the British and Roman Camps.*

Enter LUCIUS, IACHIMO, *and the Roman Army at one door: and the*
Briton Army at another: LEONATUS POSTHUMUS *following, like a*
poor soldier. They march over, and go out. Then enter again, in
skirmish, IACHIMO *and* POSTHUMUS: *he vanquisheth and disarmeth*
IACHIMO, *and then leaves him.*

Iach. The heaviness and guilt within my bosom
Takes off my manhood: I have belied a lady,
The princess of this country; and the air on't
Revengingly enfeebles me, or could this carl,

29–33. *Let . . . within*] Furness
roundly condemns these lines as
spurious, but they clearly derive from
the same hand as *Mac.*, v. v. 49–52:
'I 'gin to be aweary of the sun, / And
wish the estate o' the world were now
undone. / Ring the alarum-bell! Blow,
wind! come, wrack! / At least we'll die
with harness on our back.' Tone and
style apart, the parallel 'the guise o' th'
world': 'the estate o' the world' is
decisive.

Scene II

S.D.] Granville-Barker notes the
absence of alarums, drums, trumpets,
and the customary battle-scene trappings, and remarks: 'As it stands, the
elaborate pantomime really looks not
unlike an attempt to turn old-fashioned
dumb-show to fresh and quaint
account' (*op. cit.*, p. 259). In other
words, the audience is presented with
a battle-scene so unconventional that

suspense turns almost to bewilder-
ment.
    Enter Lucius . . . one door] Some
editors add the name of Imogen, but
it is possible that she does not appear
in this brief action. If she does, her
presence may be implicit in 'the
Roman Army'. For the use of the two
doors, cf. III. i.
    4. *this carl*] churl. The two forms
were used indiscriminately. There is a
parallel in *Philaster*, IV. iii: 'The gods
take part against me; could this boor /
Have held me thus else.' See Introduction, pp. xxxvii–xl, for discussion
of the *Cymbeline–Philaster* relationship.
Since Iachimo, like Cymbeline later,
fails to recognize Posthumus, it is
possible that the latter is wearing some
kind of visored helmet, as Granville-
Barker suggests. It was an accepted
dramatic convention in Shakespeare's
time that all disguises were impenetrable.

A very drudge of Nature's, have subdued me   5
In my profession? Knighthoods and honours, borne
As I wear mine, are titles but of scorn.
If that thy gentry, Britain, go before
This lout, as he exceeds our lords, the odds
Is that we scarce are men and you are gods.   [*Exit.*   10

*The battle continues, the Britons fly, Cymbeline is taken: then enter to
his rescue,* BELARIUS, GUIDERIUS, *and* ARVIRAGUS.

Bel. Stand, stand, We have th' advantage of the ground;
The lane is guarded: nothing routs us but
The villainy of our fears.

Gui.⎱
Arv.⎰   Stand, stand, and fight!

Re-enter POSTHUMUS, *and seconds the Britons. They rescue Cymbeline
and exeunt. Then re-enter* LUCIUS, IACHIMO, *and* IMOGEN.

Luc. Away, boy, from the troops, and save thyself:
For friends kill friends, and the disorder's such   15
As war were hoodwink'd.
Iach.   'Tis their fresh supplies.
Luc. It is a day turn'd strangely: or betimes
Let's re-inforce, or fly.   [*Exeunt.*

SCENE III.—*Another part of the Field.*

Enter POSTHUMUS *and a Briton Lord.*

Lord. Cam'st thou from where they made the stand?

5. Nature's] Natures *F* (nature's *Rowe*).

Scene III

S.D. *Another . . . Field*] *Capell.*   *Briton*] *Britaine F.*

16. *hoodwink'd*] blindfolded. 'War'
is possibly a personification.

18. *re-inforce*] *O.E.D.* 'to obtain re-
inforcements'. Hart suggests that the
meaning here may be 'renew the
attack'. He claims, rather dubiously
I think, that the word is so used in the
Play of Stucley. O.E.D. gives a like
meaning to 're-inforcement' in *Cor.,* II.
ii. 117, but this, too, is open to doubt.

Scene III

Grant White doubts the authenticity of the final part of this scene
(ll. 84–94). Furness questions occasional speeches (1–12 and, apparently,
14–51), but his doubts are not clearly
defined, and how much of the scene he
leaves to Shakespeare cannot easily be
ascertained. Holinshed's *History of
Scotland,* which Shakespeare followed

Post.   I did,
    Though you it seems come from the fliers.
Lord.   I did.
Post. No blame be to you, sir, for all was lost,
    But that the heavens fought: the king himself
    Of his wings destitute, the army broken,   5
    And but the backs of Britons seen; all flying
    Through a strait lane; the enemy full-hearted,
    Lolling the tongue with slaught'ring, having work
    More plentiful than tools to do't, struck down
    Some mortally, some slightly touch'd, some falling   10
    Merely through fear, that the strait pass was damm'd
    With dead men, hurt behind, and cowards living
    To die with length'ned shame.
Lord.   Where was this lane?
Post. Close by the battle, ditch'd, and wall'd with turf—
    Which gave advantage to an ancient soldier,   15
    (An honest one, I warrant) who deserv'd

2. come] *F;* came *F3.*

closely in *Macbeth*, supplied much of
the circumstantial detail in the present
scene, part of which looks as if it could
even have been a discarded episode
from the tragedy itself. Shakespeare's
authorship could scarcely be better
attested.

2. *I did*] Craig plausibly suggests
that 'did' is an error caught from the
preceding line, and that the original
read 'I' *sc.* 'Ay'.

3 ff.] This and Posthumus' ensuing
speeches are extremely involved.
Excitement and indignation render
him incoherent, and it is probable that
Shakespeare here employed incoherence with calculated dramatic effect,
as he had already done in *Coriolanus.*
Dr G. K. Hunter suggests that the
hanging participles give an effect of
high-strained eloquence.

4 ff.] Holinshed supplies the detail
(see Appendix A), but the incident
itself, in so far as it is a corporate part
of the plot of *Cymbeline* and a necessary
element in the wager-plot, may have
been suggested by *Frederyke of Jennen*:

'Than assembled he a grete hoost and
cam agaynst his enemyes, and slewe
them downe afore him lyke a lyon and
dyde many meruaylous faytes of
armes that daye; for he broke theyr
ordynaunce and made theim for to
scatter a brode, as it had ben loste
shepe. And so that daye had lorde
Frederyke grete vyctory, and folowed
his enemyes and toke many prysoners
of the captaynes and gret lordes, of
whome he had grete raunsome.' The
prevalence of animal imagery in this
scene and in the prose tale may be
noted.

8. *Lolling the tongue*] The image is of
a beast of prey. Dryden applies the
same phrase to tigers in *Georgics,* IV.
741, and again in *Æneid,* VIII. 843.

12. *hurt behind*] a sign of cowardice.
Old Siward (*Mac.,* v. viii. 46) asks of
his slain son, 'Had he his hurts before?'

16–17. *who deserved ... came to*] 'Who,
for this patriotic action, deserved as
long a nurture in the future as his
white beard indicated that he had been
nurtured in the past' (Furness).

So long a breeding as his white beard came to,
In doing this for's country. Athwart the lane,
He, with two striplings (lads more like to run
The country base than to commit such slaughter,   20
With faces fit for masks, or rather fairer
Than those for preservation cas'd, or shame)
Made good the passage, cried to those that fled,
'Our Britain's harts die flying, not our men:
To darkness fleet souls that fly backwards; stand,   25
Or we are Romans, and will give you that
Like beasts which you shun beastly, and may save
But to look back in frown: stand, stand!' These three,
Three thousand confident, in act as many,—
For three performers are the file when all   30
The rest do nothing,—with this word 'Stand, stand,'
Accommodated by the place, more charming,
With their own nobleness, which could have turn'd
A distaff to a lance, gilded pale looks;
Part shame, part spirit renew'd, that some, turn'd
        coward
But by example (O, a sin in war,   35

24. harts] *Pope ed. 2 (Theobald);* hearts *F.*

20. *country base*] prisoner's base, a popular boys' game.

21–2. *With faces . . . shame*] Their faces were as fair as those of ladies who wore masks either to preserve the complexion or for the sake of modesty—in fact, fairer.

24. *harts*] F 'hearts'. Theobald's emendation is, I think, correct. Ingleby defends F and interprets 'hearts' as 'courages'. These may die, but how they fly remains obscure!

our] Thirlby's 'her' is sufficiently plausible to merit notice.

25. *backwards*] Pope reads 'backwards!' but this is a statement or an aphorism, not a curse.

26. *Or we are Romans*] or we shall behave like Romans.

27. *beastly*] 'The Wallooners and High Duches fled beastly' (Gascoigne, *The Spoil of Antwerp,* 1576).

27–8. *and may . . . frown*] and which you may avert simply by turning and looking defiant.

28–39. *These three . . . hunters*] There is much parenthesis here. The run of the main sentence is: These three, with this word 'Stand, stand!' gilded pale looks and restored courage and shame, so that some of the cowards began to follow their lead and to turn on their pursuers.

30. *file*] *O.E.D.* 'The number of men constituting the depth from front to rear of a formation in line'.

32. *more charming*] winning upon others more by their noble deeds than by their words ('Stand, stand!'). I take 'Accommodated by the place' to be purely parenthetical. Dowden's suggestion: 'more influential by their own nobleness than by the advantage of position' is forced.

Damn'd in the first beginners) 'gan to look
The way that they did, and to grin like lions
Upon the pikes o' th' hunters. Then began
A stop i' th' chaser; a retire: anon   40
A rout, confusion thick: forthwith they fly
Chickens, the way which they stoop'd eagles: slaves,
The strides they victors made: and now our cowards
Like fragments in hard voyages became
The life o' th' need: having found the back-door open
Of the unguarded hearts, heavens, how they wound! 46
Some slain before, some dying, some their friends
O'er-borne i' th' former wave, ten chas'd by one,
Are now each one the slaughter-man of twenty:
Those that would die, or ere resist, are grown   50
The mortal bugs o' th' field.
Lord.   This was strange chance:
A narrow lane, an old man, and two boys.
Post. Nay, do not wonder at it: you are made

42. stoop'd] *Rowe;* stopt *F.*   43. they] *Theobald;* the *F.*   47. dying,]
dying; *F.*

40. *stop*] The sudden ending to a
horse's career by which it was thrown
upon its haunches. Possibly to be taken
literally since the Britons were
opposed by Roman cavalry (cf. IV.
iv. 17).
   retire] retreat.
   41. *confusion thick*] Hanmer plausibly reads 'confusion-thick'.
   42. *stoop'd*] Rowe's emendation
seems justified in the light of v. iv. 116.
'Stoop' is a technical term in falconry
meaning to swoop down upon prey.
   42–3. *slaves . . . made*] Theobald's
'they victors' is generally accepted but
is not absolutely necessary. Since F
seldom indicates apostrophes there is
some justification for reading 'slaves' ',
i.e. the strides of the victors were now
turned into the strides of slaves.
   44–5. *Like fragments . . . need*] like
scraps of food which maintain life in
time of need.
   47. *Some . . . friends*] F 'Some slaine
before some dying; some their
Friends'. Dowden thinks that the

third 'some' may be nominative to
'wound' understood, but it is more
likely that each 'some' refers to the
erstwhile cowards. I take it that the
line refers back, not quite exactly, to
l. 10 which uses an identical verbal
formula.
   51. *bugs*] terrors.
   53. *Nay . . . made*] Theobald reads
'Nay, do but' and Ingleby 'Nay, do
you' (making it a question). Staunton
proposes 'Ay, do but'. Hanmer inserts
'tho'' before 'you'. Vaughan would
emend 'made' to 'mad'. F, however, is
unimpeachable. The colon after 'it'
may be equivalent to 'that'. The whole
force of Posthumus' remark, however,
surely lies in the fact that the Lord is a
foppish courtier who dabbles in verse
(hence the rhymes that follow) and
who was created rather to wonder at
warlike ballads than to perform warlike deeds. Posthumus, then, scorn-
fully tells him not to wonder at fact
since he was born to wonder at fiction.

Rather to wonder at the things you hear
Than to work any. Will you rhyme upon't,   55
And vent it for a mock'ry? Here is one:

Two boys, an old man twice a boy, a lane,
Preserv'd the Britons, was the Romans' bane.

Lord. Nay, be not angry, sir.
Post.   'Lack, to what end?
Who dares not stand his foe, I'll be his friend: 60
For if he'll do as he is made to do,
I know he'll quickly fly my friendship too.
You have put me into rhyme.
Lord.   Farewell, you're angry. [*Exit.*
Post. Still going? This is a lord! O noble misery,
To be i' th' field, and ask 'what news?' of me!   65
To-day how many would have given their honours
To have sav'd their carcasses? Took heel to do't,
And yet died too! I, in mine own woe charm'd,
Could not find death where I did hear him groan,
Nor feel him where he struck. Being an ugly monster, 70
'Tis strange he hides him in fresh cups, soft beds,
Sweet words; or hath moe ministers than we
That draw his knives i' th' war. Well, I will find him:
For being now a favourer to the Briton,
No more a Briton, I have resumed again   75
The part I came in. Fight I will no more,
But yield me to the veriest hind that shall
Once touch my shoulder. Great the slaughter is

65. ask 'what news?'] *Camb.;* ask what newes *F.*

55. *rhyme*] Mr J. C. Maxwell suggests to me that as F prints 'Rime' the word may be a noun, hence 'Will you rhyme upon't' = Do you wish for rhyme upon it?

57–62. *Two boys . . . friendship too*] Posthumus has already appeared as a potential satirical poet at II. iv. 183.

64. *Still going?*] still running away—even from me?

68. *charm'd*] preserved as by a charm.

74–6. *For being . . . in*] It is possible

that Posthumus, who at v. i. 22–4 discarded his 'Italian weeds', now resumes them, and that the change of costume is implied in these difficult lines. On the other hand, it is Posthumus who proclaims himself a Roman at l. 89, and not the two British captains who recognize him as such. It is possible, therefore, that it is his retention of the British peasant's 'silly habit' that renders such disclosure necessary.

78. *touch my shoulder*] The sign of formal arrest.

Here made by th' Roman; great the answer be
Britons must take. For me, my ransom's death: 80
On either side I come to spend my breath,
Which neither here I'll keep nor bear again,
But end it by some means for Imogen.

Enter two British Captains and Soldiers.

First Cap. Great Jupiter be prais'd, Lucius is taken:
'Tis thought the old man, and his sons, were angels.   85
Sec. Cap. There was a fourth man, in a silly habit,
That gave th' affront with them.
First Cap.   So 'tis reported:
But none of 'em can be found. Stand! who's there?
Post. A Roman,
Who had not now been drooping here if seconds   90
Had answer'd him.
Sec. Cap.   Lay hands on him: a dog,
A leg of Rome shall not return to tell
What crows have peck'd them here: he brags his service
As if he were of note: bring him to th' king.

Enter CYMBELINE, BELARIUS, GUIDERIUS, ARVIRAGUS, PISANIO,
*and Roman Captives. The Captains present Posthumus to Cymbeline,
who delivers him over to a Gaoler.*

                                                      [*Exeunt.*

83. *British Captains*] Theobald; *Captaines* F.

79. *answer*] retaliation. Craig proposes: 'Great the slaughter's here /
Made by the Roman; great the
answer we / Britons must take.'

86. *silly habit*] rustic garb.

87. *affront*] attack, assault.

90. *seconds*] supporters.

91–2. *a dog . . . Rome*] Most editors
follow Theobald in making 'a dog' a
term of abuse, but F makes good sense,
i.e. not a dog, nor even a leg, of Rome
etc. 'Them' in l. 93 suggests that a
plural subject is required. Daniel
ingeniously proposes 'lag' for 'leg', but
Dowden rightly observes that 'in the
case of fliers the leg may well represent
the man' and compares *R2*, II. iii. 90.
'A leg of Rome' is the kind of phrase

that would come naturally to the
author of *Cor.*: cf. Menenius' fable of
the belly (I. i. 99–167) and his reference to the First Citizen as 'the great
toe of this assembly' (l. 159).

94. S.D. Enter . . . Gaoler] Ritson
remarks that 'this is the only instance
in these plays of the business of the
scene being entirely performed in
dumb show.' Evidently his assumption
is that the dumb show is a scene in
itself, and this may be right. The
Second Captain's 'bring him to th'
king' implies an exeunt which F does
not supply. Nor does it print one after
'*Gaoler*' where it is clearly necessary.
It is possible that the Captains lead
Posthumus off the stage, and return

SCENE IV.—*Britain. An open place near the British Camp.*

Enter POSTHUMUS *and two Gaolers.*

First Gaol. You shall not now be stol'n, you have locks
 upon you:
 So graze, as you find pasture.
Sec. Gaol.   Ay, or a stomach.

              [*Exeunt Gaolers.*

Post. Most welcome bondage; for thou art a way,
 I think to liberty: yet am I better
 Than one that's sick o' th' gout, since he had rather   5
 Groan so in perpetuity than be cur'd
 By th' sure physician, Death; who is the key
 T' unbar these locks. My conscience, thou art fetter'd
 More than my shanks and wrists: you good gods,
  give me

Scene IV

S.D. *Britain . . . British Camp*] *J. C. Adams conj.*   *two Gaolers*] *Rowe; Gaoler F.*
1. *First Gaol.*] *Rowe; Gao. F.*   2. S.D.] *Rowe.*

with him after the entry of Cymbeline and the others. Dr Alice Walker suggests (privately) that this S.D. looks almost like a note for an intended scene or a reminder of something that had been lost or cancelled.

Scene IV

S.D. Britain . . . British Camp] Most editors accept Pope's scene-location: 'Britain. A Prison'. This, if correct, would mean that the inner-stage served as the prison, but would also mean that Jupiter, whose descent could only be to the main- or the upper-stage, would be invisible to both Posthumus and the Leonati, who circle around him. Hence we must suppose that Posthumus was held prisoner on the main-stage, and this is the contention of Professor J. C. Adams (*The Globe Playhouse*, pp. 336–7) whose suggested heading I have accepted. Adams's theory, that Posthumus was chained to one of the stage posts, is eminently reasonable, and the

First Gaoler's remark in l. 2 gains something from this interpretation. Posthumus is chained like a horse in the open field and left to graze. If he were thrown into a prison cell the joke would be rather pointless.

1. First Gaol.] Julia Engelen (*Shakespeare Jahrbuch*, 1927, pp. 138–40) suggests that the First Gaoler may have been played by the actor who had previously played Cloten. W. M. Keck (*Shakespeare Association Bulletin*, 1935, pp. 68–72) accepts Engelen's view and argues that both parts were originally played by Robert Armin who introduced comic speeches of his own devising. This, Keck argues, accounts for the irregularities in Cloten. But do they have to be accounted for?

1–2. *You shall . . . pasture*] 'The wit of the gaoler alludes to the custom of putting a lock on a horse's leg when he is turned to pasture' (Johnson).

3–8. *Most welcome . . . locks*] Cf. *Meas.*, III. i. 5–41, where the theme is given extended treatment.

The penitent instrument to pick that bolt,   10
Then free for ever. Is't enough I am sorry?
So children temporal fathers do appease;
Gods are more full of mercy. Must I repent,
I cannot do it better than in gyves,
Desir'd more than constrain'd: to satisfy,   15
If of my freedom 'tis the mainport, take
No stricter render of me than my all.
I know you are more clement than vile men,
Who of their broken debtors take a third,
A sixth, a tenth, letting them thrive again   20
On their abatement; that's not my desire.
For Imogen's dear life take mine, and though
'Tis not so dear, yet 'tis a life; you coin'd it:

16. mainport] *Alice Walker conj.*; maine part *F.*

10. *penitent instrument*] Rolfe defines as 'penitential means of freeing my conscience of its guilt'. The term is, I think, synonymous with 'Death, who is the key t' unbar these locks'.

11–17. *Is't enough ... my all*] Ingleby, with acknowledgements, comments: 'In this speech Posthumus is made to employ the language of the early divines, in distinguishing the three parts (primary, secondary, and '*main*') of Repentance, as the condition of Remission of Sins. (1) Attrition, or sorrow for sin: 'Is't not enough I am sorry?' (2) Penance: which was held to convert attrition into contrition, or godly sorrow: 'Must I repent?' (3) Satisfaction: 'Must I satisfy?' And he contends that as he has fulfilled the former requirements, he is willing to fulfil the last,—to pay his debt for having taken Imogen's life,—by giving his own.' This seems to me to clarify a difficult passage.

13. *Gods . . . mercy*] i.e. they will grant him death which he desires and merits.

13–15. *Must I repent . . . constrain'd*] 'If I must repent, I cannot do it better than with the penance of voluntary

gyves' (Dowden). I take the voluntary gyves to be equivalent to death.

16. *mainport*] a small offering or tribute. Dr Alice Walker, to whom I am indebted for this brilliant emendation of F 'maine part', would paraphrase: 'if atonement consists of the small tribute of my liberty, exact no lesser forfeit from me than my life.' There is, as she points out, an attractive antithesis between the implications of 'main-port' and 'stricter render'. *O.E.D.* gives no example before 1664, but the word, a quasi-legal one associated with Latin *manus + portare*, is medieval. Mr W. J. B. Owen cites an example in Richard de Bury's *Liber Epistolaris* (ed. Denholm-Young, Roxburghe Club, 1950: Item 478) and adds that Dr Walker's emendation yields a more satisfactory scansion.

17. *No stricter . . . my all*] I take 'my all' to signify 'my life'. The most merciful penance which the gods could impose is death, and Posthumus pleads for that in preference to continued existence which, by comparison, is a 'stricter render'.

21. *abatement*] diminished amount.

'Tween man and man they weigh not every stamp;
Though light, take pieces for the figure's sake: 25
You rather, mine being yours: and so, great powers,
If you will take this audit, take this life,
And cancel these cold bonds. O Imogen,
I'll speak to thee in silence.   [*Sleeps.*

Solemn music. Enter (*as in an apparition*) SICILIUS LEONATUS, *father
to Posthumus, an old man, attired like a warrior, leading in his hand an
ancient matron* (*his wife, and mother to Posthumus*) *with music before
them. Then, after other music, follow the two young* LEONATI (*brothers
to Posthumus*) *with wounds as they died in the wars. They circle
Posthumus round as he lies sleeping.*

Sici.   No more thou thunder-master show   30
          thy spite on mortal flies:
          With Mars fall out, with Juno chide,
          that thy adulteries
          Rates and revenges.

25. figure's] *F3;* figures *F.*   26. You rather, mine] (You rather) mine *F.*
28. these] *F;* those *Ff2–4.*   29. Sleeps] *not in F.*   29. S.D. *follow*] *Rowe;*
followes F.

24–5. '*Tween man . . . sake*] The reference is to coins stamped with the
figure of the sovereign. Cf. Marlowe,
Hero and Leander, I. 265: 'Base boullion
for the stampes sake we allow.'

26. *You rather . . . yours*] You should
do so even more readily since the
light coin of my life is of your stamp-
ing.

27. *take this audit*] accept this
account. Daniel proposes 'make this
audit', but 'take' is the operative verb
throughout the second half of the
speech, being used six times.

28. *cold bonds*] Most critics think that
the reference is to legal bonds which
have become void ('cold'), but the
allusion may equally well be to the
fetters of life, or even to the manacles
on Posthumus' wrist. I incline to 'the
fetters of life' because the whole speech
seems to me to be an elaborate fan-
tasia on one simple theme: Let me die
and, by so doing, expiate my offences.
Johnson detects a pun.

29. S.D.] Solemn music. . . sleeping]
Granville-Barker notes that the solemn
music would be the customary consort
of viols. The Leonati, he thinks, enter
through curtains and form a stationary
circle round Posthumus. Very few
critics are willing to admit the whole
of the ensuing episode (ll. 30–122) as
Shakespearean, and many reject it *in
toto*. I have dealt with its authenticity
in the Introduction (pp.xxxiii–xxxvii).
See footnotes below for supporting
evidence cited by Wilson Knight and
others.

31. *flies*] So in *Lr.,* IV. i. 38–9: 'As
flies to wanton boys are we to the
gods, / They kill us for their sport.'
W. A. Armstrong (*Times Literary
Supplement,* 14 Oct. 1949, p. 665)
derives the *Lr.* passage directly from
Sidney's *Arcadia* (1590), III. x (ed.
Feuillerat, pp. 406–7). If the parallel
holds and the derivation is correct,
Shakespeare's authorship of the present lines is virtually established.

Hath my poor boy done aught but well,   35
    whose face I never saw?
I died whilst in the womb he stay'd,
    attending Nature's law:
Whose father then (as men report
    thou orphans' father art)   40
Thou shouldst have been, and shielded him
    from this earth-vexing smart.

Moth.   Lucina lent not me her aid,
    but took me in my throes,
That from me was Posthumus ript,   45
    came crying 'mongst his foes,
A thing of pity!

Sici.   Great nature, like his ancestry,
    moulded the stuff so fair,
That he deserved the praise o' th' world,   50
    as great Sicilius' heir.

First Bro. When once he was mature for man,
    in Britain where was he
That could stand up his parallel,
    or fruitful object be   55
In eye of Imogen, that best
    could deem his dignity?

Moth.   With marriage wherefore was he mock'd
    to be exil'd, and thrown

---

40. orphans'] *Theobald;* Orphanes *F.*

37–8. *I died . . . law*] Wilson Knight compares *Wint.*, II. ii. 59–61: 'This child was prisoner to the womb and is / By law and process of great nature thence / Freed and enfranchised.'

42. *earth-vexing*] Vaughan conjectures 'heart-vexing', but, as Dowden notes, 'a ghost may speak of smarts as earth-vexing in contrast to the calm of Elysium.'

43–7. *Lucina . . . pity*] Wilson Knight notes the following parallels: Lucina in *Per.*, III. i. 10–14; 'from his mother's womb / Untimely ripp'd' in *Mac.*, v.

viii. 15–46; 'When we are born, we cry that we are come / To this great stage of fools' in *Lr.*, IV. vi. 186–7.

49. *moulded . . . fair*] Wilson Knight compares I. i. 23: 'So fair an outward, and such stuff within'.

52–7. *When once . . . dignity*] Wilson Knight compares I. i. 50–4 and I. i. 22.

55. *fruitful*] Thiselton very properly connects with 'mature for man' and thereby disposes of such emendations as 'rival' (Rowe), 'frontfull' (Vaughan).

57. *deem*] judge.

From Leonati seat, and cast   60
   from her his dearest one,
Sweet Imogen?

Sici.   Why did you suffer Iachimo,
   slight thing of Italy,
To taint his nobler heart and brain   65
   with needless jealousy;
And to become the geck and scorn
   o' th' other's villainy?

Sec. Bro.   For this, from stiller seats we came,
   our parents and us twain,   70
That striking in our country's cause
   fell bravely and were slain,
Our fealty, and Tenantius' right,
   with honour to maintain.

First Bro.   Like hardiment Posthumus hath   75
   to Cymbeline perform'd:
Then, Jupiter, thou king of gods
   why hast thou thus adjourn'd
The graces for his merits due,
   being all to dolours turn'd?   80

Sici.   Thy crystal window ope; look out;
   no longer exercise
Upon a valiant race thy harsh
   and potent injuries.

Moth.   Since, Jupiter, our son is good,   85
   take off his miseries.

Sici.   Peep through thy marble mansion, help,
   or we poor ghosts will cry

79. his] *F;* her *Ff2–4.*   81. look out;] *F2;* looke, / looke out, *F.*

64. *Slight . . . Italy*] Wilson Knight
thinks the phrase complementary to
'jay of Italy' (III. iv. 50) and 'Italian
fiend' (v. v. 210). 'Slight' means
worthless.
   67. *geck*] dupe. Cf. the collocation
'geck and scorn' with 'geck and gull' in
Tw.N., v. i. 351.
   69. *came*] Dyce (ed. 2), following
Walker and Lettsom, prints 'come'.
   75. *hardiment*] deeds of valour.
   81. *look out*] F actually prints lines
81–2 thus: 'Thy Cristall window ope;
looke, looke out, no longer exercise'.
Since this involves mislineation as well
as faulty metre, there seems little point
in questioning the correction introduced into subsequent Ff.

To th' shining synod of the rest
　　against thy deity.　　　　　　　　　　90

Brothers.　　Help, Jupiter, or we appeal,
　　and from thy justice fly.

*Jupiter descends in thunder and lightning, sitting upon an
eagle: he throws a thunderbolt. The Ghosts fall on their knees.*

Jup.　　No more, you petty spirits of region low,
　　Offend our hearing: hush! How dare you ghosts
　　Accuse the thunderer, whose bolt (you know)　　95
　　Sky-planted, batters all rebelling coasts?
　　Poor shadows of Elysium, hence, and rest
　　　Upon your never-withering banks of flowers:
　　Be not with mortal accidents opprest,
　　　No care of yours it is, you know 'tis ours.　　100
　　Whom best I love I cross; to make my gift,
　　　The more delay'd, delighted. Be content,
　　Your low-laid son our godhead will uplift:
　　　His comforts thrive, his trials well are spent:
　　Our Jovial star reign'd at his birth, and in　　105
　　　Our temple was he married. Rise, and fade.
　　He shall be lord of lady Imogen,
　　　And happier much by his affliction made.

89. *synod*] used by Shakespeare to signify an assembly of the gods.

92. S.D. Jupiter descends] Normally the gods descended in an ordinary armchair, technically termed a 'throne', but the present direction (as well as the text) suggests that more elaborate devices were now being exploited. The descent of Ariel 'like a harpy' (*Tp*., III. iii) is a parallel sophistication, and J. C. Adams (*The Globe Playhouse*, pp. 336–7) argues that it is a consequence of the eagle device in *Cym*. Granville-Barker plausibly suggests that Jupiter's descent is to the upper-stage only, since mid-air would be the most fitting locus for a god. This would ensure that Posthumus is not obliterated from the view of the audience. Inigo Jones's design for an identical theophany in Townsend's *Tempe Restored* is reproduced in A. Nicoll, *Stuart Masques*, p. 94. See Appendix B.

101. *cross*] E. A. Armstrong (*op. cit.*, p. 122) notes that Shakespeare usually connects this word with some religious expression, even when it bears no sacred significance itself. Hence 'godhead' in l. 103.

102. *delighted*] Walker glosses 'endowed with delights, *deliciis exornata*'. The rule, as given by Abbott, is that a participle formed from a noun means 'endowed with (the noun)'. The phrase has a Shakespearean ring, cf. I. vi. 42, 'To be more fresh, reviving'.

104. *well*] 'well-nigh' may be the requisite reading but has not, so far as I know, been suggested.

This tablet lay upon his breast, wherein
  Our pleasure his full fortune doth confine,   110
And so away: no farther with your din
  Express impatience, lest you stir up mine.
  Mount, eagle, to my palace crystalline.   [*Ascends.*

Sici. He came in thunder; his celestial breath
  Was sulphurous to smell: the holy eagle   115
Stoop'd, as to foot us: his ascension is
More sweet than our blest fields: his royal bird
Prunes the immortal wing, and cloys his beak,
As when his god is pleased.

All.   Thanks, Jupiter!

Sici. The marble pavement closes, he is enter'd   120
His radiant roof. Away! and to be blest
Let us with care perform his great behest.
                              [*The Ghosts vanish.*

Post. [*Waking*] Sleep, thou hast been a grandsire, and begot
  A father to me: and thou hast created
  A mother, and two brothers: but, O scorn!   125
Gone! they went hence so soon as they were born:
And so I am awake. Poor wretches, that depend
On greatness' favour, dream as I have done,
Wake, and find nothing. But, alas, I swerve:
Many dream not to find, neither deserve,   130
And yet are steep'd in favours; so am I,
That have this golden chance, and know not why.
What fairies haunt this ground? A book? O rare one,
Be not, as is our fangled world, a garment
Nobler than that it covers. Let thy effects   135

123. *Waking*] *Theobald.*   126. Gone!] *Capell;* Gone, *F.*   128. greatness']
Theobald; greatnesse, *F.*

110. *Our . . . confine*] Our pleasure
confines his unrestricted good fortune
within the strict limits of this tablet.

116. *Stoop'd . . . us*] swooped as if to
seize us in its talons.

ascension] Jupiter descended in
anger, but his ascent is favourable to
the suppliants.

118. *Prunes*] preens (app. orig.

var.), trims the feathers with the beak.

cloys] claws, i.e. scratches with its
claws.

123–5. *Sleep . . . brothers*] The dream
virtually anticipates reality. At least it
forbodes the final reunion of v. v.
369 ff.

134. *fangled*] *O.E.D.* glosses 'char-
acterised by crotchets or fopperies'.

So follow, to be most unlike our courtiers,
As good as promise.
[*Reads*] When as a lion's whelp shall, to himself
    unknown, without seeking find, and be embrac'd
    by a piece of tender air: and when from a stately   140
    cedar shall be lopp'd branches, which, being
    dead many years, shall after revive, be jointed to
    the old stock, and freshly grow, then shall
    Posthumus end his miseries, Britain be fortunate,
    and flourish in peace and plenty.   145
'Tis still a dream: or else such stuff as madmen
Tongue, and brain not: either both, or nothing,
Or senseless speaking, or a speaking such
As sense cannot untie. Be what it is,
The action of my life is like it, which   150
I'll keep, if but for sympathy.

Re-enter Gaolers.

First Gaol. Come, sir, are you ready for death?
Post. Over-roasted rather: ready long ago.
First Gaol. Hanging is the word, sir: if you be ready for
    that, you are well cook'd.   155
Post. So, if I prove a good repast to the spectators, the
    dish pays the shot.
First Gaol. A heavy reckoning for you sir: but the com-
    fort is you shall be called to no more payments, fear

151. *Re-enter Gaolers*] *Capell; Enter Gaoler F.*   152. *First Gaol.*] *Capell;
Gao. F.*

140. *piece*] '"Tender air" being
mulier, a woman, the word "piece" is
probably chosen because it was often
used of persons, and often as indicating
supreme excellence' (Dowden).

146–51. *'Tis still . . . sympathy*] The
meaning of this passage is, as Johnson
says, too thin to be easily caught. I
retain F pointing and incline towards
Johnson's own paraphrase: 'This is a
dream or madness, or both,—or
nothing,—but whether it be a speech
without consciousness (as in a dream),
or a speech unintelligible (as in mad-

ness), be it as it is, it is like my course of
life.' The experience is so intangible
as to be almost inexpressible, like
Imogen's 'bolt of nothing, shot at
nothing'. Proposed emendations are
worthless. Macbeth's famous lines (v.
v. 17–28) offer a sufficiently close
parallel.

156–7. *the dish . . . shot*] 'That is, the
viands (namely himself) pay the
reckoning' (Furness). 'Hanging' (l.
154) puns on the hanging of bacon,
venison, or game. The other culinary
quibbles are obvious.

no more tavern-bills, which are often the sadness of   160
parting, as the procuring of mirth: you come in
faint for want of meat, depart reeling with too much
drink: sorry that you have paid too much, and sorry
that you are paid too much: purse and brain, both
empty: the brain the heavier for being too light; the   165
purse too light, being drawn of heaviness. O, of this
contradiction you shall now be quit. O, the charity
of a penny cord! it sums up thousands in a trice: you
have no true debitor and creditor but it: of what's
past, is, and to come, the discharge: your neck, sir,   170
is pen, book, and counters; so the acquittance
follows.

Post. I am merrier to die than thou art to live.

First Gaol. Indeed sir, he that sleeps feels not the toothache: but a man that were to sleep your sleep, and a   175
hangman to help him to bed, I think he would
change places with his officer: for, look you, sir, you
know not which way you shall go.

Post. Yes, indeed do I, fellow.

First Gaol. Your death has eyes in's head then: I have   180
not seen him so pictur'd: you must either be

170. sir] Sis *F.*

163–4. *sorry . . . much*] 'Sorry that
you *have paid* too much out of your
pocket, and sorry that you *are paid*,
or *subdued*, too much by the liquor'
(Steevens). The Gaoler, who is here
reminiscent of the *Mac.* Porter as later
of the Grave-diggers in *Ham.*, employs
the once courtly and fashionable norm
of Euphuism. 'Compare this gaoler
with his cousin german Abhorson
in *Meas.*' (Granville-Barker). *Tw.N.*,
too, affords parallels.

166. *drawn*] emptied.

O, of] Some editors omit 'O', regarding it as an error caught from the line
following.

167–8. *O, the charity . . . trice*] Craig
unhappily conjectures 'celerity' for
'charity'. The gallows, in *Ham.*, v. i.
49–50, is the frame that 'outlives a
thousand tenants'. Granville-Barker

says excellently of this phrase that it is
'actuality supercharged; there is solid
man summed up in it'.

169. *debitor and creditor*] Johnson explains as an accounting book. 'He that
dies pays all debts' (*Tp.*, III. ii. 140).
For a parallel collocation of 'debitor-
creditor–counters–hangman', cf. *Oth.*,
I. i. 31–4.

171. *counters*] used for reckoning.

177. *officer*] executioner.

180. *Your death . . . then*) Vaughan
explains 'Your death' as death in
general and compares 'your philo-
sophy' in *Ham.*, I. v. 167, but Furness
thinks that 'your' is not ethical but
emphatic and I incline to agree.

181. *pictur'd*] referring, no doubt,
to the pictorial representations of
Death in the emblem-books of the
time.

directed by some that take upon them to know, or
to take upon yourself that which I am sure you do
not know, or jump the after-inquiry on your own
peril: and how you shall speed in your journey's   185
end, I think you'll never return to tell on.

Post. I tell thee, fellow, there are none want eyes to
direct them the way I am going, but such as wink,
and will not use them.

First Gaol. What an infinite mock is this, that a man   190
should have the best use of eyes to see the way of
blindness! I am sure hanging's the way of winking.

Enter a Messenger.

Mess. Knock off his manacles, bring your prisoner to
the king.

Post. Thou bring'st good news, I am call'd to be made   195
free.

First Gaol. I'll be hang'd then.

Post. Thou shalt be then freer than a gaoler; no bolts for
the dead.   [*Exeunt all but First Gaoler.*

First Gaol. Unless a man would marry a gallows, and   200

---

184. jump] *F;* lump *F2.*   186. on] *J. C. Maxwell conj.;* one *F.*   199. *Exeunt . . .*]
Camb.; not in F; Exeunt F2.

182–3. *know, or to take*] I have retained the reading of F, though it presents syntactical difficulty. It must be
remembered, however, that the
speaker is not an educated man. The
proposed emendations, 'or take'
(Heath); 'or so take' (Vaughan); 'or
do take' (Globe, but withdrawn), are
all quite plausible, and I would also
suggest omission of 'or'. I am indebted
to Dr Harold Brooks for a helpful
paraphrase of the passage: either you
must be directed by a chaplain, or you
must be sure (as I am sure you cannot
be) of your own salvation, or you are
simply disregarding the hereafter.
He suggests that behind this passage
and the next about blindness lies a
train of ideas deriving from the ritual
of execution, with its chaplain

and blind-folding of the condemned.
186. *tell on*] I am indebted to Mr
J. C. Maxwell for this almost certain
correction of F 'tell one'. F prints 'one'
for 'on' at v. v. 134 and, as Dowden
notes, the spelling 'one' for 'on' is not
uncommon. The same explanation
may conceivably hold for II. iv. 116
(see note *ad. loc.*).
191. *of eyes*] This should, perhaps,
read 'of's eyes': cf. 'in's head' (l. 180).
192. *hanging's*] F3 has 'such hanging's'.
200–8.] 'The first gaoler's soliloquy
—if he is to speak it on the main stage
with the inner stage curtains closing
behind him—may have been put in to
make time for the shifting of the pallet
upon which Posthumus had been
lying' (Granville-Barker, p. 255).

beget young gibbets, I never saw one so prone: yet,
on my conscience, there are verier knaves desire to
live, for all he be a Roman; and there be some of
them too, that die against their wills; so should I, if
I were one. I would we were all of one mind, and 205
one mind good: O, there were desolation of gaolers
and gallowses! I speak against my present profit,
but my wish hath a preferment in't. [*Exit.*

SCENE V.—*Cymbeline's Tent.*

Enter CYMBELINE, BELARIUS, GUIDERIUS, ARVIRAGUS,
PISANIO, *Lords, Officers, and Attendants.*

Cym. Stand by my side, you whom the gods have made
Preservers of my throne: woe is my heart,
That the poor soldier that so richly fought,
Whose rags sham'd gilded arms, whose naked breast
Stepp'd before targes of proof, cannot be found: 5
He shall be happy that can find him, if
Our grace can make him so.
Bel.   I never saw

208. *Exit*] F2; *Exeunt* F.

Scene v

S.D. *Cymbeline's Tent*] Rowe.   *Lords . . . Attendants*] Capell; *and Lords* F.

201. *prone*] eager.

202–3. *there are . . . Roman*] in spite of
the fact that he is a Roman (*ipso facto* a
knave and, being Roman, indifferent
to death), there are worse knaves who
desire to live.

204. *them*] i.e. Romans. The word is
emphatic.

207. *gallowses*] Rolfe describes this
as a vulgar plural but *O.E.D.* admits it as a sixteenth-century plural
form.

208. *preferment*] promotion. The virtuous Gaoler hopes for more remunerative employment under this Utopian dispensation. This is one of
Shakespeare's verbal winks.

Scene v

This scene is incomparable in its
technical virtuosity. Wendell enumerates twenty-four distinct dénouements, 'which in my opinion o'ervalues
it something'. Nevertheless, about a
dozen of them are of sufficient magnitude to be termed dénouements.
'*Cymbeline's Tent*' is Rowe's direction
and will suffice at a push. The theatrical reality of the main-stage is now
more pregnant than imaginary localization however.

5. *targes of proof*] tested shields.
'Stepp'd before' is possibly figurative,
signifying surpassed, excelled: cf.
'went before' (I. v. 69–70).

Such noble fury in so poor a thing;
Such precious deeds in one that promised nought
But beggary and poor looks.
Cym.   No tidings of him?   10
Pis. He hath been search'd among the dead and living;
But no trace of him.
Cym.   To my grief, I am
The heir of his reward, [*To Belarius, Guiderius, and
Arviragus*] which I will add
To you, the liver, heart, and brain of Britain,
By whom (I grant) she lives. 'Tis now the time   15
To ask of whence you are. Report it.
Bel.   Sir,
In Cambria are we born, and gentlemen:
Further to boast were neither true nor modest,
Unless I add we are honest.
Cym.   Bow your knees:
Arise my knights o' th' battle, I create you   20
Companions to our person, and will fit you
With dignities becoming your estates.

Enter CORNELIUS *and Ladies.*

There's business in these faces; why so sadly
Greet you our victory? you look like Romans,
And not o' th' court of Britain.
Cor.   Hail, great king!   25

13. *To . . . Arviragus*] *Rowe.*

10. *poor looks*] Warburton proposes
'poor luck', while Vaughan cites v. iii.
34 in defence of the emendation 'pale
looks'. The change is unnecessary, but
'looks' evidently means the same thing
in both passages. Posthumus seemed
likely to confront the enemy with sorry
looks, as distinct from threatening
looks.

14. *liver, heart, and brain*] the
'sovereign thrones' of *Tw.N.*, I. i. 37–8.
Regarded by the Elizabethans as the
three vital organs in man's physical
constitution. The liver generated the
natural spirits, the heart the vital, and
the brain the animal. Hence they were

respectively the seats of the passions,
the affections, and the reason. See
E. M. W. Tillyard, *The Elizabethan
World Picture*, pp. 63–4.

17. *In Cambria . . . gentlemen*] The
Welshman's ancestral pride is often
mentioned by the Elizabethans. Thus
Overbury, in his *Characters*, says of 'A
Welchman': 'Above all men he loves a
Herrald, and speaks pedigrees natur-
ally.'

20. *knights o' th' battle*] Special distinction attached to knighthoods con-
ferred on the battle-field.

22. *your estates*] your new rank, i.e.
knighthood.

        To sour your happiness, I must report
        The queen is dead.
Cym.   Who worse than a physician
        Would this report become? But I consider,
        By med'cine life may be prolong'd, yet death
        Will seize the doctor too. How ended she?   30
Cor. With horror, madly dying, like her life,
        Which (being cruel to the world) concluded
        Most cruel to herself. What she confess'd
        I will report, so please you. These her women
        Can trip me, if I err, who with wet cheeks   35
        Were present when she finish'd.
Cym.   Prithee say.
Cor. First, she confess'd she never lov'd you: only
        Affected greatness got by you: not you:
        Married your royalty, was wife to your place:
        Abhorr'd your person.
Cym.   She alone knew this: 40
        And but she spoke it dying, I would not
        Believe her lips in opening it. Proceed.
Cor. Your daughter, whom she bore in hand to love
        With such integrity, she did confess
        Was as a scorpion to her sight, whose life   45
        (But that her flight prevented it) she had
        Ta'en off by poison.
Cym.   O most delicate fiend!
        Who is't can read a woman? Is there more?
Cor. More, sir, and worse. She did confess she had
        For you a mortal mineral, which, being took,   50
        Should by the minute feed on life and ling'ring

27. Who] *F*; Whom *F2*.   51. life and ling'ring] life, and ling'ring, *F*.

27. *Who*] whom.
36. *finish'd*] Furness suggests that
this means when she ended her confession, but the word probably means
died.
37–40. *First . . . person*] I print the
colons as in F. They evidently indicate
pauses in delivery which add impres-
siveness to Cornelius' initial disclosures.
42. *opening*] disclosing.

43. *bore in hand*] *O.E.D.* glosses as
'To profess, pretend; to lead (one) to
believe'.
47. *delicate*] used by Shakespeare in
two senses: (i) beautiful; (ii) ingenious
(cf. similar meanings of 'exquisite').
Here, I think, he plays on both.
50. *mortal mineral*] Moyes identifies
as arsenic.
51. *ling'ring*] F prints commas after
'life' and 'lingr'ing'. Some editors

By inches waste you. In which time, she purpos'd
By watching, weeping, tendance, kissing, to
O'ercome you with her show; and in time
(When she had fitted you with her craft) to work   55
Her son into th' adoption of the crown:
But, failing of her end by his strange absence,
Grew shameless-desperate, open'd (in despite
Of heaven and men) her purposes: repented
The evils she hatch'd were not effected: so   60
Despairing died.
Cym.   Heard you all this, her women?
Ladies. We did, so please your highness.
Cym.   Mine eyes
Were not in fault, for she was beautiful:
Mine ears that heard her flattery, nor my heart
That thought her like her seeming. It had been vicious
To have mistrusted her: yet, O my daughter,   66
That it was folly in me, thou mayst say,
And prove it in thy feeling. Heaven mend all!

Enter LUCIUS, IACHIMO, *the Soothsayer, and other Roman
    Prisoners, guarded;* POSTHUMUS *behind, and* IMOGEN.

Thou com'st not, Caius, now for tribute; that
The Britons have raz'd out, though with the loss   70
Of many a bold one: whose kinsmen have made suit
That their good souls may be appeas'd with slaughter
Of you their captives, which ourself have granted:
So think of your estate.
Luc. Consider, sir, the chance of war, the day   75

58. shameless-desperate] *Capell;* shamelesse desperate *F.*   62. *Ladies*] *Camb.;*
La. *F; Lady F4.*   64. heard] *F3;* heare *F.*   68. S.D.] *Enter Lucius, Iachimo,
and other Roman Prisoners, Leonatus behind, and Imogen F.*

treat 'ling'ring' as a transitive verb.
Dowden regards it as an adjective
qualifying 'mineral'.
    54. *and in time*] F2 reads 'yes and',
which restores the metre. Other proposals are 'due time' (Walker); 'so in
time' (Jervis); 'thus in time' (Hertzberg). Ingleby's 'seeming' for 'show'
rests on a bibliographical improb-
ability.

    55. *fitted*] usually explained as
shaped you or disposed of you. Is it not
possible that it means tortured, as by
fits (as in Sonnet cxix)?
    68. *And prove . . . feeling*] 'sensibly
experience it' (Dowden). Cf. III. iii. 46,
'And felt them knowingly'.
    74. *estate*] 'condition, state; mean-
ing probably your soul's state' (Dowden).

Was yours by accident: had it gone with us,
We should not, when the blood was cool, have
    threaten'd
Our prisoners with the sword. But since the gods
Will have it thus, that nothing but our lives
May be call'd ransom, let it come: sufficeth   80
A Roman with a Roman's heart can suffer:
Augustus lives to think on't: and so much
For my peculiar care. This one thing only
I will entreat, my boy (a Briton born)
Let him be ransom'd: never master had   85
A page so kind, so duteous, diligent,
So tender over his occasions, true,
So feat, so nurse-like: let his virtue join
With my request, which I'll make bold your highness
Cannot deny: he hath done no Briton harm,   90
Though he have serv'd a Roman. Save him, sir,
And spare no blood beside.

Cym.   I have surely seen him:
His favour is familiar to me. Boy,
Thou hast look'd thyself into my grace,
And art mine own. I know not why, wherefore,   95
To say, live boy: ne'er thank thy master, live;
And ask of Cymbeline what boon thou wilt,
Fitting my bounty, and thy state, I'll give it:

---

83. *peculiar care*] personal concern.

86. *duteous, diligent*] Walker proposes 'duteous-diligent'.

87. *So tender . . . occasions*] variously explained as so attentive to his master's needs, or tender beyond the bare requirements of a page's duty.

88. *feat*] dexterous, graceful in movement.

93. *favour*] face. There is a similar act of recognition at the corresponding point in *Frederyke of Jennen*.

95–6. *I know . . . boy*] I follow F punctuation. Many editors accept Rowe's 'why, not wherefore', but F (*pace* the commentators, whose alterations and glosses it would be tedious to

enumerate) is quite straightforward. 'I know not' may, as usually assumed, signify 'I do not apprehend', but 'I do not acknowledge' is equally possible: 'why, wherefore' is a perfectly normal collocation which omits an 'and' or a 'nor' for the sake of emphasis: 'To say' is a common indefinite infinitive meaning 'in saying', 'for saying':'thy master' in l. 96 is Lucius. Hence the meaning is: I do not acknowledge (or apprehend) any why, any wherefore (i.e. any reason) for saying 'Live boy'. There is no need for you to thank Lucius, for it is my instinct, which disdains reasons, that spares you—not the reasons which he has given (in ll. 85–91).

     Yea, though thou do demand a prisoner,
     The noblest ta'en.
Imo.   I humbly thank your highness.   100
Luc. I do not bid thee beg my life, good lad,
     And yet I know thou wilt.
Imo.   No, no alack,
     There's other work in hand: I see a thing
     Bitter to me as death: your life, good master,
     Must shuffle for itself.
Luc.   The boy disdains me,   105
     He leaves me, scorns me: briefly die their joys
     That place them on the truth of girls and boys.
     Why stands he so perplex'd?
Cym.   What wouldst thou, boy?
     I love thee more and more: think more and more
     What's best to ask. Know'st him thou look'st on? speak,
     Wilt have him live? Is he thy kin? thy friend?   111
Imo. He is a Roman, no more kin to me
     Than I to your highness, who being born your vassal,
     Am something nearer.
Cym.   Wherefore ey'st him so?
Imo. I'll tell you, sir, in private, if you please   115
     To give me hearing.
Cym.   Ay, with all my heart,
     And lend my best attention. What's thy name?
Imo. Fidele, sir.
Cym.   Thou'rt my good youth: my page
     I'll be thy master: walk with me: speak freely.
                    [*Cymbeline and Imogen walk aside.*
Bel. Is not this boy reviv'd from death?
Arv.   One sand another

119. S.D.] *Theobald.*

103. *a thing*] the ring, her gift to Posthumus, on Iachimo's finger.
106–7. *briefly . . . boys*] Furness rejects.
108. *Why . . . perplex'd*] Ingleby gives these words to Cymbeline,—wrongly, I think.
120–2. *One sand . . . Fidele*] The ellipsis accords with Shakespeare's

later style. Johnson prints a full stop after 'resembles' and retains Rowe's comma (for F semi-colon) after 'lad'. Other emendations include: 'than he th' sweet' (Theobald); 'resembles more than he that sweet and rosy' (Capell). *O.E.D.* shows that 're-semble' in Shakespeare's day carried several shades of meaning, and 3b 'to

Not more resembles that sweet rosy lad,   121
Who died, and was Fidele! What think you?
Gui. The same dead thing alive.
Bel. Peace, peace, see further: he eyes us not, forbear;
Creatures may be alike: were't he, I am sure   125
He would have spoke to us.
Gui.   But we see him dead.
Bel. Be silent: let's see further.
Pis.   [*Aside*] It is my mistress:
Since she is living, let the time run on,
To good, or bad.   [*Cymbeline and Imogen come forward.*
Cym.   Come, stand thou by our side,
Make thy demand aloud. [*To Iachimo*] Sir, step you
        forth,   130
Give answer to this boy, and do it freely,
Or, by our greatness and the grace of it
(Which is our honour) bitter torture shall
Winnow the truth from falsehood. On, speak to him.
Imo. My boon is, that this gentleman may render   135
Of whom he had this ring.
Post.   [*Aside*] What's that to him?
Cym. That diamond upon your finger, say
How came it yours?
Iach. Thou'lt torture me to leave unspoken that
Which, to be spoke, would torture thee.

---

121. lad,] *Rowe;* lad. *F.*   127. *Aside*] *Rowe.*   129. S.D.] *Theobald.*   130. *To
Iachimo*] *Rowe.*   134. On, speak] *F3;* One speake *F.*   135. render] *F;*
tender *F2.*   136. *Aside*] *Capell.*

copy, imitate' (example from Ben Jonson) may apply here. The situation is closely parallel to that at the end of *Tw.N.*, a play which was evidently much in the dramatist's thoughts when he wrote the present scene and that play, at v. i. 229–31, clarifies the sense of the present passage: 'How have you made division of yourself? / An apple, cleft in two, is not more twin / Than these two creatures.'

126. *But . . . dead*] Rowe's specious emendation is 'saw' (for 'see'). F is open to two interpretations: (i) but

what we see must be his ghost; (ii) unless we see him dead (Craig's suggestion), and there is a possible third: but we see him that is dead.

134. *On*] F 'One'. See note to v. iv. 186.

139–40. *Thou'lt . . . thee*] Hudson reads ''Twould' for 'Thou'lt', but Abbott's paraphrase ('You wish to torture me *for leaving* unspoken that which, *by being spoken*, would torture you'), makes emendation unnecessary. Iachimo's play on 'torture' is very involved. 'Thou'lt' may be a pure future, the idea being: You will tor-

Cym.   How? me?   140
Iach. I am glad to be constrain'd to utter that
Which torments me to conceal. By villainy
I got this ring; 'twas Leonatus' jewel,
Whom thou didst banish: and—which more may
    grieve thee,
As it doth me,—a nobler sir ne'er lived   145
'Twixt sky and ground. Wilt thou hear more, my lord?
Cym. All that belongs to this.
Iach.   That paragon, thy daughter,
For whom my heart drops blood, and my false spirits
Quail to remember—Give me leave; I faint.
Cym. My daughter? what of her? Renew thy strength: 150
I had rather thou shouldst live, while Nature will,
Than die ere I hear more: strive, man, and speak.
Iach. Upon a time, unhappy was the clock
That struck the hour: it was in Rome, accurst
The mansion where: 'twas at a feast, O, would   155

---

149. remember—] *Pope;* remember. *F.*

ture me now to make me speak, you
will then torture me again to make me
unsay that which, if spoken, would
torture you.

  141–2. *that | Which torments*] Emen-
dations are: 'what / Torments' (Pope);
'that / Torments' (Ritson); 'that /
Which it torments' (Vaughan). Capell
begins l. 142 at 'Torments', adding
'which' to 141. Dyce endorses Ritson's
reading by claiming that 'Which' is a
printer's error. One may go further
and argue that 'that / Which' is the
printer's duplication of the identical
form at ll. 139–40. If so, both words
might here be replaced by 'What'.
The possibility that an elided 'it' has
been lost (whatever reading we favour)
cannot be overlooked.

  148. *and . . . spirits*] and whom my
false spirits, etc.

  150–209.] The fact that Iachimo so
unashamedly embroiders his story has
provoked much fruitless discussion.
Granville-Barker sensibly comments
that 'Iachimo is "making a story of

it", the "Italian brain" operating as
tortuously as ever, and to no purpose
now. That, at any rate, is the obvious
effect made, and it is a very good one.'
The curious thing is that Iachimo's
story is at once boastful and apologetic. This, I think, is because Shakespeare has to conflate what, in both the
Decameron and *Frederyke of Jennen*, is
presented as two distinct confessions,
the first of which is voluntary and self-
glorifying.

  155. *'twas at a feast*] cited by
Thiselton as a piece of embroidery, but
possibly suggested to Shakespeare by
his source. In the *Decameron*, the merchants simply meet at supper, but in
Frederyke of Jennen what purports to be
a dinner involves good cheer and
making merry all day long, 'with
daunsyng and lepyng'. The stage in
I. v may be set as for a feast. Philario's
guests have presumably been invited
to come and meet Posthumus, and
some entertainment would normally
be provided.

Our viands had been poison'd (or at least
Those which I heaved to head) the good Posthumus
(What should I say? he was too good to be
Where ill men were, and was the best of all
Amongst the rar'st of good ones) sitting sadly,   160
Hearing us praise our loves of Italy
For beauty, that made barren the swell'd boast
Of him that best could speak: for feature, laming
The shrine of Venus, or straight-pight Minerva,
Postures, beyond brief Nature. For condition,   165
A shop of all the qualities that man
Loves woman for, besides that hook of wiving,
Fairness, which strikes the eye.

Cym.   I stand on fire.
Come to the matter.

Iach.   All too soon I shall,   169
Unless thou wouldst grieve quickly. This Posthumus,
Most like a noble lord in love and one
That had a royal lover, took his hint,
And (not dispraising whom we prais'd, therein
He was as calm as virtue) he began
His mistress' picture, which, by his tongue, being made,
And then a mind put in 't, either our brags   176
Were crak'd of kitchen-trulls, or his description
Prov'd us unspeaking sots.

171. lord in love] *Pope;* Lord, in love, *F.*

163. *feature*] beauty of form.

laming] rendering deformed (by comparison).

164. *shrine*] *O.E.D.* takes the word in this context as equivalent to 'temple' and regards it as 'a somewhat strained figurative application'. But 'shrine' may stand figuratively for the human body. Some critics interpret as statue, image.

straight-pight] *O.E.D.* defines 'having a tall and erect figure'.

165. *Postures . . . Nature*] variously interpreted. Warburton defines 'brief Nature' as 'hasty, unelaborate nature'. Hunter paraphrases: 'Postures of beings that are immortal', and Ingle-

by: 'Postures permanently rendered in marble which are only transient in nature.' Dowden suggests, plausibly, that 'brief' may signify 'limited, restricted (and so incapable of producing perfection)'.

condition] character, nature, disposition.

172. *lover*] usually glossed as 'mistress' (as often), but here, I think, meaning one who returned his love.

177. *crak'd*] boasted. Most editors print 'crack'd' but I have preferred F as indicating possible pronunciation. Both 'crack' and 'crake' are now dialectal.

178. *unspeaking sots*] fools incapable

Cym.   Nay, nay, to th' purpose.
Iach. Your daughter's chastity (there it begins)—
He spoke of her, as Dian had hot dreams,   180
And she alone were cold: whereat I, wretch,
Made scruple of his praise, and wager'd with him
Pieces of gold, 'gainst this (which he then wore
Upon his honour'd finger) to attain
In suit the place of 's bed, and win this ring   185
By hers and mine adultery: he, true knight,
No lesser of her honour confident
Than I did truly find her, stakes this ring,
And would so, had it been a carbuncle
Of Phoebus' wheel; and might so safely, had it   190
Been all the worth of 's car. Away to Britain
Post I in this design: well may you, sir,
Remember me at court, where I was taught
Of your chaste daughter the wide difference
'Twixt amorous and villainous. Being thus quench'd
Of hope, not longing, mine Italian brain   196
Gan in your duller Britain operate
Most vilely: for my vantage, excellent.
And to be brief, my practice so prevail'd,
That I return'd with simular proof enough   200
To make the noble Leonatus mad,

182. wager'd] *F;* wag'd *F2.*   197. operate] operare *F.*   198. vilely] *F4;*
vildely *F.*

of describing beauty (in comparison with him).

180. *as*] as if.

182. *Made scruple*] expressed doubt, disputed.

184. *honour'd finger*] 'His finger was honoured by bearing on it a token of such love and devotion' (Furness).

185. *in suit*] by urging my suit.

186. *hers*] Abbott notes that 'mine', 'hers', 'theirs' were used as pronominal adjectives before their nouns.

189–90. *a carbuncle . . . wheel*] so in *Ant.,* IV. viii. 28–9: 'He has deserved it, / were it carbuncled / Like holy Phoebus' car'. The source is Ovid, *Metamorphoses,* ii. 107. Pliny virtually

identifies the carbuncle with the ruby, but Batman enumerates twelve varieties.

197. *your duller Britain*] Dowden suggests that 'Briton' would better convey the sense, and Furness thinks that 'your duller Britain' is Posthumus. This seems absurd. In any case Iachimo and Posthumus were a thousand miles apart when these vile operations of the Italian brain began.

199. *practice*] treachery.

200. *simular*] usually glossed as 'counterfeited', but Furness suggests 'specious', 'plausible', on the grounds that Iachimo's proofs were not strictly counterfeit.

By wounding his belief in her renown,
With tokens thus, and thus: averring notes
Of chamber-hanging, pictures, this her bracelet
(O cunning, how I got it!) nay, some marks   205
Of secret on her person, that he could not
But think her bond of chastity quite crack'd,
I having ta'en the forfeit. Whereupon—
Methinks I see him now—
Post.   [*Advancing*] Ay, so thou dost
Italian fiend! Ay me, most credulous fool,   210
Egregious murderer, thief, any thing
That's due to all the villains past, in being,
To come. O, give me cord, or knife, or poison
Some upright justicer! Thou, king, send out
For torturers ingenious: it is I   215
That all th' abhorred things o' th' earth amend
By being worse than they. I am Posthumus,
That kill'd thy daughter: villain-like, I lie;
That caus'd a lesser villain than myself,
A sacrilegious thief, to do't. The temple   220
Of Virtue was she; yea, and she herself.
Spit, and throw stones, cast mire upon me, set
The dogs o' th' street to bay me: every villain

205. got it!] got *F.*   208–9. Whereupon— . . . now—] *Johnson;* Whereupon,
. . . now. *F.*   209. S.D.] *not in F.*   214. Thou, king] *Theobald;* Thou King *F.*
223. bay] *Ff1–2;* bait *Ff3–4.*

203. *averring*] Johnson regards as an
adjective meaning 'confirmatory', but
Dowden's suggestion that it is verbal
and means 'avouching' is more
probable.
    205. *O cunning . . . it*] The villain
similarly exults in his own cunning in
both the *Decameron* and *Frederyke of
Jennen.*
    208. *forfeit*] that which was for-
feited by the broken bond.
    209. Advancing] Granville-Barker
suggests that Posthumus has been
listening from behind, possibly from
the inner-stage. Cf. S.D. preceding
l. 69.

210. *Ay me*] Staunton unnecessarily
proposes 'Give me' with 'any thing' as
its object. 'Any thing' clearly means
any epithet.
    214. *justicer*] judge.
    216. *amend*] 'The thought that a
great crime or sin makes slighter sins
look less hideous, or even beautiful
by comparison, occurs several times in
Shakespeare' (Dowden). The idea is
implicit in much of III. iv. 47–65 and
may conceivably underly the perplexing passage at v. i. 15. (See note
ad. loc.)
    221. *she herself*] Virtue herself.
    223–5. *every . . . 'twas*] Again III. iv.

Be call'd Posthumus Leonatus, and
Be villainy less than 'twas. O Imogen!   225
My queen, my life, my wife, O Imogen,
Imogen, Imogen!
Imo.   Peace, my lord, hear, hear—
Post. Shall's have a play of this? Thou scornful page,
There lie thy part.   [*Striking her: she falls.*
Pis.   O, gentlemen, help!
Mine and your mistress: O, my lord Posthumus!   230
You ne'er kill'd Imogen till now. Help, help!
Mine honour'd lady!
Cym.   Does the world go round?
Post. How comes these staggers on me?
Pis.   Wake, my mistress!
Cym. If this be so, the gods do mean to strike me
To death with mortal joy.
Pis.   How fares my mistress?   235
Imo. O, get thee from my sight,
Thou gav'st me poison: dangerous fellow, hence!
Breathe not where princes are.
Cym.   The tune of Imogen!

227. hear—] *Rowe;* heare. *F.*   229. S.D.] *Rowe.*   gentlemen] *F;* Gentleman *F2.*   help!] helpe, *F.*   233. comes] *F;* come *Rowe.*   Wake,]
Rowe; Wake *F.*

47–65 offers parallels. The idea is conspicuous in *Troil.,* III. ii. 178–212; IV.
ii. 105–7; v. ii. 178–80.
        228–9. *Shall's . . . part*] Dr G. K.
Hunter suggests to me that the action
here owes something to Under-
downe's translation of the *Æthiopica*
of Heliodorus where Theagenes spurns
Chariclea: 'He seeing her foul face, of
purpose beblacked, and her apparel
vile and all torn, supposing her belike
to be one of the makeshifts of the city
and a vagabond, cast her off and put
her away, and at length, when she
would not let him go, gave her a blow
on the ear, for that she troubled him in
seeing Calasiris.' It is significant that
the *Æthiopica,* too, presents this incident in terms of a play: 'another act

was interlaced into the play', 'such
wondrous doings as commonly are but
seen upon the stage', etc.
        229. *help!*] F 'helpe,'. Some editors,
perhaps rightly, omit the comma,
making 'mistress' the object. The same
could apply at l. 231.
        233. *staggers*] 'This wild and deli-
rious perturbation' (Johnson). Normally the name of a horse-disease.
        235–59.] Furness regards the bulk
of this section as interpolated.
        238. *tune*] Eccles thinks that this
refers to the musical quality of
Imogen's voice which now serves to
establish her identity. Furness argues
for 'character, temper, disposition'.
Dowden's gloss: tone, accent, seems to
me sufficient.

Pis. Lady,
    The gods throw stones of sulphur on me, if   240
    That box I gave you was not thought by me
    A precious thing: I had it from the queen.
Cym. New matter still.
Imo.   It poison'd me.
Cor.   O gods!
    I left out one thing which the queen confess'd,
    Which must approve thee honest. 'If Pisanio   245
    Have,' said she, 'given his mistress that confection
    Which I gave him for cordial, she is serv'd
    As I would serve a rat.'
Cym.   What's this, Cornelius?
Cor. The queen, sir, very oft importun'd me
    To temper poisons for her, still pretending   250
    The satisfaction of her knowledge only
    In killing creatures vile, as cats and dogs
    Of no esteem. I, dreading that her purpose
    Was of more danger, did compound for her
    A certain stuff, which being ta'en would cease   255
    The present power of life, but in short time
    All offices of nature should again
    Do their due functions. Have you ta'en of it?
Imo. Most like I did, for I was dead.
Bel.   My boys,
    There was our error.
Gui.   This is sure Fidele.   260
Imo. Why did you throw your wedded lady from you?
    Think that you are upon a rock, and now
    Throw me again.   *[Embracing him.*

239-40. Lady . . . if] *Malone; one line F.*
F; seize *F2.*   261. from] *Rowe;* fro *F.*

252. vile] *F4;* vilde *F.*   255. cease]
263. S.D.] *Malone.*

239-40. *Lady . . . if*] F prints as one line. The change is Malone's.

240. *stones of sulphur*] thunderbolts.

243. *still.*] so F. Pope's 'still?' is generally accepted but the change adds little or nothing.

255. *cease*] end. Frequently transitive in Elizabethan English.

259. *dead*] usually explained as in-

sensible. Surely equivalent to 'as if dead' in the present context (cf. S.D. preceding IV. ii. 195).

260. *This . . . Fidele*] so F. I take 'sure' to be an adjective, cf. IV. ii. 107, 'very Cloten', and V. v. 359, 'true Guiderius'. Theobald reads 'This is sure, Fidele', making 'sure' adverbial.

262-3. *Think . . . again*] a much dis-

Post.   Hang there like fruit, my soul,
    Till the tree die.
Cym.   How now, my flesh, my child?
    What, mak'st thou me a dullard in this act?   265
    Wilt thou not speak to me?
Imo.   [*Kneeling*] Your blessing, sir.
Bel. [*To Gui. and Arv.*] Though you did love this youth,
        I blame ye not,
    You had a motive for't.
Cym.   My tears that fall
    Prove holy water on thee; Imogen,
    Thy mother's dead.
Imo.   I am sorry for't, my lord.   270
Cym. O, she was naught; and long of her it was
    That we meet here so strangely: but her son
    Is gone, we know not how, nor where.
Pis.   My lord,
    Now fear is from me, I'll speak troth. Lord Cloten,
    Upon my lady's missing, came to me   275

266. S.D.] *Rowe.*   267. *To . . . Arv.*] *Pope.*

puted passage. Textually there are three possibilities: (i) that F is correct; (ii) that, as Dowden suggests, 'rock' should read 'lock'; (iii) that the corruption is so deep-rooted as to defeat conjecture. Dowden's 'lock', a wrestling term meaning grip or embrace, is on all counts a brilliant conjecture, yet it lacks the ring of truth. Fr. Stephenson (*op. cit.*, p. 334), not quite convincingly invokes *Wint.*, v. ii. 81–4, in support of it. Those critics who follow F usually offer one of two interpretations: (i) Imogen playfully instructs Posthumus to throw her to destruction, as from a rock; (ii) she bids him think of himself as a shipwrecked sailor who has at last run upon the rock of security. L. 394 is cited in support of this second interpretation. All proposed emendations, save Dowden's, can be disregarded. Liberty to interpret remains, as anyone who consults *O.E.D.* on 'rock' and 'throw' will readily perceive. One meaning of

'throw' is to fell (a tree etc.). This would, perhaps, accord with Posthumus' reply, but is hard to reconcile with 'rock'.

263. Embracing him] a necessary condition of the oracle, see ll. 450–3.

263–4. *Hang . . . die*] Considered by Tennyson to be 'among the tenderest lines in Shakespeare'. 'Ten words which do more than anything else in the play to bring him (Posthumus) in weight and value a little nearer to Imogen' (Spurgeon, *Shakespeare's Imagery*, p. 233).

264. *my flesh*] in contrast to 'my soul' in l. 263.

267. *Though*] Eccles suggests 'That'.

271. *naught*] worthless, wicked (cf. P.E. 'naughty').

long of her] owing to her.

274. *Lord Cloten*] The appended title may be due to recollection of Ophelia's similar description of the frenzied 'Lord Hamlet' (*Ham.*, ii. i. 77 ff.).

With his sword drawn, foam'd at the mouth, and swore,
If I discover'd not which way she was gone,
It was my instant death. By accident,
I had a feigned letter of my master's
Then in my pocket, which directed him   280
To seek her on the mountains near to Milford;
Where, in a frenzy, in my master's garments,
(Which he enforc'd from me) away he posts
With unchaste purpose, and with oath to violate
My lady's honour: what became of him   285
I further know not.

Gui.   Let me end the story:
I slew him there.

Cym.   Marry, the gods forfend!
I would not thy good deeds should from my lips
Pluck a hard sentence: prithee, valiant youth,
Deny't again.

Gui.   I have spoke it, and I did it.   290

Cym. He was a prince.

Gui. A most incivil one. The wrongs he did me
Were nothing prince-like; for he did provoke me
With language that would make me spurn the sea,
If it could so roar to me. I cut off's head,   295
And am right glad he is not standing here
To tell this tale of mine.

Cym.   I am sorrow for thee:
By thine own tongue thou art condemn'd, and must
Endure our law: thou'rt dead.

Imo.   That headless man
I thought had been my lord.

---

279. *feigned letter*] See n. to III. v. 100.

280–1. *him . . . her*] Rowe emends to 'her . . . him', but the sense of 'directed' is, presumably, 'led, guided'.

284. *unchaste purpose*] Critics object that Pisanio can know nothing about this, but see note to III. v. 131.

288. *thy good deeds*] i.e. in the battle.

290. *Deny't again*] Speak again and deny what you have said.

292. *incivil*] unmannerly or, in fact 'nothing prince-like'.

297. *sorrow*] I follow F, though with some hesitation since F2 reads 'sory' and since Dyce assures us that Shakespeare uses 'I am sorry' more than fifty times. The 1608 Quarto of *Lr.* prints 'sorrow' where F prints '(I am onely) sorry' (IV. vi. 162), but its authority is dubious. The phrase could, however, be formed by analogy with 'I am woe for't, sir' (*Tp.*, v. i. 139) and 'Woe, woe are we' (*Ant.*, IV. xiv. 133).

Cym.   Bind the offender,   300
  And take him from our presence.
Bel.   Stay, sir king.
  This man is better than the man he slew,
  As well descended as thyself, and hath
  More of thee merited than a band of Clotens
  Had ever scar for. [*To the Guard*] Let his arms alone, 305
  They were not born for bondage.
Cym.   Why, old soldier:
  Wilt thou undo the worth thou art unpaid for
  By tasting of our wrath? How of descent
  As good as we?
Arv.   In that he spake too far.
Cym. And thou shalt die for't.
Bel.   We will die all three,   310
  But I will prove that two on's are as good
  As I have given out him. My sons, I must
  For mine own part unfold a dangerous speech,
  Though haply well for you.
Arv.   Your danger's ours.
Gui. And our good his.
Bel.   Have at it then, by leave: 315

305. *To the Guard*] Theobald.   311. on's] *F2;* one's *F.*   315. then, by leave:]
Pope; then, by leave *F.*

305. *scar*] F 'scarre'. Emended to
'sense' (Collier); 'soar' (Bailey);
'score' *sc.* credit (Singer, Ed. 2);
'scorse' *sc.* payment (Hudson). F
seems perfectly intelligible.

308. *tasting*] Hanmer reads 'tempting' and Warburton 'hasting'. Since
the collocation 'bondage-tasting' is
repeated at l. 404, it seems likely that
F is right. The sense of the word in this
context has provoked much discussion. Surely it is the obvious one,
here and in 404.

310. *And thou . . . for't*] Dowden
wonders whether this is addressed to
Belarius or to Guiderius. Is it not
possible that Cymbeline, in his extravagant wrath, rounds upon Arviragus,
following the latter's interruption?

Belarius (l. 310) seems to take the
death sentence as covering all three of
them.

We . . . three] This I take to signify
resigned acceptance of the doom pronounced by Cymbeline. Some editors
omit the comma after 'three' and
explain: We will die . . . if I do not
prove etc. I take 'But' in the sense of
'yet', 'even so'.

315–18. *Have . . . traitor*] I follow
F lineation. Most editors, perhaps
rightly, suspect dislocation and either
change or supplement. On the other
hand, F arrangement allows for effective dramatic pauses. Dowden notes
that it is doubtful whether 'by leave'
should be connected with either 'Have
at it' or 'Thou hadst'.

Thou hadst, great king, a subject, who
Was call'd Belarius.——

Cym. What of him? he is a banish'd traitor.

Bel. He it is that hath
Assum'd this age: indeed a banish'd man,   320
I know not how a traitor.

Cym.   Take him hence,
The whole world shall not save him.

Bel.   Not too hot;
First pay me for the nursing of thy sons,
And let it be confiscate all, so soon
As I have receiv'd it.

Cym.   Nursing of my sons?   325

Bel. I am too blunt, and saucy: here's my knee:
Ere I arise I will prefer my sons;
Then spare not the old father. Mighty sir,
These two young gentlemen that call me father
And think they are my sons, are none of mine;   330
They are the issue of your loins, my liege,
And blood of your begetting.

Cym.   How? my issue?

Bel. So sure as you your father's. I (old Morgan)
Am that Belarius, whom you sometime banish'd:
Your pleasure was my ne'er-offence, my punishment

---

332. issue?] *Rowe;* issue. *F.*   335. ne'er-offence] neere offence *F.*

319-20. *He . . . age*] Steevens, rightly I think, interprets 'assumed' as 'reached', 'attained'. The phrase means little more than 'I am he' and answers Cymbeline's 'What of him?', just as 'indeed . . . traitor' answers 'he is a banish'd traitor'.

324. *confiscate . . . soon*] The accent falls on the second syllable in 'confiscate'. Dowden, perhaps rightly, omits the comma after 'all'.

327. *prefer*] promote, advance.

335-7. *Your . . . I did*] The punctuation is Pope's. F prints: 'Your pleasure was my neere offence, my punishment / It selfe, and all my Treason that I suffer'd, / Was all the harme I did.' Both versions present a difficult

oxymoron, and in F it is impossible to parse 'that' with certainty. Possibly 'my punishment' is in antithesis to 'your pleasure'. 'All my treason' may refer to the stealing of the princes rather than the alleged dereliction. Proposed emendations: 'Itself was' (Johnson) and 'Itself made' (Vaughan) offer a solution of sorts, but there are many possibilities from which, so far as I can see, no probability emerges.

335. *ne'er-offence*] F3 converts F 'neere' into 'near'. Thiselton proposes 'near my offence', i.e. almost my offence. Johnson would emend to 'dear' but Tyrwhitt's 'meere' (*sc.* mere: whole, entire) has superseded it and has remained virtually un-

Itself, and all my treason: that I suffer'd,   336
Was all the harm I did. These gentle princes
(For such and so they are) these twenty years
Have I train'd up; those arts they have; as I
Could put into them. My breeding was, sir, as   340
Your highness knows. Their nurse, Euriphile,
(Whom for the theft I wedded) stole these children
Upon my banishment: I mov'd her to't,
Having receiv'd the punishment before
For that which I did then. Beaten for loyalty   345
Excited me to treason. Their dear loss,
The more of you 'twas felt, the more it shap'd
Unto my end of stealing them. But gracious sir,
Here are your sons again, and I must lose
Two of the sweet'st companions in the world.   350
The benediction of these covering heavens
Fall on their heads like dew, for they are worthy
To inlay heaven with stars.
Cym.   Thou weep'st, and speak'st:
The service that you three have done is more
Unlike than this thou tell'st. I lost my children: 355
If these be they, I know not how to wish
A pair of worthier sons.

336. treason:] *Pope;* Treason *F.*

challenged. It has obvious typographical probability, and 'mere' is a
fairly common Shakespearean adjective. My own reading, since 'ne'er'
sometimes appears as 'neere' in F, is a
reversion rather than an emendation.
In support of it, I would urge that
Shakespeare elsewhere coins compounds with 'ne'er' and 'never' and
that adjectival use of temporal adverbs
was a fairly common Elizabethan
device (cf. 'seldom pleasure', Sonnet
LII; 'evermore unrest', Sonnet CXLVII;
'often flames' Marlowe's *Lucan*). More
pertinent is the fact that Belarius' offence was precisely a 'ne'er-offence',
cf. III. iii. 65, 'My fault being nothing'.

338. *such and so*] Belarius emphasizes
that they are both 'princes' and

'gentle', that their princely virtues
have not been impaired by their up_
bringing.

339. *those arts*] Pope reads 'such arts',
which misses the point. Belarius considers himself a well-qualified instruc-
tor.

340. *put into them*] teach them.

342. *children*] Johnson prints a full
stop after 'children' and deletes the
colon after 'banishment'. Nothing is
gained by this.

345. *Beaten*] my having been
beaten. Nominative suppressed in a
participial phrase.

353. *To inlay . . . stars*] Steevens compares *Rom.*, III. ii. 22 ff.

355. *Unlike*] improbable, incredible.
The 'service' refers, of course, to their
deeds in the battle.

Bel.   Be pleas'd awhile;
This gentleman, whom I call Polydore,
Most worthy prince, as yours, is true Guiderius:
This gentleman, my Cadwal, Arviragus   360
Your younger princely son, he, sir, was lapp'd
In a most curious mantle, wrought by th' hand
Of his queen mother, which for more probation
I can with ease produce.

Cym.   Guiderius had
Upon his neck a mole, a sanguine star;   365
It is a mark of wonder.

Bel.   This is he,
Who hath upon him still that natural stamp:
It was wise Nature's end, in the donation
To be his evidence now.

Cym.   O, what am I?
A mother to the birth of three? Ne'er mother   370
Rejoic'd deliverance more. Blest pray you be,
That, after this strange starting from your orbs,
You may reign in them now! O Imogen,
Thou hast lost by this a kingdom.

Imo.   No, my lord;
I have got two worlds by't. O my gentle brothers,   375
Have we thus met? O, never say hereafter
But I am truest speaker. You call'd me brother,
When I was but your sister: I you brothers,
When ye were so indeed.

Cym.   Did you e'er meet?
Arv. Ay, my good lord.

369. what am I?] *Hanmer;* what am I *F;* what, am I *Dyce.*   378. brothers] *F;*
Brother *F2.*   379. ye] we *F.*

362. *curious mantle*] elaborate mantle.
'The mantle plays a part also in *Wint.*
(and in Greene's novel on which it is
founded) in the identification of the
lost child' (Dowden).

363. *more probation*] further proof.

365. *mole*] For the mole as a means
to identification cf. *Tw.N.*, v. i.
249.

370. *mother*] explained by Rolfe
as the object of the verb 'rejoic'd',

'deliverance' being the subject.

371. *pray*] Rowe emends to 'may'.

372. *orbs*] spheres. The princes are
likened to stars, which, according to
the Ptolemaic system, moved in fixed
concentric spheres, and which were
thought to 'reign' or exert influence on
human affairs.

379. *When ye*] 'If the Folio be right,
we must give the speech to Arviragus'
(Johnson).

Gui.   And at first meeting lov'd,   380
Continu'd so, until we thought he died.
Cor. By the queen's dram she swallow'd.
Cym.   O rare instinct!
When shall I hear all through? This fierce abridgement
Hath to it circumstantial branches, which
Distinction should be rich in. Where? how liv'd you?
And when came you to serve our Roman captive?   386
How parted with your brothers? how first met them?
Why fled you from the court? and whither? These,
And your three motives to the battle, with
I know not how much more, should be demanded   390
And all the other by-dependances,
From chance to chance. But nor the time nor place
Will serve our long inter'gatories. See,
Posthumus anchors upon Imogen;
And she (like harmless lightning) throws her eye   395
On him: her brothers, me: her master hitting

387. brothers] *Rowe (ed. 3);* Brother *F.*   388. whither? These,] *Theobald;*
whether these? *F.*   393. inter'gatories] *Malone;* Interrogatories *F.*

381. *he*] Hanmer unnecessarily reads 'she'. Guiderius still thinks of Imogen as Fidele.

383. *fierce*] The meanings attached to this word by Shakespeare in his final period are not always easy to define. Johnson explains it here as 'vehement', 'rapid', and Schmidt as 'wild, disordered, irregular'. I take it to mean 'drastic', i.e. like something fiercely imposed.

385. *Distinction . . . in*] i.e. each distinct detail should itself be rich in detail.

385–8. *Where? . . . whither?*] Cf. Sidney, *Astrophel and Stella,* XCII: 'I would know whether shee did sit or walke: / How cloathd: how waited on: how sighd shee or smilde: / Whereof: with whome: how often did she talke: / With what pastimes, times jorneys shee beguild.'

387. *brothers*] It is possible to defend F 'Brother' on the assumption that it refers to Cloten, but this seems most unlikely.

389. *your three motives*] the motives of you three.

391. *by-dependances*] Dowden's 'side issues' hits the sense admirably.

393. *inter'gatories*] Malone's spelling represents Shakespearean pronunciation.

394. *anchors*] Dowden following Deighton compares *Meas.,* II. iv. 3, 'my invention . . . Anchors on Isabel.' Since F prints 'Anchors' in the present passage, it is just possible that the word is a noun and that we should read 'Posthumus' anchor's upon Imogen'. Whether this could resolve the difficulty at l. 262 I do not pretend to know.

396. *On . . . hitting*] Most editors accept Rowe's pointing 'On him, her brothers, me, her master hitting, etc.' but this implies that Imogen alone 'throws her eye', whereas 'the counterchange is severally in all.' In other words there is considerable exchange of glances as F, despite its complexity, suggests. Imogen eyes Posthumus: the

Each object with a joy: the counterchange
Is severally in all. Let's quit this ground,
And smoke the temple with our sacrifices.
[*To Belarius*] Thou art my brother; so we'll hold thee
    ever.   400
Imo. You are my father too, and did relieve me,
  To see this gracious season.
Cym.   All o'erjoy'd,
  Save these in bonds, let them be joyful too,
  For they shall taste our comfort.
Imo.   My good master,
  I will yet do you service.
Luc.   Happy be you!   405
Cym. The forlorn soldier that so nobly fought,
  He would have well becom'd this place, and grac'd
  The thankings of a king.
Post.   I am, sir,
  The soldier that did company these three
  In poor beseeming: 'twas a fitment for   410
  The purpose I then follow'd. That I was he,
  Speak, Iachimo: I had you down, and might
  Have made you finish.
Iach.   [*Kneels*] I am down again:
  But now my heavy conscience sinks my knee,

---

400. *To Belarius*] Rowe.   401. father] *F*; Mother *F2*.   406. so] *F2*; no *F*.
413. you] *F*; your *F2*.   S.D.] *Hanmer*.

Princes eye Cymbeline: Imogen's master (presumably Lucius) glances from one to the other. The syntax is admittedly abnormal but is in keeping with Shakespeare's late style. The particular is universalized as it is elsewhere throughout this scene.

397–8. *the counterchange . . . all*] 'The reciprocation is in all, and individually in each' (Dowden).

401. *relieve*] The verb may conceal the image of a town being relieved after a siege: cf. III. iv. 135–6: 'That Cloten, whose love-suit hath been to me / As fearful as a siege'.

406. *forlorn*] Dowden interprets as 'lost', but Furness's 'meanly dressed' is preferable. Shakespeare several times uses the word in the sense 'poverty-stricken'.

407. *becom'd*] an irregular participial form used several times by Shakespeare.

410. *beseeming*] appearance.

fitment] O.E.D. glosses as 'a making fit, preparation' in the present context. The same authority defines it as 'that which is fitting' in *Per.*, IV. vi. 6—a sense which Furness would prefer here. I incline to define 'makeshift', 'device', as the word itself seems to imply.

413. *finish*] die.

As then your force did. Take that life, beseech you,   415
Which I so often owe: but your ring first,
And here the bracelet of the truest princess
That ever swore her faith.

Post.   Kneel not to me:
The power that I have on you, is to spare you:
The malice towards you, to forgive you. Live   420
And deal with others better.

Cym.   Nobly doom'd!
We'll learn our freeness of a son-in-law:
Pardon's the word to all.

Arv.   You holp us, sir,
As you did mean indeed to be our brother;
Joy'd are we that you are.   425

Post. Your servant, princes. Good my lord of Rome,
Call forth your soothsayer: as I slept, methought
Great Jupiter, upon his eagle back'd,
Appear'd to me, with other spritely shows
Of mine own kindred. When I wak'd, I found   430
This label on my bosom; whose containing
Is so from sense in hardness, that I can
Make no collection of it. Let him show
His skill in the construction.

Luc.   Philarmonus!

Sooth. Here, my good lord.

Luc.   Read, and declare the meaning.

Sooth. [*Reads*] When as a lion's whelp shall, to himself   436

436. *Sooth.*] *Capell.*

415–16. *Take ... owe*] The villain in
Frederyke of Jennen acknowledges that
he merits death. There is no corresponding admission in the *Decameron*.

422. *freeness*] generosity.

429. *spritely*] ghostly, spectral.

431–2. *whose containing ... sense*]
whose contents are so remote from
sense.

433. *collection*] inference, conclusion,
piecing together.

434. *Philarmonus*] Possibly Shakespeare adapted the name from that of
'the chamberlain *Harmonias*' who

appears in the dénouement of the
Æthiopica.

436–53. *When as ... air*] Several
commentators reject the 'label' and,
presumably, the subsequent interpretation. Collier regards both the scroll
and the vision as relics of an earlier
play, but oracles and visions are prominent in the Romances, nor are the
tragedies free from ghosts, witches,
soothsayers, and supernatural matters.
Granville-Barker finds the present
passage dramatically redundant, but I
think that the large-scale riddle con-

    unknown, without seeking find, and be em-
    brac'd by a piece of tender air: and when from a
    stately cedar shall be lopp'd branches, which,
    being dead many years, shall after revive, be   440
    jointed to the old stock, and freshly grow, then
    shall Posthumus end his miseries, Britain be for-
    tunate, and flourish in peace and plenty.
Thou, Leonatus, art the lion's whelp,
The fit and apt construction of thy name,   445
Being Leo-natus, doth impart so much:
[*To Cymbeline*] The piece of tender air, thy virtuous
    daughter,
Which we call *mollis aer*; and *mollis aer*
We term it *mulier*: which *mulier* I divine
Is this most constant wife, who even now,   450
Answering the letter of the oracle,
Unknown to you, unsought, were clipp'd about
With this most tender air.

Cym.   This hath some seeming.
Sooth. The lofty cedar, royal Cymbeline,
    Personates thee: and thy lopp'd branches point   455
    Thy two sons forth: who, by Belarius stol'n,
    For many years thought dead, are now reviv'd,
    To the majestic cedar join'd; whose issue
    Promises Britain peace and plenty.

446. Leo-natus] *Capell;* Leonatus *F.*

tributes to the suspense. It is, moreover, a logical consequence of the
vision and its significance is here ex-
panded since it now sets persons and
events against a broad national background. The exposition of 'In terram
Salicam mulieres ne succedant' in *H5*,
I. ii. 33 ff., is sufficiently close in tone
and style to vindicate the authenticity
of the Soothsayer's lines.

447. *The piece . . . daughter*] Wilson
Knight (*op. cit.*, p. 193) notes that the
imagery employed by Imogen is much
concerned with things of the air (birds,
wings, winds, etc.) and argues that she
and the Princes are conceived aerially,
with a hint of angelic essence. This is

perhaps over-subtle. Nevertheless,
Ariel, the spirit of air, is the final outcome.

449. mulier] The '*mollis*' etymology
is attributed to Cicero's friend Varro
by Tertullian, Lactantius, and Isidore
of Seville. '*mollis aer*' first appears in
Caxton's *Game of Chess*, the first book
printed in England.

450. *this*] Capell reads 'thy'. Other
conjectures: 'this thy' (Keightley);
'your' (Delius); 'his' (Hertzberg), are
worthless.

452. *were clipp'd*] wert embraced.

454. *The lofty cedar*] For possible implication see Introduction, pp. lxxxi–
lxxxii.

Cym.   Well,
My peace we will begin: and Caius Lucius,   460
Although the victor, we submit to Cæsar,
And to the Roman empire; promising
To pay our wonted tribute, from the which
We were dissuaded by our wicked queen,
Whom heavens in justice both on her, and hers,   465
Have laid most heavy hand.
Sooth. The fingers of the powers above do tune
The harmony of this peace. The vision,
Which I made known to Lucius ere the stroke
Of yet this scarce-cold battle, at this instant   470
Is full accomplish'd. For the Roman eagle,
From south to west on wing soaring aloft,
Lessen'd herself and in the beams o' the sun
So vanish'd; which foreshadow'd our princely eagle,
Th' imperial Cæsar, should again unite   475
His favour with the radiant Cymbeline,
Which shines here in the west.
Cym.   Laud we the gods,
And let our crooked smokes climb to their nostrils
From our blest altars. Publish we this peace
To all our subjects. Set we forward: let   480
A Roman, and a British ensign wave
Friendly together: so through Lud's town march,
And in the temple of great Jupiter
Our peace we'll ratify: seal it with feasts.
Set on there! Never was a war did cease   485
(Ere bloody hands were wash'd) with such a peace.
                                              [*Exeunt.*

---

460. *My peace*] Several editors emend to 'By peace'.

465-6. *Whom . . . hand*] The construction is irregular. Keightley's emendation 'hand on' is unnecessary but serves to clarify the meaning. 'Hers' is, of course, Cloten.

467. *fingers*] in contrast to 'hand' in l. 466.

470. *yet this*] F3 prints 'this yet' which most editors follow. I have retained the F reading as the trans-

position seems in no way exceptional. The emendation does not make for greater euphony.

486. S.D. Exeunt] Granville-Barker remarks that the characters set out 'in elaborate procession, the play dissolving into pageantry'. I have given what is, perhaps, a subjective interpretation of the ending in my Introduction. In modern theatres the curtain should not fall until the stage is cleared.

APPENDIX A

SOURCES

As indicated in the Introduction to this edition, Shakespeare's use of his sources in *Cymbeline* is extremely fluid. It seems pointless to reprint the sporadic sections of Holinshed which deal with Cymbeline and Guiderius, all of which are included in Boswell-Stone's *Shakspere's Holinshed* (pp. 6–18), but I give below Holinshed's account of the defeat of the Danes at the Battle of Luncarty since Shakespeare follows this fairly closely. Boccaccio's story of the wager is available in several editions, and I have preferred to reprint *Frederyke of Jennen* which is virtually inaccessible. Dr Josef Raith's admirable *Aus Schrifttum und Sprache der Angel-Sachsen*, which reprints the 1560 edition of the tale, is no longer obtainable, the publisher's stock having been confiscated or destroyed. Dr Raith has kindly allowed me to base my text on his. I have chosen the edition of 1560 rather than that of 1518 on the grounds that it is more likely to be the one that Shakespeare knew. A song from Underdowne's translation of the *Æthiopica* of Heliodorus, of which there are several echoes in *Cymbeline*, especially in the final act, is reprinted here since it has some bearing on the controversial Vision of v. iv. *Love and Fortune*, which is at most a minor source, is included in Hazlitt's *Dodsley* (vol. vi) and the Malone Society has published a type facsimile. The tale of Snow-white, which has been unconvincingly cited as a source, will be found in Grimms' *Household Tales*, and the tale 'told by the Fishwife of Stand on the Green', which can no longer be regarded as a source, is given in Hazlitt's *Shakespeare's Library* (i. ii) and in Furness's *Cymbeline* (pp. 462–9).

(a) Holinshed, Vol. ii, *Historie of Scotland*, p. 155

Which maner being noted of the Danes, and perceiuing that there was no hope of life but in victorie, they rushed foorth with such violence vpon their aduersaries, that first the right, and then after the left wing of the Scots, was constreined to retire and flee backe, the middle-ward stoutly yet keeping their ground: but the same stood in such danger, being now left naked on the sides, that the victorie must needes haue remained with the Danes, had not a renewer of the battell come in time, by the appointment (as is to be thought) of almightie God.

For as it chanced, there was in the next field at the same time an husbandman, with two of his sons busie about his worke, named Haie, a man strong and stiffe in making and shape of bodie, but indued with a valiant courage. This Haie beholding the king with the most part of the nobles, fighting with great valiancie in the middle ward, now destitute of the wings, and in great danger to be oppressed by the great violence of his enimies, caught a plow-beame in his hand, and with the same exhorting his sonnes to doo the like, hasted towards the battell, there to die rather amongest other in defense of his countrie, than to remaine aliue after the dis-comfiture in miserable thraldome and bondage of the cruell and most vnmercifull enimies. There was neere to the place of the battell, a long lane fensed on the sides with ditches and walles made of turfe, through the which the Scots which fled were beaten downe by the enimies on heapes.

Here Haie with his sonnes, supposing they might best staie the flight, placed themselues ouerthwart the lane, beat them backe whome they met fleeing, and spared neither friend nor fo: but downe they went all such as came within their reach, wherewith diuerse hardie personages cried vnto their fellowes to returne backe vnto the battell, for there was a new power of Scotishmen come to their succours, by whose aid the victorie might be easilie obteined of their most cruell aduersaries the Danes: therefore might they choose whether they would be slaine of their own fellowes com-ming to their aid, or to returne againe to fight with the enimies. The Danes being here staied in the lane by the great valiancie of the father and the sonnes, thought verely there had beene some great succors of the Scots come to the aid of their king, and there-vpon ceassing from further pursute, fled backe in great disorder vnto the other of their fellowes fighting with the middle ward of the Scots.

The Scots also that before were chased, being incouraged here-with, pursued the Danes vnto the place of the battell right fiercelie. Wherevpon Kenneth perceiuing his people to be thus recomforted, and his enimies partlie abashed, called vpon his men to remember their duties, and now sith their aduersaries hearts began (as they might perceiue) to faint, he willed them to follow vpon them man-fully, which if they did, he assured them that the victorie vn-doubtedlie should be theirs. The Scots incouraged with the kings words, laid about them so earnestlie, that in the end the Danes were constreined to forsake the field, and the Scots egerlie pur-suing in the chase, made great slaughter of them as they fled. This victorie turned highlie to the praise of the Scotish nobilitie, the which fighting in the middle ward, bare still the brunt of the battell, continuing manfullie therein euen to the end. But Haie, who in such wise (as is before mentioned) staied them that fled, causing them to returne againe to the field, deserued immortall fame and commendation: for by his meanes chieflie was the victorie atchiued.

(*b*) *Frederyke of Jennen*

HERE BEGYNNETH A PROPRE TREATYSE OF A MARCHAUNTES WYFE, THAT AFTERWARDE WENTE LYKE A MAN AND BECAME A GRETE LORDE, AND WAS CALLED FREDERYKE OF JENNEN

The prologue.
Our lord god sayeth in the gospel: What measure ye mete withal, ther with shall ye be mete agayn. And do your besynes ryghtfully and iustly, ye shal haue a blessyd and a good ende to your rewarde; and occupye your besynes vnryghtfully, and ye shall haue an yl rewarde therfore, as this story maketh mencion. But now a dayes euery man gyue hym selfe to occupye deceytes and vnrightfulness, but neuerthelesse at the laste commeth ryghtfulnes; and he that hath occupied that, he shal haue for his rewarde euerlastynge blisse, as this lytell story sheweth of a fals marchaunte that deceyued another marchaunte with grete falsenesse and deceyte; but at the last for his falsenesse he was hanged: and that was his rewarde for that false dede, as here after foloweth more playnely.

How foure marchauntes met al together in one waye, whiche were of foure diuers londes; and howe they woulde all to Paris.
In the yere of our lorde god M.CCCC.xxiiii it happened, that foure ryche marchauntes departed out of diuers countreis for to do their marchaundise. And as they were goyng their iourneys, by fortune they mette all together and fel in company together; for thei were al foure goyng towarde Paris in Fraunce; and for company sake they rode al iiii into one ynne; and it was about shraf-tyd in the mooste ioyfull tyme of al the yere; and their names were called as here foloweth: the firste was called Courant of Spayne, the second was called Borcharde of Fraunce, the thirde was called John of Florence, and the iiii was called Ambrose of Jennen. Than by the consent of the other marchauntes Borcharde of Fraunce went vnto the hoste and sayd: 'Hoste! Nowe is the meriest tyme of the yere, and we be foure marchauntes of foure diuers countreis, and by fortune we met altogether in one place, and oure iourney is to Paris. And therfore whyle we be so met, let vs make good chere together, and ordeine the best meet that ye can get for money against to morowe, and byd also some of your best frendes that you loue moste, that we maye make good chere together, or that we departe fro hence; and we shall contente you all your money

agayne.' And than the hoste sayd that he woulde do it with a good wil; and than went he and bad many of his good frendes and neighbours to diner. And he bought of the best meet that he coulde get for money, and brought it home; and on the morowe he dressed it and made it redy againste dyner after the best maner that he could. And whan that it was diner tyme, than came in the gestes to dyner, and the marchauntes came to them and bad them welcome. Than bad the marchauntes the hoste that he should bryng in the meete and lay the table, that they myght go to dyner. And than the hoste sayde: 'With a good wyll.' Than went the hoste and layd the table and fetched the meate and set it theron, and prayed the marchauntes to take the gestes to them and syt downe together. And so they did and made good chere all the daye longe with good honeste, tyll that it was very late with daunsyng and lepyng. And whan they had doone, the gestes toke their leue of the marchauntes and thanked them for their good chere. And than euery man departed home to his house. And than came the marchauntes to the hoste and prayed hym hertely for to come in and thanked hym, that he had ordered and doone all thynges so well and mannerly.

Howe two of the marchauntes, as Johan of Florence and Ambrosius of Jennen, hylde one another v thousande golde gyldens.

Whan all the marchauntes and the gestes had made mery together al the day long, at nyght the gestes toke their leue of the marchauntes and thanked them for theyr good chere that they had made them, and so departed euery one to their lodgyng. And as they were departed euery man to their house, then wexed it late. And than came the hoste of the house to the marchauntes and asked them, if that they would go slepe; and they aunswered vnto their hoste: yes. And than toke he a candell and brought the marchauntes in to a fayre chambre, where was iiii beddes rychely hanged with costly curtaynes, that euery marchaunt might lye by them selfe. And whan that they were so altogether in the chambre, than began they to speke of many thinges: some good, some bad: as it laye in their myndes. Than sayd Courant of Spayn: 'Sirs! We haue be all this day mery and made good chere; and euery one of vs hath a fayre wyfe at home: how fare they nowe at home, we can not tell.' Than said Bourchard of Fraunce to the other marchauntes: 'What aske you how they doe? They syt by the fyre and make good chere and eate and drynke of the beste and labour not at all; and so get they vnto them hote bloud, and than they may take another lustye yong man and doe their pleasure with him that we knowe not of; for we be often tymes long from them, and for the cause may they leen a lofe for a nede secretly to another.' Than sayd Johan of Florence: 'We may all well be called fooles and ydeotes, that trust our wiues in this maner as we do; for a womans hert is not made of so harde a stone, but that it wyll melte: for a womans nature is to be vnstedfast, and tourneth as the wynde dooeth and careth not for vs tyll the time that we come agayn. And we labour dayly both in wynde and in raine, and put often our liues in ieopardy and in auenture on the sea, for to fynde them withall; and our wyues syt at home and made good chere with other good felowes, and geue them parte of the money that we get. And therfore, and ye wyll do after my counseyll: let euery one of vs take a faire wenche to pas the time withall as wel as our wiues do; and they shall knowe no more of that than we knowe of them.' Than saide Ambrosius of Jennen to them: 'By goddes grace! That shall I neuer dooe whyle that I lyue. For I haue at home a good and a vertuous woman and a womanly: and I know wel that she is not of that disposition, but that she will eschewe her of all suche yll abusions till the tyme that I come home agayne; for I knowe wel that she wil haue none other man but me alone. And if that I should breake my wedlocke, than were I but litle worthe.' Than sayde John of Florence: 'Felowe! Ye set muche price by your wife at home and trust her with all that ye haue. I wil laye with you a wager of fyue thousande gyldens: if that ye will abyde me here, I shall departe and ryde to Jennen and dooe with your wyfe my wyll.' Than sayd Ambrosius to John of Florence: 'I haue delyuered to myne hoste fiue thousand gyldens to kepe. Put ye downe as muche againste it, and I shall tary here tyll the tyme that ye retourne agayne from Jennen. And if that you by any maner of menes can get your pleasure of my wyfe, ye shall haue all this money.' Than sayde Johan of Florence: 'I am contente.' And than putte he in his hostes hande other fyue thousande gyldens agaynste Ambrosius money. And than tooke he his leue and departed towarde Jennen. And as he rode thider warde, he thought in his mynde, by what maner of wyse that he myght come best to speke with Ambroses wyfe, that he myghte haue his pleasure of her and wynne the money that he had layde with Ambrose to a wager: whether it were by ryght or by wrong. And at the laste he had roden so long, that he came to Jennen, were that Ambrose wyfe dwelte.

How that Johan of Florence was come to Jennen for to speke to Ambroses wyfe; and whan that he came in her presence for to speke to her, he durste not, bicause that he founde her so womanly in her behauoure.
And whan that Johan of Florence was come to Jennen, he wente walkyng al aboute to se yf that he coude spy Ambrosius wyfe. And as he was walkynge, came Ambrosius wyfe to chyrche, so that Johan behelde her and spake to her and bad her good morow. And she thanked hym and gaue vnto him agayne swete wordes and womanly behauoure, so that he was a shamed and sayd to hym selfe: Alas, poore wretche that I am: what haue I done! The money is lost: I se it wel. For she semeth a worshypfull woman, and I dare not speke to her of that vylany: wherof I am sory.' And as he walked

thus, he thought in hys mynde, that yf that he shold wynne the money he must nedes come in to her chambre. And than made he a chest, that he wolde haue conueyd in to the womans chambre, and he wyst not how. Than remembred he him and sayd: 'I haue herde saye that the dyuell can not do that an olde woman can do.' And he thought to proue it. And than went he to the olde clothe marked, where he founde an olde woman that solde olde clothes, which he thought best for him. But he sayd: 'How shal I speke beste to her to shewe my mynde?'

How Johan of Florence gaue vnto the woman a cote of sylke for to sell.
Than broughte Johan of Florence with him a cote of sylke and came to the olde woman and sayd: 'Yf that ye coude sel this cote, I shold gyue you a good drinkynge penny; for it is al to heuy for me.' The woman saide to hym: 'How? Wyll you sel your sylken cote?' Than answered he: 'Yf that ye may sel it for ii ducates, let it goo.' But the cote was well worth seuen ducates. Than was the olde woman glad in her mynde, and bad that he shold come agayne the morowe after and he sholde haue his monye; and she sayd to her selfe: 'This is my marchaunt.' And than departed he home. And on the nexte daye in the mornynge came Johan of Florence to the olde woman againe. And she gaue vnto him the ii ducates, and she tolde him that she coude haue no more; but she kepte the cote too her selfe. And than Johan of Florence receyued the two ducates of the olde woman and thanked her. And than he cast downe one of the ducates to her and said vnto her: 'Take that and fetche the best meet and drynke that ye can get! For we two must make good chere or that we departe.' And that dyd he for to make the woman dronken, that he myghte haue some good counseile of her for to come in to Ambroses hous. And at dyner tyme came Johan of Florence to dyne with the olde woman; and there he made good chere and gaue vnto the olde woman soo moche wyne that she began to wexe mery. And that seynge, Johan of Florence sayd to the olde wyfe that was worser than the deuyl: 'Knowe ye not a marchaunt that is called Ambrose?' And the olde woman answered: 'Yes; I know hym wel. He is not at home; but he hath here a fayre woman to his wyfe dwellynge, that is bothe yonge and worshypfull of behauoure, curteyse in answere, gentyl, not proude, good for to speke withall.' Than sayd Johan of Florence: 'Know ye not the way that ye myght conuay a chest in to her hous, and I my selfe wil shyt me therin? And whan that the chest hath stande in her hous by the space of iii daies, than come and fetche the chest home againe. And yf that ye can do it, I shal gyue vnto you CC ducates for your laboure with a better drinkyng peny.' Than was the olde woman glad with that profer and sayde vnto him: 'O my frende! Sorowe not for that thynge. Brynge the chest in to my hous and shyt you fast therin and I shall fynde suche wayes that the cheste shall be conueyed in to her house.' Than was John of

Florence glad and did as the olde woman bad him, and fetched the cheste and brought it in to her house and put him selfe therein.

How that the olde woman desyred Ambroses wyfe to kepe a cheste in her house till the tyme that she come from saynt James.

After that John of Florence had promysed to the olde woman the CC ducates, he woulde se fyrste that she shold erne them before that she shold haue them. And the olde woman sought and ymagined many falsenes to haue the money. Than went she to Ambroses wyfe with a false herte and greted her, and louyngly thanked her and bad her welcome to her. For she semed to her for to bee a good honest woman: but she was but a dissimeler of cloked falshede; for it is a commyn saiyng of people, that an olde woman can do that the deuell hym selfe can not do, as we haue in examples more playnely thereof in many diuerse bokes, and as this litle boke maketh mencion. Than whan the olde woman had talked a good while with Ambroses wife of many diuers matters, than sayde she to her: 'Maistres! My comyng to you at this tyme is for this cause: I did vowe a pilgrimage a longe tyme to the holy apostle saint James, and nowe take I iorney; and if it please you to sende any offring thither, I shal bere it with a good will.' And than thanked Ambroses wyfe her and gaue vnto her a ducate, and said that she should offre that ducate to saynt James to saue her husbande from the perill of the sea and sodayne death. Than toke the olde woman the ducate and sayd: 'Worshypful maistres! I desire you of one thyng. I haue a cheste here that all my Jewels ben in and all my chefe plates. And I would desyre you to kepe it in youre house, tyll the tyme that I come home to you agayn; for ye be the woman that I truste and beleue aboue all other women now beyng alyue.' Than said Ambroses wife: 'That wyll I do with a good will. And I shall set it sure inough; for I will set it in my chamber, that it may be the surer kept.' Than was the olde woman glad in her mynde, and thanked her and departed homewarde for the cheste.

Howe John of Florence was in the cheste, and howe he was brought into Ambroses house.

And whan this false olde woman hadde ordeyned all thynges after her minde and knewe that Ambroses wife wolde take the cheste into her house, than wente she and put John of Florence in the cheste secretly, that no body wyste thereof, and gaue hym in the cheste meate and drinke for three or foure daies, soo that he neded nothynge. And the cheste was made with a spryng locke, so that John of Florence myght open and shitte in what that he would at his pleasure. And than did the olde woman laye the chest vpon a whelebarowe and gate twoo stronge men to cary it to Ambroses house. And whan they were come there with the chest, the olde woman came to Ambroses wyfe and tolde her that she had the chest at the dore. And than Ambroses wyfe bad her brynge the cheste in, and set it in her owne chambre, thynking of no deceyte nor falshede. Than went the olde woman to the dore and bade the two men bryng in the cheste and bere it vp in to the chambre: and so they dyd. And than whan it was in the chambre, than she payed the men; and they departed from thence. And than tooke the olde woman leue of Ambroses wyfe, and so departed homewarde very glad and mery.

How John of Florence opened the chest in the nyght and came out into Ambroses chambre and stale iii Juwels.

Whan nyght came, that euerye body was a slepe in their first slepe and at reste, than did John open the chest and went out in to the chamber. And by misfortune Ambroses wife had left her cofer open, wherein the Jewels were, and had forgot to shytte it. And that spied wel the false John of Florence, and theyr he stale three costly Jewelles. The one was a purse wrought al with perles and costly stones, beyng worth lxxxiiii ducates; and the other was a gyrdle of fyne golde set with costly perles and stoones, that was worth CCCC ducates; and the thyrde was a rynge with a point of diamond, that was worth l ducates. And the moone shone so clere that he myght see in euery corner of the chamber; and there he behelde Ambroses wife that was soundely a slepe. And than it fortuned that her lefte arme lay on the bed; and on that arme she had a blacke warte that the false traitoure John of Florence sawe well, wherwith he reioysed and sayd: 'O good lorde! What great fortune haue I. For now haue I sene a pryuy token, wherby he shall byleue me that I haue had my pleasure of his wyfe; and so shall I haue the money of hym.' Than wente the fals thefe with the Jewelles agayne in to the chest and shyt hym self fast therin. And on the thyrde day after came the olde woman to Ambroses wyfe and gaue to her agayne the ducate that she sholde haue borne to saynt James, and sayde: 'Worshypfull maystrys! I haue gote a grete sekenes that I wene wyl tary longe by me. And therfore I wel not take this Jornaye on me this yere. And therfore I praye you that I myghte haue my cheste agayne; and I thanke you hertely of youre good wyll.' Than delyuered Ambroses wyfe the cheste to the olde woman, mystrustynge nothynge; and knewe not that therof sholde come ony heuynes. And than departed the olde woman home with the chest agayne. And whan it was in the olde womans hous, than opened Johan of Florence the chest and came out; and than he gaue to the olde woman CC ducates for her laboure, and toke his leue of her and rode to Parys, where that Ambrose taryed hym. And whan that he was come to Parys, than rode he in to the ynne, where that Ambrose was; and than set he vp his horse and came to Ambrose and called hym a syde and sayde: 'Bycause that ye be a good frende of myne and we haue kepte company togyder, and that ye sholde not be a shamed, I call you asyde for to shewe vnto you that I haue wonne the

money. Se: here I haue euydente tokens for to shewe that I haue
wonne it.' And than toke Johan of Florence outte the purse, the
gyrdell, and the rynge, and shewed those thre Jeweles vnto
Ambrose. Than sayd Ambrose: 'I knowe well that those thre Jewels
be my wyues. But yet I wyll not byleue that ye haue hadde your
wyl on her; but ye must tel me some better and pryuyer token than
these be.' And than sayd Johan: 'Ye wyll byleue me and I tel vnto
you a more preuier token than these be.' Than he tolde vnto
Ambrose, that his wyfe had vpon her lefte arme a blacke wart. And
whan that Ambrose herde that, than fel he in a sownde; for he
knewe not the falsenes of Johan. Than Johan toke Ambrose vp, and
bad hym take a mans herte vnto hym and let it passe; for he coude
not therwith amende it. And whan that Ambrose was vp agayne,
than he sayde: 'Alas, what is my fortune! I had went that my wyfe
wolde neuer haue deceyued me as she hath done; for she was bothe
worshypfull and vertuous and beloued bothe of yonge and olde.'
And than bad Ambrosius Johan of Florence, that he sholde tel it no
ferther to ony bodye, and badde him goo to the hoste and fetche the
monye; and so he dyde. And there was no man, but he and
Ambrose, that knewe who had wonne the money.

How Ambrose rode home agayne towarde the towne of Jennen.
Than forth with departed Ambrose frome Parys and toke his Journey towarde Jennen with a soroweful herte. And whan he cam to
Jennen, he wente in to a certayne place of his that he had gyuen to
kepe to a certayne man of his that he knewe sure and trusty. And
than came Ambrose in and called the man to him. And than he
came; and whan that he was come, he sayd to him: 'My seruaunt!
I knowe well that you be trusty and trewe; and you muste do one
thyng for me that I shal commaunde you, and swere on a boke that
ye wyl do it.' And so the seruante dyde swere that he wolde. Than
sayd he to hym that he sholde byd his maystris come to hym there;
and whan that she was come, that he shold slee her and burye her
in the sonde. Than sayde the seruaunt to his mayster: 'That were
grete pyty.' Than sayd Ambrose: 'Yf ye do it not, I shall slee you.'
Than sayde the seruante: 'I wyll'. For he thoughte it was better to
slee his maystrys than his selfe to be slayne. And than departed he
towarde his maystrys with a sorowfull herte.

How the man wente to the towne.
And as the man was come to the towne, he came to his maystrys and
tolde her, that her husbande was come and taryed her at his house
without the towne. Than was Ambroses wyfe glad; and wente with
the man, and caryed with her a lytell lambe that she was wonte to
play with all. And whan they came without the towne in the wod,
than saide the seruaunt to his maistres: 'O good maystres! My
maister hath charged me, vpon payne of death, that I should slee
you here and bryng to hym for a token your tongue and a locke of

youre heere.' And whan she herde that, she fell downe on her knees and sayde: 'I haue neuer offended him for to dye; and therfore, good lady, delyuer me from this daunger, as I am gyltlesse!' And as soone as she had done her prayer, she sayde to the man: 'My true seruaunt! I shall geue you good counseyle. I haue a lambe here: we shall kyll it and take his tongue; and I wyll cut a locke of my here and with the bloud anoynt my clothes; and bere these tokens to your maister.' And than sayde the seruaunt to his maistres: 'That shall I doo with a good wil. But ye must departe from hence, that my maister se you not; for if he doe, than shall we bothe lese our lyues.' And than departed she. And than kylde he the lambe and did as she bad him and bare the tokens to his maister. And whan Ambrose sawe theim, than was he more sorier than he was before, because that he spake not with her before that he caused her to be put to death, to examyne her, wherfore John of Florence had the Jewels. And the man seing howe his maister that he founde no faulte with the tokens, he thanked God and our lady of the good counsayle of the woman.

Howe Ambroses wyfe came in mans clothing in to Secant.

Than clothed Ambroses wyfe her selfe in mans clothynge and came to Secant to an hauen, where she found a shyppe redy to goe. Than desired she that she might go with it. And than asked the shypman: 'What is your name?' And she aunswered hym: 'Frederike is my name; and I haue had a greate losse bothe of my frendes and my goodes, so that I am vndone.' Than sayde the shypman: 'Ye be a propre man: wil ye serue me? For I haue here hawkes, that I must bryng to the kynge of Alkare, that shall ye kepe, and I wil geue vnto you good wages.' Than sayd Frederyke: 'With a good wyll.' And than toke they their passage and came ouer, and presented the kyng the hawkes; and he rewarded theim well. And as soone as Frederyke was departed, than began the hawkes to drope. Than was the kynge angry, and sente for the shypman and asked him: what haukes he had broughte. 'We bad you bryng of the beste; and see what haukes ye haue brought!' Than sayde the shypman: 'Whan that I hadde theim in the shyppe they were fayre and good, as anye man myght see. And I hyred a propre man that came to me by fortune, that kepte theim diligentely; and for that cause they morne.' Than sayd the kynge: 'Bryng to me the man and let me se hym!' Than sayde the shypman: 'My lege! I will fetche him. But if it please your grace, I am lothe to departe with hym; for he is bothe wyse and subtyll in many causes. And if youre grace haue hym, ye muste kepe hym that no persone do to hym wrong.' Than sayde the kyng: 'Gooe fetche hym hether! And we promyse you that no man soo hardy of his head shall dooe hym wronge.' And than toke the shypman leue of the kynge and so departed.

Howe Frederyke was the kynges of Alkares faukenar.

Than was the kyng very sory for his haukes; for he went that they would haue dyed. And whan Frederike was come before the king and sawe hym, than had he a great fauoure vnto him and brought him to his haukes; and as sone as the haukes sawe him, they reioysed and flapped with their wynges and were hole, wherof the kyng was glad and meruayled gretly therat. And than gaue he Frederyke charge of his haukes; and he kept them well, so that the king loued him wel and promoted him and made him a gret officer in his court and after that a knight, and than he made him a lorde. Than in the meane tyme befel in the towne a great death, so that the king wold departe from thense. Than as he departed, he called to him lorde Frederyke and made hym lorde defender of all his londe, tyll the tyme that he retourned agayne, whan that dethe were paste. And than dyd the kynge and all his lordes take theyr leue of lorde Frederyke, and departed fro thense.

Howe Frederyke ouercame the kynges ennemyes that brenned and destroyed many townes after the departynge of the kynge.

Than as the kynge and his lordes were departed, than had his enemyes knowlege that he was departed, and came with a grete hoste and brente, and slewe, and toke many prysoners. And at the last this tydynges came to Frederyke that was lord and defender of the kynges realme. Than assembled he a grete hoost and cam agaynst his enemyes, and slewe them downe afore him lyke a lyon and dyde many meruaylous faytes of armes that daye; for he broke theyr ordynaunce and made theim for to scatter a brode, as it had ben loste shepe. And so that daye had lorde Frederyke grete vyctory, and folowed his enemyes and toke many prysoners of the captaynes and gret lordes, of whome he had grete raunsome. And whan that the warre was done and that lord Frederyke had sette the londe in peace through the grete boldenes and hardynes of hym, than tydynges was brought to the kynge: wherof the kynge was glad of the greate fayte that his newe captayne had done. Than retourned the kynge to his towne agayne, where that lorde Frederyke was. And whan that lorde Frederyke hade knowlege of his commynge, than receyued he the kynge with great honoure in to the towne. And whan that the kynge was with in, he sayde to Frederyke: 'I thanke you, my trewe and faythfull seruaunt, of the great dedes of armes that ye haue done for me, puttynge your body and lyfe in ioperdye. And for that cause I make you lorde protectoure and defender of all my londe; for I am an aged man, and you be yong and lusty and a valyaunt man.' And than thanked Frederyke the kynge and toke the charge on hym, and gouerned the realme worshipfuly, so that al the lordes and knightes loued him wel and al the comens. And he regned xii yere with greate honoure, and dayly gettynge more therto.

How Johan of Florence came to Alkaren with marchaundyse.

Upon a tyme wente Johan of Florence to the see wyth his marchaundyse, that was but lyght passage, toward the towne of
Alkare; for he coude speke many dyuerse languages. And whan he
was come to Alkare, he wente to the kynges palayce and shewed his
marchaundyse. Thanne on a daye, as lorde Frederyke and his
lordes walked aboute, lorde Frederyke sawe the marchaunte
standynge with his marchaundyse. Than wente he wyth his lordes
to Johan of Florence; and whan he was come, he loked asyde and
sawe the gyrdle, the purse, and the ryng, whiche he knewe well
inough, and sayd: 'Marchaunt! Let me se those thre costely Jewels
that ye haue there; and shewe me, I pray you, in what londe ye
bought them.' Than sayd Johan of Florence: 'I bought theym not;
but yf ye wyste how daungerously I came by them, ye wolde loue
me the better euer after.' Than sayd lorde Frederyke: 'That grete
daunger muste ye tell me.' Than tolde Johan of Florence to lorde
Frederyke, howe that he came by them: and howe that he layd v
thousande geldens with Ambrose, that he sholde haue goten his
pleasure of his wyfe; and how that he gate the Jewels vnknowen to
his wyfe; 'and than retourned I to her husbande and tolde hym
that I had wonne the money; and than retourned he home and
caused his man for to slee her' (as is before shewed more playnly).
Than sayd lorde Frederyke: 'The sleynge of hys wyfe was yll done;
but the money was goten with a wonder grete practyse and well.'
But for all that lorde Frederyke spake so, yet he thought not soo.
Than said he to the marchaunte: 'Wyll ye tary with vs here, and
we shall gyue vnto you mete and drynke out of my court. And kepe
those Jewelles that ye haue here for me: for they please me won-
derly well, and nowe haue I no leasure to gyue to you the money at
this time for they be so costly, that the money wyl be longe a
tellynge; and they shal serue for my paramoure.' Than thanked
Johan of Florence lorde Frederyke, that he was so curteyse to him,
and sayd: 'These thre Jeweles be so costely and of to hyghe a price
to gyue to his paramoure, without that he loued her very well.'
And than departed lorde Frederyke fro the marchaunt and
charged his offycers, that they sholde gyue vnto the marchaunte
his lyuery for two or thre men euery daye. And they sayde: they
wolde with a good wyll. So on the morowe came Johan of Florence
for his lyuerey; and they gaue it vnto hym, so that he neded not for
too spende, but yf he wolde. Than pryuely called lorde Frederyke
a poste and asked of hym, yf that he knewe wel where that the
towne of Jennen was. And he answered: 'Yes, lorde! I knowe it
well.' Than sayd lorde Frederyke: 'Thyder must ye as faste as ye
may go; and there is money ynoughe. And whan ye bee there, than
aske for one Ambrose, a wedower; and whan that ye speke with
hym, delyuer vnto hym this letter, and brynge hym with you.' And
this letter was wryten, as though the kynge hym selfe had sende it.

How the poste or messenger delyuered the letter to Ambrose.

Through the commaundement of lorde Frederike departed the
messengere towarde Jennen, and passed ouer the see and at the
laste came to Jennen. And whan that he was there, he asked where
that Ambrose dwelte; and he asked so longe, that at the last he
came to him and presented the letter to hym with the kynges brode
seale; and he receyued it humbly and opened it. And this was the
tenoure, as here foloweth: 'We kynge of Alkaren desyre of oure
frende Ambrose for a nedeful cause that we haue to doo: which
shall be a grete profyt vnto you, wherwith ye shal be made ryche;
so that ye wolde spede you and come with this messenger to vs, and
ye shal haue no maner of harme done to you; for we send to you
oure brode seale and Saufcoundute bothe to goo and to come fre.'
And as Ambrose reed this letter, he wondered gretly of the hasty
desyre of the kynge. Neuerthelesse he dressed his gere, and set one
in his hous to kepe it tyll the tyme that he retourned agayne; and
than departed he with the messenger. And they passed ouer the see
and came to lorde Frederyke, that bad him welcome and made him
good chere. And on the morowe came lorde Frederyke to Ambrose
and made hym come to dyner with hym. And he his owne persone
toke and set hym at the kynges owne table, and set hym selfe downe
therby; and oftentymes in the dyner he bad that Ambrose sholde
be mery. And whan dyner was done, than sayde lorde Frederyke
to the king: 'My lege! Here is come to this towne a marchaunte,
that hath broughte thre costely Jewelles, whiche that I wolde that
ye had sene; and therfore wyll I sende for hym and byd hym
brynge his thre Jewelles with hym.' And than wente a messenger
and bad Johan of Florence that he sholde make hym redy and
come before the kynge with his thre Jewels. Than was Johan of
Florence glad and thought that he sholde haue receyued moche
money, and went with the messenger to the kynge in to the halle.
And whan he was come, lorde Frederyke sayde vnto hym: 'Syr!
Shewe your marchaundyse, and shewe howe that ye came by them
to the kyng.' Than sheweth he the thre Jewels. And than Ambrose
seyng the Jewels woundered, and wente than that the kynge had
sent for hym to put him to death; and than fel he for sorowe almoste
to the grounde. This markyng lorde Frederyke came and comforted
hym and clapped him on the sholder, and sayde: he shoulde haue
no harme, but Joye. Than tolde the marchaunt to the king altogether howe that he had gotten the Jewels. Than went the lorde
Frederyke with the kyng asyde and asked the kyng: what that
marchaunt had deserued, that hadde dishonoured suche a worshipfull woman and had begyled her in that maner of her Jewels,
and after that loste her lyfe therfore. Than saide the kyng to the
lorde Frederyke: 'He hath bothe deserued the whele and the
galowes; for he caused both murder to be done, and also he stoele
the jewels.' Than sayde lorde Frederyke: 'So thynketh me also,

that he hath deserued it well for to be his rewarde. But if that it please your grace and the lordes to returne againe into the hall, ye shall see and knowe many other marueylous thinges that that false marchaunt hath done to that worshipfull woman.' Than sayde the kyng: 'With a good wyll, that shall we do.' Than retourned the kynge and all his lordes with lorde Frederyke into the hall agayne, for to here more of the marchaunte.

How lorde Frederyke came naked before the kyng and his lordes.

With those wordes tourned the king into the hall, where he and his lordes spake of manye dyuerse straunge matters. And in the meane whyle went the lorde Frederyke secretly away, and came into the chamber, where she did vnclothe her al naked sauing a clothe before her membres, and than came into the hall before the kyng and al his lordes, and before all the other persones there beynge present, all naked, saue that she had a kercher of sylke before her membres. And whan she was come in, she wente to the kyng and dyd him reuerence. And whan the kyng and his lordes sawe her, they meruayled greatly, wherefore that that fayre woman came in naked before them. Than saide the kynge to his lordes: 'That persone haue I sene before oftentymes in other arayment than she is now; and if I should tell trewe, me thynketh it is our protectour and defender lorde Frederyke.' And therfore sayd the kynge to her, 'Shew to vs what ye be and wherfore that ye come in here before vs al naked in this maner.' Than answered the woman to the kyng and saide: 'I am the same persone lorde Frederike that you spake on, your poore subiecte. And I am here come before your great maieste to complaine on this false marchaunt, that standeth here with the thre Jewels that be myne, as the purse, the gyrdle, and the rynge, that he had gotten by thefte, whiche is openly knowen before your grace by what maner of craft he came by them; and this other marchaunt, that here standeth before you, is my husbande. And I my selfe is the same woman that should haue be put to death in the wood at the same time; but I escaped by the helpe of God and oure ladye from that great perill of death; and from that day to this day I neuer had conuersacion with any man, but haue liued chaste, and no man nor woman knewe neuer none other but that I was a man. And therfore if that it please your grace to do so much for me, that this false marchaunt and traitour may suffre death, as ye knowe well that he hath deserued and none other wise.' Than said the kyng to her: 'That must I nedes do; for right and reason wil desire none other. And therefore, for that yll dede that he hathe done, we wil that he be headed, and than after that his body to be layde vpon the whele, ouer him a paire of galowes: because that he hath stolen and also caused murder to be done, and therfore take him by and by.' Than was John of Florence taken and broughte to pryson, and all his goodes giuen to Ambrose and his wyfe. Than sayde Ambrose to John of Florence: 'O poor wretche and katyf! What helpeth you now al your craft and falshed and al that yll gotten good that ye haue gotten by falshed and theft? For now at the last is your traytershype and false dede openly knowen. And nowe therfore must ye suffre a shamefull death, and that shall be your rewarde. Better ye had bene to haue done right, and than ye had not come to that ye be at.' Than aunswered John of Florence: 'That is truth. I haue well deserued my death.' Than toke the officers John of Florence and brought hym besyde of the galowes, where the Justice should be done. And whan that he had made his prayers and all doone, than made the hangman him knele downe and smote Johans of Florence head of, and after that laied his body vpon a whele, and the head he stycked on a stake and set it by, ouer the head a galowes: all after the maner as the kyng had iudged him; and than retourned home againe. And in this maner was John of Florence serued for his great falshed and thefte that he hadde done to that trewe wyfe and mayde. For it is neuer seene yet, that murdre and thefte was neuer so long kept, but at laste it is knowen; and they that dooe it at the laste be hanged, or elles they suffre some other shamefull death.

Howe Ambroses wyfe toke leue of the kyng and departed towarde home with her husbande.

And whan that Ambrose had sene that lorde Frederyke was his wyfe, he meruayled gretly therat and wened that she hadde ben deed longe agone. Neuerthelesse he was ryght heuy for the grete wronge that he had caused to be done to her in tyme past; and than went he to her and toke her in his armes and kyssed her; and whan he had done, he fell before her on his knees and asked her forgyuenes for that grete wronge that he had doone to her so hastely, not spekynge to her before. Than dydde she take hym vp and sayd to hym: 'Be contente, my good loue! I forgyue you frely, as thoughe you had neuer done it.' And than he rose and thanked her, and thought in his mynde not for to tary longe there. Neuerthelesse the kynge made them bothe good chere, and gaue vnto theym many grete gyftes bothe to Ambrose and his wyfe also; for he loued her for the grete trueth and valyaunce that she had done for hym in his abscence, puttynge her lyfe in ieopardy for hym agaynst his ennemyes. And whan she had ben a while with the kynge and made good chere, than came she to the kynge and prayed hym of lycence, that she myght departe homeward with her husbande. And whan the kynge herde that she wolde departe fro thens, he was sory and was lothe for to let her departe frome thense; but she desyred so moche, that at the laste he gaue too her lycence and saufcoundute, that they myght passe throughe all his londe without ony maner of harme or agayne sayenge. Than was Ambrose and his wyfe glad and toke theyr leue of the kynge and wente theyr way, and came to the see and toke a shyp and passed ouer the see to Jennen and hadde good passage; and whan they were come, they were receyued and met of the people. Whan they sawe that Ambroses wyfe was come agayne, that was sayde longe before to be dede, they meruayled gretly therof. And after that lyued they longe in vertue and goodnes, and loued euer after togyder and thanked god of that grete fortune that they had, and serued god deuoutely. And after that had Ambrose by hys wyfe foure chyldren: that is to vnderstande iii sonnes and a doughter. And the eldest sone was named Frederyke after the name of his moder. And whan that he began to wexe grete and myghty, than was he sente to Alkaren to the yong kynges court, the sone of the olde kynge that his mother had dwelte withal before; and he was made moch of for that his moder had done before to the olde kynge, and gate worshyp dayly more and more for his mothers sake, and became a gret lord, and was well beloued of the kyng and all his lordes. And all the kynrede of them euer after came to great worshyp and honour.—And than whan that Ambrose and his wyfe sawe that their sonne was so muche made of, than toke they their lefe of the kynge of Alkare, and than departed towarde the towne of Jennen and came therein in the viii. day of January, whiche was vpon a sonday, in the yere of our Lorde God M.CCCC and xxxvii. And thus in this maner hathe this good marchaunt Ambrose and his wyfe lyued together, and these fortunes they haue suffered. And than was Ambroses wife seke and died, and commended her soule into the handes of almyghty God, and went to the blisse euerlastyng, to the whiche blisse God bryng you and me. Amen.

And thus endeth this lytell story of lorde Frederyke.

(c) Thomas Underdowne, *An Aethiopian Historie, written in Greek by Heliodorus* (1587), p. 39ᵛ

> O *Nereus* God in surginge Seas,
>   we prayse thy daughter deare:
> Whome *Peleus* at commaundement,
>   of *Ioue* did make his feare.
> Thou art our lady *Venus* braue,
>   in Sea a glimsinge Starre:
> Who, thee *Achilles*, did bringe foorthe,
>   a very *Mars* in warre.
> And captaine good vnto the *Greekes*
>   thy glory scales the skyes:
> To thee did thy redheaded wiue,
>   cause *Pyrrhus* rough to rise.
> The *Troians* vtter ouer throwe,
>   but Stay to Greekishe host:
> Be thou good *Pyrrhus* vnto us,
>   a fauourable ghost.

Who here in graue intumbed liest,
 in Phoebus sacred grounde:
Bowe downe thine eare, to th'oly hymmes,
 that we to thee doo Sounde
And this our citie suffer not,
 in any feare to be:
Of thee, and *Thetis* is our songe,
 Thetis al hayle to thee.

(*d*) Act III, Scene i, and *The Mirror for Magistrates* (Contributed
by Harold F. Brooks)[1]

In Act III, Scene i, Shakespeare dramatizes the British refusal to pay
the tribute originally imposed by Julius Caesar, and now demanded by a successor—Augustus in the play (and for this there is a
basis in Holinshed), but Claudius in most accounts.[2] When the
scene is compared first with the materials available for it in Holinshed,[3] Grafton, Fabyan, Geoffrey of Monmouth, North's Plutarch,
and Spenser,[4] and then with Blenerhasset's 'Complaint of Guidericus' in his *Seconde part of the Mirrour for Magistrates*, 1578,[5] and
especially with the tragedies of Nennius, Irenglas, Guiderius, and
Caius Iulius Caesar, by Higgins, in *The Mirour for Magistrates*,
1587,[6] it seems plain that Shakespeare had the work of Higgins and
Blenerhasset in his head.

His scene, with its opening stage direction, 'Enter in state . . .',
presents the rejection of the Roman demand by the king in full
council. There is no specific hint for a council-scene in Holinshed
and the rest, but it would have been the natural way for Shakespeare to dramatize the episode, even apart from the precedents he
had in Higgins, whose Cassibellane, after a fiery speech, sends a
defiant reply to Caesar's ultimatum 'Through counsaile . . . of all
the nobles', and in Blenerhasset, whose Guidericus relates how

1. See the editor on *Cym.* and the *Mirror*, p. xviii above. Since he found me in
the midst of investigating the *Mirror* as a source of particular passages in Shakespeare, it seemed to both of us a happy arrangement that instead of his pursuing
a parallel inquiry, the results of mine, so far as they concerned *Cym.*, should be
included here.

2. See p. xviii above. According to Spenser, Claudius was refused the tribute
by Cymbeline; according to the chroniclers and the *Mirror*, by Guiderius (whom
Blenerhasset calls Guidericus).

3. Cf. Boswell-Stone, *op. cit.*, pp. 7–15.   4. *The Faerie Queen*, II. x. 46–52.

5. *Parts Added to The Mirror for Magistrates*, ed. L. B. Campbell, 1946, p. 386.

6. Campbell, *op. cit.*, pp. 191, 210, 311, 290; 'Nennius' had appeared in the
1574 and 'Irenglas' in the 1575 edition of Higgins's *First Parte of the Mirour
for Magistrates*.

The three estates in Court to Parle[e] I
In hast did call,

'amongst which Royal route' he delivered a harangue that 'moued
much their manly mindes to fight' against Claudius.[1] The existence
of these precedents is no proof that Shakespeare knew them; what
seems to show that he did is the series of parallels, in word and idea,
which we are now to examine.

There is a clear verbal parallel at ll. 48 f.:

> Till the injurious Romans *did extort*
> This *tribute* from us, we were *free* . . .[2]

ummistakably echoes Guiderius in Higgins:

> I sayd I would not pay them *tribute*, I,
> They *did extort* the same by force, perdy.
> Hee should not beare our *free*dom so away.[3]

Perhaps the most striking cluster of parallels comes in ll. 22–7. The
Queen speaks of Britain, fenced

> With *sands* that will not bear your enemies' boats,
> . . . .   a *kind of conquest*
> Caesar made here, but made not here his *brag*
> Of 'Came, and saw, and overcame:' with *shame*
> (The *first* that ever touch'd him) he was carried
> From off our coast, twice beaten: and his shipping

was cracked against the British rocks. Caesar's defeats and his
losses by shipwreck are in Holinshed; but the words I have italicized (and their attendant ideas) are not from him or the other
possible sources I have mentioned with him. In Higgins we find,
however:

> . . . our shatter'd *ships* . . .
> . . . that else had bulg'd themselues in *sand*;
> ('Caesar')

> I have *no cause of* Britayne *conquest* for to boast,
> Of all the regions *first* and last with whome I werd.
> ('Caesar')

> Proud Caesar he for all his *bragges* and *boste*:
> Flew back to *shippes* . . .
> The Monarche Caesar might have been *ashamde*
> From such an Islande with his *shippes recoyle*,
> ('Nennius')

---

1. Campbell, *op. cit.*, pp. 196, 387. Subsequent page-references for Higgins
and Blenerhasset are all to Professor Campbell's edition.
2. Italics mine; so thoughout.   3. P. 311.

When Caesar so, with *shameful* flight *recoylde*
And left our Britayne land *vnconquerde first*
('Irenglas')

That never erst with such repulse to foes did
turne the backe.
('Caesar')[1]

These passages do not stand alone. The Queen's opening argument (ll. 15 ff.):

That opportunity
Which then they had to take from's, to resume
We have again . . .

is Guidericus' argument in Blenerhasset:

That he who dyd subdue but yesterday
Is now subdude, and hath the lyke decay.[2]

Next, she begins her exhortation to Cymbeline (ll. 17 f.):

. . . Remember, sir, my liege,
The kings your *ancestors*

exactly as Cassibellane (in Higgins) begins his to the council:

. . . straight the king for all his nobles sent:
He shew'd them what their *auncestour's* had bene.[3]

According to Cymbeline (l. 53), the Britons reckon themselves 'a *warlike* people'; in Higgins, Caesar describes them as

The . . . *warlike* sort of Britaynes stout within.[4]

As regards the *tribute* (l. 49), it was '*Caesar's ambition*', says Cymbeline, that

Did put the *yoke* upon's (l. 52)

This is Guidericus' word in Blenerhasset:

Shal we buy *yoke* with *tribute* evermore . . .?[5]

Like Cymbeline, Irenglas complains of Caesar's ambition:

. . . should all these giltles Britaynes dye
For thine *ambicion*, fye O *Caesar* fye.[6]

Cymbeline's description of this ambition (ll. 50 f.),

---

1. Pp. 295, 294, 200, 214, 296. Italics are used to show not only parallels with *Cym.*, but also links likely to have associated the passages in Shakespeare's mind. For his familiarity with the 'Caesar', cf. *Cæs.*, e.g. II. iii. 1 ff. (the contents of Artemidorus' warning scroll), and III. i. 2 (the wording of the Soothsayers' retort); and see the most recent Arden edition.
2. P. 388.   3. P. 196.   4. P. 293.   5. P. 387.   6. Higgins, p. 214.

> Which swell'd so much, that it did almost stretch
> The sides o' the world, . . .

recalls the comment of Higgins's Caesar that when he had con-
quered the Gauls

> Mee thought I had vnto the worlde his ende
> By west subdued the Nations whilome free,[1]

until he perceived 'an Island yet / By west of Fraunce'.[2]

The comparable idea in ll. 12 f., that 'Britain is / A world by
itself', has its originals in Holinshed, Virgil (whom Holinshed
quotes), and elsewhere:[3] but it is in Higgins, following Geoffrey of
Monmouth,[4] that it appears as a retort to Roman claims of tribute.
Defying Caesar, Cassibellane there writes:

> . . . though Gods have giune, thee all the world as thine;
> Thats parted from the world, thou getst no land of mine.[5]

On review, the signs of indebtedness to Blenerhasset may look
rather slight. I have not much doubt, however, that Shakespeare
did echo him, and at v. iii. 19 f. as well as in the present scene.
There Posthumus, describing Guiderius and Arviragus as

> . . . lads more like to run
> The country base than to commit such slaughter,

is employing an image used (though differently) by Blenerhasset's
Guidericus, who announces his resolve to fall upon the Romans—

> To byd the Bace, and fetch them from their denne.[6]

In trying to show that the *Mirror* is one of the sources of *Cymbeline*,
one has to concentrate on touches that cannot have come from
Holinshed or the rest. But if it is agreed to be a source, its influence
may have to be reckoned with even where it overlaps other sources;
features in them perhaps stood out for Shakespeare partly because
he knew the same features also in the *Mirror*. Possible instances are
his form of the name Tenantius,[7] and his allusions to the annual

---

1. Cf. also *Ant.*, I. ii. 189 f. With 'whilome free', cf. ll. 49 f., cited above.
2. P. 293.
3. Cf. Boswell-Stone, *op. cit.*, pp. 10 f. (four passages); Virgil, *Ecl.* I. 66; North,
Plutarch's Lives, 'Caesar' (Tudor Translations, v. 25); and new Arden, *R2*,
II. i. 45 n.
4. 'Nos intra pericula Oceani extra orbem positos' (*Historia Britonum*, IV. ii,
Caxton Soc. 1844, p. 57).   5. P. 197.   6. P. 389.
7. I. i. 31; introduced as 'Theomantius or Tenantius', but normally Theomantius, in Holinshed; Tenantius in Spenser, Tennancius in Higgins (p. 194).
Cf. 'Temancius or Tenancius' (Fabyan); 'Theomantius or rather Tenantius',
also Temancius, Tenancius (Grafton); Tenuantius (Geoffrey). The F spelling of
Cassibulan I have found elsewhere only in Fabyan.

rate of the tribute in dispute, the incident of Caesar's sword, the victorious celebrations (in Lud's Town), Mulmutius and his laws, and the revolt of the Pannonians and Dalmatians.[1]

Finally, going outside Act III, Scene i, altogether, I hazard a guess that the episode of Hamo,[2] elaborated from Geoffrey of Monmouth by the chroniclers, and given prominently by Higgins, furnished Shakespeare with a hint for Cloten's end, and another for Posthumus' fighting in disguise against the Roman army in which he was supposed to be a soldier. Hamo, a real Roman, likewise puts on British garb, and fights the Romans, or pretends to— though it is to get the chance of killing Guiderius.[3] Afterwards he is slain (by Arviragus[4]) beside a haven, as Cloten is slain near Milford-Haven; and as Cloten's severed head is thrown into 'the creek behind our rock', so Hamo is

> ... hewde in pieces small:
> Which downe the cleeues they did into the waters cast.[5]

He is a personage otherwise quite unlike Cloten or Posthumus; but Shakespeare's mind will 'take suggestion as a cat laps milk'. And this suggestibility of Shakespeare's, as the study of his response to his sources reminds us again and again, is matched only by his power of assimilating the suggestions to his own purposes.

APPENDIX B

STAGE HISTORY

Simon Forman saw a performance of *Cymbeline*, probably at the Globe Theatre, some time before September 1611. There were doubtless earlier and later Jacobean performances but these are not recorded. Professor T. W. Baldwin (*The Organization and Per-*

---

1. III. i. 9, 31–3, 55–9, 74 f.; Holinshed, *Chronicles*, Vol. I, Bk III, ch. xviii *ad init.*; Boswell-Stone, *op. cit.*, pp. 8, 13–15; Higgins, pp. 298, 199, 215, 296, 259; Blenerhasset (the Emperor's adversaries not named, however), p. 390.

2. Eponymous hero of Southampton.

3. V. i. 22–5; Higgins, 'Guiderius', pp. 312 f.; Holinshed, *Chronicles*, Vol. I, Bk. IV, ch. ii *ad fin.*

4. In Fabyan and Geoffrey.

5. IV. ii. 150–4; Higgins, 'Hamo', p. 314; Holinshed, *loc. cit.* The hewing in pieces (present in Fabyan and Grafton) is absent from Holinshed. It is reflected, perhaps, at IV. i. 15–18, where 'Posthumus, thy head ... shall within this hour be off' ironically anticipates Cloten's own fate, and 'thy garments cut to pieces', reminiscent of Hamo's, may have originated partly in Shakespeare's subconscious linking of the two.

sonnel of the Shakespearean Company, pp. 394–415) has attempted to reconstruct the original cast as follows:

Posthumus Leonatus	.	Richard Burbage
Belarius . . .	.	Henry Condell
Guiderius . .	.	John Underwood
Arviragus . .	.	William Eccleston or Eglestone
Cloten . . .	.	Robert Armin
Pisanio . . .	.	John Heminge
The Queen . .	.	John Edmans
Imogen . . .	.	James Sands

Such conjectures cannot be trusted over far. Baldwin assumes that Posthumus is a man of forty in allotting the part to Burbage. This is unconvincing. The play, like the other romances and certain of the later tragedies, was evidently designed to give scope to the older members of the company such as Heminge, Condell, Lewin, and Burbage himself. It is possible that Shakespeare provided for the introduction of certain novel devices. Professor J. C. Adams (*The Globe Playhouse*, pp. 336–40) remarks on the use of the eagle attached to wires in place of the customary chair, throne, or chariot in v. iv.

Cymbeline was played before Charles I and Henrietta Maria in 1634. Sir Henry Herbert's account book records:

On Wensday night the first of January, 1633(4), Cymbeline was acted at court by the Kings players. Well likte by the kinge.

Professor Allardyce Nicoll (*Stuart Masques*, pp. 147–53) reproduces and discusses some stage designs by Inigo Jones, and suggests, very tentatively, that 'these scenes fit rather well the localities of *Cymbeline*.' The designs are for a king's chamber, a princess's bedchamber on the inner stage, two camps, and a dream. Nicoll's suggestion is a most attractive one, but I do not find it tenable. The dream design, which, if it had depicted Jupiter on his eagle, would have been decisive, actually shows Pallas Athene 'on a Whight Cloude wch turnes to a roke, a laurell in hir hande'. Nevertheless, these drawings, together with Jones's design for the descent of Jupiter in Townsend's *Tempe Restored* (Nicoll, p. 94) merit close attention as representing the kind of scenery probably employed in the Court performance if not in the earlier public performances.

After the Restoration, Shakespeare's play was supplanted for a period by D'Urfey's adaptation, *The Injured Princess or the Fatal Wager*, which was made in or about 1673. This was printed in 1682 and probably performed in that year. Revivals followed in 1720 and 1738. Whether the *Cymbeline* played at the Haymarket in 1744 was Shakespeare's or D'Urfey's is not clear, but the original play was revived at Covent Garden in 1746. Thereafter, eighteenth-century productions were usually of the original, with or without the alterations made by Garrick when he presented *Cymbeline* at Drury Lane in 1761. Performances in both London and the provinces were fairly frequent in the second half of the century and Mrs Siddons first played Imogen at Drury Lane in 1787. The eighteenth-century passion for adaptation is reflected in the versions, or rather perversions, of Charles Marsh (1755), William Hawkins (1759), Henry Brooke (1778), and Ambrose Eccles (1793). These efforts found print, but only Hawkins's reached the stage. Hawkins elected to rewrite the play in conformity with the classical unities. He merits the passing tribute of a sigh, for Hercules is remembered for lesser labours.

In 1801 Kemble revived *Cymbeline* at Drury Lane with very elaborate scenery. Subsequent revivals were notable for Edmund Kean's Posthumus and Helen Faucit's Imogen. Helen Faucit (Lady Martin) gives a charming but sentimental study of Imogen's character as the actress sees it in her book *On Some of Shakespeare's Female Characters*. This, and Kean's scenery, are symptomatic of the nineteenth century as a whole. Productions were vulgarly opulent and everything was made to revolve around the heroine. Nevertheless, Ellen Terry is remembered as the finest of Imogens.

The present century has witnessed yet another adaptation in Bernard Shaw's *Cymbeline Refinished*. This purely Shavian reconstitution of the final scene of the play, though spirited and witty, cannot be taken seriously, whatever may have been Shaw's intentions. In the theatre Shakespeare's play may be said to have held its own, and its inclusion in the Memorial Theatre's repertoire in both 1946 and 1949 suggests increasing popularity. Neither of these Stratford productions could be reckoned conspicuously successful. The best criticism of Nugent Monck's 1946 production is contained, ironically enough, in its programme note: 'The action of the play takes place dispersedly in Britain, Rome and Wales.' Michael Benthall in 1949 produced against vast, and often gloomy, scenic ramifications. In the main he achieved cohesion, but individual details were obscured and there was little deftness. In neither production did Arviragus and Guiderius induce the willing suspension of disbelief, and they, among other things, remain to harass producers of the future.

In 1957, *Cymbeline* was again revived at Stratford. Peter Hall's production, 'archetypal and fairy storyish', was intense, coherent, and illuminating. Peggy Ashcroft was an admirable Imogen, but team-work of a high order was the secret of Hall's triumph. Clive Revill's quasi-tragic Cloten was possibly un-Shakespearean, but none the less acceptable. The very considerable difficulties of the Cave scenes were overcome by emphasizing the comedy and, at times, the poignancy. The close of III. vii and the Dirge were both 'classical' moments, at least for the present editor, who left the theatre satisfied that the high claims he has made for *Cymbeline* are not unwarranted.

APPENDIX C

THE SONGS

(i) *Hark, hark, the lark* (II. iii. 19–25)

I reproduce above, with acknowledgements to the authorities of the Bodleian Library, an edited transcript of the early seventeenth-century setting of this lyric which is preserved in Bodleian MS. Don. c. 57.[1] This manuscript has been the subject of two articles: George A. Thewlis's 'Some Notes on a Bodleian Manuscript' (*Music and Letters*, XXII (1941), pp. 32–5) and Willa McClung Evans's 'Shakespeare's "Harke Harke Ye Larke" ' (*P.M.L.A.* LX (1945), pp. 95–101). Thewlis gives a transcript of the song in modern notation, argues plausibly that the manuscript was copied in or about 1650, and speculates on the identity of the anonymous composer. His suggestion that the choice lies between John Wilson and Robert Johnson awaits demonstration. Both men were associated with Shakespeare's company, and the music used in both *Macbeth* and *The Tempest* is attributed to Johnson.[2] Miss Evans, too, favours the view that the setting was used in Jacobean performances, claiming that it fulfils Cloten's demand for a 'wonderful sweet air' and that its high treble range fits it for an 'unpaved eunuch'. The fact that the music was actually written down leads her to the dubious conclusion that this aubade symbolizes Cloten's calculated plan of courtship and, in its presentation, reflects his dishonest nature. Miss Evans offers two possible explanations for the omission of the lines:

> His steeds to water at those springs
> On chalic'd flowers that lies.

(i) that they were a late interpolation, (ii) that they were deleted by the composer in order that the singer should not have to cope with awkward sibilants. This second explanation receives strong support from the other variants in the manuscript text.

Richmond Noble (*Shakespeare's Use of Song*, pp. 130–7) claims that the song was sung in 'consort' by a trained musician specially commissioned for the purpose, and thinks that the singer was probably a male alto rather than a boy or a eunuch. Granville-Barker (*op. cit.*) thinks that the singer may have been the actor who subsequently plays Arviragus, but the fact that the second song is spoken raises difficulties.

Wilson Knight notes that the song serves to relieve the tension, coming as it does between two gloomy scenes, and Noble argues that it introduces 'a whiff of comedy'. From the practical stand-

1. In the recent B.B.C. productions of *Cym.*, an early setting of *Hark, hark, the Lark*, discovered by Rudolph Dolmetsch, was employed. I know nothing of this.
2. Mr J. P. Cutts suggests (privately) that the setting may reasonably be assigned to Johnson on stylistic grounds. See his important article 'A Bodleian Song-Book' in *Music and Letters*, Vol. XXXIV, No. 3, July 1953, pp. 192–211.

point, Granville-Barker points out that the song and the 'very excellent good-conceited thing' which precedes it, afford time for Imogen to change back from night attire to court costume. Noble is unquestionably right in suggesting that this 'characteristically morning music' is partly intended to emphasize the fact that night has been transformed to dawn. The play has a fairly high proportion of early morning scenes, and the song is only one of a number of ingenious devices which serve to impress upon the audience that it is now dawn, though it might more fittingly be regarded as a symbol rather than a device.

Many parallels to Shakespeare's song have been pointed out, notably by Douce, but, as Furness remarks, these belong to the common stock of the aubade convention. Its affinities with one of the lyrics from Lyly's *Campaspe*, first noted by Isaac Reed, seem less fortuitous but present difficulties. In *Campaspe*, v. i, Trico sings:

> What bird so sings, yet so dos wayle?
> O, 'tis the rauish'd nightingale!
> 'Iug, iug, iug, iug, tereu,' shee cryes;
> And still her woes at midnight rise.
> Brave prick-song! who is't now we heare?
> None but the larke so shrill and cleare.
> How at heauens gats she claps her wings,
> The morn not waking till shee sings!
> Heark, heark, with what a pretty throat
> Poore Robin red-breast tunes his note!
> Heark how the iolly cuckoes sing!
> 'Cuckoe,' to welcome in the spring.
> 'Cuckoe,' to welcome in the spring.

If this song was written by John Lyly (1554?–1606), it is reasonable to conclude that Shakespeare owed something to it, but Lyly's authorship of the lyrics which appear in his plays has recently been called in question. Though they appear in Blount's 1632 edition of Lyly, they are lacking in the early quartos. Feuillerat doubts Lyly's authorship, and Greg presents internal evidence in favour of a comparatively late date. Shakespeare's debt to the *Campaspe* song is therefore much less certain than it once appeared though it cannot be ruled out altogether. If Shakespeare was the debtor, there is a strange irony underlying 'Hark, hark the lark'. The opening lines of the *Campaspe* song relate, of course, to the classical myth of the rape of Philomel by Tereus, a circumstance which Shakespeare has already used with ironic effect in the bed-chamber scene. This association of Imogen with Philomel, though the parallel is not exact, may have led Shakespeare, in the scene immediately following, to echo a song which made specific reference to the rape of Philomel. Shakespeare's joyful lyric, therefore, may, by virtue of what it omits from its source, have a dark underlying significance which was not lost upon the Jacobean audience. If the *Campaspe* lyric was extant and familiar, Shakespeare's aubade would be readily related to Iachimo's attempt and to Cloten's adulterous designs.

(ii) *Fear no more the heat o' th' sun* (IV. ii. 258–81)

Presumably this lyric was presented without any kind of musical embellishment, unless the consort of viols which served as the 'ingenious instrument' at IV. ii. 186 was again pressed into service. Noble (*op. cit.*, p. 137) concludes that Shakespeare had not the singers available to fill the Princes' parts and that 'consequently he was compelled to make excuse in the context for the lack of singing'. This envisages a state of affairs which could hardly have been permanent, and it is just possible that the Folio text reflects a stage in the company's history when the breaking of an actor's voice made the substitution of the spoken for the written word a temporary necessity. If so, lines 239–42 of the text, and possibly part of lines 234–8, must be regarded as special additions made by Shakespeare or another, and 'say', in line 254, as a substitution for 'sing'.

Noble regards the song as the kind of gruesome funeral game that appeals to children, but the 'zeal for ritual' which he attributes to the Princes is, perhaps, over-emphatic. It is couched in general, not, as some critics appear to think, in particular terms but is an appropriate threnody for Imogen. Whether it could have served equally well for Euriphile is another matter. The couplets which end the first and third stanzas are scarcely applicable to an elderly matron. This, rather than any qualitative consideration, might be held to confirm Staunton's view that the final couplets of each stanza are spurious additions to a lyric which is otherwise Shakespeare's. Such additions might be made in order to fit the lyric to some existing piece of music, but if, on the other hand, the verses were written simply to be spoken, it is inconceivable that they would receive such minimal augmentation.

If the line 'Save that Euriphile must be Fidele' (IV. ii. 238) implies, as many critics think, that the name Fidele must be substituted for the name Euriphile in the actual song, further difficulties arise. That Shakespeare was himself unaware of the discrepancy seems unlikely. It can be argued that the song in the Folio replaces an earlier lyric in which the proper name occurred. This would leave the question of authorship open. Grant White alone finds the whole song un-Shakespearean and his reasons are quite unconvincing. The theory of replacement does not inspire confidence, for it would be quite pointless to substitute the present lyric for one specially fitted to the occasion. The possibility that the Folio printer had to use the original dirge because a later substitution which specifically mentioned Fidele was not available at the time of going to press is, perhaps, too remote to admit discussion.

I have accepted the Folio version of Arviragus' lines at 234–8 and take them to mean: Let us, though our voices are now different, sing him to the ground as we once sang to our mother, using the same tune and words, though we are now singing to Fidele instead of Euriphile (see Notes *ad loc.*). This admits the possibility that the song which serves as a dirge for Imogen was one which the Princes used to sing to their mother *during her lifetime*—'once' signifying 'in bygone days', not 'on one particular occasion' (i.e. her funeral). It may be noted that to alter 'Euriphile' to 'Fidele' might involve metrical, if not musical, difficulties.

The discrepancies admit of no easy solution, but the fact that they inspired William Collins to write his charming, if stilted, *Dirge in 'Cymbeline'* renders them less distressing.

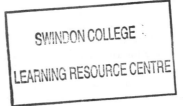